The Asbury Theological Seminary Series in Christian Revitalization Studies

This volume is published in collaboration with the Center for the Study of World Christian Revitalization Movements, a cooperative initiative of Asbury Theological Seminary faculty. Building on the work of the previous Wesleyan/Holiness Studies Center at the Seminary, the Center provides a focus for research in the Wesleyan Holiness and other related Christian renewal movements, including Pietism and Pentecostal movements, which have had a world impact. The research seeks to develop analytical models of these movements, including their biblical and theological assessment. Using an interdisciplinary approach, the Center bridges relevant discourses in several areas in order to gain insights for effective Christian mission globally. It recognizes the need for conducting research that combines insights from the history of evangelical renewal and revival movements with anthropological and religious studies literature on revitalization movements. It also networks with similar or related research and study centers around the world, in addition to sponsoring its own research projects.

This title presents Dr. Brett Knowles' important research on Pentecostalism in New Zealand (1920-2010). It is a critical study of this movement, written from an "insider's" viewpoint, that provides an in-depth, comprehensive and critical analysis. Rather than presenting a complex factual narrative, he interprets the movement as a whole, perceptively penetrating the motives and ambitions of leaders and circumstances influencing its development. He brings the perspective of a long term participant observer who is also a skilled academic historian. Conversant with principles of New Zealand Pentecostalism, his treatment is presented in light of the challenges posed to its mission by an increasingly secularized culture. Using a range of primary research data, Knowles contributes to understanding Pentecostalism as well as the related charismatic renewal that has changed the face of Christianity in New Zealand. This study is presented in the Pentecostal and Charismatic Studies subseries of the general series in Revitalization Studies.

J. Steven O'Malley
General Editor
The Asbury Theological Seminary Series in Christian Revitalization Studies

The Pentecostal and Charismatic Sub-Series

Of all the renewal traditions that have engaged the theological landscape, the Pentecostal Movement has undoubtedly made the most significant impact since it emerged at the turn of the twentieth century. Starting as a revival in a small African-American congregation on Azusa Street in Los Angeles, California, the movement soon swept the world, establishing itself in more than forty countries in the first three years. One hundred years later Pentecostalism has grown to an estimated 500 million global adherents or approximately twenty-five percent of all of Christendom. In the same manner that Wesleyanism burst beyond the bounds of Methodism to embrace an interdenominational holiness movement following the American Civil War in the nineteenth century, Pentecostalism transcended denominational lines in the form of the Charismatic Movement during the second half of the twentieth century.

This sub-series is designed to explore the historical, theological and intercultural dimensions of these twin twentieth-century restorationist traditions from a global perspective. This volume presents the definitive interpretation of Pentecostalism's history in New Zealand from its origin to the present. Unlike Australia, China, Korea, India, and Japan where the Pentecostal Movement was flourishing by 1909, the movement did not become visible in New Zealand until the English Pentecostal Evangelist, Smith Wigglesworth, held a series of crusades throughout the country in 1922. Knowles' extensive research, however, demonstrates that a Pentecostal presence *did* exist by 1903. In that year, John A.D. Adams, a disciple of John Alexander Dowie, founded the Roslyn City Road Mission in Dunedin. This group advocated "perfect liberty for the exercise of spiritual gifts," including glossolalia. Adams visited the Azusa Street Mission in 1907 and later became an Elder in the Pentecostal Church of New Zealand after its formation in 1923 in the wake of Wigglesworth's crusades. This monograph is the culmination of years of research and reflection as Knowles grounds the movement's roots in the nineteenth-century soil of New Zealand's culture and particularly in the heritage of revivalism and healing in that country. He then describes the movement's development as he analyzes its salient features decade by decade.

D. William Faupel
Sub-Series Editor

Transforming Pentecostalism

*The Changing Face of
New Zealand Pentecostalism,
1920–2010*

Brett Knowles

*Asbury Theological Seminary Series in
World Christian Revitalization Movements in Pentecostal/Charismatic Studies*

EMETH PRESS
www.emethpress.com

Transforming Pentecostalism:
The Changing Face of New Zealand Pentecostalism, 1920–2010

Copyright © 2014 Brett Knowles
Printed in the United States of America on acid-free paper

All rights reserved. No part of this book may be reproduced, or stored in a retrieval system or transmitted in any form or by any means, electronic, mechanical, photocopying, recording, scanning or otherwise, except as permitted by the 1976 United States Copyright Act, or with the prior written permission of Emeth Press. Requests for permission should be addressed to: Emeth Press, P. O. Box 23961, Lexington, KY 40523-3961. http://www.emethpress.com.

Library of Congress Cataloging-in-Publication Data
Knowles, Brett.
  Transforming Pentecostalism : the changing face of New Zealand Pentecostalism, 1920-2010 / Brett Knowles.
      pages cm. -- (The Asbury Theological Seminary series in pentecostal/charismatic studies)
  Includes bibliographical references and index.
  ISBN 978-1-60947-076-0 (alk. paper)
  1. Pentecostalism--New Zealand--History--20th century. 2. New Zealand--Church history--20th century. I. Title.
  BR1644.5.N45K56 2014
  279.3'082--dc23
                                    2014005248

Contents

Figures vii
Tables ix
Abbreviations... xi
Māori Glossary xv
Preface xvii
Chapter 1: Introduction... 1
Chapter 2: Before 1920... 5
Chapter 3: The 1920s.. 17
Chapter 4: The 1930s.. 41
Chapter 5: The 1940s.. 65
Chapter 6: The 1950s.. 87
Chapter 7: The 1960s..109
Chapter 8: Beyond the 1960s: Postmodernity, Secularization and the Relocation of Authority 137
Chapter 9: The 1970s: Part 1 151
Chapter 10: The 1970s: Part 2 169
Chapter 11: The 1980s..185
Chapter 12: The 1990s..209
Chapter 13: The 2000s..229
Appendix A..249
Appendix B..259
Appendix C..263
Bibliography 267
Name Index..289
Place Index 295
Select General Index..299
About the author 303

Figures

Figure 1: John A. D. Adams with other Pentecostal leaders associated with the Azusa Street revival, c.1907. 11

Figure 2: Smith Wigglesworth, at the time of his first campaigns in New Zealand, 1922. 19

Figure 3: Henry Roberts and his son, Harry V. Roberts, early leaders in the Pentecostal Church of New Zealand. 21

Figure 4: Rob and Beryl Wheeler and Ian and Mavis Hunt and their families on campaign 1958–59 99

Figure 5: Christian Adherence as a percentage of the total population, 1956–2013 112

Figure 6: Rob Wheeler's tent campaign in Auckland, January 1962 116

Figure 7: The exultant crowd at Parliament grounds following the Jesus March through Wellington's streets, 9 October 1972 159

Figure 8: Bishop Brian Tamaki, speaking at a Destiny Church conference in Auckland, 22 October 2006 233

Tables

Table 1: Distribution of Pentecostal Church of New Zealand adherents as per the 1926 Census and a summary of the congregational transfers resulting from the secession from the Pentecostal Church of New Zealand. 32

Table 2: Comparative Church Statistics for 1961–62, for Anglican, Presbyterian, Methodist and Baptist Churches 112

Table 3: Previous Pentecostal involvement of current mainstream church members 240

Table 4: Comparative Census Returns for Pentecostal and Quasi-Pentecostal adherents, 1901 to 2013 (part 1) 251

Table 5: Comparative Census Returns for Pentecostal and Quasi-Pentecostal adherents, 1901 to 2013 (part 2) 252

Table 6: Comparative Census Returns for Pentecostal and Quasi-Pentecostal adherents, 1901 to 2013 (part 3) 253

Table 7: Comparative Census Returns for General Population, 1901 to 2013 (part 1) 254

Table 8: Comparative Census Returns for General Population, 1901 to 2013 (part 2) 255

Table 9: Comparative Census Returns for General Population, 1901 to 2013 (part 3) 256

Table 10: Comparison of Pentecostal Churches 2002–12 260

Table 11: Dates, Origins and Trajectories of Pentecostal Denominations (part 1) 263

Table 12: Dates, Origins and Trajectories of Pentecostal Denominations (part 2) 264

Table 13: Dates, Origins and Trajectories of Pentecostal Denominations (part 3) 265

Abbreviations

am	*ante meridiem* (before noon)
ACT	Association of Consumers and Taxpayers (used as proper name, e.g., ACT Party)
ACTs	Apostolic Churches Trusts (formerly known as the Apostolic Churches)
AD	*Anno Domini* (in the year of our Lord)
ADPCM	Australian Dictionary of Pentecostal and Charismatic Movements
ANZUS	Australia, New Zealand and the United States (Defense Pact between these countries, 1951–85)
AOG	Assemblies of God
APCNZ	Associated Pentecostal Churches of New Zealand
APN	Australian Provincial Newspapers Holdings Ltd.
AV	Authorized Version (also known as the King James Version)
BA	Bachelor of Arts
BBC	British Broadcasting Corporation
BCE	Before the Common Era
BD	Bachelor of Divinity
BKRP	Brett Knowles Research Papers
BPhil	Bachelor of Philosophy
c.	*circa* (about, approximately)
C3	Christian City Churches
CA	California
CCNZ	Church of Christ (New Zealand)
CEO	Chief Executive Officer
Chas.	Charles

CNBC	Television Channel, formerly the Consumer News and Business Channel.
CO	Colorado
Co.	Company
Comp.	Compiler
CRC	Christian Revival Crusade
DAWN	Discipling A Whole Nation
DPhil	Doctor of Philosophy
Dr.	Doctor
e.g.	*exempli gratia* (for example)
Ed./eds.	Edited by
Ed.	Edition
Eph.	Ephesians
Et al.	*Et alii* (and others)
Etc.	*Et cetera* (and the rest)
F./ff.	Folio/s
FGBMFI	Full Gospel Businessmen's Fellowship International
FL	Florida
Gen.	Genesis
Hants.	Hampshire (county in England)
Hons.	Honors
IA	Iowa
i.e.	*id est* (that is)
ICNZ	Indigenous Churches of New Zealand
IN	Indiana
Inc.	Incorporated
Jer.	Jeremiah
Jr./Jnr.	Junior
KY	Kentucky
Ltd.	Limited
MA	Master of Arts
MA	Massachusetts
Matt.	Matthew

MHCF	Majestic House Correspondence Files
MI	Michigan
MMP	Mixed-Member Proportional representation
MN	Minnesota
MP	Member of Parliament
MS/MSS	Manuscript/s
MS	Missouri
MTh	Master of Theology
n.	Number
n.d.	no date
NIDPCM	New International Dictionary of Pentecostal and Charismatic Movements
NJ	New Jersey
No.	Number
n.p.	No place or No publisher
NY	New York
NZ	New Zealand
NZBC	New Zealand Broadcasting Corporation
OE	"Overseas Experience" [as in the commonly-used New Zealand phrase "The Great OE"]
OECD	Organization for Economic Cooperation and Development
OH	Ohio
OK	Oklahoma
ON	Ontario
OR	Oregon
pm	*post meridiem* (after noon)
PhD	Doctor of Philosophy
PM	Prime Minister
Ps.	Psalms
QC	Queen's Counsel
Qrtly	Quarterly
Rev.	Reverend
Rev.	Revelation

rev.	Revised
s.v.	*sub verbo* (under the word)
SA	South Australia
Sam.	Samuel
SC	South Carolina
SPCS	Society for the Promotion of Community Standards
SPUC	Society for the Protection of the Unborn Child
Sr.	Senior
St.	Saint
STh	Scholar in Theology
TN	Tennessee
Trans.	Translated by
TV	Television
TVNZ	Television New Zealand
US/USA	United States of America
UWC	United Women's Convention
v.	verse
VE Day	Victory in Europe Day, i.e., 8 May 1945
Vic.	Victoria
VJ Day	Victory over Japan Day, i.e., 15 August 1945
vol./vols.	volume/s
WA	Washington

Māori Glossary

These definitions are derived from the online version of *Te Aka Māori-English, English-Māori Dictionary and Index*.[1] Note that the use of macrons to indicate a long vowel is a comparatively recent linguistic convention. Because of quotations from earlier sources, not all Māori words are micronized consistently throughout this book.

Haka	Vigorous dance, with actions and rhythmically shouted words.
Hīkoi	March, especially the 1975 Land March of Whina Cooper and the 1998 *Hīkoi* of Hope.
Hongi	To press noses together in greeting.
Iwi	Tribe, large group of people descended from a common ancestor.
Karakia	Prayers, ritual chants, intoned incantations.
Kaumātua	Elder, old person.
Kawa	*Marae* protocol, a ceremony to remove *tapu* from a new house or a new canoe.
Kōhanga Reo	Māori-language preschools (literally, "language nest").
Kura	School, education, learning gathering.
Kura Kaupapa	Primary school operating under Māori custom and using Māori as the medium of instruction.
Māngai	Mouth, representative, "mouthpiece" (i.e., of God). The title adopted by Māori healer T. W. Rātana.
Marae	The courtyard of a Māori meeting house, and thus the venue for tribal gatherings and the center of tribal life.
Mōrehu	Remnant or survivor. Rātana's name for his followers.
Ngāi Tahu	The tribal group of much of Te Wai Pounamu (the South Island).

Ngāti Porou	The tribal group of the East Coast area of Te Ika-a-Maui (the North Island), from Gisborne to Tikirau.
Ngāti Whātua	The tribal group of the area from Kaipara to Tāmaki-Makau-Rau (Auckland).
Pākehā	Non-Māori, i.e., New Zealander of European descent.
Pōwhiri	Welcome, ritual of encounter, welcome ceremony on a *marae*.
Rangatiratanga	Sovereignty, chieftainship, right to exercise authority, chiefly autonomy.
Raupatu	Conquest, confiscation.
Tainui	The tribal group of the Hauraki, Waikato and King Country regions.
Tangata Whenua	Local people, hosts, the indigenous "People of the Land."
Tapu	Spiritual restrictions, sacred, supernatural condition.
Te Rūnanga o te Pīhopatanga o Aotearoa	The Council of the Diocese of New Zealand [i.e., the Māori Council of the Anglican Church of New Zealand]
Tikanga	Social organizations, language, laws, principles and correct procedure, customs and lore.
Tohunga	Skilled person, chosen expert, priest or artist (a specialist in any field, especially spiritual).
Wānanga	University, tertiary institution that caters for Māori learning needs.

Notes

1. *Te Aka Māori-English, English-Māori Dictionary and Index*. http://www.maoridictionary.co.nz/ (accessed 10 September 2013).

Preface

The transformation of New Zealand Pentecostalism over the decades is epitomized by the three photographs on the cover of this book. That on the left, taken about 1907, shows Dunedin lawyer John A.D. Adams, one of the pioneers of the movement in New Zealand, together with William J. Seymour—leader of the 1906 Azusa Street revival—and several other early American Pentecostals. This photograph is significant on two levels, since it highlights not only the global connections of early New Zealand Pentecostalism but also its comparative insignificance. It was one of the oldest held by the Flower Pentecostal Heritage Center in Springfield, Missouri, but the exact identity of "Brother Adams"—so named on its reverse—remained unknown for nearly a century. Australian Pentecostal historian Mark Hutchinson recognized him in 2004[1] and this enabled the Heritage Center finally to classify the photograph. The "hiddenness" of Adams' identity reflected that of early Pentecostalism in New Zealand, which did not emerge into public view until the Smith Wigglesworth campaigns of 1922 and 1923–24.

The middle photograph forms a striking contrast to this sectarian obscurity. It portrays the 1972 Jesus Marches, in which some 85,000 people took to the streets throughout New Zealand in celebration of Jesus and in protest against the declining moral standards of society. The marches both reflected and reinforced the growth of New Zealand Pentecostalism and of its emerging sister movement, the Charismatic Renewal. While they were not successful in influencing the morality of the country as their organizers had hoped, they did reflect an increasing sense of Pentecostal power and influence. They also reinforced the informal ecumenism that was one of the driving forces of Pentecostal expansion and Charismatic renewal in the 1960s and 1970s and laid the foundations for the further development of these movements. These two decades marked the peak period of primary charismatic growth; as will be demonstrated in this book, the Pentecostal movement became quite different in character in the 1980s.

The third photograph—which would be instantly recognized by most New Zealanders—is of Bishop Brian Tamaki, a Māori Pentecostal pastor who gained considerable notoriety in the first decade of the twenty-first century. His high public profile derived from his television programs, as well as from vehement controversy over his views, which was fanned by extensive—and unrelentingly hostile—media coverage. Tamaki and his Destiny Church have now also attracted academic scrutiny, with Professor Peter Lineham publishing a book on him and his movement in 2013.² It is a mark of the public's awareness of Tamaki that copies of Lineham's book were being sold, not only in bookstores, but also at discount prices in the Warehouse—a large New Zealand-based shopping chain—within weeks of its publication. For any book on a religious topic to be mass-marketed in this way in "secular" New Zealand was highly unusual; it was unprecedented for a book on a Pentecostal movement. The photographs on the cover of this book therefore illustrate the changing nature of the Pentecostal movement and of public perceptions of it.

Despite this growing interest and several histories of individual Pentecostal denominations—including Lineham's book on the Destiny Church—little has been published on the movement as a whole since its pioneer historian James Worsfold wrote his *History of the Charismatic Movements in New Zealand* in 1974.³ Like that of an earlier pioneer of church history, Eusebius of Caesarea, Worsfold's treatment remains valuable for its preservation of sources that are no longer extant. Nevertheless, it represents a narrative, rather than an analytical, account, telling "what happened" rather than "what was going on." It is also only a partial coverage of the movement up to 1974 and, at times, exhibits inaccuracies and biases. The present book will seek to comprehensively and critically analyze the history of the movement as a whole and, in particular, the ways in which its character, attitudes, perceptions and mindsets have changed—often unconsciously—over time. In so doing, it will attempt—in German-American historian Fritz Stern's words—"to penetrate beyond the descriptive fact to the causes, the material conditions, the mood, the human motives and ambitions"⁴ which underlie its growth and development. Its methodology is necessarily "broad-brush," rather than detailed; readers seeking a detailed account of each and every Pentecostal leader and church will be somewhat disappointed. The author has approached this research from the subjective perspective of an active participant in the movement for more than fifty years, as well as from the critical objectivity of an academic church historian. The book is therefore "a view from the inside" as well as an objective history and hopefully will exhibit both personal empathy and critical reflection.

In this project I have received the generous support of many people and I gladly take this opportunity to recognize my indebtedness and to extend my thanks. I wish first to thank my publishers, Emeth Press, for accepting the book for publication, and to Professor Larry Wood and Dr William Faupel for their encouragement. I also acknowledge the liberal assistance of a number of fellow historians, including Professor Peter Lineham of Massey University, Dr Tim Cooper of the University of Otago and Dr Ali Clarke of the Hocken Library. The Hocken Library provided a scholarly setting in which much of the writing of this book was done and its staff members were indefatigable in their assistance and in the provision of references and resource materials. The Hewitson library at the Knox Centre for Ministry and Leadership and the Central Library at the University of Otago were also extremely helpful at several key stages of the project. I am grateful to a number of copyright holders who granted permission to reproduce several photographic images. These include the Flower Pentecostal Heritage Center, Springfield, Missouri, USA; Carol Soukotta, Mount

Hope Foundation, Indonesia; Rob Wheeler, Auckland; and the Alexander Turnbull Library, Wellington, New Zealand. I wish also to thank Pastor David Shearer for permission to use the letter reproduced on page 201 and the Estate of James K. Baxter for permission to reproduce Baxter's "Song to the Holy Spirit" on page 243. Verbal comments from Janet Marsh and Judith Forbes are also cited with permission, as are data from a draft research paper by Dr Ali Clarke.

I want to thank my two proofreaders—Gill Trebilco and my wife Adrienne—for their diligence and careful attention to detail in their checking of the text. Any errors that remain are solely the responsibility of the author (and are likely to have been added in a fit of last-minute inspiration after proofreading was completed!) Sandi Jull and the Helpdesk team at the Univeristy of Otago also provided invaluable technical assistance. Finally, I express my thanks to friends and loved ones who have encouraged me in this project. Paul and Gill Trebilco, Bruce and Lesley Currie and Colin and Lyn Blair—to name just a few—and my family have been immensely encouraging and supportive. But my greatest debt is to my wife Adrienne, who has encouraged, cajoled and inspired many aspects of the book and without whose patience, love and support this project could not have been completed. To adequately express my gratitude would truly require the tongues of men and of angels.

Notes

1. Mark Hutchinson, "Adams, John Archibald Duncan (1844–1936)," *Australian Dictionary of Pentecostal and Charismatic Movements* [hereafter cited as ADPCM], http://webjournals.ac.edu.au/journals/ADPCM/a-to-d/adams-john-archibald-duncan-1844-1936/ (accessed 10 November 2011).

2. Peter Lineham, *Destiny: The Life and Times of a Self-Made Apostle* (Auckland: Penguin, 2013).

3. James E. Worsfold, *A History of the Charismatic Movements in New Zealand, including a Pentecostal Perspective and a Breviate of the Catholic Apostolic Church in Great Britain* (Bradford: Julian Literature Trust, 1974).

4. Fritz Stern, ed., *The Varieties of History From Voltaire to the Present* (New York: Meridian Books, 1956), 25.

Chapter 1

Introduction

Of Golliwogs and Glaciers

In August 2011, a visiting black American hip hop star created a public stir by protesting the sale of golliwog dolls in a souvenir shop at Auckland International Airport. He saw these dolls as racist and his post on Twitter resulted in their removal by airport management staff. Responses to his complaint reflected two main perspectives. The first of these was geographical, in that golliwogs seemed to have more acceptance in New Zealand than they did in countries such as the United States and the United Kingdom.[1] Race Relations Commissioner Joris de Bres noted that New Zealanders often did not realize that golliwog dolls had a controversial history in other countries where many people found them offensive. The second perspective was historical, rooted in perspectives of the past. Thus, Dunedin City Councilor Richard Thomson strongly defended the sale of the dolls, observing that "for most people, [golliwogs] are a nostalgic memory from the past. People buy them because they remind them of when they were kids, and they appreciate them for what they are."[2]

It is evident that attitudes towards the golliwog doll have evolved over time. It began life as a story book character in 1895 and was immediately embraced by the English public. James Robertson and Sons, a British manufacturer of jams and preserves, began using the golliwog image as its trademark in the early twentieth century. It was also a favorite children's soft toy in Europe (and indeed, in New Zealand). However, attitudes began to change in the 1960s as a result of racial conflict in the United States and the United Kingdom and golliwogs came to be seen as symbols of racial insensitivity. Use of the image waned, and the manufacturing of golliwog dolls declined as the demand for these decreased. The antigolliwog campaign reached its height by the late 1980s, with the term "golliwog" now being understood as a racial slur in a number of countries. Nevertheless, many collectors contend that the antigolliwog movement represents political correctness at its worst and pockets of nostalgic interest have remained, with an active secondary market for the dolls on the internet.[3]

Changing perceptions of golliwogs are only one example of the ways in which public attitudes and orientations evolve over time. This evolution has had great significance for social, political and religious landscapes. In this respect, church historian Martin Marty offers an illuminating analogy, using the environmental metaphors of hurricanes and glaciers to categorize the change in American religion in the fifty years from 1935 to 1985.[4] Marty observes that "both hurricane and glacial forces leave altered [religious] landscapes."[5] The "hurricane" represents sudden, drastic change, the product of clearly identifiable catalytic events such as, for example, the Second Vatican Council from 1962 to 1965. By contrast, the "glacier" represents a process of gradual, subtle change, which may not be attributable to any specific causative event or series of events. These glacial forces represent a slow, cumulative progression of attitudes and orientations. They are much more difficult to identify than those of the hurricane, but are also more important and powerful in influencing and shaping the course of history. One is reminded of the epigram (loosely based upon a saying from French author Victor Hugo): "There is one thing stronger than all the armies in the world; and that is an idea whose time has come."[6]

The glacial forces of attitudinal change are therefore important in the process of history and in the shaping of religious movements. However, there are other sociological factors at work also. Movements—by definition—*move*; they are dynamic, rather than static entities. Sociologist Max Weber argued that these bodies all begin as charismatic movements (i.e., associations that owe their existence to the personal power of the charismatic founder or leader). Over the course of time, they evolve into rational-legal (or bureaucratic) modes of leadership, in which power is located in the officially appointed leader and channeled through prescribed modes of action. Weber noted that this process, known as the "routinization of charisma," is an inevitable one.[7] It represents a transition from a pioneering movement to one of a different kind, one in which charisma gives way to tradition or rational socialization.[8] Thus, "Charismatic authority is often 'routinized' . . . so that [the charismatic leader] will be succeeded either by a bureaucracy vested with rational-legal authority or by a return to the institutionalized structures of tradition to which the charismatic impetus has now been incorporated."[9]

Theological ethicist Richard Niebuhr adds another element to Weber's analysis, arguing that all religious movements begin as sects (i.e., exclusive, voluntary associations) which—over the passage of time—develop into churches (i.e., natural, universalist social groups).[10] Such a transition, he insists, occurs relatively early in the movement's trajectory: "The social character of sectarianism . . . is almost always modified in the course of time by the natural processes of birth and death, and on this change in structure changes in doctrine and ethics inevitably follow. *By its very nature the sectarian type of organization is valid for only one generation.*"[11] Consequently, the character of the new movement changes from sect to church and ultimately to denomination.[12] Later sociologists have extended and modified the theories of Weber, Ernst Troeltsch and Niebuhr. Nevertheless, Pentecostal churches (as typically sectarian, charismatic movements) provide classic examples of these processes.

The Transforming of New Zealand Pentecostalism

In 2000, I was visited in my office at the University of Otago by an Australian Pentecostal pastor who had founded several assemblies during the course of his ministry in the Assemblies of God. However, during our conversation, he stated that despite this long history, he had not been in a Pentecostal church since 1986. I asked him why he had left. "Oh," he replied, "I didn't leave the movement—it left me!" What he was saying was that the Pentecostal movement itself had changed; and upon reflection, I could see numerous examples of this evolutionary process. His statement was the catalyst which has led to the subject matter of this book.

In this respect, missiologist David Bosch's magisterial book *Transforming Mission* has provided a model for recognizing and understanding these changes. Bosch posits that "transforming mission" can be understood not only as a mission that transforms society, but also as a mission which is itself being transformed.[13] These "paradigm shifts" (which are often unconscious ones) produce new ways of viewing and interpreting reality. In this book, I will argue that a number of paradigm shifts have taken place in New Zealand Pentecostalism, leading to new orientations and attitudes within the movement. And, as this Australian pastor observed, in so doing the movement has left previous models of Pentecostalism behind. In this respect, it has become a "transforming Pentecostalism."

This book will therefore address the transformation of New Zealand Pentecostalism from the 1920s to the 2010s. It will examine the perceptual changes that have occurred in the movement and in the wider society and attempt to ascertain the impact of these changes on the nature of the movement. It will also seek to explain why these changes have taken place. The book begins with an introductory chapter examining the movement prior to 1920, before devoting a chapter to each decade thereafter, except for the 1960s and 1970s, which have two chapters each.

Notes

1. *3 News*, "Big Boi's NZ Golliwog Encounter," 26 August 2011, http://www.3news.co.nz/Big-Bois-NZ-Golliwog-encounter/tabid/418/articleID/223634/Default.aspx (accessed 1 September 2011).

2. Jamie Morton, "Golliwogs offend hip hop star," *Otago Daily Times*, 27 August 2011, 3.

3. David Pilgrim, "The Golliwog Caricature," Jim Crow Museum of Racist Memorabilia, Ferris State University, MI, http://www.ferris.edu/news/jimcrow/golliwog/ (accessed 1 September 2011).

4. Martin E. Marty, "Introduction: Religion in America 1935–1985," in *Altered Landscapes: Christianity in America 1935–1985*, ed. David W. Lotz, Donald W. Shriver, Jr., and John F. Wilson, 1–2 (Grand Rapids, MI: Eerdmans Publishing Company, 1989).

5. Ibid, 1.

6. Taken from flyer for *Nation*, 15 April 1943, cited in Elizabeth M. Knowles, *Oxford Dictionary of Quotations*, 7th ed., 2012 online version, http://www.oxfordreference.com/browse?t1=ORO:GEN00170 (accessed 8 August 2013). The allusion is to Hugo's epigram *"On résiste à l'invasion des armées; on ne résiste pas à l'invasion des idées"* (Victor Hugo, *Histoire d'un Crime*, (1877), part 5, section 10).

7. Max Weber, "The Nature of Charismatic Domination," in *Max Weber: Selections in Translation*, ed. W. G. Runciman, trans. E. Matthews, 226–50 (Cambridge: Cambridge University Press, 1978). This specific passage was selected by the editor from Max Weber, *Wirtschrift und Gesellschaft* [Economy and Society], 7th ed. (Tübingen: Mohr, 1956), 2:662–79. This work, the best-known of Weber's writings, was originally published posthumously in 1922, two years after his death.

8. *From Max Weber: Essays in Sociology*, ed. and trans. H. H. Gerth and C. Wright Mills (New York: Oxford University Press, 1946), reproduced in S.N. Eisenstadt, ed. and with an introduction to *Max Weber: On Charisma and Institution Building. Selected Papers*, 28 (Chicago: University of Chicago Press, 1968). For a discussion of Weber's conception of power and the ways in which charisma emerges and is routinised, see Sik Hung Ng, *The Social Psychology of Power*, European Monographs in Social Psychology 21, 51–59 (London: Academic Press, 1980),.

9. John Scott and Gordon Marshall, eds., *A Dictionary of Sociology*, 3rd rev. ed. (New York: Oxford University Press, 2009), s.v. "Charisma."

10. For a definition of these categories and discussion of sectarianism from a New Zealand perspective, see Michael Hill, "The Sectarian Contribution: The Decline of Church-based Spirituality and the Rise of Sectarianism," in *Religion in New Zealand Society*, ed. Brian Colless and Peter Donovan, 2nd ed. (Palmerston North: Dunmore Press, 1985), 119–42.

11. H. Richard Niebuhr, *The Social Sources of Denominationalism*, 19 (1929; New York: Meridian Books, 1959). Emphasis added.

12. Ibid, 20. Niebuhr borrowed this idea from the work of Ernst Troeltsch, in particular from his *Soziallehren der Christlichen Kirchen und Gruppen*.

13. David J. Bosch, *Transforming Mission: Paradigm Shifts in the Theology of Mission*, American Society of Missiology Series 16, xv (1991; Maryknoll, NY: Orbis Books, 1995).

Chapter 2

Before 1920

In the Beginning: Were there Pentecostals in New Zealand before Wigglesworth?

The arrival of Pentecostalism in New Zealand is customarily dated to May 1922, when English Pentecostal evangelist Smith Wigglesworth began the first of his healing campaigns in Wellington. However, while both Wigglesworth and his campaigns can aptly be described as "hurricanes" in terms of their religious impact, his success built upon glacial changes of attitude and orientation. The movement did not arise in a vacuum; it emerged from the matrix of attitudes, orientations, beliefs and expectations that both shaped its theology and furnished its initial constituencies. These influences included an interest in revivalism, a belief in alternative forms of healing, the spiritual empowerment advocated by the Keswick movement and—to a lesser extent—the charismatic patterns of the Irvingite tradition. They overlapped and interpenetrated, together forming a multifaceted religious subculture that contributed to the emergence of Pentecostalism.

In the New Zealand context, the most powerful of these interconnected influences was revivalism and a "sawdust trail" of revivalist networks had emerged by the 1880s.[1] This impulse was built upon the doctrinal foundations of a sovereign encounter with the Holy Spirit—available to every person—which also provided a pattern of activity by which this encounter could be facilitated. By anchoring the precedents for this encounter in the eighteenth-century Great Awakenings, it created a revivalist mythology and stimulated a widespread network of expectation that formed a constituency for the twentieth-century Pentecostal movement. However, these expectations—and perceptions of what constituted revival—both developed over time.

Other influences formed a substratum of the revivalist impulse in New Zealand. The interest in healing[2] was the most pervasive of these and was reinforced by traditional Māori forms of spiritual healing.[3] This had some of the characteristics of a folk religion, forming a deeper level of public awareness, rekindled occasionally by specific events such as Smith Wigglesworth's campaigns in the 1920s. Since healing was also a prominent feature in Pentecostalism,[4] resurgence of this interest tended to spill over into increased openness to Pentecostalism. This was the major factor in that movement's expansion,[5] particularly in the 1920s and 1960s.

As with the development of revivalism, the histories of the Keswick and Irvingite movements provide classic examples of the way in which ideas evolve, often being transmuted and redirected by catalytic insights. The concept of holiness—and of the means by which it was achieved—had a trajectory from the "process sanctification" of Methodist founder John Wesley through nineteenth-century Oberlin theology to the "crisis sanctification" of Holiness revivalism. This understanding of sanctification in terms of a "Baptism of the Spirit" was then transmitted and transmuted through the Holiness movement[6]—and its British wing, the Keswick movement[7]—to Pentecostalism. This British offshoot contributed to the formation of New Zealand "deeper life" spirituality. It was introduced to New Zealand by English revivalist George Grubb in the 1890s,[8] becoming a networked piety through the establishment of annual conventions at Pounawea in 1910 and Ngaruawahia in 1921.[9] However, the decisive point of difference between the new Pentecostalism and its Holiness and Keswick antecedents was the insight of its founder, Charles Fox Parham, that glossolalia was the initial sign that one had been baptized in the Spirit.[10]

Similarly, the outbreak of charismatic phenomena surrounding Scottish Presbyterian pastor Edward Irving's ministry in London in the 1830s[11] quickly became a formalized structure of apostles and prophets. This took institutional form as the Catholic Apostolic Church,[12] which had established branches in Australia and New Zealand by the mid-1860s.[13] Nevertheless, the circumscribed nature of the apostolate (which was limited to the original apostles established at the formation of the church in the 1830s) meant that the movement's development was eventually truncated. On the death of the last Irvingite apostle in 1901, the Catholic Apostolic Church went into decline, ceasing to exist by the mid-twentieth century. The debated question of its influence on the development of Pentecostalism will be discussed later in this chapter.

In tracing this matrix of interrelated and interpenetrating attitudes, orientations, beliefs and expectations, two important comments must be made. Firstly, ideas are not fixed; they mutate—sometimes quite suddenly, through the integration of transforming insights—and have periods of decline and resurgence. Secondly, the intersection and interaction of these ideas can lead to altered perceptions that, in turn, produce changed expectations and, ultimately, lead in new directions. The influences that led to the emergence of Pentecostalism in New Zealand in the 1920s are the result of a combination and interaction of ideas, contexts and expectations. The movement is therefore the end product of a long process of theological evolution and it consequently continues to evolve and mutate.

This complex of expectations preceding Wigglesworth's arrival helps to explain why historians of New Zealand Pentecostalism take different positions on the issue of the movement's emergence. Assemblies of God historian Ian Clark, while acknowledging that Wigglesworth was not the first charismatic evangelist to visit New Zealand,[14] nevertheless describes him as the person who brought the Pentecostal message to this country.[15] James Worsfold, the pioneer historian of the movement, takes an opposite view. He identifies what he sees as earlier examples of charismatic activity from the 1860s on and has been particularly inclusive in his categorization of such instances as "Pentecostal."[16] However, historian Peter Lineham has been highly critical of Worsfold's tendency to incorporate diverse forms of nineteenth-century New Zealand revivalism and evangelicalism within Pentecostal/charismatic categories.[17] As will be seen, the truth lies somewhere between the two extremes. At the heart of the problem is a failure to recognize that understandings of the Baptism of the Spirit have changed over time. American historian Donald Dayton[18] has shown that the phrase "Baptism of the Spirit" had developed into a general shorthand term within the Holiness movement for a crisis experience of sanctification by the 1870s.[19] This use of Pentecostal imagery and rhetoric was widespread among popular "Higher Christian Life" institutions and movements in America and elsewhere in the 1890s. Such terminology did not necessarily imply that this experience was understood in terms of its association with glossolalia. Indeed, while Holiness groups such as the Salvation Army and the Keswick movement were comfortable with this rhetoric, they did not accept the focus on spiritual gifts that would characterize later Pentecostal versions of it. Thus, while the Holiness and Pentecostal movements were related, they were *distinct, separate* entities: the feature that distinguished the later movement from its Holiness antecedents—despite a shared rhetoric and imagery—was speaking in tongues. Worsfold fails to recognize this distinction and therefore telescopes a variety of experiences and understandings into the classical Pentecostalism of Wigglesworth and his followers.

This failure of critical differentiation leads Worsfold into a number of errors. In particular, he maintains that the Irvingite tradition of the Catholic Apostolic Church was a theological ancestor of Pentecostalism,[20] a position that is disputed by many scholars. (Scottish historian Gordon Strachan, for example, insists that the two movements were unaware of each other's existence, despite striking similarities between them.[21] Similarly, Mark Hutchinson observes that the different sociological contexts of the Catholic Apostolic Church and the new Pentecostal movement meant that contacts were comparatively minimal, despite a shared vocabulary and common expectation.[22] Lineham likewise discounts an Irvingite influence on early Pentecostalism in New Zealand.[23] Any connections between the two movements in this country were indirect, rather than direct.) Worsfold's inclusivist assumption that all references to the Baptism of the Spirit indicate instances of early Pentecostalism is also faulty. For example, he refers to a ten-day "Holiness and Divine Healing" convention in Wellington in 1888[24]—at which one of the addresses was on "The Baptism and Gift of the Holy Ghost"[25]—describing this as "Pentecostal."[26] However, given the conference theme, it is evident that this address reflected a Holiness viewpoint, rather than that of classical Pentecostalism. Similarly, prominent Evangelical and orphanage director George Müller's address on "The Gift of the Holy Spirit" during his meetings in Wellington the following month also reflected a Holiness understanding.[27] Nor is there any evidence of Pentecostal phenomena in the meetings of faith healer John Alexander Dowie,[28] who also visited New Zealand in 1888.[29] Advertisements for Dowie's meetings appeared under the heading of "Healing through Faith in Jesus," and his sermons included Holiness topics such as "Divine Healing" and "Sanctification of Spirit, Soul and Body."[30]

James Worsfold also refers to the campaigns of evangelist Rev. George Soltau, who ministered widely and effectively from 1895 to 1897 throughout New Zealand on the development of the Deeper Christian Life.[31] Soltau had been associated with Scottish Evangelical scholar Henry Drummond and had also worked with evangelists Moody and Sankey in America. Before coming to New Zealand, he had been the minister of the unsectarian Christian Mission Church in Launceston, Tasmania, in addition to conducting missions in India, Ceylon [Sri Lanka] and later in Victoria.[32] The numerous and extensive newspaper reports of his sermons demonstrate a Keswick emphasis on the Baptism of the Spirit as an enduement of power for witness.[33] This was also the case in those of his numerous writings still extant and sighted by the author.[34] There was no indication, at the time of his visit, of a classic Pentecostal understanding of the Baptism of the Spirit as being evidenced by speaking in tongues. Nevertheless, Worsfold cites from a pamphlet written by Soltau in which he describes his encounter with glossolalia, the implication being that it dates from his time in New Zealand during the 1890s. However, this is a secondary—and possibly anachronistic—reference; its source is an undated and unidentified leaflet written by Soltau, cited in a 1923 article by Dunedin lawyer John A. D. Adams. This article was reprinted in the Australian Pentecostal periodical *Good News* in 1928 and—in this form—is available online.[35] Adams' article does not identify or give the provenance of the leaflet. However, its reference to "the excitement and enquiry that have sprung up over the 'Speaking in tongues'" indicates that it was written well after the date of his visit to New Zealand, most likely after 1906.[36] Although the leaflet must have been written before 1909, the year of Soltau's death, the absence of date and provenance details vitiates its evidential value for early Pentecostalism in New Zealand.

Other errors include Worsfold's anachronistic claim that the United Christian Mission building, erected by independent evangelical missioner Henry Roberts' Wellington congregation in 1900, was "the first church building put up by Pentecostal people."[37] However, he offers no evidence that Roberts and his congregation *then* understood the reception of the Holy Spirit in anything other than Holiness categories: i.e., as the means of achieving sanctification and empowerment for witness. This objection is borne out by his description of their beliefs, which included the health and healing teachings of John Alexander Dowie and, later, some of the doctrinal emphases of the Catholic Apostolic Church. There is no mention of glossolalia; indeed, the reaction of H. V. Roberts[38]—Henry Roberts' son—to Smith Wigglesworth's meetings in 1922 indicates that these Pentecostal phenomena were a new experience for the Roberts family. On receiving a copy of the Wigglesworth campaign pamphlet, H. V. Roberts remarked "I suppose this is another of father's cranky friends." He did, however, attend the teaching meetings and was profoundly moved: "for the first time in our lives [we] realised the mighty, yet fragrant working of the Spirit of God."[39] Furthermore, three of Henry Roberts' great-grandchildren (missionary Carol Soukotta and Pastors Harvey Walker and Ian Bilby) believe that he did not speak in tongues until after Wigglesworth's visit, although this cannot now be verified. Bilby describes Roberts as more evangelical than Pentecostal up to this point.[40] (Roberts' support of Wigglesworth's visit had been on the basis of the latter's healing revivalism, rather than his Pentecostalism.) This orientation is borne out by the name adopted—under Henry Roberts' leadership—by the Wellington congregation that had resulted from Wigglesworth's meetings: the Wellington City Mission.[41] This became the New Zealand Evangelical Mission some months later.[42]

James Worsfold also refers to the Helping Hand Mission in Wellington, founded by Methodist Missioner Rev. L. O. Stanton, noting that he had preached on the Baptism of the Spirit in 1909.[43] However, this sermon was part of a wider teaching series on "The Work of the Holy Spirit," conducted in January–February 1909 and again in 1911. This was not a major emphasis in Stanton's mission. Of the 147 references in the Wellington *Evening Post* to his Helping Hand Mission over the eight years between its founding in 1907 and 1915, only eight were to sermons about the Holy Spirit. Five of these related to this specific series on the Work of the Holy Spirit. The last two lectures in the series were "The Baptism of the Holy Ghost" and "The Results of Being Filled with the Spirit."[44] The Helping Hand Mission also hosted a Ten Day's Holiness Convention in 1908 and ran weekly holiness meetings in 1913.[45] These indicate that its orientation was a Holiness, rather than a Pentecostal, one and Stanton's references to the Baptism of the Holy Spirit therefore must be understood in this sense. Finally, the Christian Covenanters Confederacy, which arrived in New Zealand about 1919 and was active in preparing the way for Smith Wigglesworth's meetings, appears to have had a standard Holiness/Revivalist focus.[46] The third paragraph of its Covenant, popularized by ex-Salvationist Herbert Booth during his campaigns in New Zealand from 1919 to 1921, reflects this perception of the Holy Spirit's work. This declares: "I believe in the Holy Ghost the promised comforter whose presence and baptism of power I claim as essential to a life of victory. I am determined to seek after the fullest measure of his infilling, the endowment of His gifts and the bestowal of his graces."[47]

This "baptism of power" was a characteristic example of Holiness rhetoric. These examples cited by Worsfold therefore all appear to reflect Holiness and revivalist views and as such, represent a pre-Pentecostal penumbra rather than a participation in the movement itself. Nevertheless, they provided a constituency from which Pentecostalism was able to derive its early converts through Wigglesworth's campaigns.

John A. D. Adams and Other Pioneers

Despite Worsfold's undifferentiated inclusivism, there are several legitimate instances of early Australasian Pentecostalism. In Australia, Pentecostal historian Barry Chant refers to the "Sounders," who were recorded as being filled with the Holy Spirit and speaking in tongues as early as 1870. He describes their gatherings as the first known Pentecostal meetings in Australia. It is not known how this group came to this understanding—which preceded that of Charles Fox Parham by thirty years—of the connection between glossolalia and the baptism of the Spirit.[48] Chant notes that while Joseph Marshall, the leader of the movement, may have possibly had some English Irvingite links, there was no evidence to support this connection.[49] There are several examples of early Pentecostalism in New Zealand also. The most significant of these was the Roslyn City Road Mission, founded by John A. D. Adams and others in 1903.[50] Worsfold notes that this Mission appeared to be organized on Brethren lines, with the exception that it offered "perfect liberty for the exercise of spiritual gifts."[51] This freedom was evidently understood in a classical Pentecostal sense, since Adams was espousing glossolalia and other spiritual gifts as early as 1906. In one of his pamphlets, he discusses the infilling of the Spirit, asking: "But what are the effects of this filling? This we can inquire into and discover, and the answer is upon the surface. The first effect is perhaps the one which the Church of today most dislikes to consider. They spoke with OTHER TONGUES."[52] Adams strongly argues against the cessationist view that the gifts of the Spirit were not for today.[53] He is therefore a genuine example of early Pentecostalism in New Zealand.

While it is difficult to ascertain the point at which Adams moved into a Pentecostal orbit, the influence of John Alexander Dowie appears to have been a key factor. Chant notes that although Dowie "never spoke in tongues, nor did he specifically advocate it,"[54] "a significant number of pioneer Pentecostal leaders [including Adams] trace their spiritual heritage" to him.[55] Indeed, J. Ellis, a follower of Dowie for twenty-three years, and later a Pentecostal, testified that he "taught the truths of the Scriptures, with the one exception of the Baptism of the Holy Spirit with speaking in tongues."[56] Adams received healing through Dowie in the 1880s and he and his wife were guests in the Adams' home during their 1888 visit to Dunedin.[57] (Mark Hutchinson appears to be inaccurate on the dating of this healing—which Adams testified took place in Dunedin—since he locates it during "Dowie's visit to New Zealand in 1904." However, Dowie's only visit to Dunedin was in 1888. He was briefly in the port of Auckland on his way to Australia in February 1904, but only conducted an informal meeting on board ship. He does not appear to have landed during his stopover.[58] Furthermore, Adams' allusion to his healing "39 years ago"—prior to his writing in 1926—places it within the time frame of the 1888 visit, rather than that of 1904.)

Adams and others later felt constrained to secede from the Roslyn Methodist Church in 1900 over the issue of healing and the Roslyn City Road Mission was opened three years later. This mission continued for a number of years and fully supported Smith Wigglesworth's Dunedin campaign in 1922. Adams also had personal links with the most significant figures in global Pentecostalism, as evidenced by a famous photograph of him with Pentecostal pioneers William J. Seymour,[59] John G. Lake,[60] F. F. Bosworth[61] and Tom Hezmalhalch,[62] taken about 1907.[63] Adams was well-known as a Christian apologist and a strong supporter of causes such as the temperance movement. His keen mind and legal training enabled him to be highly effective in communicating the Pentecostal message, both within New Zealand and later in Australia. He eventually became an elder in the Pentecostal Church of New Zealand after its formation in the wake of the Wigglesworth campaigns of 1922 and 1923–24. Following a shift to Australia in the mid-1920s, he also became prominent in Australian Pentecostalism, being elected national President of the Apostolic Faith Mission in 1927, a position he held for several years.[64] He later returned to Dunedin, where he died in 1936.

Figure 1: John A. D. Adams with other Pentecostal leaders associated with the Azusa Street revival, c.1907. Standing (left to right): Adams, F. F. Bosworth, and Tom Hezmalhalch. Seated (left to right): William J. Seymour and John G. Lake. Source: "Azusa Street Mission (Los Angeles, CA) [P0624]," location P0624—AZUSA, Flower Pentecostal Heritage Center, Springfield, MS, USA. Reproduced by permission from Flower Pentecostal Heritage Center.

Other early Pentecostal meetings in New Zealand included a prayer gathering in Whangarei in the home of a Mrs. Leonard, who had been baptized in the Spirit in 1913. This was later relocated to Auckland, where Mr and Mrs Bailey, Pentecostal missionaries returning from India, continued the leadership of the prayer group.[65] Other Pentecostal meetings began in Freeman's Bay, Auckland, in 1918 under the leadership of a Miss Jacobson, a missionary who had worked in the Pacific Islands. This group later amalgamated with the Auckland congregation that was formed after Smith Wigglesworth's campaign there in late 1923.[66] There was also a small Pentecostal church in Christchurch, the Church of God: Sydenham Gospel Mission Hall. This had been established in 1903, following a series of evangelistic missions, but had become Pentecostal in 1920. It was pastored by Scottish Pentecostal minister Andrew Reid, who had arrived in New Zealand in 1921.[67] This church supported—and provided the venue for—Wigglesworth's Christchurch campaign in June 1922.

A second Pentecostal Mission in Dunedin—separate from John A. D. Adams' Roslyn City Road Mission—was led by Pastor Abraham Lind. Prior to the Smith Wigglesworth campaign, this Mission was advertised in the *Evening Star* each week under heading of "Lind's Sunday Night Lectures." These lectures were held each Sunday evening in the Oddfellows' Hall, Roslyn and later at Tailoress' Union Hall in Dowling Street.[68] Since Adams' group met nearby in its own building in City Road, it seems that the two Missions were not connected. Lind took over the pastorate of the congregation that resulted from the Wigglesworth campaign.

While it is evident that there were some small Pentecostal groups in New Zealand prior to Wigglesworth's arrival, there was also a wider, fluid network of revivalist and holiness expectations. This pre-Pentecostal penumbra provided a reservoir of support for the new movement. Historian David Maxwell observes that "existing networks of radical Evangelical Protestantism ... facilitated Pentecostalism's rapid uptake."[69] This was not a process unique to New Zealand, since, as he also notes, "The key to the [Pentecostal] Movement's rapid spread across the globe lay in the religious networks already in place."[70] Wigglesworth's campaigns brought these constituencies together and provided the catalyst that precipitated them into a movement with its own distinctive identity.

Notes

1. Much has been written on New Zealand revivalism. For a comprehensive bibliographical list, see Peter Lineham, "New Zealand Religious History, a Bibliography: Section Q-R-S," s.v. "Revivalism," http://www.massey.ac.nz/~plineham/RelhistNZ.htm (accessed 29 August 2012). Also see Lineham, "Brethren Revivalism: A Second Look at New Zealand," in *Growth of the Brethren Movement: National and International Experiences. Essays in Honour of Harold H. Rowdon*, ed. Neil T. R. Dickson and Tim Grass, 154–75 (Carlisle: Paternoster, 2006); and, for a particular example of New Zealand revivalism, David Jull, "The Knapdale Revival (1881): Social Context and Religious Conviction in 19th Century New Zealand," *Australasian Pentecostal Studies*, no. 7 (March 2003), http://webjournals.ac.edu.au/journals/aps/issue-7/02-the-knapdale-revival-1881-social-context-and-re/ (accessed 10 November 2011).

2. See W. J. Shiels, ed., *The Church and Healing: Papers read at the twentieth Summer meeting and the twenty-first Winter meeting of the Ecclesiastical History Society*. Studies in Church History 19 (Oxford: Basil Blackwell, 1982); David Edwin Harrell, Jr., *All Things are Possible: The Healing and Charismatic Revivals in Modern America* (Bloomington, IN: Indiana University Press, 1975); and Douglas B. Ireton, "A Time to Heal: The Appeal of Smith Wigglesworth in New Zealand 1922-24" (BA (Hons.) dissertation in History, Massey University, 1984).

3. See Edward Shortland, *Maori Religion and Mythology*, 31–32 (London: Longmans, Green and Co., 1882); Elsdon Best, *Maori Religion and Mythology: Being an Account of the Cosmogony, Anthropogony, Religious Beliefs and Rites, Magic and Folk Lore of the Maori Folk of New Zealand, Part 1*, 370–75 (Wellington: Government Printer, 1976);

Bronwyn Elsmore, *Like Them That Dream: The Maori and the Old Testament*, 120, 134, 148–49, 152, 156 and 159 (Tauranga: Tauranga Moana Press, 1985); and Elsmore, *Mana from Heaven: A Century of Maori Prophets in New Zealand*, 95–159 (Tauranga: Moana Press, 1989).

4. Jonathan R. Baer, "Redeemed Bodies: The Functions of Divine Healing in Incipient Pentecostalism," *Church History: Studies in Christianity and Culture* 70, no. 4 (December 2001): 735–72.

5. M. M. Poloma, "An Empirical Study of Perceptions of Healing Among Assemblies of God Members," *Pneuma* 7.1 (1985): 61–77, cited in Thomson K. Mathew and Kimberly Ervin Alexander, "The Future of Healing Ministries," in *Spirit-Empowered Christianity in the 21st Century*, ed. Vinson Synan (Lake Mary, FL: Charisma House, 2011), 317, note 9.

6. For a concise discussion of the Holiness Movement, see C. E. Jones, "Holiness Movement," in *New International Dictionary of Pentecostal and Charismatic Movements* [hereafter cited as NIDPCM], ed. Stanley M. Burgess and Eduard M. van der Maas, 726–29 (Grand Rapids, MI: Zondervan, 2002).

7. See Donald W. Dayton, *Theological Roots of Pentecostalism*, Studies in Evangelicalism 5, 106–8 (Metuchen, NJ; London: Scarecrow Press, 1987); and D. D. Bundy, "Keswick Higher Life Movement," in NIDPCM, 820–21.

8. See Edward C. Millard, *What God Hath Wrought: An Account of the Mission Tour of the Rev G. C. Grubb, M.A. (1889–1890) Chiefly From the Diary Kept by E. C. Millard One of His Companions, in Ceylon, South Africa, Australia, New Zealand, Cape Colony*, 188–248 (London: E. Marlborough, 1891); Millard, *The Same Lord: An Account of the Mission Tour of the Rev. George C. Grubb in Australia, Tasmania and New Zealand From April 3rd 1891, to July 7th, 1892*, 283–347 (London: E. Marlborough, 1893); and Robert Evans and Roy McKenzie, *Evangelical Revivals in New Zealand: A History of Evangelical Revivals in New Zealand and an Outline of Some Basic Principles of Revivals*, 107–11 (Paihia: Colcom Press, 1999).

9. H. R. Jackson, *Churches and People in Australia and New Zealand 1860–1930*, 63–65 (Wellington: Allen and Unwin/Port Nicholson Press, 1987); Peter J. Lineham, "Tongues must cease: The Brethren and the Charismatic Movement in New Zealand," *Christian Brethren Research Journal*, no. 34 (November 1983): 7–52, at 11.

10. For a brief biography of Parham, see J. R. Goff, Jr., "Parham, Charles Fox," in NIDPCM, 955–57.

11. See Andrew Landale Drummond, *Edward Irving and his circle; including some consideration of the "Tongues" Movement in the light of modern psychology* (London: James Clarke and Co., [1934]); H. C. Whitley, *Blinded Eagle: An Introduction to the Life and Teaching of Edward Irving* (London: SCM Press, 1955); and D. D. Bundy, "Irving, Edward," in NIDPCM, 803–4. For a discussion of Irving's theology, see C. Gordon Strachan, *The Pentecostal Theology of Edward Irving* (London: Darton, Longman and Todd, 1973).

12. D. W. Dorries, "Catholic Apostolic Church," in NIDPCM, 459–60.

13. Worsfold, *History of the Charismatic Movements in New Zealand* 64–79.

14. Ian G. Clark, *Pentecost at the Ends of the Earth: The History of the Assemblies of God in New Zealand (1927–2003)*, 15 (Blenheim: Christian Road Ministries, 2007).

15. Ibid, 13.

16. Worsfold, *History of the Charismatic Movements in New Zealand*, particularly chapters 9 and 10.

17. Peter Lineham, review of *The History of a New Zealand Pentecostal Movement*, by Brett Knowles, *Stimulus* 10:1 (February 2002): 65.
18. For a brief biography of Dayton, see R. M. Riss, "Dayton, Donald Wilbur," in NIDPCM, 573.
19. Dayton, *Theological Roots of Pentecostalism*, 173–74, 186.
20. Worsfold, *History of the Charismatic Movements in New Zealand*, chapters 2–8, particularly pages 64–79.
21. Strachan, *The Pentecostal Theology of Edward Irving*, 19.
22. Mark Hutchinson, "Edward Irving's Antipodean Shadow," *e:Oikonomia: The Sydney College of Divinity e-journal of theology, ministry and the arts* 3, no. 1 (April 2008), http://oikon.webjournals.org/articles/1/04/2008/7063.htm?id={756C09C7-58E5-41DC-9B5B-0F6C94A7EE79} (accessed 13 April 2009). For a contrary view, see Peter Elliott, "Nineteenth-Century Australian Charismata: Edward Irving's Legacy," *Pneuma: The Journal of the Society for Pentecostal Studies* 34, no. 1 (2012): 26–36.
23. Lineham, "Tongues must cease": 9.
24. Reports of this conference appeared in *Evening Post*, 25 January 1888, 2, National Library of New Zealand—Te Puna Mātauranga o Aotearoa, "Papers Past," http://paperspast.natlib.govt.nz/cgi-bin/paperspast/ [hereafter cited as "Papers Past"]; and in *Evening Post*, 26 January 1888, 2, "Papers Past" (both accessed 24 March 2010). "Papers Past" was created by the National Library of New Zealand (Te Puna Mātauranga o Aotearoa). It is a valuable online collection of digitised historic New Zealand newspapers, covering the years from 1839 to 1945 and including 83 publications from all regions of New Zealand. It contains more than three million pages of text and offers both browsing and full text searching.
25. *Evening Post*, 21 January 1888, 2, "Papers Past" (accessed 24 March 2010).
26. Worsfold, *History of the Charismatic Movements in New Zealand*, 85.
27. Ibid., 85–86. This address was reported in *Evening Post*, 3 March 1888, 2, "Papers Past" (accessed 24 March 2010).
28. For a brief biography of Dowie, see E. L. Blumhofer, "Dowie, John Alexander," in NIDPCM, 586–87. For a more extensive coverage, see Barry Chant, *Heart of Fire: The Story of Australian Pentecostalism*, rev. ed., 11–26 (Plympton, Vic.: Tabor Publications, 1997); and Chant, *The Spirit of Pentecost: The Origins and Development of the Pentecostal Movement in Australia 1870–1939*. Asbury Theological Seminary Series in World Christian Revitalization Movements in Pentecostal/Charismatic Studies 5, 59–82 and 341–42 (Lexington, KY: Emeth Press, 2011).
29. Worsfold, *History of the Charismatic Movements in New Zealand*, 86.
30. E.g., "Page 1 Advertisements Column 7," *Timaru Herald*, 2 May 1888, 1, "Papers Past" (accessed 25 March 2010).
31. Worsfold, *History of the Charismatic Movements in New Zealand*, 86–87. Worsfold consistently misspells Soltau's name as "Solatu."
32. Biographical details in "Rev. George Soltau: Opening of his Mission at Gore," *Mataura Ensign*, 11 June 1895, 5, "Papers Past" (accessed 25 March 2010).
33. Ibid. This article reports that his opening message was "We must all appear before the judgement seat of God" and "Sanctification." Also *Tuapeka Times*, 26 February 1896, 3, "Papers Past"; and "Christian Endeavor Rally," *North Otago Times*, 12 February 1897, 3, "Papers Past" (both accessed 25 March 2010).
34. For example, George Soltau, *The Inquiry Room: Hints for Dealing with the Anxious* (London: Morgan and Scott, 1884), http://www.inquiryroom.com/the_inquiry_room_by_george_soltau.htm (accessed 31 August 2013); Soltau, *The Person and Work of the*

Holy Spirit. The "Bible-Talk" Series 1 (London: John F. Shaw and Co., [1886]); and Soltau, *The Person and Work of the Holy Spirit* (London: Jas. Nisbet, [1920?]).

35. John A. D. Adams, "The Scriptural Statement Concerning the Baptism with the Holy Spirit, Chapters XIII–XVI," *Good News*, 1 May 1928, 6–7, http://webjournals.alphacrucis.edu.au/journals/GN/gn-vol19-no5-may-1928/03-scriptural-statement-concerning-bapt-XIII-XVI/ (accessed 7 March 2012).

36. Ibid., 6–7.

37. Worsfold, *History of the Charismatic Movements in New Zealand*, 87. For a brief biography of Henry Roberts, variously (and confusingly) called both Henry Roberts and Harry Roberts in Worsfold's account, see B. Knowles, "Roberts, Henry," in NIDPCM, 1026.

38. For a brief biography of H. V. Roberts, see B. Knowles, "Roberts, H. V. (Harry)," in NIDPCM, 1025–26.

39. H. V. Roberts, *New Zealand's Greatest Revival*, 10 (Auckland: New Zealand Pelorus Press, 1951). A photostated copy of this book is held in Brett Knowles Research Papers [BKRP], MS-3530/005, Hocken Library, Dunedin.

40. Carol Soukotta, Mount Hope Foundation, Indonesia, email message to author, 25 November 2012.

41. Worsfold, *History of the Charismatic Movements in New Zealand*, 127.

42. Ibid, 141.

43. Ibid, 92–93.

44. "Page 2 Advertisements Column 6," *Evening Post*, 30 January 1909, 2, "Papers Past"; and "Page 2 Advertisements Column 5," *Evening Post*, 6 February 1909, 2, "Papers Past" (both accessed 28 March 2010).

45. "Page 6 Advertisements Column 5," *Evening Post*, 18 April 1908, 6, "Papers Past"; and "Page 2 Advertisements Column 8," *Evening Post*, 5 July 1913, 2, "Papers Past" (both accessed 29 March 2010).

46. Worsfold, *History of the Charismatic Movements in New Zealand*, 95–97; 107–8, 126.

47. Cited in Ibid, 95.

48. Chant, *Heart of Fire*, 35–36; and Chant, *The Spirit of Pentecost*, 2 and 42–44.

49. Chant, *The Spirit of Pentecost*, 54, note 102.

50. Worsfold, *History of the Charismatic Movements in New Zealand*, 89–92. For biographies of Adams, see B. Knowles, "Adams, John A. D.," in NIDPCM, 308; and, in greater detail, Hutchinson, "Adams, John Archibald Duncan (1844–1936)."

51. Roslyn City Road Mission, Trust Deed, Land and Deeds Office, 19 December 1903 and Memorandum, cited in Worsfold, *History of the Charismatic Movements in New Zealand*, 90.

52. John A. D. Adams, *The Church as Revealed in Scripture*, 87–88 (Dayton, OH: John J. Scruby, [1906]). Pamphlets 156/21, Hocken Library, Dunedin. Capitalisation as cited.

53. Ibid, 107–9.

54. Barry Chant, "The Nineteenth and Early Twentieth Century Origins of the Australian Pentecostal Movement," in *Reviving Australia: Essays on the History and Experience of Revival and Revivalism in Australian Christianity*. Studies in Australian Christianity 3, ed. Mark Hutchinson and Stuart Piggin, 107 (Sydney: Centre for the Study of Australian Christianity, 1994).

55. Chant, *The Spirit of Pentecost*, 59, 75–77; also Chant, *Heart of Fire*, 11 and 24.

56. J. Ellis, in *Australian Evangel*, July 1926, 10, cited in Chant, *Heart of Fire*, 24, and Chant, *The Spirit of Pentecost*, 76.

57. Hutchinson, "Adams, John Archibald Duncan (1844–1936)."
58. "'The Prophet of Zion.' Dr. J. A. Dowie in Auckland. A Gathering of Friends. An Interview. American Reports Denied." *New Zealand Herald*, 10 February 1904, 3. "Papers Past" (accessed 21 June 2013).
59. For a brief biography of Seymour, see C. M. Robeck, Jr., "Seymour, William Joseph," in NIDPCM, 1053–58.
60. For a brief biography of Lake, see J. R. Ziegler, "Lake, John Graham," in NIDPCM, 828.
61. For a brief biography of Bosworth, see R. M. Riss, "Bosworth, Fred Francis," in NIDPCM, 439–40.
62. For a brief biography of Hezmalhalch, see W. E. Warner, "Hezmalhalch, Thomas," in NIDPCM, 712.
63. See Figure 1 above, 11.
64. Chant, *Heart of Fire*, 105, 108 and 111; and Chant, *The Spirit of Pentecost*, 135, 286 and 367.
65. *New Zealand Evangel*, June 1930, 10.
66. Worsfold, *History of the Charismatic Movements in New Zealand*, 93–94.
67. Ibid, 115, notes 1 and 2.
68. "Religious [Notices]," *Evening Star*, April-June 1922.
69. David Maxwell, "'Networks and Niches': The Worldwide Transmission of the Azusa Street Revival," in *The Azusa Street Revival and Its Legacy*, ed. Harold D. Hunter and Cecil M. Robeck, Jr., 129 (Cleveland, TN: Pathway Press, 2006).
70. Ibid, 139.

Chapter 3

The 1920s

The "Roaring Twenties"?

Classic Hollywood films such as *Little Caesar*—based in part on gangster Al Capone—have provided potent images of "the Roaring Twenties" as a period characterized by Prohibition, gangsters and illicit alcohol.[1] However, these portrayals are only partial refractions of a reality which, in any case, existed only in America. If the 1920s can be characterized at all, they are best described as a decade of anxiety. This insecurity, continuing from the global dislocations of the previous decade, was both economic and existential. In New Zealand, the chief cause of economic unease was the fluctuating overseas market for the country's primary produce.[2] Although the mid-1920s saw a marked improvement in the economy, people were conscious of its fragility rather than of its prosperity.[3] At a deeper level, the massive death tolls of the First World War, together with the effects of the worldwide 1918 influenza epidemic, produced an awareness of mortality and a search for reassurance. It is therefore not surprising that in the 1920s

> there was an unquestionable demand for exotic religion.... One extreme manifestation of this development was the interest shown in the visits to England of [Indian Christian] Sadhu Sundar Singh in 1920 and 1922. A more predictable sign was the great increase of interest in spiritualism, starting initially with an understandable desire to make contact with the dead, but soon extending to interest in the use of spiritualism for healing.[4]

Although this observation describes the English religious context, the "demand for exotic religion" was also characteristic of religion here during the 1920s also, as evidenced in the "Religious Notices" columns in the newspapers of the period.

This quest for reassurance led to a resurgence of revivalism. The phenomenon had previously had a heyday in the 1880s, but was revitalized and reached new heights in the 1920s. Although historian Hugh Jackson insists that Australasian revivalism had always been peripheral to colonial life,[5] History student Douglas Ireton notes that revivalists were far more common in this decade than in any previous period of New Zealand's religious history.[6] The frequent reportage of revival meetings in the New Zealand media in the 1920s might indicate that Jackson's dismissal of the phenomenon may not be entirely accurate. This religious revitalization was paralleled by a resurgence of interest in healing; Tahupōtiki Wiremu Rātana[7] was the most significant of the faith healers active during the decade. Others included Anglicans James Moore Hickson—who visited New Zealand in 1923[8]—and curate Henry Braddock, who conducted itinerant healing ministry throughout the South Island until his death in 1932.[9]

Rātana's activity began in November 1918, at the height of the influenza epidemic. The Māori death toll from this was almost five times that of non-Māori;[10] only three of the twenty-one members of his family survived.[11] Rātana had a vision of a small cloud rising from the sea, calling him to be the *māngai*, or "Mouthpiece" of God, to unite the Māori people and turn them to "Jehovah of the thousands." He soon gained national fame and attracted large numbers of Māori to his farmhouse at Whangaehu, south of Whanganui, to seek his prayers. This grew into a settlement, which came to be known as Rātana Pa. His reputation was extended by his tours throughout New Zealand and especially through the testimony of Nelson woman Fannie Lammas, who had been in a metal frame for nineteen years and was healed after corresponding with him. Rev. Joseph Kemp, the prominent pastor of the Auckland Baptist Tabernacle and founder of the influential Bible Training Institute, published an account of Miss Lammas' healing, which went through four reprint editions.[12] Kemp's support of Rātana's ministry contributed to its wide influence in the Pākehā community. Rātana was steeped in the Bible—which he expressed in terms of Māori language and metaphor—and strongly opposed those traditional aspects of Māori life that he believed to be superstitious and harmful. Although his theology was broadly orthodox, theological differences eventually emerged with the Anglican and Methodist churches—which hitherto had strongly supported his healing movement—leading to the formation of the Rātana Church in 1925.

The activities of Rātana and of other healers in New Zealand during the 1920s reflected what Ireton has called a "national fascination" with healing.[13] Although the roots of this go back to the nineteenth century, it was reinforced by three specific factors in the 1920s. The first was the consciousness of mortality following the First World War and the influenza epidemic of 1918. Secondly, Ireton notes an interest in new extensions of psychoanalytic theory and aspects of "mental hygiene." The third element was a reaction to theological demystification and to the move away from an emphasis on the supernatural.[14] These factors helped to foster public receptivity towards healing, thus extending the constituency of the healing revivalists and—by association—of the nascent Pentecostal movement. This provided it with a reservoir of support upon which it was able to build.

Pentecostal Pioneer: Smith Wigglesworth in New Zealand

Former Salvationist Smith Wigglesworth had received the baptism of the Spirit under the ministry of early British Pentecostal leader Rev. A. A. Boddy[15] in Sunderland, Northeast England, in 1907. This empowerment enabled him to launch into healing evangelism throughout Britain and in other countries around the world. Although Wigglesworth had little formal education, his straightforward Yorkshire manner and vigorous faith preaching made a strong impression on his audiences. By the time of his campaigns in New Zealand, he was one of the better known evangelists in the Pentecostal movement and had been conducting healing campaigns for fifteen years.[16]

Figure 2: Smith Wigglesworth, at the time of his first campaigns in New Zealand, 1922. Source: "WIGGLESWORTH, SMITH [P5605]," location P5605-WIGGLESWORTH, Flower Pentecostal Heritage Center, Springfield, MS, USA. Reproduced by permission from Flower Pentecostal Heritage Center.

Wigglesworth was influenced to come to New Zealand by John Fullerton, a spirit-filled China Inland Mission missionary whom he had met during the latter's furlough in Denmark in 1921. Australian-born Fullerton[17] and his Danish wife

Martha had both been baptized with the Spirit during a Pentecostal revival in South Yunnan, China, where they were stationed. However, H. V. Roberts' eyewitness account mistakenly describes him as Danish, thereby obscuring his connection with Australia and New Zealand;[18] this error is repeated by both James Worsfold[19] and Ian Clark.[20] Fullerton had been impressed to pray for revival in Australasia and seized the opportunity of asking Wigglesworth to pray about the possibility of a visit to this part of the world. Wigglesworth felt led to come and was brought out to Australia by Pentecostal pioneer "Mother" Sarah Jane Lancaster[21] and the Good News Hall in Melbourne later that year. (Lancaster's assembly paid for Wigglesworth's sea-fares from the United Kingdom and all expenses of his campaigns in Australia. This was a considerable sacrifice as the fares alone were equivalent to six months' wages for a working man at the time.)[22] Following the conclusion of his Australian campaigns, Wigglesworth then crossed the Tasman to New Zealand in May 1922. However, he had no local contacts and was personally unknown in New Zealand, despite several Australian Pentecostal members of the Christian Covenanters Confederacy—an interdenominational prayer group for revival and holiness, founded by Herbert Booth—having arrived in Wellington in November 1921 to pave the way for Wigglesworth's campaigns.[23] W. A. Buchanan, one of these Australian advance agents, was Lancaster's son-in-law.[24] Fullerton therefore came to Wellington in April to facilitate an introduction to local ministers, but since Wigglesworth missed his boat from Australia, he had to return to China without making contact with him. Fullerton consequently got in touch with Henry Roberts—a regular contributor to his mission in China—and arranged for him to meet Wigglesworth on his arrival. Roberts, a longtime advocate of revival and healing, saw Wigglesworth's arrival as an answer to prayer, having started numerous prayer meetings for revival, nine of which were in full swing in Wellington at the time.[25] He inserted advertisements in the newspapers and booked the Wellington Town Hall—the largest venue in the city—for the first night of the campaign as a step of faith.

Smith Wigglesworth eventually arrived in late May 1922 and spent the next two months in New Zealand.[26] More than half of this time was spent in Wellington, where he conducted two highly successful healing campaigns. The first of these, which opened in the Town Hall on 28 May with an attendance of 800 supporters, raised expectations and set the pattern for his campaigns in other centers. By the third night of the campaign, the number present had grown to a full house of 3,000, with hundreds more being turned away. This attendance continued until the final night of the campaign on 7 June.[27] Wigglesworth's ministry to the sick captured wide public attention, tapping into a pervasive interest in healing. The Wellington newspapers were generally positive, with the *Dominion*'s sympathetic and detailed report noting that a large percentage of those prayed for had received healing and observing that their testimonies "rang with the spirit of real conviction."[28] A more critical approach was taken by the controversialist *New Zealand Truth*, which lamented the "polite reports of the revival meetings" in the Wellington dailies, which it said had "dealt very tenderly" with Wigglesworth's claims.[29] The impact of the campaign appears to have sparked a response from the pulpits of several other Wellington churches, the ministers of which preached sermons on the subject of healing in following weeks.[30] In addition to the evening healing meetings, Wigglesworth also conducted preliminary morning teaching meetings for Christians. This had the effect of introducing Pentecostal subjects such as the Enduement of Power and the Gifts of the Spirit to his supporters. He also preached on Pentecostal themes such as the Baptism of the Spirit, Sanctification, the Second Coming, Divine Healing and Exorcism in the main evening meetings.[31] Spiritual gifts were witnessed for the first time—Wigglesworth's sermons frequently being interspersed with tongues and interpretation—and healings and miracles took place.[32]

Figure 3: Henry Roberts (left) and his son, Harry V. Roberts (right), early leaders in the Pentecostal Church of New Zealand. Carol Soukotta, Mount Hope Foundation, Indonesia. Reproduced by permission from Carol Soukotta.

Following this campaign, Smith Wigglesworth and his party travelled to the South Island for further meetings. As was the case in Wellington, local contacts provided a base from which to work. In Christchurch, a small Pentecostal church—the Church of God: Sydenham Gospel Mission Hall, pastored by Andrew Reid—arranged the venue and the advertising for the campaign. This ran for five days from 11 June to 16 June and, as in Wellington, the hall where the services were held was filled to overflowing. However, there was some strong opposition: Christchurch papers were less positive than their Wellington counterparts in their reports of the campaign.[33] The *New Zealand Truth* also continued its trenchant criticism of Wigglesworth's activities and methods[34] and some ministers lambasted the campaign from their pulpits. An example of the latter was Baptist minister Rev. Dr. J. J. North, who launched a stinging attack on the campaign, his sermon topic on the following Sunday being "The Miracles that Did Not Happen in Sydenham."[35]

North also wrote a highly critical letter about the campaign to the Editor of the *Sun*.[36] Nevertheless, as Henry Roberts responded in a letter to the *Sun*, a number of healings took place in the meetings, including a desperate case of internal cancer, incurable heart trouble and other complaints.[37] To its credit, the *Sun* published Roberts' letter alongside its leading article on the campaign, thus giving a balanced perspective. Considerable debate ensued in the "To the Editor" columns of the *Sun* over the next few days, with both critics and supporters of the campaign expressing their point of view.[38]

In Dunedin, the campaign was supported by two local Pentecostal groups: the Roslyn City Road Mission—founded by John A. D. Adams and others in 1903[39]—and another Pentecostal group led by Pastor Abraham Lind. However, backing for the campaign went wider than this. The *Otago Daily Times* reported that the Council of Churches in Dunedin was offering prayer "in regard to the soul-winning campaign" and that an influential committee of local businessmen was also assisting the mission.[40] (This wider support may reflect both memories of the highly successful Chapman-Alexander campaign of ten years earlier[41] and the personal standing of Adams, who had been a prominent barrister and solicitor in Dunedin.) Nevertheless, control of the campaign appeared to be in the hands of the Wellington campaign committee, since the main advertisements appeared above the signature of Henry Roberts,[42] rather than of these local groups. Several anonymous advertisements for the campaign—apparently inserted by local supporters—also appeared in these papers. The campaign began on 18 June in the Early Settlers Hall and after a moderate attendance at the beginning, soon reached capacity[43] with hundreds being turned away, necessitating shifts to several larger venues. The campaign attracted people from all levels of society, with Adams noting the presence of "respected and prosperous" Dunedin businessmen in the audience.[44]

Despite the churches' support for the Dunedin campaign, newspaper reports were mixed. The *Evening Star* was ambivalent in its attitude, combining an acknowledgement of positive results with acid comments about the campaign.[45] The *Otago Daily Times* was more critical, heading its report "A Questionable Display" and taking particular issue with the roughness of Smith Wigglesworth's approach to praying for the sick. "He gripped the patients firmly and roughly and pulled about the part said to be afflicted, all the time loud[ly] rebuking the devil within, adjuring it to leave and never return."[46] This was Wigglesworth's standard practice, since he did not believe in being gentle where the devil and his works were concerned. He was noted for his strenuous efforts while praying for the sick and for his tendency towards aggressive physical contact with those to whom he ministered. (This could occasionally backfire, as once happened in South Africa, where it was reported that "A big Afrikaans woman came for prayer, and Wigglesworth hit her as he prayed. She said, 'Oh, that's the way, is it?' and hit him back! But the next night she was back and asked for an opportunity to make a public apology for hitting the servant of the Lord. After she got home the night before, she had discovered that every trace of her illness was gone.")[47] In Dunedin, this rough treatment, together with Wigglesworth's forthright denunciations from the platform, gave some sections of his audience an impression of bullying and the same article noted that there was "growing resentment at the whole business in one corner of the building at least, and the indignant mutterings of some returned soldiers might have developed into something more serious had the end [of the meeting] not been at hand."[48] As was the case in Christchurch, debate over the campaign ensued in the "To the Editor" columns of the two local newspapers over the next few days.[49]

After the end of the campaign on 26 June, services continued under the leadership of Pastor Lind, continuing to meet in the Queen's Picture Theatre[50] and later adopting the name "Dunedin Evangelistic Mission." Lind seems to have taken the leadership by default, since John A. D. Adams was seventy-eight years old at the time of Smith Wigglesworth's campaign. Nevertheless, Adams later became an elder in the Pentecostal Church of New Zealand, a position which he held until his emigration to Australia in early 1926. He came back to New Zealand in 1932. Wigglesworth and his party returned to Wellington, conducting a second campaign in the Town Hall—from 2 July to 13 July—which built upon and consolidated the results of the first campaign. (H. V. Roberts also refers to a campaign in Blenheim immediately after the Wellington campaign and within the same time frame as the other campaigns in the South Island, but his recollection may be inaccurate.[51] As his eyewitness account was published thirty-nine years after the event, his memory may have been at fault and it is difficult to see how a visit to Blenheim could have fitted into Wigglesworth's itinerary. The only available dates were 8 June, 27–29 June and 16–20 July 1922, but no mentions of a visit to Blenheim appear in the *Marlborough Express* for these dates. Furthermore, no advertisements for, or accounts of, the Blenheim campaign appear in the *Marlborough Express* for these dates.[52] However, Wigglesworth did conduct a later campaign in Blenheim in December 1923, during his second visit to New Zealand in 1923–24.) Wigglesworth then left New Zealand, not returning until October 1923, when he conducted campaigns in Auckland, Palmerston North and Blenheim, before returning to Wellington in December to address the first national Pentecostal conference. He also conducted a final series of meetings in the Wellington Town Hall in January 1924.

What were the long-term results of Wigglesworth's ministry in New Zealand? Statistics are available only for Wellington, where an estimated two thousand people were converted to Christ during the two campaigns (500 of these on a single night).[53] Roberts also notes that many were healed through the laying on of hands by Wigglesworth and his assistants and that 800 people were baptized in the Spirit and spoke in tongues.[54] It is therefore evident that Wigglesworth made a considerable impression on the religious life of the capital, an impact noted by the media. In a larger sense, he is usually credited with introducing Pentecostalism to New Zealand. However, this categorization is only *partly* accurate, since there were several Pentecostal groups in New Zealand before his arrival and other Pentecostal campaigners (such as Aimee Semple McPherson)[55] also visited New Zealand in 1922.[56] What is true is that—as with the Azusa Street revival in Los Angeles in 1906—a previously little-known, under-the-radar movement was brought to public notice in no uncertain terms. Wigglesworth should therefore be seen as the *popularizer* of the Pentecostal movement in New Zealand, rather than its *founder*. His campaigns tapped into a widespread interest in healing and thus received extensive public attention; and his teaching about, and demonstration of, Pentecostal gifts built a new constituency upon the foundation of this interest. In so doing, Wigglesworth's campaigns provided a focus and center of identity for the new movement.

From Mission to Movement: New Zealand Pentecostalism after Wigglesworth

The end of Smith Wigglesworth's healing campaigns marked a transition from an evangelistic mission to the beginnings of an organized movement. A committee was immediately set up to look after the prayer meetings that had emerged and to provide pastoral care for the converts of the Wellington campaign. Import merchant E. E. Pennington was elected to the chair of this committee, Henry Roberts was appointed as its missioner and his son H. V. Roberts was elected secretary. The committee adopted the name of "Wellington City Mission"[57] and placed an advertisement in the daily newspapers advising that it was continuing the work of the Wigglesworth mission.[58] This was a necessary step, since while some churches and ministers had supported Wigglesworth's campaigns, antagonism from others produced boundaries of differentiation between them and Wigglesworth's converts. Consequently, as the *New Zealand Evangel* commented, "these newly-formed believers . . . were like sheep without a shepherd, [and] something had to be done to conserve the fruit gathered from the Smith-Wigglesworth Mission."[59]

This was no easy task, as Wigglesworth had not established any structures for the movement's continuance; his only official action had been the ordination of Henry Roberts, the Secretary of his campaign committee.[60] The Wellington City Mission therefore had to deal with some urgent major issues. The first of these was the lack of a generally recognized authority structure; consequently there was a proliferation of "Pentecostal" meetings in private homes, not subject to any authority and tending to extremism. Nor had provision had been made for the pastoral care for the converts of the mission. Furthermore, there was no clearly defined and generally accepted set of beliefs and practices, since the converts of the mission had come from a variety of religious backgrounds and held a wide diversity of beliefs.[61] There were also disciplinary problems, exemplified by the unfortunate experience of the Dunedin church. Pastor Lind had taken the responsibility for this church following Wigglesworth's campaign there in June 1922. However, he was later involved in sexual offences against women members of his congregation and was eventually brought before the Dunedin Supreme Court in August 1923 on charges of rape and indecent assault. He was found guilty and sentenced to seven years jail with hard labor, the maximum penalty available. The trial generated strong public condemnation, as indicated by the reports in the *Otago Daily Times*.[62] This incident adversely affected the growth of the Pentecostal movement in Dunedin for many years and James Worsfold notes—with masterly understatement—that the church there "did not grow to any great extent."[63]

In Wellington, the City Mission committee, under Henry Roberts' leadership, set about its task with vigor. Its immediate concern was to bring the spontaneous formation of independent prayer meetings in Wellington and elsewhere under centralized control. To this end, it established two congregations in the central city and in Newtown and insisted that all "tarrying meetings" for the Baptism of the Spirit were to be under its central oversight.[64] It also produced a Constitution, formulated an official Doctrinal Statement (which was later reproduced on the back page of each issue of the *New Zealand Evangel*),[65] established guidelines for the selection of future leaders and purchased a centrally located building in Te Aro, Wellington. However, the Committee's perspective soon expanded beyond Wellington, as is indicated by a change of name to the "New Zealand Evangelical Mission" in January 1923.[66] It clearly felt some degree of responsibility for other cities and assumed a role of guidance on a national basis.[67] Consequently, it selected, appointed and financially supported workers to the pastorates of Pentecostal congregations in other towns,[68] thus creating a network of pastoral control. The movement's identity was further strengthened by the holding of annual Christmas conventions, usually in Wellington, and by the publication of a national monthly magazine, the *New Zealand Evangel*, from June 1924 on.[69] The return of Smith Wigglesworth for further campaigns in October 1923—which coincided with those of the Anglican healing missioner, James Moore Hickson—also reinforced the momentum of the movement. (Several other Pentecostal campaigners had also made brief visits to New Zealand in the interim.) Wigglesworth conducted campaigns in Auckland, Palmerston North and Blenheim, before returning to Wellington for the first national Pentecostal Christmas Convention and a further series of revival meetings in the Wellington Town Hall in January 1924.

Despite this energy, however, there were several signs that augured badly for the movement's future. Attendances at Wigglesworth's meetings in the Wellington Town Hall in January 1924 were not as great as those eighteen months earlier and only a minority of the converts had continued in the movement. (Indeed, of the nineteen people identified by James Worsfold from among the hundreds of participants in the campaigns, only six reappear as members of the New Zealand Evangelical Mission—a retention rate of only 31.58%. This small sample may reflect a larger trend, since many of those who had been influenced in the campaigns had returned to their churches.)[70] Furthermore, the New Zealand Evangelical Mission Executive Committee had taken the opportunity of holding several administrative meetings during the 1923 Christmas Convention. Its Minute Book noted, however, that although Wigglesworth had been the catalyst for the movement's beginnings and was the main speaker at the Convention, he did not attend any of these Committee meetings.[71] His absence appeared to reflect his charismatic focus on evangelism and lack of concern for organizational niceties. This tension between charismatic authority and bureaucratic organization intensified over the next three years. This was exemplified by Edward R. Weston, a Baptist pastor who had been baptized in the Spirit during Wigglesworth's Dunedin campaign. Weston, who was appointed to the Wellington South congregation in 1924, was an exceptionally gifted Bible teacher and was to have a strong influence on the future trajectory of the movement in the 1920s and 1930s.[72] However, his ministry also seems to have created an alternative locus of authority to that of the Executive Committee for some members of the movement, reinforcing a tendency towards fragmentation.[73] The arrival of A. C. Valdez in New Zealand in September 1924 brought these issues to a head.[74]

Valdez was a Spanish-American Pentecostal evangelist, having associations with—but not formal ordination in—the American Assemblies of God.[75] (He had been divorced and remarried, which automatically disbarred him from ordination in that body.)[76] He was to have great influence on the shape of Pentecostalism in both Australia and New Zealand, hence Mark Hutchinson's reference to him as the "second founder" of Pentecostalism in Australia (after Sarah Jane Lancaster).[77] He received an enthusiastic welcome from New Zealand Pentecostals[78]—who expected him to continue the momentum generated by Smith Wigglesworth's visits—and conducted campaigns in Wellington, Blenheim, Christchurch and Dunedin. However, he appears to have rapidly become perturbed at the disorganization of the movement and proposed that the New Zealand Evangelical Mission hold a New Zealand-wide conference in November 1924 to consider how it should be governed.[79] This conference, which was chaired by Valdez himself, was crucial for the future trajectory of the movement. Ian Clark makes the significant comment that Valdez's chairmanship indicates that there was insufficient confidence in the New Zealand leadership's ability to deal with these fundamental issues.[80]

At the conference, Valdez taught on the Scriptural patterns of Church structure, emphasizing its basis as a Biblical, divine institution[81] and apparently stressing the roles of elders and deacons in the local church. This teaching was well-received, with the conference unanimously expressing an "earnest desire to get all assemblies established in Divine Order" and calling for a Christmas convention to formalize this.[82] The conference also decided to change the name of the movement to the "Pentecostal Church of New Zealand."[83] He afterwards travelled with the South Island delegates to Christchurch, where he called a joint meeting of the two Pentecostal churches there and publicly ordained elders and deacons to work in these local churches. This was the first such ordination in the New Zealand Pentecostal movement. It is significant that it should have taken place in Christchurch, rather than in the movement's headquarters in Wellington, possibly reflecting an initiative on the part of Valdez rather than of the Executive Committee. He also ordained elders and deacons in Wellington the following month; it is noteworthy that his sermon on that occasion was on "the symptoms of a division maker."[84]

The 1924 Christmas convention endorsed the decisions made in November and declared itself to be the first official gathering of the Pentecostal Church of New Zealand, transferring all property of the New Zealand Evangelical Mission to the new body. The election of nine elders—the majority of whom were from Wellington—was confirmed, a Credentials Committee was set up and trustees were appointed.[85] The February 1925 issue of the *New Zealand Evangel* advised that the periodical was now the official organ of the Pentecostal Church of New Zealand and that all branches of the movement would bear this name.[86] Furthermore, all future campaigns would be held only under the name of the Pentecostal Church of

New Zealand.⁸⁷ It is therefore evident that, from the point of view of its leadership, matters were firmly under control and a successful incorporation had taken place. The events of the next two years would prove this optimism to be ill-founded.

A hardening of attitudes is observable in some of the articles in the *New Zealand Evangel* immediately after the Conference. The January 1925 issue warned of division and insisted that no one was to be received into fellowship without written approval from the Credentials Committee. It also advised that all communications relating to the Pentecostal Church of New Zealand were to be addressed to its secretary, Harry Roberts, Jnr. [i.e., H. V. Roberts], in Wellington.⁸⁸ The following month's issue also indicated that there was some doctrinal divergence, since it included a warning against literature being distributed which was a distortion of the Word of God.⁸⁹ (This literature was not identified, but since Australian Pentecostal leader Sarah Jane Lancaster found it necessary, twenty-one months later, to warn New Zealand readers of her periodical *Good News* that "people were circulating false statements that the editors [of *Good News*] did not believe in the deity of Christ or the personality of the Holy Spirit," the *New Zealand Evangel* warning may be about her somewhat unorthodox views.)⁹⁰ It is not surprising that these doctrinal disagreements should have arisen, since some of the pastors in the movement—such as E. R. Weston—had strong teaching gifts and their ministries created alternative sources of authority to that of the Executive Committee in Wellington. Similarly, the arrival of American evangelist/teacher Kelso Glover at the invitation of the Executive Committee in August 1925 introduced eschatological views that were quite different from those held by the New Zealand churches. Glover taught that Christians would go through the end-time Tribulation, in contrast to the rest of the New Zealand Pentecostal movement, which believed that the Church would be "raptured" out of this. Although he only remained in New Zealand for six months, these variant views were adopted by some Pentecostal Church of New Zealand pastors, adding to tensions within the movement.⁹¹

The most severe conflicts, however, were about organization. These were particularly acute over the role of Harry Roberts, its General Secretary, as is demonstrated in the minutes of the 1925 Christmas convention. These were reported in the *New Zealand Evangel* and recorded that the duties of this office were discussed in committee, rather than in open session.⁹² The committee was conscious of "the danger that the General Secretary may use his office to control the movements of workers and other activities of the church." Consequently, it emphasized that "[The Secretary's] duties were confined to that of an agent of the Church rather than a managing officer of the Church. He forms one member of the Credential Committee, but has no power to decide on matters of the Church, but is subject to the decision of the Elders of the Incorporated Assemblies."⁹³ This decision failed to fully resolve the issue. Despite the final authority theoretically being vested in "the Elders of the Incorporated Assemblies" (i.e., the ordained elders of all the local assemblies), this group only met at the Annual Conference. No body had been set up to administer the affairs of the Pentecostal Church of New Zealand between these conferences. Consequently, much of the day-to-day running of the movement devolved upon the General Secretary (despite the official limitation of his role). This did little to dissipate the perception that the movement was run from the Wellington headquarters.

It is therefore not surprising that a number of secessions from the Pentecostal Church of New Zealand—many of these involving key figures in the movement—took place throughout 1926. These included one led by Hugh Bruce and A. J. Cobb—both elders of the Pentecostal Church of New Zealand[94]—and C. J. Lovatt; Cobb was also the movement's General Secretary and Lovatt its General Treasurer.[95] Since all three of these men were national leaders in the Pentecostal Church of New Zealand, their departure reflected tensions at the highest levels of the movement. These splits obliged the movement's leaders—together with A. C. Valdez, who had recently returned from Australia—to convene a national conference of Elders in August 1926 to deal with the issue. The conference agreed to set up a widely representative Interim Control Board to deal with matters affecting the administration of the national Church between the annual conferences. By contrast to the earlier Wellington-dominated Elders' Council, this had only two members from Wellington, the remainder being from Christchurch, New Plymouth and Auckland.[96] This action, however, was too little, too late. It failed to restore confidence in the movement's leadership and a rash of resignations followed over the next five months, including that of Valdez himself in September 1926.[97]

By the time of the 1926 Christmas conference, a rival conference had been organized in New Plymouth with Valdez as the guest speaker;[98] this was attended by most of the churches in the movement, with delegates from twelve centers registered as attending.[99] This Conference was more inclusive and less authoritarian than in previous years, with shared leadership of its sessions. It was also fully reported in the *New Zealand Evangel*,[100] which also expressed the hope that the coming year would be one of "fruitful ministry for the Pentecostal Church of New Zealand."[101] (This sentiment was an indication that the conference was seen as a gathering of that body, rather than a breakaway movement). By contrast, a smaller—and much less representative—"official" Pentecostal Church of New Zealand conference was simultaneously held in Wellington on 29–30 December 1926, with representatives from only six of the movement's churches; thirty-one of the forty-three attendees were from Wellington. Nevertheless, this conference ruled that the New Plymouth conference was unconstitutional, since the arrangement of the annual conference was a matter for the Wellington committee. However, the majority of the membership of the Pentecostal Church of New Zealand—who had attended the New Plymouth conference in preference to that in Wellington—was ready to support a new leadership structure in the movement. The rulings of the Wellington conference were therefore quietly ignored and no report of it appeared in the *New Zealand Evangel*.[102]

It is therefore clear that a substantial secession was under way, with a large proportion of the movement's membership having moved out from under the control of the Wellington committee. Despite the perception of this faction that it represented a continuation of the Pentecostal Church of New Zealand, moves were already in progress to form a new, less Wellington-dominated alliance. Several factors appear to have been significant. The first was a typical Pentecostal antipathy towards organization. A classic exemplar of this attitude was Frank Bartleman,[103] the diarist of the 1906 Azusa Street revival. Just four months after its beginning, he records, with a mixture of dismay and righteous indignation, that

> "Azusa" began to fail the Lord also early in her history. God showed me one day that they were going to organize, though not a word had been said in my hearing about it. The Spirit revealed it to me. He had me get up and warn them against making a "party" spirit of the Pentecostal work. The "baptized" saints were to remain "one body," even as they had been called, and to be free as His Spirit was free, not "entangled again in a yoke of (ecclesiastical) bondage." . . . That spirit has been the curse and death of every revival body sooner or later.
>
> Sure enough the very next day after I had spoken this warning in the meeting I found a sign outside the building reading "Apostolic Faith Mission." [This title represented an association with the "Apostolic Faith Movement" of Charles Fox Parham, since William J. Seymour, the leader of the "Azusa Street" mission, had links with Parham.[104]] The Lord said: "That is what I told you." They had done it.[105]

Frank Bartleman's response was to leave this group and to start up another independent Pentecostal Mission.

The speed with which the Wellington Evangelical Mission had adopted a formal institutional structure reinforced this suspicion of organizational control and this distrust grew as the movement developed. A second factor, allied to this, was the vigor with which the Wellington church pursued its agenda. This reflected the personalities involved. Ian Clark alludes to Harry Roberts' "desire to control the local churches from Wellington"[106] and E. E. Pennington, the movement's first superintendent, was noted for the firmness with which he spoke his mind.[107] By contrast, A. C. Valdez was loved and trusted by the majority of the movement's adherents.[108] E. R. Weston—although remaining loyal to the Pentecostal Church of New Zealand leadership until 1933, when he joined the Apostolic Church—offers a scathing assessment of this period:

> We tried first an autocratic form of control—under an autocratic President, who was elected to that office by the people as King Saul was chosen by Israel of old and, as with Saul, this President's reign turned out to be a tyranny. Like Nebuchadnezzar, "whom he would, he slew, and whom he would he kept alive" (the writer was one of those he slew). No doubt he meant well, but a company of saints revolted, naturally, from the reign of terror.[109]

The careful circumscription of the Secretary's role at the 1925 Pentecostal Church of New Zealand Christmas convention and the secession of more than one-third of the movement's membership in 1926 were both reactions to this perception of autocracy.

As has already been noted in chapter 1, a central factor in the development of movements is the Weberian evolution from charismatic to rational-legal (or bureaucratic) modes of leadership.[110] The changes in the Pentecostal Church of New Zealand following Smith Wigglesworth's campaigns reflect this process, known as the "routinization of charisma." The movement was evolving from a pioneering movement, gathered around the charismatic endowment of its founder, to a different kind of movement, one in which authority was located in rational or legal forms of leadership. The rapid establishment of a bureaucratic framework within the Wellington churches, followed by an extension of this structure over other churches in the movement, is a classic example of the process. Indeed, one of the consequences of routinization is "centralized rule over territories"[111] (or, in this case, churches). While such structures are necessary for the long-term survival of a charismatic movement, they create a tension between memories of the charismatic pioneer and the "official" bureaucracy that has succeeded him or her. Furthermore, the absence of Scriptural models of leadership—such as elders and deacons—in the movement's early stages meant that there was no external source of authority that could legitimate this bureaucratic model. It is therefore not surprising that Bible teachers such as A. C. Valdez, E. R. Weston and Kelso Glover tended to be divisionary figures in the early movement. Thus, although the Pentecostal Church of New Zealand saw itself as continuing and conserving the momentum of the Wigglesworth campaigns, it was in fact a different kind of movement. Its focus on disciplinary controls—such as the selection of ministers, an official doctrinal statement and a comprehensive organizational structure—identified it as bureaucratic, rather than charismatic. Its struggle to define its leadership structures in the face of increasing distrust made it almost inevitable that alternative Pentecostal polities, such as those of the Assemblies of God, should gain a following in New Zealand.

New Wineskins?
The Assemblies of God in New Zealand

The arrival of the Assemblies of God introduced an inclusive, congregationally governed model of church government into New Zealand. This Pentecostal denomination had been formed in Hot Springs, Arkansas, in 1914 as an association of churches to conserve and extend the momentum of Azusa Street and other Pentecostal revivals. It took the form of an incorporated cooperative fellowship of locally governed churches, presided over by an Executive Structure having some similarities to that of the Pentecostal Church of New Zealand. However, it was much less centralized and restrictive. As Ian Clark notes, it provided "maximum liberty for local churches to govern their own affairs," while at the same time "enabling them to enjoy the benefits of belonging to a national group of like-minded believers."[112] At the time of its arrival in New Zealand, the Assemblies of God had already been operating successfully in America and elsewhere for twelve years.

Valdez was the key figure in the introduction of the Assemblies of God to Australia and New Zealand.[113] His concern at the increasing disorganization of the New Zealand Pentecostal movement had compelled him to seek for some form of church government that was not centrally controlled. He therefore contacted the leadership of the Assemblies of God in America shortly after the formation of the Interim Control Board at the Pentecostal Church of New Zealand's

August 1926 national conference of Elders. Valdez's approach reflected his view that this Board would not resolve the movement's administrative problems. As he saw it, the New Zealand churches would benefit from an affiliation with a Pentecostal body which allowed for a cooperative association of churches. His overtures were successful and the proposal to affiliate with the Assemblies of God was widely discussed within the New Zealand movement. The editor of the *New Zealand Evangel* reported on this discussion in April 1927, noting that "it has been practically settled that all the Assemblies are in favour of this co-operative fellowship."[114] (This slightly overstated the case, as not all the Pentecostal Church of New Zealand churches joined the new body.) In reality, the report also lagged behind the event, since the first Assembly of God already had been formed in Palmerston North two months earlier, following Valdez's evangelistic campaign there in February 1927. This was followed by the secession of a number of assemblies from the Pentecostal Church of New Zealand; the Assemblies of God was formally inaugurated in New Zealand at a meeting of their leaders in Wellington at the end of March. Seven assemblies were initially represented in the new movement; this number had grown to eleven by the end of 1927. The *New Zealand Evangel*, previously the official publication of the Pentecostal Church of New Zealand, was taken over in early 1927 and made the official organ of the new movement. Under the editorship of Wellington pastor Len J. Jones, it became noticeably livelier in tone.[115]

Although James Worsfold correctly observes that many of those who had seceded regarded themselves as remaining in some kind of loose federation with the Pentecostal Church of New Zealand,[116] this secession had a severe impact. By 1926, the Pentecostal Church of New Zealand comprised five organized and nine unorganized assemblies. (Organized assemblies—i.e., Auckland, Blenheim, Christchurch, New Plymouth and Wellington—were those which had been incorporated by the appointment of elders and deacons. Unorganized assemblies were those which had not yet been incorporated and whose delegates did not have voting rights at the national Annual Conventions. The result was a two-tier system in which some assemblies had greater standing than others.) The geographical distribution of Pentecostal Church of New Zealand adherents in 1926 is shown below in Table 1, together with an analysis of the responses of Pentecostal Church of New Zealand congregations—both organized and unorganized—to the crisis and the outcomes of these defections.

This table shows that Blenheim was the only one of the organized assemblies to remain loyal to the Wellington leadership.[117] Two other organized assemblies—Christchurch and New Plymouth—transferred their allegiance to the Assemblies of God, while the Auckland church split into separate Pentecostal Church of New Zealand and Assemblies of God groups. The Wellington church had already split; this breakaway group now became an Assembly of God. All of the unorganized assemblies in the Pentecostal Church of New Zealand—with the sole exception of the small Picton assembly—either joined the Assemblies of God or disbanded. Although two new Pentecostal Church of New Zealand congregations—Onehunga and Nelson—were started over the next six years, by 1932 that denomination's national adherence was only about 400, a 45% drop from the 726 members six years earlier.[118]

Place	Number	Assemblies as at January 1926 (as per Worsfold, *History of the Charismatic Movements in New Zealand*, 171).		Outcomes
		Organized	**Unorganized**	
Wellington City	324	Wellington		Had already split
Christchurch	109	Christchurch		Transferred to AoG
Auckland City	56	Auckland		Split
Wellington other	54		Masterton	
Marlborough	39	Blenheim	Picton	Both remained in PCNZ
New Plymouth	32	New Plymouth		Transferred to AoG
Canterbury other	28		Geraldine, Temuka, Pleasant Point	Temuka transferred to AoG
Dunedin	19		Dunedin	Transferred to AoG
Auckland other	18			Remained in PCNZ?
Palmerston North	17			Transferred to AoG
Taranaki other	9		Eltham, Hawera	
Wanganui	9		Wanganui	Transferred to AoG
Nelson other	5		Motupiko	
Otago other	4			
Hamilton	2			Transferred to AoG?
Hawkes Bay	1			
Total	**726**			

Table 1: Distribution of Pentecostal Church of New Zealand adherents as per the 1926 Census[119] and a summary of the congregational transfers resulting from the secession from the Pentecostal Church of New Zealand.

The effect of this division was also reflected in the decline of individual congregations. The adherence of the two Wellington Pentecostal Church of New Zealand assemblies—which together comprised 44% of the movement's national membership—dropped by 32% (from 324 to about 220) between 1926 and 1932.[120] Furthermore, of the ninety-five people identified by James Worsfold as Assemblies of God members after its formation, thirty-three (or 34.74%) had previously been members of the Pentecostal Church of New Zealand.[121] (It should be noted that these ninety-five people were only that part of the movement's adherents named by Worsfold; the Assemblies of God were larger than this.) Indeed, many of these transferees had been leaders in the

Pentecostal Church of New Zealand churches from which they came. However, not all withdrawing Pentecostal Church of New Zealand members joined the Assemblies of God; others later provided a constituency for new Pentecostal groups such as the Apostolic Church and the Revival Fire Mission in the 1930s.[122] As well as this, several of the new Assemblies of God sprang up in areas in which the Pentecostal Church of New Zealand had not previously been represented—e.g., Ellerslie, Hamilton, Palmerston North and Timaru. This indicates that not all New Zealand Pentecostals had been linked to the Pentecostal Church of New Zealand. In summary, then, the Pentecostal Church of New Zealand lost more than one-third of its members, with the Assemblies of God providing a new associative center for many of these members and for Pentecostals previously unconnected to the Pentecostal Church of New Zealand.

Despite this parting of the ways, there was little doctrinal difference between the two movements, a comparison of their respective statements of faith revealing only slight variations of wording. Similarly, there was little organizational dissimilarity between the Pentecostal Church of New Zealand and Assemblies of God models of polity. Each movement had a Chairman, Secretary and an Executive Committee or—in the case of the Assemblies of God—an Executive Presbytery. The difference lay in the ways in which these bodies operated and to some extent also reflected the personalities involved. The central leadership of the Pentecostal Church of New Zealand was strongly autocratic, limiting the right to participate in the leadership of the movement to the pastors and elders of its organized assemblies, meeting in committee. By contrast, the Assemblies of God stressed the local government of the churches and allowed for greater democracy in its decision making. This was reflected in the new movement's first Annual Conference, held on the Palmerston North farm of Cecil C. H. Scadden in December 1927. Both James Worsfold and Ian Clark note that this Conference was the first time that lay representatives were allowed to vote together with the ordained ministry on decisions affecting the New Zealand Pentecostal movement. This is a reflection of the Assemblies of God emphasis on democratic congregational government and stands in marked contrast to the rather dictatorial Pentecostal Church of New Zealand model.[123]

The more participatory character of the Assemblies of God was only one of the benefits of the new movement; another was its links with a wider, global community of Pentecostal churches. These international links facilitated the development of an Assemblies of God culture in New Zealand. It is noticeable that an increasing number of overseas Pentecostal visitors to New Zealand were from Assemblies of God backgrounds and that these stayed in New Zealand for longer periods, sometimes taking up permanent residence. This compounded their influence in the new movement. There were also short-term visits from overseas Assemblies of God ministers and ministerial exchanges between the New Zealand and Australian Assemblies of God.[124] However, there were also visits from well-known Pentecostal ministers such as Donald Gee[125] and Stephen Jeffreys,[126] who ministered in joint Pentecostal Church of New Zealand/Assemblies of God campaigns wherever possible. This cooperation indicates that barriers between the two churches were not great. (There were also a number of attempts to heal the breach at official level; the Pentecostal Church of New Zealand annual conference in 1928 attempted to pass a unity motion, but this was defeated by twenty-nine votes to three.)

Thus, by the end of the decade, much of the Pentecostal movement in New Zealand had coalesced into two bodies: the Pentecostal Church of New Zealand and the Assemblies of God. A. C. Valdez returned to America in April 1927, shortly after receiving the first ministerial credential issued by the New Zealand Assemblies of God. He intended to later return for further ministry; in fact, he did not return to New Zealand until 1962. Nevertheless, he had left a legacy behind him in the form of a new, more congregational group of Pentecostal churches. These Assemblies of God would grow to become the largest Pentecostal denomination in New Zealand by the 1980s. However, the process of division was not yet over: the arrival of the Apostolic Church in the 1930s would further fragment the Pentecostal Church of New Zealand and the Assemblies of God.

Conclusion

What were the attitudes and orientations that led to the emergence of the Pentecostal movement in New Zealand? What hurricane or glacial forces shaped its contours during the 1920s? And in what ways did its paradigms shift during this initial decade? The public anxiety and insecurity that characterized the decade, together with a resurgence of revivalism and the pervasive interest in healing, contributed to Pentecostalism's emergence as a distinct, identifiable movement. Smith Wigglesworth was indeed the hurricane that launched the movement; but the longstanding mix of public religious attitudes and orientations was the more significant glacial factor in its emergence.

The structure of this new movement took some time to come together. The efforts of Harry Roberts and his Wellington associates represented a precipitous shift to a bureaucratic mode of leadership. Although the intention was to preserve and maintain the charismatic momentum of the Wigglesworth campaigns, the effect was to create a different type of movement, one in which power was exercised through centralized control. This created its own set of tensions, since it was incompatible with the movement's theological emphasis on Pentecostal freedom. It also was at variance with the early history of the movement, exemplified by Frank Bartleman's account of the changes at Azusa Street. In sociological terms, it represented a routinization of the movement's charisma.

The movement's struggles to define and refine its corporate shape continued throughout the decade and—as will be seen in the next chapter—also into the 1930s. The shape of its leadership evolved from a Wellington-based autocracy, to the appointment of local elders and deacons and ultimately, through the influence of Valdez, to the arrival of the Assemblies of God. This paradigm shift to the more inclusive congregationalism of the new movement proved attractive to many Pentecostals, stimulating the defection of at least one-third of the Pentecostal Church of New Zealand's adherents to the Assemblies of God. However, conflict over the shape of Pentecostal polity would continue in the next decade with the arrival of the Apostolic Church. This would create further division that would last for a generation.

Notes

1. Tim Dirks, "Filmsite Movie Review: Little Caesar (1930)," http://www.filmsite.org/littc.html (accessed 14 June 2009).
2. Keith Sinclair, *A History of New Zealand*, rev. ed. (Harmondsworth: Penguin, 1984), 244–45.
3. Ibid, 238–39.
4. Stuart Mews, "The Revival of Spiritual Healing in the Church of England 1920–26," in Shiels, *The Church and Healing*, 316.
5. Jackson, *Churches and People*, 76.
6. Douglas B. Ireton, "'O Lord How Long?': A Revival Movement in New Zealand 1920–1933" (MA thesis in History, Massey University, 1986), 5.
7. For accounts of Rātana, see J. M. Henderson, *Ratana: The Man, The Church, and the Political Movement*. Memoirs of the Polynesian Society, 2nd ed., 36 (Wellington: A. H. and A. W. Reed in association with the Polynesian Society, 1972); Elsmore, *Like Them That Dream*, 166–71; Elsmore, *Mana From Heaven*, 337–46; Keith Newman, *Ratana Revisited: An Unfinished Legacy* (Auckland: Reed, 2006); and Newman, *Rātana: The Prophet* (North Shore: Penguin, 2009). Also see Angela Ballara, "Ratana, Tahupotiki Wiremu," from the *Dictionary of New Zealand Biography. Te Ara Encyclopedia of New Zealand*, Biographies, updated 30 October 2012 http://www.TeAra.govt.nz/en/biographies/3r4/ratana-tahupotiki-wiremu (accessed 2 December 2013).
8. Worsfold, *History of the Charismatic Movements in New Zealand*, 147–48.
9. Mark Hutchinson, "Braddock, Henry (1857–1932)," ADPCM (accessed 10 November 2011).
10. I.e., 5,516 to 1,200. Michael King, *The Penguin History of New Zealand* (Albany: Penguin, 2003), 335.
11. Henderson, *Ratana: The Man, The Church, and the Political Movement*, 24–25.
12. Rev. Joseph Kemp, *How I was healed, or, A New Zealand miracle: An autobiographical sketch of Miss Fannie Lammas, Nelson, New Zealand* (Auckland: Book Room, [Baptist] Tabernacle, [1923]).
13. Ireton, "A Time to Heal," 25–29.
14. Ibid.
15. For a brief biography of Boddy, see D. D. Bundy, "Boddy, Alexander Alfred," in NIDPCM, 436–37.
16. Colin C. Whittaker, *Seven Pentecostal Pioneers* (Basingstoke, Hants: Marshall, Morgan and Scott, 1983), 19–46; and W. E. Warner, "Wigglesworth, Smith," in NIDPCM, 1195. Warner notes that no fewer than six biographies of Wigglesworth are currently in print.
17. Douglas Fullerton, "How Christianity came to South Yunnan," http://www.dofu.dk/pages/1a.%20How%20Christianity%20came%20to%20South%20Yunnan.pdf (accessed 29 July 2009; site now discontinued).
18. Roberts, *New Zealand's Greatest Revival*, 8.
19. Worsfold, *History of the Charismatic Movements in New Zealand*, 109.

20. Clark, *Pentecost at the Ends of the Earth*, 15.
21. For a brief biography of Lancaster, see B. Chant, "Lancaster, Sarah Jane (Jeannie)," in NIDPCM, 828–29. A brief note is also given in Chant, *The Spirit of Pentecost*, 347–49. Chant also gives an example of her preaching in Chant, *Heart of Fire*, 285–90.
22. Chant, *Heart of Fire*, 48.
23. Worsfold, *History of the Charismatic Movements in New Zealand*, 95–97, 108.
24. Mark Hutchinson, "'Second Founder': A C Valdez Sr and Australian Pentecostalism," *Australasian Pentecostal Studies*, no. 11 (January 2009), http://webjournals.alphacrucis.edu.au/journals/aps/issue-11/02-second-founder-a-c-valdez-sr-and-australian-pen/ (accessed 2 June 2010).
25. Roberts, *New Zealand's Greatest Revival*, 8.
26. Accounts of Wigglesworth's campaigns in New Zealand include H. V. Roberts' eyewitness description of his first campaign in Wellington (Roberts, *New Zealand's Greatest Revival*); and the histories of Worsfold and Clark (Worsfold, *History of the Charismatic Movements in New Zealand*, 107–26, 149–55; Clark, *Pentecost at the Ends of the Earth*, 13–20).
27. Roberts, *New Zealand's Greatest Revival*, 12.
28. "Faith Healing—Extraordinary Scenes at Town Hall—The Deaf Made to Hear," *Dominion*, 31 May 1922, 5. This report is reproduced in its entirety in Roberts, *New Zealand's Greatest Revival*, 13–15.
29. "'Take Up Thy Bed And Walk'—Is Smith-Wigglesworth A Miracle Man?—'Truth' Analyses Claims Of Yorkshire Revivalist—Ethics of Faith Healing Reverently Discussed," *New Zealand Truth*, 10 June 1922, 5; "Faith Healer Wigglesworth—Operating In Cathedral City—'Miracles' While You Wait On Tap," *New Zealand Truth*, 1 July 1922, 4.
30. Sermon titles listed in Worsfold, *History of the Charismatic Movements in New Zealand*, 112–13.
31. Ibid, 113.
32. For examples of these charismatic utterances, see the stenographically recorded sermons in Roberts, *New Zealand's Greatest Revival*, 41–42 and 49; and Worsfold, *History of the Charismatic Movements in New Zealand*, 124.
33. Worsfold, *History of the Charismatic Movements in New Zealand*, 115–17.
34. "Faith Healer Wigglesworth—Operating In Cathedral City—'Miracles' While You Wait On Tap," *New Zealand Truth*, 1 July 1922, 4.
35. "The Miracles that Did Not Happen in Sydenham—the Damages done to the Innocent Sick—The Sort of Miracles that would Convince Christchurch—The Only Sort of Miracle that Christ Cared for," "Religious Announcements," *[Christchurch] Press*, 17 June 1922, 18.
36. *Sun*, 19 June 1922, cited in Worsfold, *History of the Charismatic Movements in New Zealand*, 118.
37. H. Roberts, "Letters to the Editor," *Sun*, 16 June 1922, cited in Worsfold, *History of the Charismatic Movements in New Zealand*, 117.
38. Cited in Worsfold, *History of the Charismatic Movements in New Zealand*, 117–19.
39. Ibid, 90; see also Hutchinson, "Adams, John Archibald Duncan (1844–1936)."
40. "Smith-Wigglesworth Mission," *Otago Daily Times*, 17 June 1922, 10.
41. Evans and McKenzie, *Evangelical Revivals in New Zealand*, 146.
42. "Late Advertisements," *Evening Star*, 19 June 1922, 7; "Religious," *Evening Star*, 24 June 1922, 6; "Sunday Meetings," *Otago Daily Times*, 24 June 1922, 11.

43. "Smith-Wigglesworth Mission," *Evening Star*, 19 June 1922, 5; "Faith Healing: Nission [sic] of Mr Smith-Wigglesworth: Remarkable Scenes in Burns Hall: A Questionable Display," *Otago Daily Times*, 20 June 1922, 8.

44. John A. D. Adams, "Mr Smith-Wigglesworth's Meetings: To the Editor," *Otago Daily Times*, 22 June 1922, 10.

45. "The Devil of Disease: Strange Scenes in Burns Hall: The Smith-Wigglesworth Revival," *Evening Star*, 20 June 1922, 6.

46. "Faith Healing: Nission [sic] of Mr Smith-Wigglesworth," *Otago Daily Times*, 20 June 1922, 8. A further report the following day was also critical. "Faith Healing: Wigglesworth Mission: Miracles That Were Not Worked: Another Series of Disappointments," *Otago Daily Times*, 21 June 1922, 6.

47. Justus du Plessis, cited in George Stormont, *Smith Wigglesworth: A Man Who Walked with God* (Chichester: Sovereign World, 1990), 16. Du Plessis (the brother of the well-known Pentecostal ecumenist David du Plessis) was Wigglesworth's interpreter during his South African campaign.

48. "Faith Healing: Nission [sic] of Mr Smith-Wigglesworth," *Otago Daily Times*, 20 June 1922, 8.

49. Cited in Worsfold, *History of the Charismatic Movements in New Zealand*, 120–23.

50. "Sunday Meetings," *Otago Daily Times*, 1 July 1922, 11.

51. Roberts, *New Zealand's Greatest Revival*, 18.

52. Mary Cobeldick, Librarian, Research Services, Alexander Turnbull Library, e-mail message to Library Central Interloans, University of Otago, 3 September 2009; Cherie Howie, Journalist, *Marlborough Express*, e-mail message to author 11 May 2010.

53. Roberts, *New Zealand's Greatest Revival*, 24.

54. Ibid, 34.

55. For a biography of McPherson, see C. M. Robeck, Jr., "McPherson, Aimee Semple," in NIDPCM, 856–59. A brief note is also given in Chant, *The Spirit of Pentecost*, 351. Chant also gives an example of her highly dramatic preaching style in Chant, *Heart of Fire*, 297–302.

56. *Dominion*, 28 August 1922, 6, cited in Worsfold, *History of the Charismatic Movements in New Zealand*, 136–37.

57. Worsfold, *History of the Charismatic Movements in New Zealand*, chapters 15, 17, 19 and 20; and Clark, *Pentecost at the Ends of the Earth*, 21–26. Clark's treatment, although largely based on Worsfold's account, offers a much clearer analysis of events.

58. "Religious Services," *Dominion*, 29 July 1922, 7.

59. *New Zealand Evangel*, 6 June 1924, 1.

60. Worsfold, *History of the Charismatic Movements in New Zealand*, 166.

61. Clark, *Pentecost at the Ends of the Earth*, 22–23.

62. "Supreme Court: Criminal Sessions: Charges against Lind," *Otago Daily Times*, 9 August 1923, 11; "The Lind Case: Accused Convicted: Strong Comments by Judge: 'Mixture of Lust and Blasphemy': Seven Years Hard Labour," *Otago Daily Times*, 10 August 1923, 4.

63. Worsfold, *History of the Charismatic Movements in New Zealand*, 90.

64. Ibid, 145.

65. *New Zealand Evangel*, 20 August 1925, 1, 8–9.

66. Worsfold, *History of the Charismatic Movements in New Zealand*, 141.

67. Ibid, 156.

68. Ibid, 146.

69. Ibid, 157. The magazine's full title was *The New Zealand Evangel of the Apostolic Faith*.
70. Worsfold, *History of the Charismatic Movements in New Zealand*, 156–58.
71. Minute Book, New Zealand Evangelical Mission, Wellington, ff.70–90, cited in Ibid, 156. Although Worsfold does not include a date, these meetings would have taken place in late December 1923.
72. *New Zealand Evangel*, 6 October 1924, 12; Worsfold, *History of the Charismatic Movements in New Zealand*, 159–60. For biographies of Weston, see B. Knowles, "Weston, Edward (Ned) R.," in NIDPCM, 1192–93; and James E. Worsfold, *The Reverend and Mrs Edward and Eily Weston*, New Zealand Apostolic Pioneer Breviate Series 1 (Wellington: Julian Literature Trust, 1994).
73. Worsfold, *History of the Charismatic Movements in New Zealand*, 159.
74. *New Zealand Evangel*, 6 October 1924, 14. For biographies of Valdez, see J. R. Ziegler, "Valdez, A. C., Sr.," in NIDPCM, 1169; and Hutchinson, "'Second Founder': A C Valdez Sr and Australian Pentecostalism." A brief note is also given in Chant, *The Spirit of Pentecost*, 354. Chant also gives an example of his preaching in Chant, *Heart of Fire*, 307–12.
75. See Hutchinson, "'Second Founder': A C Valdez Sr and Australian Pentecostalism."
76. Clark, *Pentecost at the Ends of the Earth*, 31, footnote 3.
77. Hutchinson, "'Second Founder': A C Valdez Sr and Australian Pentecostalism."
78. *New Zealand Evangel*, 6 October 1924, 12; *New Zealand Evangel*, 16 December 1924, 12–13.
79. *New Zealand Evangel*, 16 December 1924, 13.
80. Clark, *Pentecost at the Ends of the Earth*, 25.
81. *New Zealand Evangel*, 16 December 1924, 13.
82. Ibid.
83. E. E. Pennington, *Conferences of Delegates of the Pentecostal Assemblies in New Zealand* (Wellington: Wright and Carmen, 1924), 41, cited in Worsfold, *History of the Charismatic Movements in New Zealand*, 163.
84. *New Zealand Evangel*, 16 December 1924, 13.
85. Worsfold, *History of the Charismatic Movements in New Zealand*, 168; "First Annual Conference," *New Zealand Evangel*, 20 March 1925, 11.
86. *New Zealand Evangel*, 20 February 1925, 2.
87. Ibid, 6.
88. "Division," *New Zealand Evangel*, 20 January 1925, 6.
89. *New Zealand Evangel*, 20 February 1925, 8.
90. *Good News*, October 1926, 19, cited in Chant, *The Spirit of Pentecost*, 134 and 149, note 26.
91. Worsfold, *History of the Charismatic Movements in New Zealand*, 169. For a biography of Glover, see Mark Hutchinson, "Glover, Kelso R. (1884–1965)," ADPCM (accessed 10 November 2011). A brief note is also given in Chant, *The Spirit of Pentecost*, 344; Chant also gives an example of his preaching in Chant, *Heart of Fire*, 313–19.
92. "MINUTES OF ANNUAL CONFERENCE OF THE PENTECOSTAL CHURCH OF NEW ZEALAND, held at Orange Hall, Worcester Street, Christchurch, commencing at 10.30am on Monday, 28th December, 1925, and ending Sunday Night, 3rd January, 1926," *New Zealand Evangel*, February/March 1926, 5–8.
93. Ibid, 5–6.
94. Clark, *Pentecost at the Ends of the Earth*, 29.

95. Worsfold, *History of the Charismatic Movements in New Zealand*, 172–73.
96. *New Zealand Evangel*, October/November 1926, 8.
97. Clark, *Pentecost at the Ends of the Earth*, 29–30.
98. *New Zealand Evangel*, December 1926, 4.
99. Worsfold, *History of the Charismatic Movements in New Zealand*, 175.
100. *New Zealand Evangel*, February 1927, 2–4.
101. Ibid, 1.
102. Worsfold, *History of the Charismatic Movements in New Zealand*, 176.
103. For a brief biography of Bartleman, see C. M. Robeck, Jr., "Bartleman, Frank," in NIDPCM, 366.
104. Edith L. Blumhofer, *The Assemblies of God: A Chapter in the Story of American Pentecostalism* (Springfield, MS: Gospel Publishing House, 1989), 1:104–5.
105. Frank Bartleman, *Another Wave Rolls In! [formerly What really happened at "Azusa Street?"]*, ed. John Walker; rev. and enlarged ed., ed. John G. Myers ([1925]; Northridge, CA: Voice Publications, 1970), 70. Reproduced http://www.arlev.co.uk/azusa/ (accessed 16 November 2011).
106. Clark, *Pentecost at the Ends of the Earth*, 28.
107. Dorothy Walker (retired long-term missionary to Indonesia), Interview, Wellington, 27 June 1996, cited in Brett Knowles, *The History of a New Zealand Pentecostal Movement: The New Life Churches of New Zealand from 1946 to 1979*, Studies in Religion and Society 45 (Lewiston, NY: Edwin Mellen Press, 2000), 13.
108. *New Zealand Evangel*, 16 December 1924, 12–13.
109. Worsfold, *The Reverend & Mrs Edward and Eily Weston*, 27–28; Worsfold, *History of the Charismatic Movements in New Zealand*, 244–46.
110. See above, 2.
111. Arpad Szakolczai, "Charisma," in *Encyclopedia of Social Theory*, ed. Austin Harrington, Barbara l. Marshall and Hans-Peter Müller, 53 (London and New York: Routledge, 2006).
112. Clark, *Pentecost at the Ends of the Earth*, 32–33.
113. Hutchinson, "'Second Founder': A. C. Valdez Sr and Australian Pentecostalism," 1–2, 5–9.
114. "General Council Assemblies Of God: Proposed Advance Step For New Zealand Towards World-Wide Fellowship," *New Zealand Evangel*, April 1927, 26.
115. Worsfold, *History of the Charismatic Movements in New Zealand*, 197–98; Clark, *Pentecost at the Ends of the Earth*, 33–36.
116. Worsfold, *History of the Charismatic Movements in New Zealand*, 175.
117. "MINUTES OF ANNUAL CONFERENCE OF THE PENTECOSTAL CHURCH OF NEW ZEALAND," *New Zealand Evangel*, February/March 1926, 5.
118. Worsfold, *History of the Charismatic Movements in New Zealand*, 179.
119. See Appendix A.
120. Worsfold, *History of the Charismatic Movements in New Zealand*, 179.
121. Ibid, 104, 115, 127, 144–46, 152, 156–90, 197–223.
122. Ibid, 224 and 237–38.
123. Ibid, 207–8; Clark, *Pentecost at the Ends of the Earth*, 38.
124. Worsfold, *History of the Charismatic Movements in New Zealand*, 207; Clark, *Pentecost at the Ends of the Earth*, 36–37.
125. For a brief biography of Gee, see D. D. Bundy, "Gee, Donald," in NIDPCM, 662–63. A fuller account is given in Whittaker, *Seven Pentecostal Pioneers*, 79–99.

126. For a brief biography of Jeffreys, see D. W. Cartwright, "Jeffreys, Stephen," in NIDPCM, 808–9. A fuller account is given in Whittaker, *Seven Pentecostal Pioneers*, 47–78.

Chapter 4

The 1930s

The "Great *Im*pression"?
The Effects of the Depression in New Zealand

It is commonplace to refer to the 1930s as a benchmark for economic catastrophe.[1] Thus, the attempts of the British government to stave off a new credit crisis in 2011 were reported as "the most serious financial crisis we've seen, at least since the 1930s, if not ever."[2] Such a comparison categorizes that decade as the *Great* Depression, the high-tide mark of economic collapse. It could also be dubbed "the Great *Im*pression," since it and its counterpart, the creation of the Welfare State, were watersheds for social change in New Zealand, shaping the attitudes of the next two generations. Part of the reason for the post-war generation gap was that the "Baby Boomers" [i.e., those born between 1945 and 1961] had never experienced this kind of economic adversity. The affluent youth of the 1960s could not identify with their parents' frugal attitudes, born of the hardships of the 1930s. Nor could they conceive of what it was like to live in a world without a Social Welfare safety net.

Even before the Depression began, New Zealand was already in economic difficulty, with the value of its exports falling 40% between 1928 and 1931.[3] The adversity brought about by declining prices was exacerbated by the Wall Street stock market crash of 1929, leading to unprecedented levels of unemployment and suffering. By the peak of the Depression in 1933, there were more than 80,000 unemployed, or about 12% of the workforce. (The actual figure may have been higher still at 100,000 unemployed, since Māori and women were not included in the unemployment figures.)[4] Social historian Tony Simpson's harrowing oral history *The Sugarbag Years*[5] starkly portrays the desperation and hopelessness of the period; Simpson's title refers to the sack in which the down-and-out unemployed carried their worldly possessions.

It should be noted, however, that this suffering was not borne equally by all: while the poor grew poorer, the rich remained relatively untouched by the Depression. The widening gap between rich and poor created a perception of "us and them," which, together with hunger and desperation, fuelled rioting in

Dunedin, Auckland and Wellington in April 1932.[6] In part, the anger of the rioters was directed at the failure of the United Government under Sir Joseph Ward and George Forbes (1928–31) and the United-Reform Coalition under Forbes (1931–35) to resolve the crisis. The financial improvidence of Ward and, later, the inability of Forbes to grasp what needed to be done exacerbated the plight of the unemployed and set the stage for radical political change. Ward had a reputation for being a financial wizard, but was decrepit and ill, dying in 1930; Forbes, although known for his honesty, doggedness and loyalty, was not an intellect of the first rank. (His junior colleague Keith Holyoake—to be Prime Minister himself in the 1960s—later unkindly said that the only reason his leader had graduated from Lyttelton Primary School was that the school had burned down.)[7] Under Ward and Forbes, the Government cut spending—including wages and pensions—in order to balance the books and created work schemes for the unemployed. The philosophy behind these schemes was "no pay without work." As a result, increasing numbers of unemployed men were engaged in pointless and often soul-destroying work or else sent to work camps under "Scheme 5." These work camps were engaged in building roads, planting forests and tussock grasslands in remote areas; those sent to these camps were paid for three weeks, followed by a unpaid one week stand-down period. This had the effect of removing the support of married men from their families, who had to survive as best they could for three weeks, followed by a further week of no income at all. It is therefore not surprising that resentment against the Government was extreme; although conditions began to alleviate after 1933, the stage was set for radical political change later in the decade.

The landslide success of the Labour Party under Michael Joseph Savage[8] in the 1935 elections led to a socioeconomic revolution. The new Government reversed the reductions of the Forbes administration, set a basic minimum wage, raised pensions and created a Public Works program to provide productive employment on full wages instead of relief handouts. Other major initiatives in its first term included the building of low-rental state houses to alleviate the deteriorating housing conditions of the inner cities. The passing of the 1938 Social Security Act—which increased pensions, extended family allowances and provided almost free medical care—further established a comprehensive and integrated social welfare system.[9] By 1939, New Zealand's standard of living was the third highest in the world; one economist estimated that New Zealanders then had the highest level of real income per head in the world.[10] The benefits of the Welfare State—with government-provided welfare provided literally "from the cradle to the grave"—continued until its dismantling under "Rogernomics" in the 1980s.[11] These developments shaped the mind-set of the New Zealand public for the next fifty years.

The Depression also produced something of a paradigm shift on the part of the mainstream churches. Initially, they were maintainers of the status quo and supporters of the powers that be, although many churches were also heavily involved in palliative charitable work such as soup kitchens. The churches saw the Depression in moralist terms, with greed and slothfulness at the core of the problem. Consequently, they insisted that the solution lay in religious revival, rather than in seeking social change; their instinctive response was to organize national days of prayer for the government and for the unemployed. However, these attitudes began to change as the Depression intensified from 1929 to 1931.[12] The constant involvement of the Methodist and Catholic churches in welfare led them to insist on workable solutions to the unemployment problem, although they still tended to be simplistic in their analysis of its causes. This reflected a shift from a theological emphasis on personal piety to a "social gospel" based upon the Sermon on the Mount. Consequently, these churches became more critical of the Government's inability to resolve the crisis, and by 1934, some of their leaders were beginning to articulate radical social ideas. Because the Government was seen to be not doing anything except institutionalizing misery, the political and economic systems were perceived as immoral and unjust, and a radical change was needed. This marked the beginnings of a Crusade for Social Justice—born out of direct involvement with the needy—in 1934–35, in which the churches provided support for radical social and political change. Although this was not a political endorsement, it translated into support for the opposition Labour Party (which had formerly been seen as a radical Socialist party). Labour could now be promoted as "the truly Christian party[,] as the party which most adequately expressed Christianity in practice, and which came closest to translating into reality the religious values which the churches' spokesmen had been expounding over three years."[13] This legitimation was reinforced when ten clergymen stood for Parliament as Labour candidates in the 1935 elections, three of whom were elected. Taking into account the change in public attitudes—which the churches had helped to foster—it is not surprising that Labour won by a landslide.

Given the perception of Pentecostalism as a "vision of the disinherited,"[14] one might expect that the members of Pentecostal churches might have been more adversely affected by the Depression than were those in mainstream churches. Such does not appear to have been the case, since New Zealand Pentecostalism attracted professional and well-to-do people as well as those from the unskilled working class. The audience at Smith Wigglesworth's Dunedin campaign had included "respected and prosperous" businessmen.[15] (Similarly, Barry Chant notes that Australian Pentecostalism was primarily a middle-class movement, not a movement of the disenfranchised. In the 1930s, the percentage of professionals involved in the Australian Pentecostal movement was approximately double that of their representation in the community.)[16] And, although tradesmen and working-class people were predominant in the membership of—for example—the Apostolic Church during the 1930s,[17] successful professionals and businessmen were also members (and often leaders) of New Zealand Pentecostal churches. Examples of these businessmen/leaders include Pentecostal Church of New Zealand elder and retired barrister John A. D. Adams of Dunedin,[18] and Assemblies of God leaders Hugh Bruce of Wellington, Cecil Scadden of Palmerston North and Wallace Thompson of Taumarunui. (Bruce had run his own bakery in central Christchurch before becoming a partner in the New Zealand-wide cake and confectionery firm of Adams Bruce and was "a person of some means."[19]

Similarly, Scadden owned a farm near Palmerston North;[20] Thompson was a master plumber with a large and very successful business in Taumarunui during the 1930s and was described as "an astute businessman.")[21]

It is noteworthy, however, that Pentecostal churches seem seldom to have been involved in the alleviation of social distress amongst those adversely affected by the Depression. The only extant reference to this was the activity of the Pentecostal Church of New Zealand in "distributing clothes, food and funds from their poor fund to the destitute" in 1929.[22] Furthermore, there was no social critique of the Depression, with the predominant Pentecostal attitude exemplified by Apostolic pastor Gilbert White's response to financial need as a "test of faith":

> On some occasions Alice [White] would be burdened as to how she was to provide meals for her growing family. The children remember one occasion when their mother was seeking the Lord, standing in front of the cupboard which was almost bare, and praying for Divine help. To the surprise of the children a knock sounded at the door. On opening it a box of food was found on the doorstep and a retreating figure (a member of the congregation) was disappearing through the gate. Gilbert had often preached on the subject "Jehovah-Jireh," (the Lord will supply) and once again this family experienced the reality of the promise that God would not see the righteous begging for bread. . . .[23]

Both the attitude of "the Lord will supply" and the surreptitious assisting of fellow believers seem typical of Pentecostalism during the Depression. Nevertheless—as with the mainstream churches, which suffered severe financial stringencies[24]—the impact on Pentecostal churches was considerable. The Wellington Pentecostal Church of New Zealand congregation introduced drastic measures to reduce expenditure, but eventually was forced to sell its building in order to repay the mortgage on the property. Thereafter it met in rental premises.[25] The Assemblies of God were also hard hit. By the end of 1930, workers in the smaller assemblies were being recommended to engage in some outside work to supplement their support.[26] The following year, it was noted that the ability of delegates to afford attendance at the movement's national conferences was being severely curtailed and that the superintendent was not able to itinerate around the assemblies.[27] Nor could the movement provide for the return of its missionaries who were home on furlough to their mission fields, or to financially support students studying in the movement's Bible School.[28] Its national publication, the *New Zealand Evangel*, continued to appear throughout the 1930s, but was reduced in format from a twelve-page printed magazine to a typed and duplicated newsletter.[29] However, the movement was still able to open new churches—such as the Lower Hutt Assembly of God in 1930—and to send out missionaries.[30] Nevertheless, as will be seen, the impact of the Depression on the Assemblies of God was exacerbated by the arrival of the Apostolic Church.

In contrast to the difficulties faced by the Pentecostal Church of New Zealand and the Assemblies of God, several other Pentecostal groups were thriving during the Depression. A vigorous new Pentecostal stream espousing the British Israel theory emerged in the 1930s. The best-known of these British

Israel churches, the Mount Roskill Church of Christ (New Zealand)—established after World War Two by Fred Wilson—was to become the largest Pentecostal congregation in New Zealand until the 1970s.[31] Secondly, the Revival Fire Mission, headed by healer A. H. Dallimore in Auckland, came to public attention in 1930 and went from strength to strength during the early Depression years.[32] Finally, the arrival of the Apostolic Church in 1934 changed the configuration of New Zealand Pentecostalism for several decades to come. These churches will be discussed in the next three sections.

A. H. Dallimore and the Revival Fire Mission

The most prominent Pentecostal group in New Zealand in the early 1930s was Dallimore's Revival Fire Mission.[33] His healing campaigns in the Auckland Town Hall attracted capacity crowds, generated controversy and created media frenzy for several years, and left a lasting legacy for other Pentecostal groups. Dallimore's early life was somewhat migratory. He was born in England—where he was healed from typhoid fever at the age of seven—and moved to New Zealand in 1886. He later left New Zealand for Alaska, eventually returning to England, where he married in 1911. Shortly after his marriage, he and his wife emigrated from England to Canada. Here he went into several business ventures which failed, bringing about a nervous breakdown. Later, he was inspired by the writings of John Alexander Dowie and Aimee Semple McPherson, also coming under the personal influence of Pentecostals John G. Lake and Charles S. Price in Vancouver. Dallimore returned to New Zealand in 1927, where he began healing meetings with a small handful of people.[34] These meetings grew into the Revival Fire Mission, which, after 1930, was attracting hundreds of people to receive his ministry. Reports of his meetings began to appear in the newspapers, particularly after he shifted to the Auckland Town Hall in August 1932 in order to accommodate the crowds. (The *Evening Post* reported that 550 people came to the platform for healing in one meeting and that, for about an hour and a half, the large platform was covered with the prostrate forms of men, women and children who had received ministry from the evangelist.)[35] This coverage was most intensive between October and December 1932.[36]

Part of the reason for this media attention lay in the flamboyant nature of his "cures." Although not personally extroverted, Dallimore's methods made good media copy. In addition to praying for the sick in his meetings—which the *Auckland Star* described as "the main feature of the gathering"[37]—he adopted the practice of praying over handkerchiefs which were then laid on those seeking healing.[38] This included the healing of animals[39] and, in at least one case, a motorcycle with a flat battery was induced to start after a blessed handkerchief was laid on it.[40] A particular feature of his meetings was the way in which people were "slain in the Spirit" when he prayed for them. A newspaper article in *New Zealand Truth* described some young men—who had come to mock—"collaps[ing] to the floor like a felled ox" on being prayed for, much to their consternation.[41] (It was claimed that this phenomenon had occurred between 20,000 and 40,000 times in five years of his ministry without any mishap.)[42] The newspapers seized upon stories like these and this publicity added to his popularity. Eventually, however, the veracity of his healings was challenged and a committee of medical doctors, clergymen and university lecturers was set up to investigate the meetings. Dallimore refused to cooperate with the committee (which was not surprising, given his trenchant opposition to the medical profession).[43] Nevertheless, the committee examined forty-three claimed cases of healing but failed to substantiate any of these.[44] As a result, public controversy erupted and the Auckland City Council rescinded his right to use the Town Hall.[45] Dallimore's supporters, including an Auckland Stipendiary Magistrate—today equivalent to a District Court Judge—Mr. E. C. Cutten, protested this decision and, through the presentation of a 7,000-signature public petition, won a reversal. Cutten's leadership of a delegation to the City Council was instrumental in regaining the use of the Town Hall.[46] All of this controversy was reported in the press, further publicizing his activities. However, numbers at his meetings began to drop after the Council's decision was overturned and Dallimore seems to have become somewhat less newsworthy in the eyes of the press. Letters to the editors, both for and against his campaigns, also declined after this.[47]

There seem to be a number of reasons why A.H. Dallimore was so successful. Firstly, although his preaching did not address the social context of the Depression, his meetings were lively, dramatic and colorful and the claimed miracles gave people a messianic hope.[48] This reflected the social context of the period; Labour politician Michael Joseph Savage, who became Prime Minister of New Zealand in 1935, also held near-messianic status in the eyes of some of his supporters.[49] Secondly, his campaigns represented a scale of Pentecostal evangelism not seen in New Zealand since Smith Wigglesworth and A. C. Valdez in the 1920s. They therefore tapped into a vacuum of expectation; this was heightened by the comparative lack of success of other Pentecostal groups. Dallimore himself claimed not to be Pentecostal—in fact, disliking Pentecostalism because of its enthusiasm and overt manifestations[50]—and his meetings were "extremely sober."[51] Nevertheless, his healing methods were recognizably Pentecostal ones, and instances of glossolalia in his meetings were reported in the press on a number of occasions and in the report of the Committee that investigated the Dallimore Mission.[52] Thirdly, although born in England, he was not an overseas visitor—as were Wigglesworth and Valdez—but was resident in New Zealand and was therefore able to build a long-term base. The effects of this were reflected both in the Revival Fire churches that grew out of his campaigns as well as the considerable number of future Pentecostal leaders who trace their spiritual empowerment to him.[53] In this way, Dallimore had a seeding effect on other New Zealand Pentecostal churches that went far beyond the boundaries of his own movement. Fourthly, the influence of the media appears to be significant and much of his success in 1932 was media fed.[54] The press coverage given to his campaigns extended their constituency as people came to his meetings to investigate for themselves. This included those who came to scoff; the article in the *New Zealand Truth* on the young men who were "slain in the Spirit" gives a particularly good example of this.[55] The role of the media has also been significant in the expansion of other Pentecostal and revival movements. As an Australian church historian neatly puts it, commenting on revivalism in Australia during the 1860s, "revivalistic hopes and activity . . . [were] fanned by . . . reports of revivals overseas: *the fame of revival is the flame of revival.*"[56] The opposition to Dallimore's meetings also played a role in his success; as sociologists Luther Gerlach and Virginia Hine note, persecution—either real or imagined—is one of the five key factors that are crucial for the "lift-off" of a movement.[57] Dallimore gloried in opposition and in the media attention that resulted. E. C. Cutten later noted that the "period of persecution and attack . . . gave such publicity to Mr Dallimore's work that he could fill the Town Hall to overflowing."[58] The decline of his meetings after the rescinding of his exclusion from the Auckland Town Hall and the resultant reduction in media coverage, demonstrate the nexus between perceived opposition and the attractiveness of a movement. Finally, the support from influential people such as Cutten contributed to the reservoir of resources available to him, thus increasing his effectiveness.

What was A.H. Dallimore's legacy to New Zealand Pentecostalism? Only a few Revival Fire churches survived the end of the 1930s; these were the three congregations in Auckland, Hamilton and Thames, with branch services in Avondale and Onehunga.[59] Another group started in Tauranga in 1939, but this did not continue as a Revival Fire congregation, eventually becoming allied with the Latter Rain movement at the end of the 1940s. (This was effectively the first congregation in the movement that later became the New Life Churches of New Zealand.)[60] Dallimore contributed to the development of other New Zealand Pentecostal churches as well as his own, although his emphasis on British Israelism and his increasingly unorthodox views on the Trinity combined to limit his long-term effectiveness. His movement therefore fell into obscurity after the 1930s.

Dallimore's British Israelite views predated his involvement with Pentecostalism, since he was introduced to the latter through the influence of John G. Lake, who he had met at a British Israel conference in Vancouver in 1920.[61] Dallimore argued that the British enjoyed a special Divine covenant, with the promises to ancient Israel being appropriated to Britain—and to Anglo-Saxon peoples in general—claiming that "we British people are none other than 'Lost' Israel [i.e., the lost ten tribes]."[62] He made a number of predictions, based on his British Israel beliefs and also his interpretation of the Great Pyramid of Gizeh. Thus "the heir to the British throne would be a second Davidic messiah, never marrying, but ushering in the reign of Jesus Christ in 1936. Unfortunately, the future Edward VIII failed to live up to expectations."[63] While he was by no means the only Pentecostal preacher to make such assertions, his views helped to stimulate an emerging Pentecostal British Israel movement during the 1930s. This was perpetuated in the churches formed by the Wilson brothers, particularly the Church of Christ (New Zealand) in Mount Roskill and the Commonwealth Covenant Church. The influence of this movement on New Zealand Pentecostalism will be discussed next.

Prophecy, British Israelism and New Zealand Pentecostalism

Pentecostals have always had an orientation towards the end times.[64] Their world view is implicit in their understanding of the outpouring of the Spirit as a fulfillment of end-time prophecy.[65] A classic example of this was Frank Bartleman, who asked of the events surrounding the Azusa Street revival: "may not this be our Lord's 'last call'?"[66] This eschatology determines their view of world historical events, both in the ways in which they interpret these events and also in their social and political responses to them. Most Pentecostals are futurist premillennialists, believing that the coming of Christ would occur in the future, inaugurating the 1,000-year reign of Christ described in Rev.20:1–6. As a subset of this belief, they also tend to be pretribulationists, expecting the rapture, or removal, of the church prior to the time of the Tribulation and the rise of the AntiChrist. Some Pentecostals also espoused premillennial dispensationalism, namely, an emphasis on the return of the Jews to Palestine and the rise of the State of Israel as sure signs of the imminent return of Christ.[67]

In the light of this eschatological framework, Pentecostals have tended to interpret world events as signs of the times and as indicators that the end was nigh. It follows, then, that times of increased international tension—such as the Depression or threats of war—would be reflected in a greater focus on eschatological subjects. Barry Chant notes that in *Good News* (a Pentecostal periodical published in Australia by Sarah Jane Lancaster from 1913 to 1934),

> Almost universally, world events were seen as pointing towards the time of the end. Over ten percent of published articles commented on what was happening in the world and related this to Biblical prophecies and their fulfilment. If the features on the Second Coming and those on world events are combined, they represent over one quarter (27.27 per cent) of all articles [in *Good News*]. Developments in Italy, for example, pointed to the resurrection of the Holy Roman Empire under Mussolini, and events in the Middle East suggested that Turkey's Mustapha Kemal Pasha might well be the AntiChrist. Furthermore, a study of the prophecies of Daniel and Revelation showed that time was almost running out and the year 1934 looked like being the beginning of the Tribulation.[68]

Chant also notes that there were twice as many articles on eschatology—interest in which was clearly heightened by the incidence of war—in issues of *Australian Evangel* between 1939 and 1945, than between 1930 and 1939.[69] Similarly, Pentecostal pastor Luke Worsfold observes that in New Zealand,

> Pentecostalism of the Depression era saw in the prevailing world situation early warning of a future total collapse.... In 1935 the memory of the Great War was still quite fresh, only three years had passed since the Russian famine, the world-wide 'flu epidemic had claimed 22 million by 1920, an earthquake in Kansu Province, China the same year killed 200,000 and the employment difficulties associated with the Depression were expected to rise. Added to this, Nazism was on the increase.... For a premillennialist in 1935 the world events of the

previous 15 years provided ample fulfilment of the Matthean text [Matt.24:7], further justifying an expectation of an imminent world end.[70]

It is therefore not surprising that there should be numerous sermons preached on the subject in Pentecostal churches and missions. Some of these were simply exhortations on the Second Coming; others specifically addressed current world issues in the light of the imminent end. For example, Sarah Jane Lancaster was reported as preaching on "Behold He Cometh" and "Anti-Christ: That Wicked One" in her Australian *Good News* magazine.[71] Contemporaneous sermons in the *New Zealand Evangel* included "The Second Coming of Christ,"[72] "The Coming One"[73] and "Signs of the Times."[74] Apostolic leader William Cathcart preached sermons on "The Coming Age-End Climax," "Will the Church go through the Tribulation?" and "War Clouds" during a revival campaign in Auckland in 1934.[75] Similarly, E. R. Weston's sermon titles in Christchurch in 1935 and 1936 included, "Six Downward Steps in Italy's final History Predicted in Scripture," "Abyssinia's part in the comming [sic] World Crisis," and "Current Events foreshadowing the approaching return of Christ."[76] He also spoke on "A World Empire Expected to Rise in Europe."[77] The Italian invasion of Abyssinia was likewise the topic of Apostolic pastor J. F. D. Thompson's sermon "Can Italy Hold Abyssinia? What is the Future of this Remarkable Race?" preached in Palmerston North in 1935.[78]

However, there was one particular prophetic emphasis that was increasingly popular during and following the First World War: British Israelism. The core of this widely held genealogical theory was a "Two-House Theology," which asserted that while all Jews were Israelites, not all Israelites could be considered Jews. Rather, the House of Judah (i.e., the Jews) was descended from the two tribes of Judah and Benjamin. Conversely, the House of Israel (i.e., the "lost" ten tribes, taken into captivity by Assyria in 721BCE) comprised the Anglo-Saxon races of Northern Europe.[79] Thus the British nation enjoyed a covenantal relationship with the God of Israel, with the promises made to ancient Israel being appropriated to Britain.[80] Some of the more extreme adherents of the theory—such as A. H. Dallimore—even argued that the name "British" was derived from two Hebrew words: *berith* (covenant) and *ish* (man); hence "British" meant "covenant man."[81]

Three specific promises were emphasized in most varieties of British Israelism. The first of these was the promise that Abraham's descendants would spread across the face of the earth (Gen.28:14), becoming "a nation and a community of nations" (Gen.35:11). This was held to have been historically fulfilled in the British Commonwealth, "the Empire on which the sun never set." British Israel advocates claimed that only the Anglo-Saxon races could be said to have spread around the world in this way.[82] Secondly, the Bible prophesied that the descendants of Abraham would possess the gates of their enemies (Gen.22:17 AV). British Israel advocates pointed to British control of the key sea-lanes around the world—e.g., the English Channel, Gibraltar, Suez, Aden, the Straits of Malacca, etc.—as evidence of this prophecy's fulfillment.[83] Thirdly—and perhaps most importantly—the British Monarchy was seen as a continuation of the Davidic monarchy of ancient Israel and, as such, heir to the promises that David's kingdom would be everlasting (Jer.33:17).[84] Some British Israelites placed special significance on the Stone of Destiny which lay under the throne upon which British monarchs were crowned. This was asserted to be the stone which Jacob had anointed at Bethel (Gen.28:18) and which thereafter was "the Rock of Israel" (Gen.49:24).[85] Other variants of British Israel belief included an emphasis on the Pyramid of Gizeh, the dimensions of which functioned as a time line of end-time prophetic events.[86]

British Israelism appears to have arrived in New Zealand in the early 1880s, with early local British Israel associations being formed in Dunedin[87] and Christchurch.[88] By 1900, there were reports of further British Israel meetings and associations in Wellington, Invercargill, Auckland, Sydenham, Timaru, Napier and Oamaru. Although formal membership in the movement remained small, there was sufficient interest for a Dunedin bookseller to advertise British Israel books for sale to the general public in 1883.[89] This interest grew steadily over the years, occasionally becoming more overt and explicit in response to social changes. The formation of a national British Israel Federation helped to stimulate the movement's growth in the 1930s. Reports to the Federation's Annual Congress reflect this expansion. The 1932 branch reports note that "membership [was] increasing rapidly,"[90] while the 1934 Congress was the largest yet held, with the membership and the number of local British Israel centers both doubling during that year.[91]

This growth indicates that in the early twentieth century British Israelism was not the sectarian, "lunatic fringe" topic that it is today. It enjoyed support from prominent people such as William Ferguson Massey, Prime Minister of New Zealand from 1912 to 1925, who was a patron of the movement.[92] It is noteworthy that an address from the British Israel Association was included among the official speeches welcoming the Prince of Wales to Christchurch in 1920.[93] Furthermore, British Israel meetings were often chaired by local dignitaries and extensively reported in the media, indicating that this was a relatively mainstream belief. Part of the reason for this wide—but not universal—public acceptance was the way in which the theory reinforced the imperialism of the time. One British Israel supporter specifically made this equation during the Boer War: "'British Israelism'," he said, "had an intimate connection with the Imperial struggle that was being waged in South Africa."[94] This imperialism was viewed in jingoistic, yet deeply religious terms, an example of which was a resolution passed by the Methodist Annual Conference in 1915. This declared that "We regard the British Empire, with all its defects, as being, in practical righteousness, the largest instalment of the Kingdom of God that has yet arisen among men" and celebrated "that dispensation of righteousness and liberty which it has been the glory of our Empire to spread over the world."[95] Thus, just as the churches provided a "sacred canopy" for New Zealand's involvement in the Boer War and the First World War,[96] the British Israel movement represented a sanctification of the imperialist impulse. This process continued, although less stridently, during the Second World War.[97] It is noteworthy that official speeches in Christchurch to celebrate VE Day in 1945 did not—in contrast to the welcome to the Prince of Wales in 1920—include representation from the British Israel movement.[98]

However, strains began to emerge as the movement grew in the 1930s. It was criticized both by the 1934 Presbyterian General Assembly[99] and by the Anglican bishops in 1936.[100] There were also internal tensions when British Israel churches—as distinct from the broader, nonsectarian movement—began to emerge in the 1930s. This trend appears to have begun with A. H. Dallimore, since the British Israel World Federation specifically dissociated itself from his meetings.[101] Dallimore's convert A. J. Ferris—who was a prolific British Israel author, publishing at least three books on the subject under the auspices of the British-Israel World Federation[102]—began conducting British Israel lectures in the Hutt Valley in early 1933. Wellington appears to have been the early epicenter of the British Israel church movement. The 1936 Census notes that 341 (or 48.44%) of the 704 members of British Israel churches in New Zealand resided in the Wellington urban area. Surprisingly, only seven members resided in that most English of New Zealand cities, Christchurch.[103] The Pentecostal connection and the incipient development of these churches became more explicit in October 1933, when advertisements included references to the Baptism of the Spirit as well as to a Communion Service following the meeting.[104] Ferris was later joined by W. E. Wilson and the meetings were thereafter advertised as being under Ferris' auspices, rather than those of the British Israel Federation.[105] Later W. E. Wilson became the leader of these meetings, the name of which was changed from "British Israel Assemblies" to "Commonwealth Covenant Assemblies" in 1939, thus forming the basis of what became the Commonwealth Covenant Churches.[106] The four Wilson brothers were the principal figures in the Pentecostal British Israel movement, all becoming founders and leaders of Pentecostal British Israel churches. Charles S. Wilson helped to found the Commonwealth Revival Crusade in 1941, while Frank Wilson (together with his brother W. E. Wilson) founded the Commonwealth Covenant Church in 1939. Frederick Wilson, a Dallimore convert, founded the Church of Christ (New Zealand) in Mount Roskill in 1946; this eventually became the largest Pentecostal congregation in New Zealand up to the 1970s. Another Pentecostal British Israel group—unconnected to either Dallimore or the Wilson brothers—was started by Pastor Vin Brown in Wellington in 1939. This amalgamated with Pastor Leo Harris' Australian-based Christian Revival Crusade in 1944 to form the National Revival Crusade,[107] which was renamed Christian Revival Crusade in the late 1950s and still exists today as CRC New Zealand. However, Brethren writer Murray Darroch notes that although British Israelism was still advocated by a significant minority of Christian Revival Crusade members, it was no longer a major doctrinal emphasis by the 1980s.[108]

It should be noted that British Israelism has a long history in the Pentecostal movement: Charles Fox Parham had espoused the doctrine,[109] as did John G. Lake.[110] Nevertheless, both the British Israel emphasis and the new groups that espoused it created problems for other Pentecostal churches. It exacerbated tensions within the Pentecostal Church of New Zealand, the Assemblies of God and the newly arrived Apostolic Church and stimulated defections from these churches into the new movement. The Pentecostal Church of New Zealand consequently issued a repudiation of the new teaching in 1933. This led to the resignation of Charles Wilson, then the Pentecostal Church of New Zealand pastor in Nelson, and the commencement of an independent church,[111] which later became part of the Apostolic movement and eventually, of the Commonwealth Covenant Churches. The Apostolic churches were also adversely affected, with Apostolic Church National Superintendent Dr. A. L. Greenway[112] having his hands full trying to defuse tensions in Wilson's Nelson congregation, recently transferred from the Pentecostal Church of New Zealand.[113] This did not end the problem, as at least one very senior and prominent Apostolic leader was reported as "flirting" with the new teaching in the early 1940s.[114] The Assemblies of God, already weakened by the advent of the Apostolic Church, were further damaged by the British Israel controversy. As Ian Clark notes, "the rise of the Commonwealth Covenant Churches pastored by the Wilson brothers . . . served to retard the recovery of the Assemblies of God for a decade or more."[115]

The focus on prophecy meshed with the global anxieties of the decade and contributed to Pentecostal expansion in the 1930s. However, in its British Israel form, it proved a catalyst for division as well as for growth. The large and vigorous British Israel Pentecostal churches that emerged did so at the expense of already-struggling Pentecostal churches such as the Pentecostal Church of New Zealand and the Assemblies of God. By the end of the 1930s there already were two Pentecostal British Israel denominations: the Revival Fire Mission of A. H. Dallimore and the Commonwealth Covenant Assemblies of W. E. Wilson. Two more would emerge in the 1940s: the Christian Revival Crusade and the Church of Christ (New Zealand). However, the greatest impact on the Pentecostal movement came from the arrival of the Apostolic Church in 1934; this created a further legacy of division and bitterness that would last for a generation.

The Apostolic Church

The Apostolic Church claims to have originated in the Welsh Revival of 1904–5;[116] this perception has been reinforced by Apostolic Church literature.[117] In fact, the movement emerged as a result of the expulsion of D. P. Williams, its Welsh founder, from the independent Evangelistic Church and his subsequent alliance with the Apostolic Faith Church, from which he and his followers then seceded to form the Apostolic Church. The conflation of the movement's early history has served to obscure its confrontational origins in the interests of emphasizing its divine arrangement.[118] Its arrival introduced a new model of Pentecostal polity into New Zealand. In contrast to locally governed Pentecostal churches such as the Assemblies of God, it was strongly centralized and tightly organized. Its world headquarters were located in Penygroes, Wales[119] and its overseas outposts—such as Australia and New Zealand—were superintended by the church's Missionary Council at Bradford.[120] The work in New Zealand therefore followed the patterns which had been established in Great Britain. Its affairs were administered by a General Superintendent sent out from Britain and—until becoming an autonomous Apostolic Church in 1943—all important matters were referred to the British Church Council for final decision.[121] However, the key distinctive in its polity was the operation of apostles and prophets in the Biblically legitimated theocratic government of the church. These offices were, in theory, simply two of the five ministry gifts of apostles, prophets, evangelists, pastors and teachers (Eph.4:11). In practice, they were senior ministers, with the apostles exercising a governmental role and the prophets providing guidance and direction. This practice was particularly evident in the appointment and location of ministers. The movement therefore had strong and well-established governmental structures, but also an emphasis on the direction of the Holy Spirit in this government by means of the prophetic ministry.[122]

These apostolic and prophetic ministries also played an important part in the setting up—or as Apostolic terminology had it, "setting in order"—of a local assembly. This was an intentional, formalized procedure. It involved teaching on the doctrines and tenets of the church. (These tenets were extensive. The detailed Constitution of the British Apostolic Church came to over 200 typed pages; this was accepted by the Australian Apostolic Church in 1939 with little change.)[123] This teaching was followed by an invitation to those members of the audience who so desired to receive "the right hand of fellowship" at a Communion service. Those who responded and were thus "received in" by the presiding apostolic or prophetic minister formed the basis of the new congregation. From this group, appointments were made—usually at the directions given by prophetic ministry—to the local offices of elders, deacons and deaconesses in the congregation. James Worsfold notes that as the movement developed, superintendent ministers also appointed these officers.[124] These "set apart" local leaders thereafter had the responsibility for the local congregation, subject to the overall governing authority of the apostles and prophets. It therefore followed that no congregation could be formally set in order without the ministry of apostles and prophets. This authority structure provided a security and a clear pattern of Biblically legitimated responsibility that new adherents found attractive, given the organizational turmoil previously experienced in the New Zealand Pentecostal churches. Luke Worsfold notes that "the orderly authority of the church, particularly the practice of divine government, has developed into a distinctive which historically has set the Apostolic Church in New Zealand apart from other pentecostal groups."[125] E. R. Weston, a prominent convert to the Apostolic Church, later summarized what he found attractive about this theocratic format:

> Now, if the autocratic and democratic form of government for the church are alike hopeless, what then remains? To this question no one offered any solution until the Apostles of a new (yet very old) method came along. Their simple solution lies in the fact that they allow the Lord Himself to speak through His prophets (as has ever been God's way with prophets whenever He sent them) and so declare plainly His will for the people, which will is then enforced by the authority of God's appointed Apostles. Of all officers thus called into office by the Word of the Lord through the prophets, it can truly be said "The Holy Ghost hath made you overseers." Acts 20:28.
>
> ...The Apostle whose authority enforces obedience to God's will, and the Prophet who is the channel through which God's will can be revealed in the matters of

guidance and order and appointment of officers, etc., Hallelujah! The Lord can at least have a say in the affairs of His Church. The Head of the Body at least is given an opportunity to control His members and bring order out of chaos....[126]

The Apostolic Church had arrived in Australasia in response to invitations from members of the Apostolic Church in Great Britain who had emigrated there. The number of these members was not large. Twelve people claimed membership of the Apostolic Church of Great Britain in the 1926 New Zealand Census.[127] Similarly, William Cathcart,[128] the Scottish pioneer Apostolic missionary to Australasia knew of only a solitary "isolated member" on his arrival in Melbourne.[129] Cathcart was sent out in response to a letter of petition to the Apostolic Church leaders and the prophetic conviction that "the Lord was preparing a servant to go to Australia." The witness of a Miss Flett, who had been a member of the Apostolic Church in the Orkney Islands before emigrating to Australia, seems to have been a significant factor in the generation of this letter of petition, as was her distribution of Apostolic Church literature.[130] Cathcart arrived in Perth in early 1930, to be greeted by a welcoming committee of some twenty-five people. From this small beginning, the first Apostolic congregation was established and the movement spread from there across Australia and into New Zealand over the next five years. Similarly, a small group of people in Wellington had contacted the Apostolic Church leaders in Wales in 1928 and eventually a small congregation began to meet following Apostolic principles. This came to be regarded as the first Apostolic community in New Zealand, although not, as yet, set in order as an Apostolic church.[131] Cathcart was later joined by other Apostolic leaders from the United Kingdom (Apostle A. S. Dickson and Prophet Joshua McCabe). He also worked closely with former Assemblies of God minister John H. Hewitt[132] and his brother Isaac, both of whom had become members of the Apostolic Church in Australia. These men provided the apostolic and prophetic ministry necessary to formally set in order local Apostolic churches in Australia and New Zealand.

When William Cathcart eventually arrived in Wellington in late October 1933 to conduct a revival campaign, he taught on end-time prophetic subjects and Apostolic Church governmental tenets.[133] Attendance at these Wellington meetings grew steadily to 700 people.[134] This systematic instruction formed an essential part of the establishment of Apostolic congregations in New Zealand. Cathcart's ministry, together with that of his co-worker John H. Hewitt, attracted much attention, being reported in the local *Evening Post*.[135] Cathcart apparently delegated his apostolic authority to Hewitt when he returned to Australia in December. Hewitt was then joined by Joshua McCabe, whose prophetic ministry enabled the Wellington church to be set in order as the first official Apostolic church in New Zealand in January 1934. E. R. Weston was set in as the pastor of this congregation, most of which had transferred *en masse* with him from the Pentecostal Church of New Zealand. As such, Weston was the first person ordained in New Zealand under Apostolic auspices[136] and 112 members were reported as receiving the right hand of fellowship.[137] Within five months, other Apostolic churches also had been established at Nelson, Blenheim, New Plymouth, Auckland, Onehunga and Te Kuiti. The first four of these churches were set in order by Hewitt and McCabe, working together as apostle and prophet (and accompanied in several of these events by Weston and Len J. Jones). McCabe seems to have given prophetic instructions to the Onehunga congregation before returning to Australia and the congregation was officially established by Jones, who had transferred from the Assemblies of God and had recently been set apart to the Apostolic ministry. Jones also set the Te Kuiti congregation in order, although there is no record of who provided the prophetic ministry in this instance.[138] Furthermore, Dr. A. L. Greenway had been sent out from England to be the National Superintendent, working with Weston in the Wellington church.[139] Other churches were established over the next two years;[140] by the time of the 1936 Census, there were eleven Apostolic churches in New Zealand.

Why was the Apostolic Church so attractive to New Zealand Pentecostals? Given the controversy over the centralized administration of the Pentecostal Church of New Zealand in the 1920s, it seems surprising that a similar Pentecostal polity should have been so successful less than a decade later. The answer lies partly in the means by which this centralization was legitimated. The Apostolic Church saw itself as a theocratic—or rather, Christocratic—government in the Church, the leadership of which was vested in the ministries of apostle, prophet, evangelist, pastor and teacher.[141] Thus the central leadership of the Church was a charismatic one, appointed by means of prophetic revelation.[142] This view appealed strongly to Pentecostal perceptions of Biblical precedent, spiritual legitimation and charismatic empowerment. As well as this, the Pentecostal Church of New Zealand and the Assemblies of God had both been weakened by the schisms of the previous decade. The Apostolic Church brought a new sense of Pentecostal power and zeal that these churches had lost. Ian Clark observes that

> by the early 1930s the Assemblies of God were lamenting their loss of Pentecostal power and zeal, for no ministries for some years had come close to those of Wigglesworth and Valdez. The latent hunger for the power of Pentecost and solid, well-established church order and discipline based on the scriptures was satisfied when the Apostolic Church arrived in this country, for it had a set code of beliefs that were convincingly presented through its anointed prophetic, evangelistic, healing and teaching ministries.[143]

Nevertheless, the arrival of the Apostolic Church exacerbated the damage to existing Pentecostal churches. Some churches—for example, the Nelson, Blenheim, Palmerston North and New Plymouth Assemblies of God[144] and the Onehunga Pentecostal Church of New Zealand—appear to have transferred *en masse* to the new movement. Other churches which had already left their parent movements—as, for example, E. R. Weston's Wellington Pentecostal Church of New Zealand congregation[145] and the Blenheim Assembly of God—now found homes within the Apostolic Church. Still other churches remained in existence, but suffered a loss of congregational members. By 1935, the Assemblies of God had retained "only 11 affiliated assemblies, six of them being in the Auckland area, with 'adherents here and there in twos and threes'."[146] Furthermore, the rise of the Apostolic Church removed the financial base of those Assemblies of

God that had survived, condemning them to decades of small congregations and dingy, uninviting halls.[147] By contrast, the Apostolic Church was seen as the aristocracy of New Zealand Pentecostalism. Their impact on other Pentecostal churches was reinforced by the rise of the British Israel churches. The Pentecostal Church of New Zealand, already under pressure after the arrival of the Assemblies of God in the 1920s, was now struggling for survival. By the 1940s, it could claim only three remaining assemblies: Wellington, Auckland and Blenheim.

Thus, by building on their initial success, the Apostolic Church became the leading Pentecostal group in New Zealand for the next thirty-five years. For their part, the Pentecostal Church of New Zealand and the Assemblies of God were reduced to the status of marginal groups.[148] This reinforced a sense of suspicion and mistrust, which lasted until the 1960s. In 1945, the Assemblies of God passed a motion "that all leaders and elders of the Assemblies of God refrain from any association with the Apostolic Church."[149] Ian Clark commented to the author in 1990 that

> Despite what would be said by Apostolics, they *did* tear the Assemblies of God to pieces, and many of the old leaders of the Assemblies of God ended up in the Apostolic Church as Apostles and Prophets and what not. Whole congregations had problems over it.... There was that ... "heritage" of splits and divisions [that] took a long time to heal; there was a lot of mistrust. When I became ... General Secretary [of the Assemblies of God] in 1971, I was warned *never* to trust the Apostolic Church.... It was still very real at that time.[150]

As will be seen, these divisions did not begin to heal until the 1970s.

Conclusion

The 1930s were a decade of significant shifts in perception. The Great Depression—and its corollary, the creation of the Welfare State—shaped the attitudes of the next two generations of New Zealanders. The experience of the Depression molded attitudes of frugality and caution in the minds of those who had lived through it. By contrast, the "cradle to the grave" welfare system—created in 1938—cocooned those born after the 1930s from the harsher realities of economic life. The dismantling of this Social Welfare system in the 1980s would usher in a precarious new world for almost all New Zealanders.

Changes in the New Zealand Pentecostal movement in the 1930s were also significant and, in most cases, long-lasting. A. H. Dallimore's successful campaigns, although seemingly ephemeral, had the effect of filling a vacuum of expectation for a return of the glory days of Smith Wigglesworth and A. C. Valdez. Of greater significance was the fact that many of the future leaders of several Pentecostal bodies had been converted or had received the Baptism of the Spirit in his meetings. Dallimore's British Israelism was also significant in helping to launch a Pentecostal version of the British Israel movement. This found its expression in several new Pentecostal denominations and in a number of large British Israel churches which prospered until the 1970s. This emphasis on Britain's role reflected both the increasingly gloomy geo-political outlook of the 1930s and also the intensified perception of many students of the Bible that end-time prophecy was rapidly being fulfilled.

For New Zealand Pentecostalism, the most significant change of the 1930s was the "invasion"[151] of the Apostolic Church. This new movement brought a solid, well-established order and discipline, together with a set code of beliefs which was Biblically legitimated and powerfully presented. However, it also brought a legacy of division and distrust. Congregations were split and in some cases transferred *en masse* into the new movement, with a resultant sense of bitterness and mistrust in those left behind. A number of leaders in the Pentecostal Church of New Zealand and Assemblies of God transferred their allegiance to the Apostolic Church, sometimes taking precious ministry resources with them. The most striking example of this was Cecil C. H. Scadden, one of the founding members of the Assemblies of God in 1927. Scadden resigned from this movement in 1938, feeling that it was going nowhere. He took the Onehunga Assembly of God and the Onehunga Bible School—the Assemblies' only major training institution—with him and shortly thereafter joined the Apostolic Church, which soon ordained him as an apostle.[152] Such incidents did nothing to resolve the antipathy and distrust between the Apostolic Church and the other Pentecostal groups.

The effects of the divisions of the 1930s can be quantified from a comparison of the Census Statistics for 1926 and 1936. In 1926, almost all of the 742 Pentecostals in New Zealand identified themselves as "Pentecostal"—most likely referring to the Pentecostal Church of New Zealand—in the Census. By 1936, the movement had grown to 1,274 adherents, but the proportion of "Pentecostals" had fallen to 490 (or 38.46% of the total). The Apostolic Church and the Assemblies of God had almost identical numbers (390 and 389 adherents, respectively).[153] Thus, although the Pentecostal movement had grown in the 1930s, it had also become more diversified and divided. The Pentecostal Church of New Zealand and the Assemblies of God, which were already struggling to maintain a sense of spiritual direction[154] and which now merely maintained parity of adherence with the Apostolic Church, became marginalized second-class citizens in the movement. This reinforced their incipient sectarianism and strengthened a sense of difference between them and—in particular—the Apostolic Church. The latter church became an aristocracy within New Zealand Pentecostalism, giving them a sense of status that lasted for the next three decades. The emergence of a new and vibrant group of British Israel Pentecostal churches at the end of the decade also contributed to the developing diversity of the movement. Both division and diversity would increase in the 1940s.

Notes

1. Charles Duhigg, "The Nation: Depression, You Say? Check Those Safety Nets," *New York Times*, 23 March 2008, www.nytimes.com/2008/03/23/ weekinreview/23duhigg.html?pagewanted=all&_r=0 (accessed 14 August 2013).
2. Sir Mervyn King, Governor of the Bank of England, cited in James Kirkup, "World facing worst financial crisis in history, Bank of England Governor says," *Telegraph*, 6 October 2011, http://www.telegraph.co.uk/finance/financialcrisis/8812260/World-facing-worst-financial-crisis-in-history-Bank-of-England-Governor-says.html (accessed 11 October 2011).
3. Sinclair, *History of New Zealand*, 255; King, *Penguin History of New Zealand*, 346.
4. Tom Brooking and Paul Enright, *Milestones: Turning Points in New Zealand History*, with picture research by Harry Mills (Lower Hutt: Mills Publications, 1999), 150 and 154.
5. Tony Simpson, *The Sugarbag Years: An Oral History of the 1930s Depression in New Zealand*, 2nd ed. (Auckland: Hodder and Stoughton, 1984).
6. Brooking and Enright, *Milestones*, 151.
7. King, *Penguin History of New Zealand*, 345.
8. For a biography of Savage, see Barry Gustafson, "Savage, Michael Joseph," from the *Dictionary of New Zealand Biography*. Te Ara Encyclopedia of New Zealand, Biographies, updated 30 October 2012, http://www.TeAra.govt.nz/en/biographies/4s9/savage-michael-joseph (accessed 2 December 2013).
9. Sinclair, *History of New Zealand*, 270.
10. Ibid. 278.
11. See below, 188.
12. Kevin Clements, "The Religious Variable: Dependent, Independent or Interdependent?" in *A Sociological Handbook of Religion in Britain*, ed. Michael Hill, IV: 36–45 (London: SCM Press, 1971). Clements' argument is summarized in Allan K. Davidson, *Christianity in Aotearoa: A History of Church and Society in New Zealand* (Wellington: Education for Ministry, 1991), 109–10.
13. Clements, "The Religious Variable," 43.
14. Robert Mapes Anderson, *Vision of the Disinherited: The Making of American Pentecostalism* (New York: Oxford University Press, 1979). For a discussion of Anderson's thesis and its applicability (or otherwise) to the New Zealand context, see Brett Knowles, "Vision of the Disinherited? The Growth of the Pentecostal Movement in the 1960s, with particular reference to the New Life Churches of New Zealand," in *"Be Ye Separate": Fundamentalism and the New Zealand Experience*. Waikato Studies in Religion 3, ed. Bryan Gilling (Hamilton: University of Waikato and Colcom Press, 1992): 107–41.
15. John A. D. Adams, "Mr Smith-Wigglesworth's Meetings: To the Editor," *Otago Daily Times*, 22 June 1922, 10.
16. Chant, *The Spirit of Pentecost*, 3.
17. W. Luke Worsfold, "Subsequence, Prophecy and Church Order in the Apostolic Church, New Zealand" (DPhil thesis in Religious Studies, Victoria University of Wellington, 2004), 72.
18. Knowles, "Adams, John A. D.," in NIDPCM, 308.
19. Clark, *Pentecost at the Ends of the Earth*, 33.

20. B. Knowles, "Scadden, Cecil C. H.," in NIDPCM, 1039–40; Clark, *Pentecost at the Ends of the Earth*, 38.
21. Clark, *Pentecost at the Ends of the Earth*, 55, 60.
22. Minute Book, Pentecostal Church Board of Deacons, Wellington, November 1929, cited in Worsfold, *History of the Charismatic Movements in New Zealand*, 177–78.
23. James E. Worsfold, *The Reverend Gilbert and Mrs Alice White*, New Zealand Apostolic Pioneer Breviate Series 2 (Wellington: Julian Literature Trust, 1995), 46–47.
24. Davidson, *Christianity in Aotearoa*, 108–9.
25. Worsfold, *History of the Charismatic Movements in New Zealand*, 178.
26. Clark, *Pentecost at the Ends of the Earth*, 47.
27. Ibid, 48.
28. Worsfold, *History of the Charismatic Movements in New Zealand*, 211.
29. Clark, *Pentecost at the Ends of the Earth*, 55.
30. Ibid, 47.
31. Ibid, 57–58.
32. Ibid, 48–49.
33. The best critical analysis of Dallimore's ministry is given in Guy's two articles (Laurie Guy, "Miracles, Messiahs and the Media: The Ministry of A. H. Dallimore in Auckland in the 1930s," in *Signs, Wonders, Miracles: Representations of Divine Power in the Life of the Church*. Studies in Church History 41, ed. K. Cooper and J. Gregory, 453–63 (Woodbridge: Ecclesiastical History Society, 2005); and Guy, "One of a Kind? The Auckland Ministry of A. H. Dallimore," *Australasian Pentecostal Studies*, no. 8 (July 2004), http://webjournals.ac.edu.au/journals/aps/issue-8/06-one-of-a-kind-the-auckland-ministry-of-a-h-dall/ (accessed 9 November 2011).
34. Additional biographical details from B. Knowles, "Dallimore, A. H.," in NIDPCM, 570; Worsfold, *History of the Charismatic Movements in New Zealand*, 224, note 2; and Bryan D. Gilling, "Dallimore, Arthur Henry," from the *Dictionary of New Zealand Biography. Te Ara Encyclopedia of New Zealand*, Biographies, updated 7 June 2013 http://www.TeAra.govt.nz/en/biographies/4d2/dallimore-arthur-henry (accessed 2 December 2013).
35. "Mass Faith-Healing: Patients Stretched Out: Scenes in Auckland," *Evening Post*, 24 August 1932, 9, "Papers Past" (accessed 12 November 2011).
36. Guy, "One of a Kind?"
37. *Auckland Star*, 31 October 1932, 3, cited in Guy, "One of a Kind?"
38. A number of letters testifying to healing are given in A. H. Dallimore, *Healing by Faith: including many Testimonies of healing received by people in New Zealand*, 2nd ed. (Auckland: n.p., 1932?), for example 27–28, 77–78, 84–85, etc. Guy, "One of a Kind?" notes that nearly half of these published letters refer to this means of healing.
39. "Healing by Faith: A Cow and a Rooster," *Evening Post*, 25 October 1932, 9, "Papers Past" (accessed 11 November 2011).
40. The letter testifying to this event was reproduced in *Revival Fire Monthly* 1.7 (November 1934), 8, cited in Guy, "One of a Kind?"
41. "Collapsed as if Pole-Axed! The Remarkable Power of Evangelist Dallimore: Turns Tables on the 'Slick Alecs'," *New Zealand Truth*, 20 November 1930, 1.
42. E. C. Cutten, cited in *New Zealand Herald*, 16 December 1932, 13, and thence in Guy, "Miracles, Messiahs and the Media," 457.
43. Guy, "Miracles, Messiahs and the Media," 458–59.

44. "Faith Healing: Dallimore's Mission: Report of Committee: No Cures Proved," *Evening Post*, 14 December 1932, 5, "Papers Past" (accessed 11 November 2011). The full report of the Committee was published as Auckland Council of Christian Congregations, *The Dallimore campaign exposed: the full report of the joint clerical medical, and professional committee of inquiry into the faith healing mission conducted by Mr. A.H. Dallimore, 1932* (Auckland: Wilson and Horton, 1932).

45. Gilling, "Dallimore, Arthur Henry," *Te Ara Encyclopedia of New Zealand*, Biographies.

46. Guy, "One of a Kind?"

47. Worsfold, *History of the Charismatic Movements in New Zealand*, 234.

48. Guy, "Miracles, Messiahs and the Media," 453.

49. John A. Lee, *Simple on a Soap-Box: A Political Testament* (Auckland/London: Collins, 1963), 50 and 62, cited in Guy, "Miracles, Messiahs and the Media," 454.

50. *Revival Fire Monthly*, I.5 (September 1934), 5, cited in Guy, "Miracles, Messiahs and the Media," 455. Guy also discusses whether Dallimore was Pentecostal, despite his explicit claims not to be (Guy, "One of a Kind?").

51. Gilling, "Dallimore, Arthur Henry," *Te Ara Encyclopedia of New Zealand*, Biographies.

52. "Faith Healing: Dallimore's Mission: Report of Committee: No Cures Proved," *Evening Post*, 14 December 1932, 5, "Papers Past" (accessed 11 November 2011). Guy cites other reports of glossolalia appearing in *New Zealand Herald*, 14 July 1930, 10; 31 October 1932, 10; 12 December 1932, 10; and *Auckland Star*, 7 November 1932, 9; 14 November 1932, 3, cited in Guy, "One of a Kind?" See also Gilling, "Dallimore, Arthur Henry," *Te Ara Encyclopedia of New Zealand*, Biographies.

53. Worsfold, *History of the Charismatic Movements in New Zealand*, 236, note 1.

54. Guy, "Miracles, Messiahs and the Media," 460.

55. "Collapsed as if Pole-Axed!" *New Zealand Truth*, 20 November 1930, 1.

56. Darrell Paproth, "Revivalism in Melbourne from Federation to World War I: the Torrey-Alexander-Chapman Campaigns," in Hutchinson and Piggin, *Reviving Australia*, 160. Emphasis added.

57. Luther P. Gerlach and Virginia H. Hine, *People, Power, Change: Movements of Social Transformation* (Indianapolis: Bobbs-Merrill, 1970), xvii.

58. E. C. Cutten, letter in *Revival Fire Monthly* XI.6 [actually X.6] (October 1943), 7, cited in Guy, "Miracles, Messiahs and the Media," 460, footnote 46.

59. Gilling, "Dallimore, Arthur Henry," *Te Ara Encyclopedia of New Zealand*, Biographies.

60. Tauranga Christian Fellowship, "Jubilee Reunion 1939–1989," 2 (mimeographed), BKRP, MS-3530/014, Hocken Library, Dunedin.

61. Worsfold, *History of the Charismatic Movements in New Zealand*, 224, note 2; and Gilling, "Dallimore, Arthur Henry," *Te Ara Encyclopedia of New Zealand*, Biographies. Guy summarises Dallimore's "British Israel" beliefs in Guy, "One of a Kind?"

62. Gilling, "Dallimore, Arthur Henry," *Te Ara Encyclopedia of New Zealand*, Biographies; and A. H. Dallimore, *Britain-Israel: Chats about our Empire, our People and our Origin*, 2nd ed. (Auckland: n.p., 1932?), 70.

63. Guy, "Miracles, Messiahs and the Media," 457.

64. For a survey of Pentecostal understandings of eschatology, see D. J. Wilson, "Eschatology, Pentecostal Perspectives on," in NIDPCM, 601–5.

65. For example, Joel 2:28 and Acts 2:17.

66. Bartleman, *Another Wave Rolls In!* 26.

67. For a brief discussion of these terms, see Alister E. McGrath, *Christian Theology*, 2nd ed. (Oxford: Blackwell, 1999), 552.
68. Chant, *The Spirit of Pentecost*, 303.
69. Ibid, 318, note 2.
70. Luke Worsfold, "Subsequence, Prophecy and Church Order," 67–68.
71. Chant, *The Spirit of Pentecost*, 110–11.
72. "The Second Coming of Christ," *New Zealand Evangel*, 6 July 1924, 7–8.
73. "The Coming One," *New Zealand Evangel*, 6 August 1924, 9–10.
74. "Signs of the Times," *New Zealand Evangel*, 20 May 1926, 5–8.
75. Worsfold, *History of the Charismatic Movements in New Zealand*, 247; Chant, *The Spirit of Pentecost*, 236, note 35.
76. *Christchurch Star-Sun*, 16 and 23 November 1935, 7 and 29 December 1935, 4 and 11 January 1936, April 1936, cited in Worsfold, *History of the Charismatic Movements in New Zealand*, 253.
77. Worsfold, *The Reverend & Mrs Edward and Eily Weston*, 39.
78. Worsfold, *The Reverend Gilbert and Mrs Alice White*, 65.
79. Christopher J. Richmann, "Prophecy and Politics: British-Israelism in American Pentecostalism," *Cyberjournal for Pentecostal Research*, no. 22 (January 2013), http://www.pctii.org/cyberj/cyberj22/richmann.html (accessed 14 August 2013).
80. Gilling, "Dallimore, Arthur Henry," *Te Ara Encyclopedia of New Zealand*, Biographies.
81. Dallimore, *Britain-Israel*, 9.
82. "Local & General," *Star*, 18 May 1888, 3, "Papers Past" (accessed 21 November 2011).
83. Letter from "British Israelite," cited in "Passing Notes," *Otago Witness*, 21 June 1900, 3; and "Chapter VIII," *Taranaki Herald*, 5 November 1898, 2, para.24, "Papers Past" (both accessed 19 November 2011).
84. "Literary Notes," *Evening Post*, 11 March 1922, 15, "Papers Past" (accessed 22 November 2011).
85. "The British Empire's Stone Witness," *Auckland Star*, 14 May 1900, 2, "Papers Past" (accessed 21 November 2011).
86. "The Pyramid's Message," *Evening Post*, 15 June 1932, 5, "Papers Past" (accessed 19 November 2011); and "Pyramid Symbolism: The Predictions," *Evening Post*, 18 September 1936, 3, "Papers Past" (accessed 20 November 2011).
87. See "The Lecturer: Britain, The Stone People," *Otago Witness*, 11 December 1880, 25.
88. See "Local and General," *Star*, 2 September 1887, 3, "Papers Past" (accessed 18 November 2011).
89. "Business Announcements, Page 3 Advertisements Column 3," *Otago Daily Times*, 3 March 1883, 3.
90. "British-Israelites: New Zealand Branch: Annual Congress," *Evening Post*, 30 March 1932, 12, "Papers Past" (accessed 19 November 2011).
91. "British-Israel: Conference in Wellington," *Evening Post*, 31 March 1934, 4, "Papers Past" (accessed 19 November 2011).
92. Guy, "One of a Kind?"
93. "Prince and People: A Day of Extraordinary Enthusiasm: Civic Reception and Loyal Addresses: Fine Military Spectacle in Hagley Park," *Press*, 15 May 1920, 8.
94. C. E. R. Mackesy, cited in "British-Israel Society: Lecture by Mr. C. E. R. Mackesy," *Southland Times,* 6 June 1900, 2.

95. Methodist Annual Conference, 1915, 117, cited in Allan Davidson and Peter J. Lineham, eds., *Transplanted Christianity: Documents Illustrating Aspects of New Zealand Church History*, 2nd ed. (Palmerston North: Dunmore Press, 1988), 180.

96. Davidson, *Christianity in Aotearoa*, 95–100.

97. For a discussion of the religious motivations behind support for New Zealand's war effort in the Second World War, see Peter J. Lineham, "The Religious Face of Patriotism," in *Kia Kaha: New Zealand in the Second World War*, ed. John Crawford, 199–220 (Auckland: Oxford University Press, 2000).

98. Jock Phillips, "New Zealand celebrates victory," in Crawford, *Kia Kaha*, 313.

99. "British-Israelism: Menace to Peace: An Involved Debate," *Evening Post*, 14 November 1934, 7, "Papers Past" (accessed 19 November 2011).

100. "British Israel: World Federation: Congress in Wellington," *Evening Post*, 13 April 1936, 10, "Papers Past" (accessed 20 November 2011).

101. "British Israel Federation: To the editor," *Evening Post*, 7 February 1930, 8, "Papers Past" (accessed 19 November 2011).

102. A. J. Ferris, *Armageddon is at the Doors* (Lower Hutt: Lower Hutt Branch of the British-Israel World Federation, [1934]); Ferris, *British-Israel teaching Concerning the signs of the approaching end of the age* (Wellington: British-Israel World Federation, 1934); and Ferris, *Why the British are Israel: Nine conclusive facts proving that the Anglo-Saxons represent the House of Israel of Scripture* (Lower Hutt: British-Israel World Federation, 1934).

103. Census and Statistics Department, *Dominion of New Zealand Population Census, 1936* (Wellington: Government Printer, 1940), "Vol. VI.—Religious Professions," 3–4.

104. "Church Services," *Hutt News*, 18 October 1933, 4, "Papers Past" (accessed 23 November 2011).

105. "Page 6 Advertisements Column 2," *Hutt News*, 8 November 1933, 6, "Papers Past" (accessed 23 November 2011).

106. "Religious Services," *Evening Post*, 14 January 1939, 5, "Papers Past" (accessed 23 November 2011).

107. Chant, *Heart of Fire*, 181–99; Worsfold, *History of the Charismatic Movements in New Zealand*, 292–96. Worsfold erroneously dates Harris' arrival and the formation of the National Revival Crusade as 1941.

108. Murray Darroch, *Everything you ever wanted to know about Protestants but never knew who to ask*, New Zealand ed. (Wellington: Catholic Supplies, 1984), 146.

109. Gastón Espinosa, "Ordinary Prophet: William J. Seymour and the Azusa Street Revival," in Hunter and Robeck, *The Azusa Street Revival and Its Legacy*, 33.

110. Gilling, "Dallimore, Arthur Henry," *Te Ara Encyclopedia of New Zealand*, Biographies.

111. Worsfold, *History of the Charismatic Movements in New Zealand*, 179.

112. For a brief biography of Greenway, see B. Knowles, "Greenway, Alfred L.," in NIDPCM, 680–81.

113. Worsfold, *History of the Charismatic Movements in New Zealand*, 249.

114. Worsfold, *The Reverend and Mrs Eily Weston*, 47.

115. Clark, *Pentecost at the Ends of the Earth*, 58.

116. Chant, *The Spirit of Pentecost*, 221.

117. For example, Thomas N. Turnbull, *What God Hath Wrought: A Short History of the Apostolic Church* (Bradford: Puritan Press, 1959), 13, cited in Luke Worsfold, "Subsequence, Prophecy and Church Order," 1–2.

118. Luke Worsfold, "Subsequence, Prophecy and Church Order," 1–6, 21–32.
119. Worsfold, *History of the Charismatic Movements in New Zealand*, 237.
120. Ibid, 248.
121. Ibid, 252.
122. Chant, *The Spirit of Pentecost*, 221–23, 229–32.
123. Ibid, 221.
124. Worsfold, *History of the Charismatic Movements in New Zealand*, 239, note 5, and 257.
125. Luke Worsfold, "Subsequence, Prophecy and Church Order," 15.
126. E. R. Weston, cited in Worsfold, *The Reverend & Mrs Edward and Eily Weston*, 28 and 30.
127. Worsfold, *History of the Charismatic Movements in New Zealand*, 237.
128. For a biographical account of Cathcart and his activities in Australia, see Chant, *The Spirit of Pentecost*, 220–21 and 224–26; and (in greater detail), B. Chant, "Cathcart, William," in NIDPCM, 458.
129. Chant, *The Spirit of Pentecost*, 225.
130. James Worsfold, *The Reverend Gilbert and Mrs Alice White*, 29.
131. Worsfold, *History of the Charismatic Movements in New Zealand*, 237–38.
132. For a biographical account of John H. Hewitt, see Chant, *The Spirit of Pentecost*, 226–28 and 344–45.
133. Worsfold, *History of the Charismatic Movements in New Zealand*, 239.
134. Clark, *Pentecost at the Ends of the Earth*, 49.
135. "Forecast," *Evening Post*, 25 November 1933, 5, "Papers Past" (accessed 5 December 2011).
136. Worsfold, *History of the Charismatic Movements in New Zealand*, 244.
137. Clark, *Pentecost at the Ends of the Earth*, 49. Worsfold, *History of the Charismatic Movements in New Zealand*, 240–41.
138. Worsfold, *History of the Charismatic Movements in New Zealand*, 242–44.
139. Ibid, 246; Worsfold, *The Reverend & Mrs Edward and Eily Weston*, 33.
140. These were Dargaville (Worsfold, *History of the Charismatic Movements in New Zealand*, 247), Hastings (Worsfold, *The Reverend & Mrs Edward and Eily Weston*, 34; Worsfold, *History of the Charismatic Movements in New Zealand*, 250–52), Christchurch (Ibid, 253) and Napier (Ibid, 252).
141. Worsfold, *The Reverend & Mrs Edward and Eily Weston*, 38.
142. For examples of prophetic appointment, see James Worsfold, *The Reverend Gilbert and Mrs Alice White*, 34–36, 48–49, 55–56 and 62. However, tensions began to develop between the prophetic and organisational modes of leadership in the 1940s. Worsfold, *The Reverend & Mrs Edward and Eily Weston*, 41–42.
143. Clark, *Pentecost at the Ends of the Earth*, 50.
144. Ibid.
145. Worsfold, *History of the Charismatic Movements in New Zealand*, 179.
146. *New Zealand Evangel*, January/February 1936, 6, cited in Clark, *Pentecost at the Ends of the Earth*, 55.
147. Clark, *Pentecost at the Ends of the Earth*, 51.
148. Ibid, 50.
149. Ibid.
150. Clark, Interview, Auckland, 28 February 1990, cited in Knowles, *The History of a New Zealand Pentecostal Movement*, 248. Emphasis as cited. The audio cassette of this interview is held in BKRP, MS-3530/024, Hocken Library, Dunedin.

151. The word is Clark's. Clark, *Pentecost at the Ends of the Earth*, 50.
152. Ibid, 57.
153. See Appendix A.
154. Clark, *Pentecost at the Ends of the Earth*, 49.

Chapter 5

The 1940s

As the World Turns . . .

The Second World War was the dominant event of the 1940s, the axis upon which the world turned. The war in Europe, ignited by Germany's invasion of Poland in September 1939, was replicated in the Pacific by Japan's air attack on Pearl Harbor in December 1941, bringing America into the War. By early 1942, the rapid Japanese advance southward had placed Australia and New Zealand under real danger of invasion, especially after the fall of Singapore.[1] New Zealand was committed to both conflicts, contributing more than 200,000 men and women to the war effort, although most of these troops served abroad in the European theatre, rather than in the Pacific. Of these, 11,500 were killed, the highest *per capita* casualty rate in the Commonwealth.[2] Another 250,000 men and women served within New Zealand in the Home Guard, providing a defense reserve in the event of a Japanese invasion.[3] This comprehensive mobilization had an economic dimension as well as a human one, especially in agricultural production. Between 1942 and 1944, war-related expenditure consumed more than half the national income, with Britain purchasing almost all New Zealand's agricultural exports and New Zealand also providing food for United States forces in the Pacific.[4] This resulted in shortages and rationing of petrol, food and clothing and the imposition of social and economic controls on New Zealand life. Wartime restrictions such as butter and petrol rationing were not removed until the election of the National Government in October 1949.[5]

Historian Jock Phillips has observed that New Zealand's way of life was conformed, body and soul, during the War. Social freedom was vitiated by conscription into the army, where one followed orders, having no say about what one did, where one worked, or with whom one associated. Nor was this control limited to those in armed service. Employment was regimented by conscription into essential industries; economic controls fixed prices and prevented sales of housing and land—except at set prices—and rationing limited access to produced goods and food. There was also a mental conformity imposed by censorship.[6] The effect of this was to reinforce attitudes already present within the

New Zealand psyche. These had been built up over the years by the lower middle-class values enshrined in the state school system.[7] They were also strengthened by the moralist efforts of the churches[8] and by public campaigns against alcohol. These pressures had served to break down older codes of larrikinism and revelry; consequently, New Zealanders had internalized expectations about respectable behaviors in public places.[9] This is tellingly demonstrated in the way in which the rule of regulation had been embraced by the end of the War and by New Zealanders' respect for "red tape" in the VE Day celebrations. When the government suppressed spontaneous celebrations of the end of the War, ordering the public to wait for a go-ahead to begin celebrations following the official Government commemorations, this was largely accepted. The *New Zealand Herald* noted at the time: "The feeling of victory was in the air, but no-one was inclined to let off steam without official authorisation."[10] Only in Dunedin—where VE Day coincided with the Otago University "Capping" (or Graduation) ceremony on the afternoon of 8 May—did a degree of spontaneity emerge.[11] This social decorum generally held firm, with the only loss of control being in Auckland on VJ Day three months later.[12] The general conformity and respect for government and regulation demonstrates the accuracy of historian Graeme Dunstall's observation that "the basic social pattern was disrupted only temporarily. In many respects the war merely accentuated the uniformity and drabness of life inherited from the depression of the 1930s."[13] This pattern prevailed until the 1970s, although the seeds of social change had already been sown and would germinate in the next three decades. Future long-term developments include the urbanization and rising expectations of Māori, arising from their military service in the Second World War[14] and an increased American cultural radiation. This latter development contrasted with the "essentially nineteenth-century British ideas ... expressed in a distinctively New Zealand manner" that characterized New Zealand's "provincial culture" by 1940.[15] A breakout from conformity and increased consumerism, as opposed to the discipline and rationing of the war years, would emerge in the 1950s.

Despite these continuities, the post-war world was significantly different from what had gone before. In the geo-political sphere, a division had been drawn between East and West and an "Iron Curtain" (in British Prime Minister Winston Churchill's phrase) had descended across Europe. The Cold War between the Soviet bloc and the West began in 1948; this would shape the bipolar configuration of world politics until the collapse of Communism in the late 1980s. The advent of the atomic bomb exacerbated fears for the future of humanity and fuelled the insecurity and defensiveness inherited from the Second World War. This country, although remote from the rest of the world, was not immune from these tensions and the post-War period was marked by the formation of new alliances and orientations. New Zealand was already mapping out an independent path from Great Britain in foreign affairs—in part, a product of its "amputation" from Britain after the fall of Singapore[16]—and was involved in the promotion of new international agreements, including the formation of the United Nations.[17] Parallel to this increasingly independent international involvement was the adoption of the 1931 Statute of Westminster in 1947. This

Statute gave this country the status of a fully independent state—although maintaining allegiance to the British throne—rather than a dominion of the British Empire. Britain's declining imperial influence was matched by an increasing American dominance in the Pacific. Indeed, historian Sir Keith Sinclair wryly notes that it was effectively the Americans—in the person of their servicemen—rather than the Japanese, who invaded New Zealand.[18] This American dominance had been predicted by Carl Berendsen, New Zealand's ambassador to the United States in 1945.[19] New Zealand was therefore acutely aware of its vulnerability to world events.[20] Consequently, new ties were—of necessity—forged with the United States and trans-Tasman relations with Australia were strengthened.[21] The most obvious example of these new alliances was the ANZUS defense pact between Australia, New Zealand and the United States. This lasted until the nuclear-free policy of the New Zealand Labour Government ended it in 1985.

Within New Zealand, there were—despite the tendency to uniformity and drabness of life—significant changes underway. Firstly, the Second World War represented a hinge between periods of depression and affluence[22] and signaled the emergence of trends that would continue into the 1970s. By the end of the 1940s, an economic boom was beginning that would last for the next two decades. Sinclair describes this as

> over twenty years of prosperity, a prolonged boom which . . . continued into the early nineteen-seventies. New Zealanders continued to enjoy one of the highest standards of living in the world, measured by any of the popular indicators, such as the number of automobiles or telephones per thousand people. The "real standard of living" was always among the top half dozen in lists of comparative standards. . . . This prosperity was the all-pervasive fact in New Zealand life for the first two post-war decades; it was the dominant influence on social attitudes and on politics alike.[23]

This prosperity—together with the social protectionism of the Welfare State—helped to maintain the high degree of uniformity in New Zealand life.[24]

Nowhere was this uniformity more evident than in the increasing national birthrate and the growth of the new housing suburbs. During the Baby Boom of 1946–61, Pākehā birthrates increased from a low point of sixteen per 1000 in 1935–36 to just over twenty-six per 1000 by the late 1940s, a level it maintained until 1961. Māori birthrates were higher and family sizes were larger.[25] Government measures such as the liberalization of the Family Benefit in 1946 effectively sponsored this population growth.[26] Its effects were most clearly seen in the sprawling State Housing suburbs in which most of these new families lived, with housing in suburbia becoming a central motif in the post-war social pattern.[27] Historian Michael King identifies several trends resulting from this "idyll of suburban domesticity."[28] The first of these was the rapid development of suburbia and of suburban culture together with a concentration on the nuclear family, reinforced by the effects of the Baby Boom. A second was the growth of philosophical and political conservatism which led to the dominance of the center-right National Party for most of the next quarter-century. There was also an

"American-led build-up of Cold War mentality and a minor outbreak in the 1950s of something resembling McCarthyism" in Wellington. This incipient paranoia was exemplified by the Holmes "Snatchel Case" in 1948, which involved the theft of a briefcase belonging to Cecil Holmes, an apprentice filmmaker who had left-wing sympathies, but who was nevertheless employed by the Information Section of the Prime Minister's Department. This affair built upon fear of Communism leading up to the Communist takeover of China in 1949 and the beginning of the Korean War in 1950.[29]

Also significant, as the nation moved from war-time rationing to peacetime prosperity, was the growth of overt forms of consumerism, which came to be known as "keeping up with the Joneses." "By 1957," Keith Sinclair drolly observes, "New Zealand was a 'materialist's paradise'."[30] This cult of domesticity turned New Zealanders in on themselves, both as individuals and as families, and confirmed some of the most profoundly imprinted social patterns of the prewar years.[31] These trends began in the 1940s and accelerated in the 1950s. Nevertheless—as will be seen in later chapters—there were also incipient tensions in the 1940s that would surface in decades to come. These included concerns over freedom as opposed to regulation, unease about moral order, and issues of class conflict and Māori-Pākehā relations. The last of these was the most significant, since the issue of bicultural relations would occupy the nation in one way or another for the next fifty years.[32]

War, Society and the New Zealand Churches

New Zealand, despite its claims to be "Godzone," has never been a Christian country in the sense that the majority of its citizens were church adherents. The peak of church attendance—at 29.8% of the population—was reached in 1896;[33] thereafter it gradually fell until the 1960s, when the decline in church membership accelerated dramatically. Historian Oliver Duff noted in 1941 that

> When you enter a church you do not get the impression that zeal for God's house is eating us up. Congregations are small, collections very small, and a majority of those present are not young. Though there has been a noticeable change in all these respects during the war, only a blind man could suppose that most New Zealanders go to church. The proportion who [sic] regularly go is smaller than it has ever been in our history.[34]

While the churches had little influence and nominalism was increasing,[35] they continued in their attempts to shape the wider society by sharing their beliefs, upholding their understandings of public morality and promoting community values. These attempts were not usually successful. The churches were "more adept at reinforcing and sanctifying values such as patriotism, loyalty and sacrifice, than shaping national ... values that promoted and achieved the peace they preached." They therefore had little influence beyond their own constituency.[36]

A significant change in New Zealand Christianity came with the formation of the National Council of Churches in 1941. This had developed from the growing cooperation of members of different Protestant churches in organizations such as the Student Christian Movement, the Bible Society, the Bible in Schools League and the Council for Religious Education. This ecumenical impulse was reinforced by the initiatives of a number of influential church leaders—particularly in Christchurch—during the 1930s. These leaders were convinced that the churches needed to come together in order to have an impact on society. The new body was made up of the main Protestant churches, i.e., the Presbyterians, Anglicans, Methodists, Baptists, Associated Churches of Christ and Congregationalists, later joined by the Society of Friends and the Salvation Army. However, support was not unanimous: Evangelical groups already had their own networks and were highly suspicious of the new body's theological pluralism and political orientation. Catholics and Pentecostals were also strongly opposed to ecumenism in principle: the former, since they alone were the authoritative true Church; the latter, because unity was a product of the Spirit, not of organization.

One of the first acts of the National Council of Churches was to organize a Campaign for Christian Order, which sought to prepare society for post-war reconstruction on a Christian foundation. The need for Christian principles in shaping the social order was emphasized, with the main objective being the promotion of "a Christian New Zealand."[37] This was reflected in a set of convictions and standards, consisting of "God, family, work in God's service, and a belief that the government of the country should reflect Christian values."[38] These Christian values—according to a Study Guide published for the use of women's groups—included the viewing of marriage for a woman as a "career." It was suggested that "one way for a mother to deal with vocational ambition was to find her reward in 'seeing her children grow up and do the things she had always longed to do.'"[39] Attitudes such as this maintained and reinforced social conformity and fostered the "cult of domesticity." Both of these social orientations, incipient in the 1940s, would become more explicit in the 1950s.

The churches' attitudes to the war were varied. While there was no repeat of the unthinking jingoism that had characterized most public attitudes to war in 1914,[40] they played a supportive role for participants in the war as well as for conscientious objectors. Church attendance increased at times of crisis, with the highest levels being reached in the middle and later months of 1940, i.e., from the evacuation of Dunkirk to the Battle of Britain.[41] Several national days of prayer were held throughout the country in 1940 and 1941, with even denominations—such as the Brethren—which had an ambivalent attitude to the war observing these.[42] The churches also contributed to the war effort, with more than 170 chaplains being posted overseas; many more served within New Zealand.[43] Some churches—most particularly the Methodist Church and Brethren groups—advocated pacifism and supported their members who applied for conscientious objector status. Members of these churches had a better than average chance of successful appeal to the Conscientious Objector Appeal boards.[44] Pentecostal churches also tended towards pacifism although official pronouncements generally left this to the conscience of the individual.[45] Military historian J. E. Cookson mistakenly singles out Pentecostal churches for condemnation over their pacifism, apparently confusing the Assemblies of God and the Christian Assemblies and incorrectly calling the latter body "the largest Pentecostal group." His accusation is that "while [the Christian Assemblies] posed as a church that respected individual conscience, to a man they refused military service."[46] However, the Christian Assemblies were not a Pentecostal group and certainly are not to be identified with the Assemblies of God. A newspaper report describing their beliefs and practices identifies them as the exclusivist sect known as the Cooneyites or "Two by Twos."[47] In October 1944, the Cooneyites comprised the largest single group of incarcerated military defaulters; 107 out of the 592 inmates were members of this sect. This number greatly exceeded that of larger groups such as Jehovah's Witnesses and Methodists (seventy-eight and sixty-seven defaulters, respectively).[48] Cookson's criticism is therefore justified, but misdirected.

Despite the restrictions of the period, innovative new patterns of ministry were emerging and new ways of recruiting membership and raising financial support were also being developed after the War.[49] The churches would enjoy a period of almost unprecedented opportunities in the new suburbs in the 1950s. This boom reflected the parallels between their position as providers of security and respectability on the one hand and the uniformity and domesticity of the expanding new suburbia on the other. These factors will be discussed in the next chapter.

Pentecostal Churches in the 1940s

In New Zealand, the Pentecostal movement of the 1940s was characterized by sectarian isolation, division and, conversely, by the emergence of several new trends that would radically shape the future of the movement. By the end of the 1930s, there were three main Pentecostal denominations: the Pentecostal Church of New Zealand, the Assemblies of God and the Apostolic Church. The Revival Fire Mission, established after the heyday of A. H. Dallimore's meetings in the Auckland Town Hall in the early part of the decade, was rapidly losing momentum and only three congregations survived the 1930s. Other groups, such as the British Israel Pentecostal churches, tended to be isolated individual congregations. Of the three denominations, only the Apostolic Church was thriving, largely at the expense of the other two. The Assemblies of God were suffering a prolonged loss of spiritual and organizational impetus: as Ian Clark notes,

> In the years leading up to the War the Assemblies of God made no perceptible progress.... Nothing really altered.... Without a change in the leadership and the injection of new ideas it is clear that the Assemblies of God would have remained a small, inward-looking, marginal group.... [I]n the end they would have exerted no influence on the life of New Zealand.[50]

These difficulties were compounded during the war years. Despite the opening of several new churches during the decade, the Wellington Assembly of God—the leading church in the movement—was forced to sell its building in 1943.[51] When the New Plymouth Assembly opened its new building in 1944, this was the first such building since the Assemblies of God was formed in 1927. Despite this advance, by 1945 the Assemblies of God were little further ahead than they had been eighteen years before.[52] The only other Assembly with its own building was the Sydenham Assembly in Christchurch and even its premises had been inherited from the Sydenham Gospel Mission when it became Pentecostal in 1922.[53] Furthermore, there were only ten credentialed ministers in the New Zealand Assemblies of God in 1948, with a further four holding licenses to preach.[54] The Pentecostal Church of New Zealand had also shrunk into a small sectarian body by the 1940s. It therefore is not surprising that its Wellington congregation should have approached the Assemblies of God and the Apostolic Church for unification talks in 1945. However, although this proposed unification was agreed to in principle in early 1946, the terms for amalgamation eventually proved unacceptable and the proposal was quietly dropped several months later. The Apostolic Church's insistence on the roles of the apostle and prophet proved to be the sticking point in the negotiations.[55]

Even the comparatively healthy Apostolic Church had its share of problems, with tensions over church government emerging in 1942[56] and some doctrinal difficulties arising during the 1940s.[57] Tensions were also beginning to develop between the prophetic and organizational modes of leadership.[58] In particular, there was disagreement over the role of prophecy in appointing Apostolic Church officers; while some felt that this had not reached its full potential,[59] others were concerned at its potential for erroneous appointments. This was also an issue in the Australian Apostolic Church; Barry Chant notes that "because of the unique system of calling into office [by prophetic direction], unfortunate mistakes occurred. Some who were called into office either became frustrated, through trying to do what they could not do; or they tried to exercise an authority they did not really have."[60] Consequently, one senior New Zealand Apostolic pastor refused to attend an Apostolic Church Council—where he knew that he would receive prophecy ordering a change of pastorate—since he did not want to relocate. Only intervention by the President of the Apostolic Church motivated him to accept the transfer.[61] After 1943, such appointments were no longer purely a charismatic appointment by prophetic direction, but were subject to confirmation by the full Apostolic Church Council.[62] However, many Apostolics were increasingly uneasy with this new subordination of the prophetic role. A further issue for the Apostolic Church was the granting of autonomy to both the Australian and New Zealand wings of the movement from its world headquarters in Bradford, England in 1942. This necessitated the formation of Councils and the drawing up of Constitutions, based on United Kingdom models of Apostolic Church polity.[63] These provided for a strongly centralized form of church government, vested in the Apostolic Church Dominion Council. Gilbert White, who was entrusted with the preparation of this Constitution, later came to see it as "too centralised" and to advocate a more regional form of church government.[64]

There were also several emerging groups in the 1940s, including several nascent British Israel Pentecostal churches. Vin Brown had started a Pentecostal British Israel group in Wellington in 1939. Advertisements of its services demonstrate an emphasis on Bible prophecy and British Israelism.[65] On purchasing a building in August 1941, it changed its name to "New Covenant Assembly" and Brown began to itinerate throughout New Zealand. The arrival of Australian pastor Leo Harris in 1944[66] changed the scale of this group's activities. Harris was leader of an identical, but stronger, group in Australia and his meetings in New Zealand led to the formation of the National Revival Crusade, which absorbed and incorporated the churches established by Brown.[67] This new group—now known as the Christian Revival Crusade Churches—continued into the 1980s, although its British Israel emphasis became much less prominent as time went on.[68] Another highly successful, but strongly sectarian, British Israel group—the Church of Christ (New Zealand)—was started by Frederick A. Wilson in Avondale, Auckland in 1946. Although numbers were initially small, the building of a church at Mount Roskill in 1951 extended its influence[69] and it became one of the largest individual Pentecostal congregations in New Zealand until the 1970s. Ironically—despite its continuing British Israel emphasis—it now attracts a strongly Chinese clientele, as is evident from its website.[70] Its statement of faith on the website contains a reference to "the 'lost' 10 tribes, which may be identified as the Celtic-Anglo-Saxon and associated peoples."[71]

Pentecostal Seed-time: The Emergence of Significant Trends

As with the wider society, trends were emerging in the Pentecostal movement in the 1940s that would come to fuller fruition in later years. In particular, two seemingly unconnected events during the decade were to have considerable long-term effects on the future configuration of New Zealand Pentecostalism. The first of these was the arrival of a party of Bethel Temple missionaries, evacuated from Indonesia, who passed through Wellington en route back to the United States in March 1942. Several of these missionaries returned to New Zealand in 1945 to take up pastoral positions in the Pentecostal Church of New Zealand.[72] The second was the emergence of a new generation of healing evangelists in America, spearheaded by William Branham, together with the related outbreak of the Latter Rain movement in North Battleford, Saskatchewan, Canada. The healing movement stimulated similar evangelism in New Zealand in the late 1950s, providing a catalyst for Pentecostal expansion. The Latter Rain movement would shape this expansion and contribute to the emergence of the Charismatic movement in the 1960s and 1970s.

For the Sake of "the Name"

Three of the evacuated Bethel Temple missionaries—Ray Jackson, Al Edmondson and John Banks—returned to New Zealand in 1945–46 and were enthusiastically welcomed by the Pentecostal Church of New Zealand.[73] Their revelatory Biblical hermeneutics and imaginative use of typology quickly attracted a following and Jackson and his colleagues were rapidly appointed to leadership positions in the movement. However, they brought with them a doctrine that created controversy, resulting in a schism in April 1946 and in the ultimate demise of the Pentecostal Church of New Zealand. This was a characteristic emphasis known as "the Name." This doctrine, which had originated with Bethel Temple Pastor W. H. Offiler in Seattle,[74] insisted upon baptism in the name of "Lord Jesus Christ" rather than using the Matthean formula of "Father, Son and Holy Spirit" (Matt.28:19). Pentecostal historian Professor Walter Hollenweger comments that almost the entire Indonesian Pentecostal movement uses the baptismal formula of "Lord Jesus Christ."[75] (This may have been due to the influence of the Bethel Temple Bible School in Surabaya, at which Jackson had taught before coming to New Zealand.) Its proponents maintained that the name of the Father was "Lord," that of the Son was "Jesus" and the name of the Holy Spirit "Christ." The name "Lord Jesus Christ" therefore symbolized and actualized the triune presence of the Father, the Son and the Holy Spirit; its invocation was seen as the validating factor in baptism.[76] Because, in the Bethel Temple view, only those baptized in this name were in the Bride of Christ, other baptismal formulas were insufficient and rebaptism in "the Name" was therefore necessary. Consequently, a number of Pentecostal Church of New Zealand congregational members were rebaptized. Pastor H. V. Roberts later lamented that these "now adopted a superior air to those who had not, and ... little groups were [gathered] around corners and in separate places whispering away and forming cliques. Here was my assembly ... split in two factions."[77] The teaching was viewed by the elders of the Pentecostal Church of New Zealand as divisionary; this perception proved to be correct, with about twenty to thirty members of the Auckland church seceding with Jackson.[78] This loss represented a substantial segment of its congregation of sixty members; about thirty members also left the Wellington congregation with Edmondson.[79] These secessionists formed the nucleus of what eventually would become a new network of independent Pentecostal churches.[80] This subsequently would grow to become one of the largest and most vigorous Pentecostal groups in the country by the 1980s.

The legacy of "the Name" controversy was a painful one. Although not numerically large, the secession of these members severely weakened the Pentecostal Church of New Zealand, which struggled on for several years before eventually amalgamating with the Elim Church of Great Britain in 1952.[81] Those who had seceded faced decades of opposition from other Pentecostal churches. This became particularly acute in the early 1960s, when they were excluded from a new ecumenical fellowship known as the New Zealand Pentecostal Fellowship.[82] Despite "the Name" proponents being strongly Trinitarian, literature published by this Fellowship in the 1960s attacked their imputed Unitarianism, insisting that baptism in "the Name" implied a view of God known as "Jesus Only."[83] This implication formed the core of opposition to the teaching, but appears to be a later, but mistaken, characterization, since none of the primary records of the dissension make any reference to this Unitarianism. No condemnation of Bethel Temple views on the Trinity appears in the various Minute Books of the Pentecostal Church of New Zealand,[84] or in the correspondence between the protagonists in the controversy.[85] Furthermore, neither the extracts cited by James Worsfold from Pastor H. V. Roberts' pamphlet *Beware of the New Revelation on Water Baptism*,[86] nor Pastor E. E. Pennington's mimeographed pamphlet on "the Name"[87] make any reference to Unitarian tendencies. These silences are significant, for if the doctrine had indeed been perceived as Unitarian, this would have been sufficient to totally damn its teachers in the eyes of their Pentecostal colleagues. Although some opponents of "the Name" teaching have continued to insist that it was Unitarian,[88] the arrival of the "Jesus Only" Pentecostal church in New Zealand in 1969[89] demonstrated the differences in approach.

However, there were also some significant positive legacies: the Bethel Temple teachers insisted that the truths of the Bible could only be known through "revelation" by the Holy Spirit. This was particularly true of its use of types and shadows, whereby Old Testament incidents and events became foreshadowings of the New Testament and of "heavenly things." This provided a hermeneutical methodology that gave full rein to the imaginative use of allegory and typology. For example, "the Sun, the Moon and the Stars, are a magnificent revelation of the Godhead Bodily [W. H. Offiler uses this phrase to denote the Trinity], as The Father, The Son, and The Holy Spirit."[90] The Tabernacle of Moses was a particularly abundant source of allegorical types. The effect of this focus created a strong emphasis on Bible teaching in the Bethel Temple movement. This was reflected in the various Bible Schools conducted in Australia by Ray Jackson and in New Zealand by his students—Rob Wheeler, Ron Coady and others—in the 1950s and 1960s. This teaching ethos inherited from the movement enabled its successors to make a significant contribution to the beginnings of the New Zealand Charismatic movement in the 1960s.

Overseas Developments

Other overseas developments in the 1940s also contributed significantly to the development of New Zealand Pentecostalism from the late 1950s on. Towards the end of the Second World War, a major resurgence of religion began to occur in many parts of the world. It is not accurate to describe this as an American Evangelical Awakening,[91] since it took no single form, and was not limited to any theological perspective or geographical area. Nevertheless, it was most prominent in the United States,[92] where it built upon a pervasive sense of public anxiety reflecting the altered realities of the Cold War era. This insecurity enhanced the perceived desirability of traditional American religion, which now functioned as a patriotic bulwark against the dreaded "Reds," particularly in the McCarthy era of the 1950s. Traditional forms of religion therefore provided a source of reassurance in the face of a frightening new world. In America, this religious revival manifested itself in a number of different ways and American historians offer a variety of characterizations. American historian Winthrop Hudson, for example, describes it as "formless and unstructured, manifesting itself in many different ways and reinforcing all religious faiths quite indiscriminately."[93] (Conversely, his fellow-historian Sydney Ahlstrom is able to distinguish five overlapping types of revival that made up the post-war religious revival in America.)[94] At one level, it reflected new generalized forms of American civil religion,[95] in which religious tradition became a constituent part of the American way and patriotism and religious commitment merged into congruent terms. This convergence was exemplified by President Dwight Eisenhower's statement in 1954 that "our government . . . makes no sense unless it is founded on a deeply felt religious faith—and I don't care what kind it is."[96] The revival of American religion was therefore as much a cultural, civil and social resurgence as a purely religious one and its eventual worldwide impact owed much to an American cultural radiation.[97]

Although this resurgence of religion was not limited to the Evangelical movement, one of its most prominent manifestations was the New Evangelicalism, exemplified by American evangelist Billy Graham and his colleagues. However, this was not a monolithic fundamentalism, but formed a multifaceted Evangelical subculture,[98] subsets of which extended from the Billy Graham Crusades to the healing campaigns of Oral Roberts and to the Latter Rain movement. The influence of this subculture was most significant in the 1950s and beyond. Nevertheless, the emergence of the healing and Latter Rain movements in the 1940s had an immediate impact on the Pentecostal movement in America and later, around the world.

The Healing Movement[99]
The emergence of a new generation of healing revivalists in America, initially led by William Branham in 1946 and, later, by Oral Roberts, created a catalyst for Pentecostal expansion after 1947.[100] A number of factors underlay this emergence. These included a sense of public anxiety and the increasing social and economic mobility of the population—especially in the move to the cities—together with a concomitant sense of social dislocation. This generalized unease augmented a perception that things were changing rapidly and that the world was no longer the same. The claims of the evangelists and revivalists brought reassurance by reinforcing the traditional beliefs of the faithful in the providence and power of God.[101] Changes within Pentecostalism also contributed to the emergence of these healing revivalists. Church historian David Harrell notes that expectancy for the miraculous pervaded the American Pentecostal movement after the Second World War and that "the times were ripe. Pentecostalism had become affluent enough to support mass evangelism . . . [and] tolerant enough to overlook doctrinal differences. Convictions were still deep enough that there was a longing for revival. As the older generation thrilled to memories of the miracle ministries of the 1920s, the young yearned for a new rain of miracles."[102] Furthermore, as Donald Gee commented, "The deaths of Charles Price and Smith Wigglesworth [two pioneers of the earlier healing evangelism of the 1920s who had both prophesied of a coming great revival] within a few days of each other early in 1947 certainly fired many pure young hearts to pick up the torch of their ministry and carry it forward to new achievements."[103]

William Branham, the spearhead of the new movement, was born in 1909 in Cumberland County in the Kentucky Appalachians, to an impoverished, nominally Catholic family with little contact with organized religion.[104] Nevertheless, he was always oriented towards mysticism, reporting several divine visitations during his childhood. He was converted at the age of twenty-two and became an assistant pastor at an independent Baptist church in Jeffersonville, Indiana. He later began his own tent church, conducting healing and revival campaigns for some years, particularly with Oneness Pentecostal groups. He came to public attention after an angelic appearance in May 1946 in which he was commissioned to "take a gift of divine healing to the peoples of the world."[105] Branham had an extraordinary spiritual power, particularly in discerning people's illnesses and thoughts. Professor Walter Hollenweger—who, as a young man, had interpreted for his campaigns in Zurich in the 1950s—noted that he was not aware of any case in which Branham was mistaken in the often detailed statements he made.[106] Consequently, the power of Branham's meetings "remains a legend unparalleled in the history of the charismatic movement"[107] and inspired other Pentecostals—for example, missionary evangelist T. L. Osborn—to begin similar healing ministries.[108] Perhaps the best example of the awe in which Branham was held is a famous photograph of a halo surrounding his head in the Sam Houston Coliseum in Houston, Texas.[109] Although he later became increasingly doctrinally unorthodox, Branham's influence amongst Pentecostals continued until his death in a car accident in 1965.

The catalytic effect of Branham's ministry was reinforced by a network of other healing evangelists, such as Osborn, Gordon Lindsay, Jack Coe, A. A. Allen, Rex Humbard and Kathryn Kuhlman.[110] Of these, the most notable was Oral Roberts, who became known as America's premier healing evangelist.[111] Like Branham, Roberts was also born into an impoverished environment (but, unlike him, into a Christian family, since his father was a Pentecostal minister). After being healed of tuberculosis and stuttering at the age of seventeen in 1935, he was ordained by the Pentecostal Holiness Church and pastored churches in that denomination for a number of years. He launched into healing evangelism in 1947 in response to a sense of divine call to "take the healing power of God to your generation." Roberts' tent campaigns across America built his reputation as the leader of a new generation of dynamic evangelists and his numerous publications on healing—and, after 1955, his weekly television program—spread his influence worldwide. While his campaigns were significant for their size—his "tent cathedral" could seat crowds of over 12,500 people—they also promoted a Pentecostalism acceptable to people who had never previously been receptive to its message. Between 1947 and 1968, Roberts conducted over 300 major crusades and his television programs lifted the healing message from the Pentecostal subculture of American Christianity to its widest audience in history. By 1980, a Gallup poll revealed that his name was recognized by 84% of the American public[112] and he has been viewed by one historian as the major person behind the emergence of the Charismatic movement in the 1960s and the most important religious figure of the twentieth century.[113]

The campaigns of William Branham, Oral Roberts and other healers active in America and elsewhere did much to extend the constituency of Pentecostalism. Later, as the healing revival subsided in the United States, this influence spread around the world. A key figure in the globalization of healing evangelism was T. L. Osborn, who conducted numerous mass-healing crusades around the world in the late 1940s and 1950s. Pentecostal scholars Thomson Mathew and Kimberley Alexander credit him with the invention of the mass prayer method for healing in his crusades. Given the tens of thousands of people who attended, there was no way that he could possibly have laid hands on each individual for healing, as did Roberts.[114] Osborn's numerous publications were highly influential in spreading Pentecostal ideas worldwide.

In New Zealand, Pentecostal groups were well informed about what was happening in the United States. The Slavic and Oriental Mission in Wellington—founded by Len J. Jones in 1932 and later renamed "World Outreach"—ran a well-stocked bookshop known as the "Evidence Book Depot," which engaged in the importing and distributing of Pentecostal books and publications. Such publications were influential in spreading the beliefs and practices of the healing movement. Independent American evangelist A. S. Worley—who was to be instrumental in the ignition of the neo-Pentecostal movement in New Zealand in 1960—was reported as carrying two books, the Bible and Osborn's book *Healing the Sick and Casting out Devils*, with him wherever he went in his early ministry, believing that he could do the same things that Osborn did.[115] The Slavic and Oriental Mission also published a monthly magazine called *The Evidence*, which gave extensive publicity to the healing revival in America. This helped to spread the ideas and theology behind the healing movement long before the arrival of a number of American Pentecostal evangelists in New Zealand in the later 1950s. This played an important part in fostering receptivity to Pentecostalism in this country in the early 1960s.

The Latter Rain Movement[116]
The Latter Rain movement (also known as the "New Order of the Latter Rain") was a further significant element in the shaping of New Zealand Pentecostalism.[117] This radically independent Pentecostal group had emerged in 1948 in a revival at North Battleford, Saskatchewan, Canada, quickly attracting worldwide attention and drawing participants from every part of North America and from other countries. In sociological terms, the Latter Rain movement was restorationist and perfectionist in doctrine, charismatic in ethos and strongly anti-organizational in church polity. It saw itself as bringing about a restoration of the fivefold ministry of apostles, prophets, evangelists, pastors, and teachers (Eph.4:11) to the Church for the "perfecting of the saints." It also emphasized the Feast of Tabernacles as symbolizing a forthcoming end-time outpouring of the Spirit by which the church would be brought to perfection. However, the movement's most significant legacy lay in its charismatic ethos and anti-organizational church polity.

The charismatic ethos of the Latter Rain movement was reflected in several key emphases and practices. The first of these was the impartation of the gifts of the Spirit through the laying on of hands. This contrasted with the traditional Pentecostal method of "tarrying," or waiting in prayer, until God sovereignly baptized the seeker in the Holy Spirit. (In New Zealand, the practice of "tarrying" continued in the Apostolic Church[118] and Assemblies of God[119] well into the 1960s.) However, the difference in method was not that great. The laying on of hands for the Baptism of the Spirit does appear in the early history of Pentecostalism, although the right to lay hands on the seeker was restricted to recognized ministers.[120] The Latter Rain movement restored and extended—rather than created—this practice, which has now become standard practice in Pentecostal and Charismatic groups. The significance of this restoration was that it represented the democratization of a function hitherto restricted to the official ministry; any spirit-filled believer could impart the spirit in this way. The laying on of hands was also a means, together with prophecy, of recognizing and setting apart charismatically gifted individuals as ministries to the Body of Christ. The movement—particularly in its Australasian form—saw this as the coming together of the Body of Christ, in which any believer could minister as the Spirit anointed them.

A second feature was the movement's charismatic emphasis on praise and worship. This incorporated several practices such as Singing in the Spirit, raising of hands and other physical expressions of worship, which have now become standard features in Pentecostal and Charismatic churches. Again, these were reintroductions of practices that had been a feature of early Pentecostalism, but which had fallen into disuse due to the increasing organization and denominationalization of the movement. Singing in the Spirit was also allied with the Latter Rain practice of setting Scripture verses to music. In New Zealand, this found expression in the Scripture in Song series (published from 1971 on); these worship songs had a worldwide influence on the Pentecostal and Charismatic movements in the 1970s. The changing nature of the songs in the series reflected the changes in New Zealand Pentecostal theology and spirituality in the 1970s and 1980s.[121]

The anti-organizational polity of the Latter Rain movement was also highly significant. Since this polity represented a reaction to the growing denominationalism of Pentecostalism, it brought it into conflict with other Pentecostal churches.[122] Although the movement did not become a sect of "come-outers," their emphasis on the autonomy and sovereignty of the local church prevented these independent churches from coalescing into an organized denominational movement. They claimed—with some justification—that Pentecostalism had lost its charismatic fervor, becoming more organized and hence more denominational. It considered all such organization to be "Babylonian" and antithetical to the freedom of the Spirit. Consequently the denominational Pentecostal churches were deemed apostate, backslidden and deserving of rebuke. Believers had to come out of these churches into independent, autonomous Pentecostal churches where the Spirit of God was free to work, unfettered by external forms of denominational authority. This autonomy was a central characteristic and was not to be vitiated by any external constraints; any church that vested authority in a central body was denominational and therefore "Babylonian." This view did not go down well with the existing Pentecostal denominations. James Worsfold, for example, describes the Latter Rain movement as a "serious but misguided attempt to bring renewal to Christians," noting that it had a "phobia of appointed or ordained leadership."[123] Since he was speaking from the viewpoint of the Apostolic Church, the most centralized of the Pentecostal denominations, his view is not surprising. His son, Luke Worsfold, agrees that the alternative model of the Latter Rain movement represented a reaction against centralism, and that it therefore posed "a challenge to the Apostolic Church leadership."[124] This abrogation of denominational constraints reinforced its democratization of the charismatic function. Although it had highly sectarian attitudes towards denominationalism and denominational churches, this democratic participatory approach and the lack of formal membership qualifications made it attractive to those seeking the Baptism of the Spirit. These characteristics enabled it to contribute strongly to the emergence of the Charismatic movement in the 1960s; Luke Worsfold observes that elements of the Latter Rain revival were catalytic for the later Charismatic Renewal.[125]

Ray Jackson was the channel through which the Latter Rain movement reached New Zealand. During a visit to America in 1947–48, he heard of the events in North Battleford and went there to see it for himself. Despite some initial hesitations, he became convinced of the reality of the Latter Rain revival and was ordained by the movement as an apostle to New Zealand. This led to considerable opposition from Bethel Temple in Seattle—to which he was still affiliated—and John Banks, his successor as pastor in the Auckland Bethel Temple church, also had strong reservations. However, he was eventually convinced and Jackson and Banks—together with Pastor Allan Thrift, an early convert to the new teaching—attempted to spread the Latter Rain message throughout New Zealand. The effect of their conversion was to align the Bethel Temple churches in New Zealand with the Latter Rain movement and to integrate their Bible teaching ethos with its radical independence. This combination helps to explain the opposition that the new movement received; in the late 1940s memories of the split from the Pentecostal Church of New Zealand were still fresh. Consequently, the movement made little headway, with only three small churches in the North Island by 1950, i.e., Auckland, Lower Hutt and Tauranga, and three house-meetings in the South Island, i.e., Blenheim, Christchurch and Timaru. Although most of these Bethel Temple/Latter Rain churches would not survive the 1950s, those that did remain began to expand and multiply at the end of that decade. They would later contribute significantly to the emergence of the Charismatic movement in the 1960s; by the 1970s, they would be regarded as "among the most dynamic forces in the religious life in New Zealand."[126]

Conclusion

The 1940s were a transitional decade, reflecting both continuities and discontinuities. Much of its significance lay in the incipient trends—both in the social and religious fields as well as in denominational and in Pentecostal churches—that emerged in the 1940s but flourished in later decades. The social conformity and conservatism of the war years continued into the 1950s; but the start of a prolonged economic "boom," together with a substantial increase in the birthrate, also marked the beginnings of demographic change. Conversely, social tensions—which Jock Phillips notes were implicit in the ways in which VE Day was celebrated—germinated in this decade and developed in the 1950s and beyond. While the churches sought to maintain the status quo in society with their Campaign for Christian Order, new patterns of ministry and ways of recruiting membership and support were also emerging. These led into the almost unparalleled opportunities of the domesticated 1950s. Finally, the 1940s were a decade of difficulty for Pentecostal churches; but developments already emerging overseas reached New Zealand in the late 1950s, transforming the shape of Pentecostalism in this country. The divisiveness and schism generated by the controversy over "the Name" in the 1940s would, in the end, have a positive outcome, setting the stage for the emergence of neo-Pentecostalism and the Charismatic movement in the 1960s.

Notes

1. Carl Bridge, "Australia, New Zealand and Allied grand strategy, 1941–43," in Crawford, *Kia Kaha*, 54.
2. King, *Penguin History of New Zealand*, 407.
3. John Crawford, "Introduction," in Crawford, *Kia Kaha*, 3.
4. Ibid, 4.
5. King, *Penguin History of New Zealand*, 408–9.
6. Phillips, "New Zealand celebrates victory," in Crawford, *Kia Kaha*, 306–8.
7. Syllabus of Instruction, Para.22 Man and Society, Section P Moral Instruction, in "Regulations for the Organization, Examination, and Inspection of Public Schools and the Syllabus of Instruction," published in *New Zealand Gazette*, 1919, vol. 3, 2897–98, cited in P. J. Gibbons, "The Climate of Opinion," in *Oxford History of New Zealand*, ed. Geoffrey W. Rice, 2nd ed., 321 (Auckland: Oxford University Press, 1996).
8. For a discussion of the (usually moralist) issues in which the churches attempted to influence public attitudes in New Zealand, see Laurie Guy, *Shaping Godzone: Public Issues and Church Voices in New Zealand 1840–2000* (Wellington: Victoria University Press, 2011).
9. Phillips, "New Zealand celebrates victory," in Crawford, *Kia Kaha*, 312.
10. "Scene in City: Marked Anti-climax: News of Surrender: Gaiety Efforts Lapse," *New Zealand Herald*, 9 May 1945, 8.
11. "Dunedin Celebrates: Why Wait? Impromptu Holiday: Informal Rejoicing," *Otago Daily Times*, 9 May 1945, 6; "Capping Ceremony: Conferring of Degrees: Oration by Professor John Henderson," *Otago Daily Times*, 9 May 1945, 8.
12. Phillips, "New Zealand celebrates victory," in Crawford, *Kia Kaha*, 309. By contrast, see King, *Penguin History of New Zealand*, 407.
13. Graeme Dunstall, "The Social Pattern," in Rice, *Oxford History of New Zealand*, 451.
14. Michael King, "Between Two Worlds," in Rice, *Oxford History of New Zealand*, 289–90 and 302–3.
15. Gibbons, "The Climate of Opinion," 308 and 334.
16. John Battersby, "Post-war security policy: The formation of the United Nations," in Crawford, *Kia Kaha*, 292.
17. King, *Penguin History of New Zealand*, 402, footnote and 406–7.
18. Sinclair, *History of New Zealand*, 282. See also King, *Penguin History of New Zealand*, 403.

19. Carl Berendsen, cited in Battersby, "Post-war security policy: The formation of the United Nations," in Crawford, *Kia Kaha*, 293.
20. Battersby, "Post-war security policy: The formation of the United Nations," in Crawford, *Kia Kaha*, 292.
21. W. David McIntyre, "From Dual Dependency to Nuclear Free," in Rice, *Oxford History of New Zealand*, 525–26.
22. Dunstall, "The Social Pattern," 451.
23. Sinclair, *History of New Zealand*, 288.
24. Dunstall, "The Social Pattern," 452.
25. Ibid, 454.
26. Sinclair, *History of New Zealand*, 270–71.
27. Dunstall, "The Social Pattern," 458.
28. King, *Penguin History of New Zealand*, 413–14.
29. For an entertaining journalistic treatment of the episode, see Redmer Yska, *All Shook Up: The Flash Bodgie and the Rise of the New Zealand Teenager in the Fifties* (Auckland: Penguin, 1993), 15–21.
30. Sinclair, *History of New Zealand*, 289.
31. King, *Penguin History of New Zealand*, 413–14.
32. Phillips, "New Zealand celebrates victory," in Crawford, *Kia Kaha*, 315.
33. Department of Statistics, Census of Population and Dwellings, for the listed years [1871–1911]. Adherence figures usually in Part 3, "Religions of the People"; attendance figures from Part X or Appendix A, "Industries, &c." Cited in Davidson and Lineham, *Transplanted Christianity*, 176–80.
34. Oliver Duff, *New Zealand Now*. New Zealand Centennial Surveys, 13 (Wellington: Department of Internal Affairs, 1941), 35–36, cited in Davidson and Lineham, *Transplanted Christianity*, 246.
35. Geoffrey M. R. Haworth, "'Higher in rank than a General and lower than a private': Anglican Army Chaplaincy in World War Two, and its impact in the Post-war Church," in Crawford, *Kia Kaha*, 172.
36. Davidson, *Christianity in Aotearoa*, 104.
37. Ibid, 121.
38. Presbyterian General Assembly, 1949, 83, cited in ibid, 146.
39. B. Cochran, "Marriage—Good-bye to other Careers?" in *1944 Studies for Women's Groups* (Christchurch: Presbyterian Bookroom, 1944), study 13, cited in Davidson, *Christianity in Aotearoa*, 146.
40. Crawford, "Introduction," in Crawford, *Kia Kaha*, 2.
41. Lineham, "The Religious Face of Patriotism," in Crawford, *Kia Kaha*, 202.
42. Ibid, 203.
43. Davidson, *Christianity in Aotearoa*, 103.
44. J. E. Cookson, "Appeal Boards and Conscientious Objectors," in Crawford, *Kia Kaha*, 191.
45. As, for example, the Apostolic Church (Worsfold, *History of the Charismatic Movements in New Zealand*, 265–66) and the Assemblies of God (Clark, *Pentecost at the Ends of the Earth*, 61).
46. Cookson, "Appeal Boards and Conscientious Objectors," in Crawford, *Kia Kaha*, 191.
47. "Exemption Sought: Military Training. Evangelist's Claim: Question of Status," *Evening Post*, 12 December 1940, 15, http://paperspast.natlib.govt.nz/cgi-bin/ paperspast/

(accessed 3 February 2012); and Research and Information Services, "Who are the Two-by-Twos?" http://www.workersect.org/2x201.html (accessed 15 August 2013).

48. Guy, *Shaping Godzone*, 269.
49. Davidson, *Christianity in Aotearoa*, 154.
50. Clark, *Pentecost at the Ends of the Earth*, 58–59.
51. Ibid, 59.
52. Ibid, 65.
53. Ibid, 63.
54. Ibid, 67.
55. Ibid, 65–66; for an Apostolic perspective on these talks, see Luke Worsfold, "Subsequence, Prophecy and Church Order," 118; and Worsfold, *History of the Charismatic Movements in New Zealand*, 311–12.
56. Worsfold, *History of the Charismatic Movements in New Zealand*, 263–64; Worsfold, *The Reverend Gilbert and Mrs Alice White*, 62; Worsfold, *The Reverend & Mrs Edward and Eily Weston*, 45–47; and Luke Worsfold, "Subsequence, Prophecy and Church Order," 35–36.
57. Worsfold, *History of the Charismatic Movements in New Zealand*, 263–65 and 267.
58. Worsfold, *The Reverend and Mrs Edward and Eily Weston*, 38.
59. Luke Worsfold, "Subsequence, Prophecy and Church Order," 35–36.
60. Chant, *Heart of Fire*, 176–77.
61. James Worsfold, *The Reverend Gilbert and Mrs Alice White*, 63.
62. Worsfold, *History of the Charismatic Movements in New Zealand*, 274.
63. Ibid, 263–64, 267, 269–74; Worsfold, *The Reverend Gilbert and Mrs Alice White*, 62.
64. James Worsfold, *The Reverend Gilbert and Mrs Alice White*, 62.
65. See, for example, "Religious Services, Page 6 Advertisements Column 1," *Evening Post*, 16 December 1939, 6, "Papers Past" (accessed 1 March 2012).
66. Reported in "Revival Campaign," *Evening Post*, 11 March 1944, 5, "Papers Past" (accessed 16 August 2013). See also Chant, *Heart of Fire*, 183.
67. Worsfold, *History of the Charismatic Movements in New Zealand*, 292–94.
68. Darroch, *Everything you ever wanted to know about Protestants* ... , 146.
69. Worsfold, *History of the Charismatic Movements in New Zealand*, 304–8.
70. Church of Christ New Zealand, http://www.chinese.ccnz.org.nz/ (accessed 3 February 2012).
71. Church of Christ New Zealand, "About CCNZ/What we believe," para.13, http://www.chinese.ccnz.org.nz/about/default.asp?id=213&page=8 (accessed 3 February 2012).
72. "Editorial Notes," *Pentecostal Messenger*, December 1943, 2 (copy held in BKRP, MS-3530/006, Hocken Library, Dunedin). See also Minute Book 1934–1951, Board of Elders of the Pentecostal Church of N.Z. (Inc.), Wellington, 10 December 1943, ff.73, 75 (held by Wellington City Elim Church); Worsfold, *History of the Charismatic Movements in New Zealand*, 181–82; and Knowles, *The History of a New Zealand Pentecostal Movement*, 9–16.
73. This section is drawn from Knowles, *The History of a New Zealand Pentecostal Movement*, 9–26.
74. See W. H. Offiler, *God, and His Name* (Seattle, WA: Temple Publishing House, [1932?]).
75. Walter J. Hollenweger, *The Pentecostals*, trans. R. A. Wilson (London: SCM Press, 1972), 71.

76. For a summary of "the Name" teaching (as the later movement understood it), see Kevin J. Conner, *The Name of God* (Portland, OR: Conner Publications, 1975).

77. H. V. Roberts to Pastor S. T. Douglas, 27 May 1952, cited in Kevin J. Conner, *This is My Story: With Lessons I've Learnt Along the Way* (Vermont, Vic.: Published by author, 2007), 161.

78. H. V. Roberts to Ray Jackson, 3 July 1946, James Worsfold Research Papers, Private collection, Wellington.

79. Roberts to Douglas, 27 May 1952, in Conner, *This is My Story*, 160–62.

80. For a critical account of the emergence and development of this new movement, see Knowles, *The History of a New Zealand Pentecostal Movement*. Worsfold also includes an account of its genesis (including extended extracts from protagonists in the controversy), but this is rather one-sided and inaccurate. Worsfold, *History of the Charismatic Movements in New Zealand*, 182–90 and 297–300.

81. Worsfold, *History of the Charismatic Movements in New Zealand*, 191.

82. See below, 122–123.

83. See Vinson Synan, *The Holiness-Pentecostal Tradition: Charismatic Movements in the Twentieth Century*, 2nd ed. (Grand Rapids, MI: William B. Eerdmans, 1997), 156–64, for an account of the "Jesus Only" movement and its beginnings. A comprehensive analysis of its history, organizational development and theology is given in D. A. Reed, "Oneness Pentecostalism," in NIDPCM, 936–44.

84. Minute Book 1934–1951, Board of Elders of the Pentecostal Church of N.Z. (Inc.), Wellington; Minute Book 8 July 1942–3 December 1951, Wellington Pentecostal Evangelical Mission, Wellington; and Minute Book 1934–1951, Executive Council, Representing the Board of Elders of the Pentecostal Church of N.Z. (Inc.), Wellington. These Minute Books are all held by Wellington City Elim Church.

85. H. V. Roberts to Al Edmondson, 11 February 1944; Ray Jackson to General Secretary of Pentecostal Church of New Zealand [Chas. Bilby], 18 December 1945; Harry [H. V.] Roberts to Chas. Bilby, 23 May 1946; Roberts to Jackson, 3 July 1946; Harry [H. V.] Roberts to General Secretary, Pentecostal Church of New Zealand, 8 July 1946; all in Worsfold Research Papers, Wellington; and Roberts to Douglas, 27 May 1952, in Conner, *This is My Story*, 159–63.

86. Roberts, *Beware of the New Revelation on Water Baptism*, 24–31, cited by Worsfold, *History of the Charismatic Movements in New Zealand*, 182–90.

87. E. E. Pennington, Pamphlet on "the Name" controversy, 1946, Worsfold Research Papers, Wellington.

88. James Worsfold, for example, continued to hold this view until the 1990s. James Worsfold to Brett Knowles, 14 January 1989, cited in Knowles, *The History of a New Zealand Pentecostal Movement*, 23, footnote 19.

89. *World Christian Encyclopedia: A Comparative Study of Churches and Religions in the Modern World, AD 1900–2000*, ed. David B. Barrett (Nairobi: Oxford University Press, 1982), s.v. "New Zealand," Table 2, "Organized Churches and Denominations in New Zealand."

90. For the essence of Offiler's teaching, see W. H. Offiler, *God and His Bible or the Harmonies of Divine Revelation* (Seattle, WA: Bethel Temple, Inc., 1946), 172. Punctuation as cited. He discusses this particular "type," which forms the basis of his Trinitarian understanding, at greater length in Offiler, *The Majesty of the Symbol, or Bible Astronomy* (Seattle, WA: By the Author, 1933).

91. As, for example, does Richard M. Riss, *Latter Rain: The Latter Rain Movement of 1948 and the Mid-Twentieth Century Evangelical Awakening* (Etobicoke, ON, Canada: Honeycomb Visual Productions, 1987).

92. Sydney E. Ahlstrom, *A Religious History of the American People* (New Haven: Yale University Press, 1973), 949–63; Winthrop S. Hudson, *Religion in America* (New York: Charles Scribner's Sons, 1965), 382–91.

93. Hudson, *Religion in America*, 383.

94. Ahlstrom, *Religious History*, 954–63.

95. For an introduction to the much-debated issue of civil religion in the United States, see Richard V. Pierard, "Civil Religion: Parallel Development or Replacement for Traditional Christianity in the West," in *Christianity in the Post Secular West*, ed. John Stenhouse and Brett Knowles (Hindmash, SA: ATF Press, 2007), 163–76.

96. *Christian Century* 71 (1954), cited in *Christianity Today*, 8 May 1961, and thence in Ahlstrom, *Religious History*, 954.

97. Knowles, *The History of a New Zealand Pentecostal Movement*, 51–52.

98. For an articulate, critical and empathetic account of this subculture, see Randall Balmer, *Mine Eyes Have Seen the Glory: A Journey into the Evangelical Subculture in America* (New York: Oxford University, Press, 1989).

99. For a useful discussion of evolving Pentecostal approaches to healing up to the second decade of the twenty-first century, see Mathew and Alexander, "The Future of Healing Ministries," 313–36. A fuller account, covering the practice of healing throughout Christian history, is R. A. N. Kidd, "Healing in the Christian Church," in NIDPCM, 698–711.

100. The best critical account of this healing revivalism is Harrell, *All Things are Possible*.

101. Knowles, "Vision of the Disinherited?" 121.

102. Harrell, *All Things are Possible*, 20.

103. Donald Gee, "The Deliverance Campaigns," *Pentecost* 36 (June 1956): 17, cited in Ibid.

104. Accounts of Branham's life and ministry are given in Hollenweger, *The Pentecostals*, 354–56; and, in more detail, in Harrell, *All Things are Possible*, 227–41 and 159–65. See also the brief summary of D. J. Wilson, "Branham, William Marion," in NIDPCM, 440–41.

105. Wilson, "Branham, William Marion," in NIDPCM, 440.

106. Hollenweger, *The Pentecostals*, 354.

107. Harrell, *All Things are Possible*, 162.

108. R. M. Riss, "Osborn, Tommy Lee," in NIDPCM, 950–51.

109. For this photographic image and an uncritical account of the events surrounding it, see William Branham Home Page, "The Pillar of Fire Photographed," http://www.williambranhamhomepage.org/lhoust.htm (accessed 26 November 2013).

110. Paul L. King, "Healing," in *The Encyclopedia of Christian Civilization. Volume II: E-L*, ed. George Thomas Kurian, 4:1103 (Oxford: Wiley-Blackwell, 2011).

111. While a résumé of Roberts' career is given in Harrell, *All Things Are Possible*, 41–52, the major critical biography is Harrell, *Oral Roberts: An American Life* (Bloomington, IN: Indiana University Press, 1975). See also the brief summary in P. G. Chappell, "Roberts, Granville Oral," in NIDPCM, 1024–25.

112. Chappell, "Roberts, Granville Oral," in NIDPCM, 1024–25.

113. Harrell, *Oral Roberts, An American Life*, cited in Vinson Synan, "The Charismatic Renewal After Fifty Years," in Synan, *Spirit-Empowered Christianity in the 21st*

Century, 10; Harrell, *All Things are Possible*, 225–38, cited in Synan, *The Holiness-Pentecostal Tradition*, 223.

114. Mathew and Alexander, "The Future of Healing Ministries," 328–29.

115. Robert E. Grice, *Apostle to the Nations: An Authorized Biography of A. S. Worley, a Man of Faith and Miracles* (Walhalla, SC: Faith Training Center, n.d.), 10.

116. This section is drawn from Knowles, *The History of a New Zealand Pentecostal Movement*, 27–42.

117. The best account of this movement is Riss, *Latter Rain*. Riss also contributed the brief entry on the movement in the *New International Dictionary of Pentecostal and Charismatic Movements*. R. M. Riss, "Latter Rain Movement," in NIDPCM, 830–33. Blumhofer, *The Assemblies of God*, 2:53–67, offers a critical perspective on the movement.

118. Luke Worsfold, "Subsequence, Prophecy and Church Order," 80. See also James Worsfold, *The Reverend Gilbert and Mrs Alice White*, 32–33 for an account of the practice in the Apostolic Church.

119. Luke Worsfold, "Subsequence, Prophecy and Church Order," 103. See also Laurie Murray, *Where to World 1977?* (Palmerston North: By the author, 1977), 8–10.

120. Luke Worsfold, "Subsequence, Prophecy and Church Order," 84. Worsfold discusses the Apostolic Church's theology and practice of "tarrying," including the role of the ministry in the laying on of hands (Ibid, 75–84 and 100–106) and contrasts this with that of the Latter Rain movement. Ibid, 106–12.

121. Brett Knowles, "'From the Ends of the Earth We Hear Songs': Music as an Indicator of New Zealand Pentecostal Theology and Spirituality," *The Spirit and Church* 3, no. 2 (November 2001): 227–49. This article was also (with permission) published online, in four parts, in *Australasian Pentecostal Studies*, no. 5–6 (April 2002), http://aps.webjournals.org/Issues.asp?index=9&id={CE149387-42E6-48C3-801C-7ED675022C60} (accessed 27 May 2005).

122. Blumhofer, *The Assemblies of God*, 2:53–55, 64–67; John Thomas Nichol, *The Pentecostals [formerly Pentecostalism]* (Plainfield, NJ: Logos International, 1966), 238; Riss, *Latter Rain*, 77.

123. Worsfold, *History of the Charismatic Movements in New Zealand*, 183.

124. Luke Worsfold, "Subsequence, Prophecy and Church Order," xxiii.

125. Ibid, 106, footnote 52.

126. Lineham, "Tongues must cease": 16.

Chapter 6

The 1950s

"Golden Weather" and the Cult of Domesticity

The 1950s formed part of a prolonged period of prosperity that started with the Korean War boom and lasted, with only minor interruptions, until the early 1970s. This post-war prosperity, Keith Sinclair observes, "was the all-pervasive fact in New Zealand life. . . ; it was the dominant influence on social attitudes and on politics alike."[1] The title of New Zealand playwright Bruce Mason's *The End of the Golden Weather* provides an apt metaphor for the ethos of the era and for the sense of transition that marked its passing.[2] The analogy was also appropriated by economic historian John Gould to describe the changes in the New Zealand economy that took place after 1967.[3] Prosperity was reflected in increasing expectations of the "good life"; although Government post-War austerity policies still continued, public demand for consumer goods was increasing. While there was still only a limited range, these goods were both affordable and readily available. The desire for modern appliances was reinforced by the influence of popular radio quiz shows such as Selwyn Toogood's *It's in the Bag*, where competitors sought to win prizes such as washing machines and refrigerators.[4]

As well as increasing prosperity, the decade was characterized by domesticity, conservatism and conformity. The cult of domesticity was exemplified by the Royal Visit of the Queen and the Duke of Edinburgh in 1953–54, the first visit to New Zealand by a reigning monarch.[5] As a result, the Royal couple were idolized and feted to a degree that would not be seen again until the worldwide public adoration of Princess Diana thirty years later. However, this enthusiasm was directed towards the Queen as an attractive model of femininity and motherhood, rather than her role as Head of State. The Queen, the Duke and their children were seen as the ideal family, a patriotic model for their subjects to follow. This provided a paradigm of domesticity in the sprawling State Housing suburbs that dotted the New Zealand landscape. These new suburbs of low-cost Government-built housing reflected both a standard of domestic bliss—based on the pro-natalist emphases of the Baby Boom from 1945 to 1961—and an idealized image of women. The stable family was the bedrock of society; this ideal defined what was natural and normal.

There were, however, cracks in this model of romanticized domesticity. Job opportunities were increasingly open to women—many of whom worked to obtain the new consumer appliances for their families—and women's educational achievements were rising. Although the economic independence achieved by women during the War was soon reversed, expectations of a life beyond domesticity still remained. Furthermore, the domestic bliss of the State Housing suburbs was only superficial; these tended to be mono-cultural and sterile, with no age mix and little variety. Housewives had little opportunity to escape the world of nappies, isolation and boredom in the suburbs.[6] It is therefore not surprising that when the phenomenon of suburban neurosis later became recognized, it had emerged amongst housewives in the suburbs.[7]

There was also a dark side to the conservatism and conformity of the decade. To some extent, this built upon the tensions already noted by Jock Phillips in his analysis of the VE Day celebrations.[8] Issues of class conflict emerged in the 1951 Waterfront dispute, the longest and most costly strike New Zealand had experienced up to that point. This bitter conflict, which lasted 151 days, was seen as a strike by the National Government and as a lockout by the workers. The Government declared a state of emergency and deployed armed servicemen on the wharves; this reflected its fears over the rise of Communism, which New Zealand troops were then fighting in Korea.[9] These anxieties built on the hysteria over the Cecil Holmes "Snatchel Case" in 1948[10] and strengthened the Government's mandate to maintain order by regulation and political control. The effect of this reinforced the sense of public conformity that pervaded the 1950s.

Nevertheless, there were several breakouts from conformity and control during the decade, especially over issues of adolescent morality.[11] These came to a head in June 1954 with the Parker-Hulme murder trial and the emergence of juvenile delinquency in the Hutt Valley. The murder of a Christchurch mother, Honora Parker, by her daughter Pauline and Pauline's friend Juliet Hulme—which became the basis of director Peter Jackson's film *Heavenly Creatures*[12]—created international headlines and sparked shock and revulsion. This was due not only to the cold-blooded callousness of the murder but also—to a greater extent—on the perceived sexual deviancy of the two girls, who shared a lesbian relationship. This sense of moral outrage was reinforced by the simultaneous emergence of public awareness of juvenile delinquency in the Hutt Valley. The *Dominion* for July 6 reported that police investigations there had revealed a "shocking degree of immoral conduct which spread into sexual orgies perpetuated in private homes during the absence of parents, and in several second rate Hutt Valley theatres, where familiarity between youths and girls was commonplace."[13] The police investigation which led to this statement resulted in fifty-nine teenagers being charged with 107 delinquency charges before the Children's, Magistrate's and Supreme Courts.[14] The publicity surrounding these charges reinforced a perception exemplified by a headline in *New Zealand Truth*: "Moral Delinquency Said To Be Widespread."[15] Ultimately, these charges led to the setting up in late July of an official enquiry headed by lawyer Dr. Oswald Mazengarb, QC. The findings of this enquiry, published in September 1954, laid the blame on a number of factors. These included the precocity of teenage girls, the rise of working mothers and the consequent decline in family life, the influence of Hollywood movies and—especially—the availability of American pulp fiction.[16]

An exacerbating factor in this moral delinquency was the increased affluence of New Zealand youth in the 1950s. Unlike their parents, they had no mortgage to service and consequently had high levels of disposable income. This enabled their participation in music, leisure and the adoption of unconventional "mod" dress styles such as that of the "Bodgies" and "Widgies."[17] Music was particularly important in this regard and the radio and record industry fostered this participation, with programs such as the *Lifebuoy Hit Parade* beginning on the non-State Broadcasting radio stations in 1954. Up to this time, the only place where "hit" music could be heard was on jukeboxes, which created their own problems as young people congregated in the milk bars where these were located. In the late 1950s, dance clubs and bands followed overseas models and movies such as *Rebel Without a Cause*[18] reinforced the point that youth were different and had different goals in life from their parents. While the Youth Culture did not develop in New Zealand during the 1960s to the extent that it did overseas, there was sufficient deviation from societal norms to provide grounds for parental concern. The Parker-Hulme murder, the Mazengarb Report, the fantasy world of youth culture and the fears of American influence and of increasing sexual experimentation, all reinforced the anxieties of the older generation. Thus, despite the surface conformity of the 1950s—which was reflected in expectations, rather than in specific events—a deeper tension was emerging. This came to be known as the "Generation Gap" and would become more general in the 1960s.

Decade of Opportunity:
The Mainstream Churches in the 1950s

Despite this concern over deviant youth morality and the flouting of societal norms, the 1950s were nevertheless a boom decade for the churches. As with the United States, New Zealand also experienced a post-war resurgence of religion and almost all sections of mainstream Christianity exhibited a much more self-confident, energetic and authoritarian ethos than is the case today. This reflected the expansionist mood of the wider society and demonstrated the strength of the traditional institutions of the period. Furthermore, the churches all enjoyed vigorous growth from the end of the Second World War to the end of the 1950s; this trend was repeated in Australia, where there was vigorous evangelism throughout the decade.[19] In response to the opportunities of the post-war Baby Boom and the urbanization—or rather, suburbanization—of New Zealand society, many churches undertook church building and extension programs and placed a conscious emphasis on evangelism. In so doing, they were utilizing the almost unprecedented opportunities made available to them. Examples of these programs included the Presbyterian, lay-oriented New Life Movement. This "created a mood of optimism, giving a renewed sense of mission"[20] and contributed to the formation of sixty-six new Presbyterian parishes between 1948 and 1958.[21] (It should be noted that the title of the later Pentecostal group known as the New Life Churches of New

Zealand has no apparent connection with the Presbyterian New Life Movement.) Another example was the Baptist Church Extension program, which had its period of maximum effectiveness in the late 1950s, with some twenty-four churches being established in the five years from 1955 to 1960.[22]

The fruits of this expansion were also reflected in the comparatively high church membership and attendance figures for almost all churches during the 1950s and into the mid-1960s. Presbyterian attendance reached an all-time high of 119,041 in 1960; in the 1960s, Methodist membership peaked at 32,749 in 1965 and the high point of 95,842 for Anglican Easter communicants was reached in 1965/66.[23] Despite the perceptions of teenage delinquency in the wider society, strong Christian youth movements flourished in the churches during the 1950s. Both Sunday Schools and Bible Classes were large, although not all of their young members would later move on to active adult church involvement. The Bible Class movement, in particular, flourished during the 1950s, supplying teenagers with opportunities for study and social pursuits. Indeed, for many young people growing up in that era, Bible Classes provided their primary locus of socialization. This was particularly the case in rural areas, where in earlier decades, Bible Classes were often the only social activity outside the public house or the sports ground.[24] This social appeal continued into the 1950s.[25]

Other developments in the late 1940s and 1950s included the creation of new parachurch agencies for evangelism, such as Youth for Christ, formed in Auckland in 1948. Groups such as these had the indirect effect of producing an informal ecumenism, whereby people related to one another across ecclesiastical boundaries in terms of common evangelical faith and task, rather than of denominational identity. This both provided an alternative Christian network and reinforced the emerging ecumenical movement, formally represented by the National Council of Churches. Ecumenism was now being reflected in the beginnings of formal negotiations for Church Union between the Presbyterian, Methodist and Congregational churches. Other denominations later joined these negotiations. Although these eventually collapsed in the 1970s, there was nevertheless considerable interchurch cooperation and a number of Union parishes—comprising Presbyterian, Methodist and Congregational partners—were set up in the new State Housing suburbs. The first of these was formed at Raglan in 1943, followed in the later 1940s and 1950s by Corstorphine (Dunedin), Taita (Wellington) and Marchwiel (Timaru).[26]

The apogee of church life in the 1950s was the Billy Graham Crusade, held over two weeks in April 1959.[27] Graham and his team came to New Zealand at the invitation of the National Council of Churches (which, as church historian Allan Davidson observes, was an indication of the "remarkable consensus" that existed amongst church leaders at that time.[28] However this consensus was not total, since Anglo-Catholics on both sides of the Tasman were dismissive of Graham's theology and methods.)[29] Interdenominational local committees in Auckland, Wellington and Christchurch organized the large meetings in these centers, which were addressed by Graham's associate evangelists during the first week of the Crusade. Graham himself spoke on the final six days. Relay landline broadcasts of the Crusade carried its message to more than sixty subsidiary meetings, led by local ministers, in provincial centers and small towns. Crowds were large, with newspapers reporting that some 60,000 had attended in Auckland to hear him on the Saturday night.[30] He later claimed that he had "preached to more people in six days in New Zealand than in any other week of my ministry."[31]

The Crusade was therefore, on the face of it, highly successful and was hailed by some of its supporters as "the time when New Zealand has been closest to a general spiritual revival."[32] The official statistics give some indication of its impact—at least in the short term—on the religious consciousness of the country. These show that an estimated 574,300 people had attended during the twelve days of the Crusade, 185,000 of them at the landline meetings in other centers, and that 17,493 decisions for Christ had been recorded.[33] However, these impressive statistics do not necessarily tell the whole story, since, as historian Bryan Gilling points out, the attendance figures make no allowance for people who may have attended more than once.[34] Furthermore, the decisions did not always represent conversions to Christianity. Of these, 6,606 (or 37.76% of the total) were for "re-affirmation of faith," "assurance of salvation" or "restoration," rather than an "acceptance of Christ" for the first time.[35] The numbers of decisions falling into these categories—which presuppose previous Christian involvement—indicate that a sizable proportion, at least, of the attendance at the Crusade comprised those already within the ambit of the churches. This suggests that "mass evangelists have little real effect on people who are not already within the churches' orbit; ... the evangelists are moving 'in the company of the converted,' or at least the sympathetic."[36] It therefore appears that while the Crusade was successful in gaining the support of the churches, it had failed to evoke a significant response from the unchurched majority of the New Zealand public.

Nevertheless, the Crusade did have some long-term effects on New Zealand Christianity. These became more evident in the 1960s and 1970s. Graham's evangelism was thoroughly American in both scope and style and the Crusade represented an importation of a largely self-sufficient American evangelical subculture. Some sections of the New Zealand Church welcomed this new subculture and its innate dynamism helped to orient Evangelicalism in this country towards a less institutional style. This informality was reinforced by the absence in New Zealand of an interdenominational evangelical organization equivalent to the American National Association of Evangelicals (formed in 1942).[37] The identity of evangelical Christians became more firmly centered in their personal relationship to Christ and denominational labels became comparatively unimportant. This was later reflected in the steep rise in the "Christian—No Other Designation" category in the five-yearly Censuses from 1961 on. A second legacy was the emphasis on "the Bible says" that characterized Graham's ministry. This provided a source of authority—and hence, of security—in the face of the erosion of many of the old value standards of family and community life over the next two decades.

However, there were also several negative consequences arising from the Crusade. Some sections of the New Zealand Church had the somewhat unrealistic expectation that the momentum of the Crusade would continue after Billy Graham and his team had left the country. This continuation did not—and indeed *could* not—happen, due to the key role that Graham's glamorous American image and gifted oratory had played in the campaign. Others saw the Crusade as a short-term phenomenon; this left a vacuum of expectation in some sections of the church community.[38] A further issue was that not all converts of the Crusade appeared to have been adequately followed up by the churches to which they were referred. (John Pollock, Graham's biographer, lamented—in the context of a discussion of the New Zealand Crusade—that "on the basis of evidence from crusades all over the world, many of those [converts] lost to sight because of the unsympathetic attitude of a church found a spiritual home elsewhere, even if after a temporary lapse."[39] A contrary view is that of a Methodist commentator, who referred to the "thorough and worthy" follow-up of the Crusade's converts.[40] However, the writer has interviewed some of these converts who had later joined Pentecostal churches and their experience tends to confirm Pollock's claim.)[41] This unfulfilled anticipation—together with the less institutional style of Evangelicalism and the insistence on "the Bible says"—would contribute towards sustained Pentecostal expansion in the 1960s and 1970s. These factors, together with the informal ecumenism of the Christian parachurch network, also fostered the emergence of the Charismatic movement in the later 1960s.

The Character of New Zealand Pentecostalism in the 1950s

Although isolated from the mainstream of New Zealand church life, Pentecostals also benefited from the religious fertility of the 1950s. A comparison of the Census figures for 1951 and 1961 show that their numbers had more than doubled—from 2,449 to 5,208—during the decade. Particular beneficiaries were the Assemblies of God, which increased 123.16% from 475 to 1,060 adherents and the Apostolic Church, up 85.05% from 756 to 1,399. Several new Pentecostal groups, such as the Elim Church, also emerged during the decade. Nevertheless, these numbers, although increasing, still remained a miniscule portion of the population and totaled a mere 0.24% of all Christians in 1961.[42] However, not all Pentecostals identified themselves as such in the Censuses; this is reflected in the increasing number of returns for "Christian—no other designation."

Nevertheless, Pentecostal churches had entered the 1950s with some optimism and some—although not all—experienced growth during the decade. A number of British Assemblies of God pastors arrived in New Zealand from 1949 on, bringing with them fresh ideas, experience and great energy.[43] Later groups of British Assemblies of God pastors also arrived in 1951[44] and 1958.[45] This rejuvenated the New Zealand assemblies and Superintendent Wallace Thompson's annual report to their 1950 Conference consequently "was the most positive for many years."[46] The next three years saw many significant changes for the Assemblies of God. In the words of the minutes of the 1950 Annual Conference, its Constitution was "revolutionised";[47] these radical changes were undertaken at the suggestion of the British ministers.[48] As well as this, a Bible School was opened,[49] three more small churches joined the movement[50] and several New Zealand-born pastors were appointed.[51] An evangelistic campaign in Auckland in 1951 recorded forty-four decisions for Christ, which Ian Clark describes as "an event unprecedented since the 1930's."[52] By 1954, there were sixteen congregations in fellowship with the Assemblies of God.[53] The Apostolic Church followed a similar trajectory in the 1950s, beginning the decade with eleven churches[54]—the strongest New Zealand Pentecostal body numerically[55]—although with a continuing dependence on British and Australian ministers.[56] A notable exception to this policy of dependence was R. Louis Arnold, the vigorous Zealand-born superintendent of the movement's Māori work from 1939 to 1952.[57] The Apostolic Church attempted to move into evangelism in 1955, when Gilbert White linked up with other Apostolic ministers to form a short-lived evangelistic team to minister in Apostolic Churches throughout New Zealand.[58] A Bible School was opened in 1957 to provide training for prospective ministers;[59] this reflected the continuing growth of the Apostolic Church during the 1950s. Other Pentecostal groups were also flourishing. The British Israel-oriented Church of Christ (New Zealand) built a large church in Mount Roskill in 1951; although strongly sectarian, this became the largest Pentecostal congregation in New Zealand for the next twenty years.[60] The Christian Revival Crusade also prospered, in part benefiting from the considerable dynamism generated by Leo Harris in its sister movement in Australia.[61] Harris had espoused a positive message about the believer's position in Christ and faith in the confident declaration of the Word of God. This "positive faith" became a popular theme and would be a dominant motif of Pentecostal expansion in New Zealand in the 1960s.[62] Consequently, the Christian Revival Crusade had grown to twelve churches by 1953—up from ten in the 1940s—and remained at this level until the end of the decade.[63]

However, there were also several less positive developments. The Assemblies of God were severely impacted by a crisis in 1953–54, due to financial mismanagement by their energetic but overworked General Secretary/Treasurer and lost their momentum for several years. Building projects were halted and the Wellington church—the largest church in the Assemblies of God since its founding in the 1920s—had to sell its building; it was not able to rebuild until 1985.[64] Furthermore, in both the Assemblies of God and the Apostolic Church, the tendency to rely on overseas ministers was not always beneficial, particularly in the latter body. Although the last expatriate joined the New Zealand Apostolic pastoral staff in 1954, it was not until 1962 that a New Zealand-born pastor, Ivor Cullen, was appointed to the presidency of the Apostolic Dominion Council. This dependency created a situation where New Zealand pastors were seen as less experienced than their British counterparts, resulting in lowered expectations and opportunities.[65] While criticism of this reliance on overseas ministers had emerged in the Apostolic Dominion Council minutes as early as 1947, the practice continued until the 1960s.[66] Similarly, the first New Zealanders of the next generation to be appointed to the Assemblies of God Executive Council—Pastors Bob Midgley and Bruce Uren—were not elected until 1959.[67]

For other Pentecostal groups, the 1950s were a less positive decade. The Pentecostal Church of New Zealand, decimated by the schism over "the Name," wound up at the end of 1952, amalgamating with the Elim Church of Great Britain.[68] British Elim pastor Gilbert Dunk had arrived in New Zealand earlier that year to facilitate this transition and became the General Superintendent of the new Elim Church of New Zealand, remaining in office until 1962.[69] Initially this movement consisted of a single church, the remnants of the Wellington Pentecostal Church of New Zealand. Although progress was slow, a church was reestablished in Blenheim in 1954; this effectively was a continuation of the Pentecostal Church of New Zealand assembly in Blenheim after a recess of several years.[70] A new Elim Church also resulted in Christchurch from the emigration of three Elim families from Great Britain in 1956. Another church was pioneered in Nelson in 1959[71] and the Wellington congregation was able to purchase a hall the same year.[72] There was also some evangelism, particularly in Wellington. Nevertheless, by the end of the decade, there were only four Elim churches—Blenheim, Christchurch, Nelson and Wellington—with an additional work being pioneered at Richmond, Nelson.[73]

The weakest body of Pentecostal churches during the 1950s was the Latter Rain churches. This small group had arisen in 1949 from the secession over "the Name" from the Pentecostal Church of New Zealand three years earlier. Although Allan Thrift had amalgamated his small independent church in Takapuna with the new Latter Rain work[74] as did a Revival Fire Mission church in Tauranga,[75] only three small churches had resulted by 1951, i.e., Auckland, Tauranga and Lower Hutt.[76] Ray Jackson, its founder, had toured the country together with Thrift, visiting every Pentecostal church they could, asking if they could share the Latter Rain message. "Without exception, the door was shut in their faces. . . . This opposition was [due] not only to the Latter Rain message, but also to Jackson's Bethel Temple origins; memories of the split from the Pentecostal Church of New Zealand were still fresh."[77] However, this view may require some qualification. Luke Worsfold notes that the New Zealand Apostolic Church was somewhat ambiguous in its approach to the new movement. On one hand, it ostensibly supported the Latter Rain move of the Spirit, seeing it as a repeat of the awakening in Great Britain of forty years previously. Nevertheless, it was very concerned about its doctrinal and organizational impact, since the Latter Rain emphasis on decentralization and on autonomous local authority constituted an enormous threat to the Apostolic Church's central control mechanisms. New Zealand Apostolic leaders appear to have been more conservative towards the Latter Rain movement than were their overseas colleagues (for example, Australia, where there was some Apostolic support for it, as well as much opposition). Nevertheless, despite official cautionary letters being sent to all New Zealand Apostolic pastors, some remained supportive of the movement, although these supporters were later forced to resign from the Apostolic Church.[78]

The Latter Rain movement would be highly significant for the future shape of New Zealand Pentecostalism, although the foundations of this impact would be laid in Australia. Ray Jackson shifted across the Tasman in 1951, where he opened a Bible School in Sydney the following year.[79] Jackson attracted some very talented students among the twenty or so that attended the school, with some of these becoming leaders in the expansion of New Zealand Pentecostalism in the 1960s.

These included Rob Wheeler, Peter Morrow, Ron Coady, David Jackson, Kevin Conner and others.[80] As will be seen, Wheeler's tent campaigns, Coady's campaigns in the South Island and Morrow's ministry in Christchurch were all significant factors in the later breakout of New Zealand Pentecostalism. This will be discussed in the next chapter.

Thus, despite its growth in the 1950s, Pentecostalism remained a small and ingrown movement, restricted in outlook and prone to sectarianism and introversion.[81] Writer Hazel Houston described the Assemblies of God as then being "small and hardly recognisable as Pentecostal," the sole exception being the Queen Street Assembly of God.[82] (This was then the only Assembly of God with a congregation of more than 100 people.) Similarly, Ian Clark defines New Zealand Pentecostals as "at best a marginal grouping within society"[83] at the time and vividly portrays them as

> a very small and a very ingrown movement. They were making all sorts of efforts to break out of a very constricted kind of a mode, but I think in modern terms, they were *totally* irrelevant. That would be a good way of describing it. Nice people, who met in little upstairs halls above a butcher shop (things like that).... [They] met at Oddfellows' Halls and that sort of thing, and it really was pretty grotty.... It was like David: all those who had a grudge, or owed money, or trouble with the law; they would join themselves to him. [The reference is to 1 Sam.22:2 "And every one that was in distress, and every one that was in debt, and every one that was discontented, gathered themselves unto [David]; and he became a captain over them" (King James Version).] But [now] there's been a transformation: you get people from many different professions in [the Pentecostal movement] today.[84]

Clark was specifically referring to the Assemblies of God, of which he was General Secretary for some years. His observation is, however, valid for the whole Pentecostal movement.

Laurie Murray, an Assemblies of God worker in Timaru during 1959 and 1960, also described his Pentecostal congregation in quite unflattering terms. They were "about half-a-dozen old-timers who had either just managed to hold on in the face of general despising and rejection; or maybe their forthright and ever-exuberant witness had frightened people for miles around."[85] While there is an element of self-mockery in Murray's account, it makes the point that there was a general antipathy towards Pentecostalism. This aversion was especially acute with Evangelicals. Peter Lineham notes that "in the years after the second world war interest in Pentecostalism was almost universally taboo among evangelical Christians."[86] This led to a policy of exclusion. Pentecostals were not permitted to be involved in the counseling of converts at the Billy Graham Crusade[87] and—in Timaru, at least—their young people were barred from membership of the local Youth for Christ.[88] A specific example of this exclusion was Apostolic minister Gilbert White, who was initially barred from participation in the Crusade because of his Pentecostal beliefs. He was later permitted to be a subcommittee supervisor.[89] There was also a deep misunderstanding of Pentecostal practices. These misunderstandings—and the policy of exclusion that they generated—would not begin to change until the mid-1960s. In this respect, the landmark illustrated article on the "Third Force in Christendom" in *Life* magazine in 1958 contributed to the beginnings of a clearer public perception of Pentecostals.[90] Another significant factor was their increased public visibility, brought about by a new wave of Pentecostal evangelism.

Day of Small Beginnings: Pentecostal Evangelism in the Late 1950s

Shortly after the middle of the decade a breakout began to emerge in several Pentecostal groups. The Assemblies of God were beginning to regain their lost momentum by 1956. This was evidenced by an increased number of ordained ministers, the opening of an up-market new auditorium for its Queen Street, Auckland, congregation and the emergence of a new generation of New Zealand-born ministers.[91] The most significant of these new ministers were Ray Bloomfield[92] and Frank Houston.[93] Ian Clark later commented that "although [Bloomfield] held AOG [Assemblies of God] credentials, [he] was always a very free spirit, and he ... wasn't typical of many AOG people at the time."[94] As Bloomfield's assistant, Houston shared his enthusiasm and exuberance; he would later have great influence as General Superintendent of the New Zealand Assemblies of God from 1966 to 1977. Bloomfield commenced evangelistic meetings in September 1957 under the banner of the Ellerslie-Tamaki Faith Mission in the Ellerslie War Memorial Hall.[95] Although initial results were small—with only five adults in attendance—these meetings grew into a substantial revival and people came to Ellerslie from miles around to receive healing. There was standing room only on many occasions and on most Sunday nights up to thirty people responded to receive Christ; more than 1,000 people would be converted over the course of the mission.[96] These meetings continued until 1959, initially under Bloomfield's leadership and later under that of Houston. From Ellerslie, these two men also began meetings among Māori at Waiomio, near Kawakawa in Northland, in late 1958.[97] Here, too, many were healed and converted, sparking revival in a district formerly known as "Drunkard's Valley." Every home in the valley was touched by the revival, with the single exception of that of the *tohunga* [literally, "skilled person," "chosen expert," "priest" or "artist" in any field, especially spiritual[98]], who refused to relinquish his traditional spiritual role.[99] However, the Waiomio revival did not generate a significant long-term Māori constituency. Victoria University Religious Studies student Philip Carew and lecturer Geoff Troughton attribute this to a number of factors, including the failure of Bloomfield and Houston to develop Māori leadership and engage with Māori culture, or to develop relationships with the local *kaumātua* [tribal elders] and the *marae* [the courtyard of a Māori meeting house, and thus the venue for tribal gatherings and the center of tribal life].[100] Nevertheless, Clark observes that the Kawakawa Assembly of God was a direct legacy of this revival. After Bloomfield's departure for Canada, Houston continued to lead these meetings until he moved to Lower Hutt to pastor the Assembly there in December 1959.[101]

Although these two revivals marked a significant advance in Pentecostal evangelism, it should not be assumed that no evangelistic efforts had been undertaken since the times of Smith Wigglesworth, A. C. Valdez and A. H. Dallimore. The Assemblies of God had appointed a Dominion Evangelist as early as 1927[102] and had engaged in tent campaigns and caravan evangelism from the 1930s to the 1950s.[103] The Pentecostal Church of New Zealand was similarly exercised during the 1940s. Discussions on "the question of evangelising" took place at its 1943 Conference, resulting in the passing of a motion "that we evangelise New Zealand as God leads us."[104] Two years later, the 1945 Conference authorized "immediate inquiries with a view to purchasing a tent for campaign purposes, accommodating 200 to 300."[105] In the end, events overtook the project's implementation, since the Pentecostal Church of New Zealand was decimated by the schism over "the Name" the following year. With few exceptions, these outreaches bore little fruit. The Assemblies of God experienced an awakened interest in evangelism after the War. American evangelist Harvey Ferrell conducted fruitful campaigns in 1946 while ministering under its auspices in New Zealand[106] and Assemblies of God pastors Benny Finch and Freddie Rogerson also successfully evangelized in 1951.[107] As well as this, the Apostolic and Elim churches undertook several evangelistic campaigns in the 1950s, but with limited success.[108] Nevertheless, Luke Worsfold notes that a manifesto issued by the Apostolic Church Council in 1960 represented a call to return to its evangelistic origins, thus implying a previous departure from these.[109]

However, the arrival of American evangelist Tommy Hicks[110] in New Zealand in October–November 1957—almost simultaneously with the start of Ray Bloomfield's Ellerslie-Tamaki Faith Mission—added a potent accelerant to the fires of evangelism. (Unsuccessful attempts had been made during the 1950s to bring other prominent American Pentecostal evangelists to New Zealand. Missionary evangelist T. L. Osborn was expected to visit New Zealand in early 1951.[111] Similarly, there are references to a proposed visit by William Branham in 1958.[112] Neither of these visits eventuated.) Hicks had been invited to New Zealand by the Full Gospel Ministers Association, an ecumenical Pentecostal association, chaired by Vin Brown.[113] He was best-known for his spectacularly successful campaign in Argentina in 1954. Here "the attendance never dropped below 60,000 a night, and on at least one night ... was reported by the Buenos Aires papers to have passed 200,000."[114] Even President Perón himself had been healed of eczema in response to Hicks' prayers.[115] Hicks therefore arrived in New Zealand with a considerable reputation and all Pentecostal churches strongly supported his healing campaigns in Christchurch and Wellington.[116] He appears to have had some success, with numbers of decisions for Christ being recorded and people testifying of having received healing.[117] However, his campaigns had a more important indirect effect in that they stimulated others to adopt this style of evangelism. Rob Wheeler, for example, recalled that Hicks represented "our first exposure to an evangelist, really. ... Ron Coady and myself got fired up on evangelism."[118] Others were similarly inspired, including brothers Norman and Gilbert White of the Apostolic Church, independent Pentecostal pastor Ian Hunt and Wheeler's Latter Rain colleague Mike Bensley.

Tommy Hicks' campaigns—together with the successes of Ray Bloomfield and Frank Houston in Ellerslie and Waiomio—therefore marked the beginnings of a new era of Pentecostal evangelism in New Zealand. While some of this represented a continuation of traditional institutional evangelism, the most successful forms of this were largely independent "faith" ministries. Church-based forms of evangelism were less potent, often being limited by the lack of institutional resources. An example of this was Assemblies of God pastor T. W. Whiting, who was appointed full-time Home Missions Promoter, with a focus on evangelism, in 1958. However, the Assemblies of God was not able to provide funding for this position and Whiting suffered financially as a result. Eventually he left for Australia after only a few months in the position.[119] A more positive example was the launching of a new Gospel Caravan—the New Zealand for Christ campaign—by several Assemblies of God ministers in 1958. Nevertheless, the *New Zealand Evangel*, while lauding the initiative, took care to stress that it was a "private venture" on the part of the campaigners.[120]

Wheeler became the best-known example of this new independent Pentecostal evangelism.[121] Within weeks of Hicks' campaigns, he had resigned his Latter Rain pastorate in Tauranga and began tent campaigns using a 36-foot by 18-foot ex-army tent as a transportable church. Wheeler regarded Oral Roberts as his "hero" and consciously modeled his campaigns on Roberts' tent crusades in the United States. Early results were meager. His first campaign—in Mount Maunganui, across the harbor from his home base in Tauranga—in late 1957 yielded "practically nothing" by way of results.[122] Similarly, Coady recalls that one of his first campaigns on his own account, in Te Araroa in June 1960, was "quite a flop."[123] However, Wheeler had greater success on the East Coast in the remote Hicks Bay-Rangitukia area, where he had been invited to conduct a campaign among Ngāti Porou [the main Māori *iwi* (tribal grouping) on the East Coast of the North Island][124] in early 1958. This invitation had come from independent Latter Rain pioneer couples Allan and Alva Thrift and Bruce and Fay McGregor, who had been carrying out "missionary" work in the area since the mid-1950s.[125] There was a spectacular breakthrough during Wheeler's campaign, when a Māori woman was sovereignly healed of blindness while sitting in the meeting. As a result, this campaign became, in Wheeler's words, an "absolute landslide."[126] This led to further successes on the East Coast and in the Bay of Plenty and to the establishment of a number of Māori churches there by 1960.[127] (These were called "Full Gospel" churches; the term "Latter Rain" was not used.) Thrift was also having considerable success among Bay of Plenty Māori, setting up congregations and eventually a Bible School in Te Teko.[128] From these early beginnings among rural Māori, Wheeler began to conduct campaigns in a number of larger urban North Island centers, sometimes at the invitation of Pentecostal churches. He also set up a Winter Bible School in Tauranga in 1959. This Bible School, together with the momentum generated by his campaigns and those of other evangelists, would lay the foundations for the rapid expansion of a new group of independent Pentecostal churches. This group would be the spearhead of Pentecostal expansion in the 1960s and will be explored in the next chapter.

Figure 4: Rob and Beryl Wheeler (left) and Ian and Mavis Hunt (right) and their families on campaign 1958–59. Taken from cover of *Bible Deliverance*, May 1959. Rob Wheeler, Auckland. Permission to reproduce requested 28 October 2013.

Conclusion

Why, despite its best efforts, did the New Zealand Pentecostal movement not begin to emerge from its isolation until the end of the 1950s? And what catalysts account for its increasing public acceptability from the late 1950s on? A number of influences lay behind this expansion; these can be categorized as external and internal factors.

External Factors

The most significant factor in the emergence of Pentecostalism from the religious ghetto was an intensified public interest in alternative forms of healing in the late 1950s. It has already been noted in Chapter 2 that this interest was long-standing and had previously contributed to the success of Smith Wigglesworth—and thus to the emergence of New Zealand Pentecostalism—in the 1920s.[129] The activities of Oral Roberts and other healing evangelists in the United States and elsewhere in the 1940s and 1950s represented only one subset of this alternative healing movement. A number of different forms of healing were extant in New Zealand during the 1950s and early 1960s. Examples of these included Chinese herbalist Kwong Salaman-Simpson, who had begun his practice in Dunedin in the 1940s, later establishing offices in Auckland and in Christchurch.[130] Another alternative treatment was Color Therapy, with a network of these clinics being formed in the 1950s. (The basis of this therapy was that different physical conditions could be alleviated by the application of specific wavelengths of color. It involved connecting the patient by means of an electrical circuit to a skein of thread. The color of this was shown by means of a diviner's rod or pendulum to be appropriate for the treatment of the condition.) Pentecostals strongly condemned this therapy because of its use of divination, which they saw as anti-Christian.[131] Other forms of faith healing were represented in the visits to New Zealand of faith healers Dr. Christopher Woodard in 1958 and Brother Mandus in 1963. Dr. Woodard's views carried some public weight, since he was a Harley Street physician and author of several books on healing.[132] His approach to sickness was based on positive thinking, since he believed that "all disease originates in the spirit and can be cured by a right attitude to things."[133] Nevertheless, his visit created vigorous public debate on the subject of healing.[134] Similarly, Mandus' ideas, based on those of the New Thought movement, utilized the "creative power of mind"—which he viewed as being identical with the creative power of God—to achieve physical and spiritual healing.[135] Despite the theological heterodoxy of his views, Mandus' speaking venues during his visit to New Zealand included large mainstream churches such as Dunedin's Presbyterian First Church.[136]

Pentecostal literature such as Oral Roberts' books and healer Agnes Sanford's best-selling *Healing Light* also stimulated the public interest in healing.[137] This was not a fringe phenomenon, since there were also healing orders—such as the Order of St. Luke the Physician and the Guild of St. Raphael—within the major churches by 1960. The first New Zealand member of the Order of St. Luke the Physician was Anglican cleric Cecil Marshall, who later became prominent in the Charismatic Movement. Another example of mainstream involvement was Wellington Congregationalist minister Rev. Jim Chambers, who began praying for the sick in 1957 and whose radio broadcasts helped to spread an awareness of this aspect of Christian ministry.[138] The resurgence of interest in healing was therefore widespread and created a constituency for Pentecostal healing movements in New Zealand from the late 1950s on.

A second factor was the renewed attraction towards Evangelicalism and Fundamentalism—which functioned as institutions of reassurance—and towards a restoration of traditional values.[139] The arrival of Billy Graham both reinforced and modified this attraction. His emphasis on "the Bible says. . ." provided Evangelicals with an authoritative foundation for faith; at the same time, his careful distancing of himself from radical fundamentalism modeled a more nuanced and acceptable form of Evangelicalism. The new Pentecostal evangelism that had begun with Ray Bloomfield and Frank Houston in 1957—and, almost simultaneously, with Rob Wheeler's campaigns—received a significant boost from the receptivity to Evangelicalism generated by the Graham Crusades.

The third external factor in the emergence of Pentecostalism in the late 1950s—and, more particularly in its expansion in the 1960s—was the beginnings of a breakout from conformity. While the conventionality of the 1950s continued into the 1960s, there were increasing signs that this social homogeneity was beginning to unravel. Pentecostal groups—as religious exemplars of unconventionality—benefitted from this willingness to move beyond the accepted status quo. This would later be reinforced by the increasing prominence of youth and by the relocation of authority that accompanied the challenge of traditional institutions. These changes will be discussed in the next chapter.

Internal Factors

Although Pentecostalism in New Zealand remained quite restricted and sectarian in the 1950s, there were signs that this was beginning to change. The most prominent example of this was the emergence of a network of vigorous Pentecostal evangelists such as Ray Bloomfield and Frank Houston. These evangelists were not necessarily church-based, but moved—as did independent tent evangelist Rob Wheeler—into venues of evangelism outside the confines of the Pentecostal churches. In this, they were following the example of the American healing evangelists such as William Branham, Oral Roberts and T. L. Osborn, and exemplified, in the New Zealand setting, by the Tommy Hicks campaigns.

However, the Latter Rain groups were the most significant contributors to, and beneficiaries of, this new Pentecostal expansion. Their refusal to be constrained by denominational parameters gave them a freedom of movement and ministry that church-based evangelists generally did not have. The churches that resulted from their campaigns were able to demonstrate a greater flexibility and independence than were the Pentecostal denominations such as the Apostolic Church and—to a lesser extent—the Assemblies of God. It is therefore not surprising that these Latter Rain-type churches grew tenfold—from six to sixty churches—in the five years from 1960 to 1965.

At the end of the 1950s, the Pentecostal movement therefore stood poised for expansion. Developments that had germinated in the late 1950s would blossom in the 1960s, resulting in the beginnings of exponential Pentecostal growth and in the emergence of the Charismatic movement. This expansion would also lead to major reshaping and reorientation of New Zealand Pentecostalism over the next two decades.

Notes

1. Sinclair, *History of New Zealand*, 288.
2. Bruce Mason, *The end of the golden weather: A voyage into a New Zealand childhood* (Wellington: Price Milburn, [1962]).
3. John Gould, *The Rake's Progress? The New Zealand Economy Since 1945* (Auckland: Hodder and Stoughton, 1982), 113.
4. Yska, *All Shook Up*, 37, 39–40.
5. King, *Penguin History of New Zealand*, 414.
6. Mark Derby, "Suburbs—New suburbs, 1950s–1970s," *Te Ara Encyclopedia of New Zealand*, updated 13 July 2012 http://www.TeAra.govt.nz/en/suburbs/page-5 (accessed 2 December 2013).

7. David Thorns and Ben Schrader, "City history and people—Suburban life," *Te Ara Encyclopedia of New Zealand*, updated 10 July 2013 http://www.TeAra.govt.nz/en/video/23528/suburban-neurosis (accessed 2 December 2013).

8. Phillips, "New Zealand celebrates victory," in Crawford, *Kia Kaha*, 315.

9. King, *Penguin History of New Zealand*, 424–25.

10. Yska, *All Shook Up*, 15–21. See above, 68.

11. For an extensive account, see Ibid, 9–11, 58–84.

12. IMDb, "Heavenly Creatures," http://www.imdb.com/title/tt0110005/ (accessed 20 August 2013).

13. *Dominion*, 6 July 1954, cited in Yska, *All Shook Up*, 63.

14. The Special Committee on Moral Delinquency in Children and Adolescents, *Report of the Special Committee on Moral Delinquency in Children and Adolescents*. Appendix to the Journals of the House of Representatives of New Zealand; H.47 (Wellington: Government Printer, 1954), 9 [hereafter cited as Mazengarb Report].

15. "Moral Delinquency Said To Be Widespread," *New Zealand Truth*, 14 July 1954, 9.

16. Mazengarb Report, 59–62.

17. Yska, *All Shook Up*, 171–76.

18. IMDb, "Rebel Without a Cause," http://www.imdb.com/title/tt0048545/ (accessed 20 August 2013).

19. Samantha Frappell, "Post-War Revivalism in Australia: the Mission to the Nation, 1953–1957," in Hutchinson and Piggin, *Reviving Australia*, 249–61.

20. Allan Davidson, "1931–1960: Depression, War, New Life," in *Presbyterians in Aotearoa 1840–1990*, ed. Dennis McEldowney, 124 (Wellington: The Presbyterian Church of New Zealand, 1990). See also I. G. Marquand, "The New Zealand Presbyterian New Life Movement: A Case Study in Church Growth" (MTh thesis in Church History, University of Otago, 1977). Marquand's study is supplemented at several key points by Owen Rogers, "The New Zealand Presbyterian New Life Movement" (BD dissertation in Church History, University of Otago, 1990).

21. Davidson, *Christianity in Aotearoa*, 159.

22. S. L. Edgar, *A Handful of Grain: The Centenary History of the Baptist Union of New Zealand*, vol. 4, 1945–1982 (Wellington: New Zealand Baptist Historical Society, 1982), 23–29.

23. Church statistics derived from the comparative tables given in "Appendix A: Church Statistics 1958–1971," in Brett Knowles, "Some Aspects of the History of the New Life Churches of New Zealand 1960–1990" (PhD thesis in Church History, University of Otago, 1994), 381–82.

24. Laurie Barber, "1901–1930: The Expanding Frontier," in McEldowney, *Presbyterians in Aotearoa*, 96–97.

25. Davidson, "Depression, War, New Life," in McEldowney, *Presbyterians in Aotearoa*, 131.

26. Davidson, *Christianity in Aotearoa*, 124.

27. The impact of the Crusade is described in Warner Hutchinson and Cliff Wilson, *Let the People Rejoice* (Wellington: Crusader Bookroom Society, 1959).

28. Davidson, *Christianity in Aotearoa*, 161.

29. Ian Breward, *A History of the Churches in Australasia*. Oxford History of the Christian Church, ed. Henry and Owen Chadwick (Oxford: Oxford University Press, 2001), 315.

30. *Auckland Star*, 7 April 1959, 6, cited in Davidson and Lineham, *Transplanted Christianity*, 310–11.
31. Billy Graham, cited in *Christchurch Star*, 9 April 1959, and thence in Hutchinson and Wilson, *Let the People Rejoice*, 130.
32. Cited in Bryan Gilling, "Mass Evangelism in Mid-Twentieth-Century New Zealand," in *"Rescue the Perishing": Comparative Perspectives on Evangelicalism and Revivalism*. Waikato Studies in Religion 1, ed. Douglas Pratt (Auckland: College Communications, 1989), 49. Gilling does not record the source of this claim.
33. Hutchinson and Wilson, *Let the People Rejoice*, 142–46.
34. Gilling, "Mass Evangelism," in Pratt, *"Rescue the Perishing,"* 49.
35. Hutchinson and Wilson, *Let the People Rejoice*, 144.
36. Gilling, "Mass Evangelism," in Pratt, *"Rescue the Perishing,"* 52. Gilling further argues this point in a companion article in the same volume (Gilling, "Convinced Christians convincing convinced Christians? A Study of Attenders at a Luis Palau Crusade Meeting," in Ibid, 77–95) and, at greater length, in his doctoral thesis. Bryan D. Gilling, "Retelling the Old, Old Story: A Study of Six Mass Evangelistic Missions in Twentieth-Century New Zealand" (DPhil thesis in History, University of Waikato, 1990).
37. Knowles, "Vision of the Disinherited?" 117–18.
38. Ibid, 119.
39. John Pollock, *Billy Graham: The Authorised Biography* (London: Hodder and Stoughton, 1966), 263.
40. *New Zealand Methodist Times*, 25 April 1959, 697, cited in Gilling, "Retelling the Old, Old Story," 288.
41. Knowles, *The History of a New Zealand Pentecostal Movement*, 55.
42. See Appendix A.
43. Clark, *Pentecost at the Ends of the Earth*, 69–70.
44. Worsfold, *History of the Charismatic Movements in New Zealand*, 215.
45. Clark, *Pentecost at the Ends of the Earth*, 91.
46. Ibid, 72.
47. Worsfold, *History of the Charismatic Movements in New Zealand*, 214.
48. Clark, *Pentecost at the Ends of the Earth*, 71.
49. Worsfold, *History of the Charismatic Movements in New Zealand*, 214; and Clark, *Pentecost at the Ends of the Earth*, 72.
50. Clark, *Pentecost at the Ends of the Earth*, 76–77.
51. Ibid, 77.
52. Ibid, 75.
53. Worsfold, *History of the Charismatic Movements in New Zealand*, 215.
54. Ibid, 277.
55. Luke Worsfold, "Subsequence, Prophecy and Church Order," 45, footnote 24.
56. Worsfold, *History of the Charismatic Movements in New Zealand*, 276, 278–79.
57. B. Knowles, "Arnold, R. Louis," in NIDPCM, 332.
58. James Worsfold, *The Reverend Gilbert and Mrs Alice White*, 88.
59. Worsfold, *History of the Charismatic Movements in New Zealand*, 277. See also Luke Worsfold, "Subsequence, Prophecy and Church Order," 55–56 and footnote 55, for the attitude of the Apostolic Church to theological training.
60. B. Knowles, "Wilson, Frederick A.," in NIDPCM, 1199; Worsfold, *History of the Charismatic Movements in New Zealand*, 304–5.
61. Chant, *Heart of Fire*, 158–60.
62. Ibid, 190.

63. Worsfold, *History of the Charismatic Movements in New Zealand*, 293–95.
64. Clark, *Pentecost at the Ends of the Earth*, 79–81.
65. Luke Worsfold, "Subsequence, Prophecy and Church Order," 36.
66. Worsfold, *History of the Charismatic Movements in New Zealand*, 276.
67. Clark, *Pentecost at the Ends of the Earth*, 92.
68. Worsfold, *History of the Charismatic Movements in New Zealand*, 191; also Colin Brown, "The Charismatic Contribution: How significant is the Charismatic Movement?" in Colless and Donovan, *Religion in New Zealand Society*, 100.
69. B. Knowles, "Dunk, Gilbert T. S.," in NIDPCM, 588–89.
70. Worsfold, *History of the Charismatic Movements in New Zealand*, 194.
71. Elim Church of New Zealand, "Guidelines for Credentialled Ministers: Elim in New Zealand," 7, in BKRP, MS-3530/022, Hocken Library, Dunedin.
72. Worsfold, *History of the Charismatic Movements in New Zealand*, 192.
73. Ibid, 194–95.
74. Riss, *Latter Rain*, 133–37.
75. Tauranga Christian Fellowship, "Jubilee Reunion 1939–1989," 2–3, in BKRP, MS-3530/014, Hocken Library, Dunedin.
76. Worsfold, *History of the Charismatic Movements in New Zealand*, 298.
77. Knowles, *The History of a New Zealand Pentecostal Movement*, 32.
78. Luke Worsfold, "Subsequence, Prophecy and Church Order," 107–9, 111–12; see also Riss, *Latter Rain*, 137–39.
79. B. Knowles, "Jackson, Ray, Sr.," in NIDPCM, 806. See also, in more detail, Knowles, *The History of a New Zealand Pentecostal Movement*, 43–47. For an account of the school's impact on one of its students, see Conner, *This is My Story*, 147–52.
80. For an account of some of these students, including photographs, see Fay McGregor, *My Testimony* (Auckland: Fayth Russell, 2006), 35–42. I am grateful to Professor Peter Lineham for directing my attention to this book.
81. B. Knowles, "New Zealand," in NIDPCM, 188.
82. Hazel Houston, *Being Frank: The Frank Houston Story* (London: Marshall Pickering, 1989), 100.
83. Clark, *Pentecost at the Ends of the Earth*, 93.
84. Clark, Interview, cited in Knowles, *The History of a New Zealand Pentecostal Movement*, 47. Emphasis as cited.
85. Murray, *Where to World 1977?* 25.
86. Lineham, "Tongues Must Cease": 16–17.
87. Rev. J. A. Clifford, principal of the Baptist Bible College from 1961 to 1973, cited in Gilling, "Retelling the Old, Old Story," 253.
88. Knowles, "Vision of the Disinherited?" 133, note 27.
89. James Worsfold, *The Reverend Gilbert and Mrs Alice White*, 75.
90. "Photographic Essay, 'The third force in Christendom: gospel-singing, doomsday-preaching sects emerge as a mighty movement in world religion,' photographed for Life by Carl Mydans," *Life*, 9 June 1958, 113–21; Henry P. Van Dusen, "Force's Lessons for Others," Ibid, 122–24.
91. Clark, *Pentecost at the Ends of the Earth*, 87–88.
92. For a brief biography of Bloomfield, see B. Knowles, "Bloomfield, Ray," in NIDPCM, 435–36.
93. For biographies of Houston, see Houston, *Being Frank*; B. Knowles, "Houston, Frank," in NIDPCM, 774; and Andrew MacFarlane, "Houston, William Francis (Frank)

(1922–)," ADPCM http://adpcm.webjournals.org/articles/23/10/2002/4731.htm?id={71D D550D-8D8A-4ED1-92B6-D927F5D7741F} (accessed 12 April 2009).

94. Clark, Interview, cited in Knowles, *The History of a New Zealand Pentecostal Movement*, 148.

95. Ray Bloomfield, "Thus hath God wrought...," *New Zealand Evangel*, May 1958, 15–16. Hazel Houston incorrectly gives this date as c.1955–56 (Houston, *Being Frank*, 76, 88), a mistake repeated by Knowles, *The History of a New Zealand Pentecostal Movement*, 57. However Clark correctly dates this as September 1957 (Clark, *Pentecost at the Ends of the Earth*, 89) and this is confirmed by Bloomfield's report.

96. Clark, *Pentecost at the Ends of the Earth*, 89; Houston, *Being Frank*, 70–90.

97. "Faith Healing Mission at Waiomio," *New Zealand Evangel*, December 1958, 19; Clark, *Pentecost at the Ends of the Earth*, 89–90.

98. So, *Reed Essential Māori Dictionary [Te Papakupu Taketake a Reed]: Māori-English/English-Māori* (Auckland: Reed Publishing, 1999), s.v. "*tohunga*." For a discussion of the *tohunga*'s function as "expert" in the spiritual dimension of Māori life, see King, *Penguin History of New Zealand*, 80, 85–86. See also Simon Moetara, "An exploration of notions of Māori leadership and a consideration of their contribution for Christian leadership in the Church of Aotearoa-New Zealand today" (MTh dissertation in Theology, Laidlaw College/Tyndale Graduate School of Theology, 2009), 21–22. For a discussion of Māori spirituality in general, see Michael P. Shirres, *Te Tangata: The Human Person* (Auckland: Accent Publications, 1997).

99. Clark, *Pentecost at the Ends of the Earth*, 89–90; Houston, *Being Frank*, 91–100.

100. Philip Carew and Geoff Troughton, "Māori Participation in the Assemblies of God," in *Mana Māori and Christianity*, eds. Hugh Morrison, Lachy Paterson, Brett Knowles and Murray Rae (Wellington: Huia Publishing, 2012), 95.

101. Clark, *Pentecost at the Ends of the Earth*, 90.

102. Ibid, 39.

103. Ibid, 56–57, 66–67; Worsfold, *History of the Charismatic Movements in New Zealand*, 215–16; *New Zealand Evangel*, October 1958, 8–10.

104. "Minutes of meeting of Elders and Delegates of The Pentecostal Church of N.Z. (Inc.) of the TWENTY-FIRST Annual Convention held at 101/103 Vivian St. Wellington on Friday 10th Dec. 1943 at 6-30 pm." Minute Book 1934–1951, Board of Elders of the Pentecostal Church of N.Z. (Inc.), Wellington, 10 December 1943, ff.74–75.

105. "Minutes of Meeting of Board of Elders and Delegates of The Pentecostal Church of New Zealand (Incorporated) at the 23rd Annual Conference, held at Assembly Hall, 101–103 Vivian Street, Wellington on 8th December 1945 at 6-30 pm." Minute Book 1934–1951, Board of Elders of the Pentecostal Church of N.Z. (Inc.), Wellington, 8 December 1945, f.87A; "Minutes of Meeting Held on Monday the 17th Dec. [1945] at 6 pm." Minute Book 1934–1951, Board of Elders of the Pentecostal Church of N.Z. (Inc.), Wellington, 17 December 1945, f.87G.

106. Clark, *Pentecost at the Ends of the Earth*, 66–67.

107. Ibid, 75.

108. James Worsfold, *The Reverend Gilbert and Mrs Alice White*, 88; Worsfold, *History of the Charismatic Movements in New Zealand*, 194.

109. Luke Worsfold, "Subsequence, Prophecy and Church Order," 36.

110. For a brief biography of Hicks, see S. Shemeth, "Hicks, Tommy," in NIDPCM, 713.

111. "Visit of Rev. T. L. Osborne [*sic*] to N.Z.," *New Zealand Evangel*, November 1950, 14.

112. "William Branham's Visit," *New Zealand Evangel*, August 1958, 19.
113. Worsfold, *History of the Charismatic Movements in New Zealand*, 312.
114. "But What About Tommy Hicks?" *Christian Century* 71 (7 July 1954): 814, cited in Nichol, *The Pentecostals*, 234. For an extended account of this revival, see Edward Miller, *Thy God Reigneth: The Story of the Revival in Argentina* (Burbank, CA: World Missionary Assistance Plan, 1968).
115. Miller, *Thy God Reigneth*, 35.
116. Worsfold, *History of the Charismatic Movements in New Zealand*, 312. Hicks was given a Mayoral reception while in Wellington. "Texan Evangelist Finds City Alive to Religion," *Dominion*, 31 October 1957, 12.
117. Worsfold, *History of the Charismatic Movements in New Zealand*, 194.
118. Rob Wheeler, Interview, Waikanae, 22 September 1987, cited in Knowles, *The History of a New Zealand Pentecostal Movement*, 58. The audio cassette of this interview is held in BKRP, MS-3530/039, Hocken Library, Dunedin.
119. Worsfold, *History of the Charismatic Movements in New Zealand*, 215; Clark, *Pentecost at the Ends of the Earth*, 90.
120. *New Zealand Evangel*, October 1958, 8–10.
121. For biographies of Wheeler, see B. Knowles, "Wheeler, Rob," in NIDPCM, 1193–94; and, in greater detail, Mark Hutchinson, "Wheeler, Rob (1931–)," ADPCM (accessed 12 April 2009).
122. Wheeler, Interview, cited in Knowles, *The History of a New Zealand Pentecostal Movement*, 58 and 63.
123. Ron Coady, Taped Interview in response to Questionnaire, Davis, CA, 24 March 1988, cited in ibid, 63, footnote 1. The audio cassette of this interview is held in BKRP, MS-3530/041, Hocken Library, Dunedin.
124. See Rice, *Oxford History of New Zealand*, 588–89, for maps of the major Māori tribal locations in New Zealand.
125. McGregor, *My Testimony*, 43–50.
126. Wheeler, Interview, cited in Knowles, *The History of a New Zealand Pentecostal Movement*, 63.
127. For a map showing the location of these churches, see Knowles, *The History of a New Zealand Pentecostal Movement*, 64. See also McGregor, *My Testimony*, 44.
128. Worsfold, *History of the Charismatic Movements in New Zealand*, 298.
129. See above, 5–6. See also Lineham, "Tongues must cease": 11–13, and R. J. Thompson, "Sects in New Zealand," in *Towards an Authentic New Zealand Theology*, ed. John M. Ker and Kevin J. Sharpe (Auckland: University of Auckland Chaplaincy Publishing Trust, 1984), 89.
130. "Noted Chinese Herbalist dies," *Otago Daily Times*, 13 June 1962, 17.
131. See "Spiritism—Colour Therapy—Are They Christian?" *Revival News*, May 1963, 10–11; "Fetishism in New Zealand," *Revival News*, August 1963, 5; and "The Sorcerer," *Revival News*, November 1963, 4–5, 11; and Leith Samuel, "Witchcraft: A Biblical Attitude," *New Zealand Evangel*, November 1968, 17. For a full photostated set of *Revival News* from March 1962 to December 1966, see BKRP, MS-3530/001, Hocken Library, Dunedin.
132. Christopher Woodard, *A Doctor Heals by Faith* (London: Max Parrish, 1953), and Woodard, *A Doctor's Faith Holds Fast* (London: Max Parrish, 1955).
133. Woodard, *A Doctor Heals by Faith*, 55–56.
134. See the "Letters to the Editor" column in the *Otago Daily Times* from 18 June to 14 July 1958.

135. "Biography of Brother Mandus," http:brothermandus.wwwhubs.com/ (accessed 18 March 2009).

136. "'Breakthrough' in Divine Healing," *Evening Star*, 22 January 1963, 18.

137. For example, Oral Roberts, *If you need Healing, Do these Things* (Tulsa, OK: Healing Waters, 1947); Agnes Sanford, *The Healing Light*, 8th ed. (St. Paul, MN: Macalester Park Publishing Co., [1949]). For a biographical note on Sanford, see P. D. Hocken, "Sanford, Agnes Mary," in NIDPCM, 1039. She visited New Zealand in 1962.

138. See J. B. Chambers, *To God be the Glory* (Christchurch: Presbyterian Bookroom, 1965).

139. Knowles, "Vision of the Disinherited?" 115 and 120.

Chapter 7

The 1960s

The Swinging Sixties? Stasis and Social Turbulence

The Swinging Sixties—which British historian Arthur Marwick extends into a long decade covering from about 1958 to 1974[1]—are a difficult period to categorize. At one level, the certainties of the past continued; at another, turbulence and change was beginning to emerge, sometimes forcefully. To picture the decade, one might use the metaphor of a well-made *crème brûlée*: the top layer forming a hard and unyielding crust, with a much more fluid core lying beneath the surface. These encrusted continuities had both social and political dimensions. The social conformity of the 1940s and 1950s remained largely intact, although there were already signs of an emerging breakout, particularly—but not exclusively—amongst youth. In politics, the stasis of the 1960s was due both to the natural philosophy of the ruling center-right National Party and to the personality and inclination of its Prime Minister, Keith Holyoake. Political historian Robert Chapman has observed that Holyoake's "greatest feat as a Prime Minister [during the 1960s] was the slowing down of every process which, if speedily dealt with, might have represented change and political harm."[2] This conservatism also reflected the propensity of National Party leaders to administer, rather than to change, the system.[3] Furthermore, the prosperity of the decade removed much of the stimulus for social or economic change. This prosperity was reflected in the full employment that had characterized New Zealand since the end of the Second World War. It was famously said by the Minister of Labour, Tom Shand, that there were fewer than "a hundred genuinely unemployed people [in the 1960s]—and I know the file on every one of them."[4]

Despite this overarching sociopolitical stasis, which continued until the 1970s,[5] there was also evidence of increasing societal fluidity, as currents of attitudinal change emerged during the decade. These stimulated a ferment of pluralism and turbulence, which affected perceptions of political and religious authority and, in turn, transformed social, familial and personal relationships. Thus, Michael King observed—possibly with a degree of hyperbole—that, by the end of the decade, there was "a maelstrom of diversity on a scale that the country had never seen before. ... New Zealand, after two decades of somnolence, was suddenly advancing on dozens of fronts simultaneously."[6] These changes should not be overstated, however. Robert Chapman has cautioned that "the underlying changes in the golden 1960s were social rather than political, ... individual rather than public. If they took a mass form, they did so as protest movements confronting, or, at the most, working alongside party structures."[7] In the 1960s, then, the individual—rather than the institution—was the focal point of social transformation.

What produced this array of social and individual change? Four sets of factors—demographic, economic, educational/aspirational, and changed attitudes to sexuality—seem to be particularly significant. The key demographic dynamic was the coming of age of the Baby Boom generation, i.e., those born from 1946 on. These Baby Boomers were important both as consumers—with comparatively high levels of disposable income—and as an expanding proportion of the population. This shift changed the economic and demographic mix of New Zealand society and reinforced the Generation Gap that underlay many of the changes from 1967 to 1973. The economic effects of the Baby Boomers were reinforced by the general prosperity of the 1960s, which enabled access to trendy fashion and music styles and gave greater freedom to do what one wanted. This was reflected in—for example—the proliferation of miniskirts and nonconformist hairstyles, as well as in the popularity of American music which encouraged resistance to authority and participation in the drug culture. Educational and aspirational factors were reflected in the increasing participation in tertiary education and, after 1964, in the growing access to overseas tourism as a result of the opening up of jet air travel. For many young people of the Baby Boom and succeeding generations, the "Big O. E. [Overseas Experience]" became a standard rite of passage after the mid-1960s, exposing them to the influence of other cultures and lifestyles. The effects of these factors, together with the advent of television in 1960,[8] contributed to the formation of a broader world view and a more sophisticated society. This sophistication was reflected in the abolition of the barbarous Six O'clock Swill in 1967[9] and the gradual development of a licensed restaurant industry where one could dine out on an increasing variety of cuisines.

The 1960s have come to be characterized as a decade of protest—particularly against the unpopular Vietnam War—and of challenge to institutional authority. Ian Clark notes the weakening of long held values and attitudes and a growing lack of respect for tradition and authority as the 1960s progressed. [10] Young people were to the fore in the antiwar protests after 1967. While New Zealand's involvement in the war was small—with only 543 volunteers serving in Vietnam—an estimated 10% of New Zealand's population had been involved in street demonstrations against it by 1971.[11] Television and photographic images were influential in fanning the flames of this growing protest movement. An example of the power of this new medium was the summary execution, in full view of the camera, of a Viet Cong suspect by a South Vietnamese police chief in 1968. The cold-bloodedness of the execution came across clearly and added fuel to the fires of protest.[12]

However, one of the most significant changes in the 1960s was the liberalization of attitudes to sexuality.[13] In England, this Sexual Revolution was sparked by the publication of the unexpurgated version of D. H. Lawrence's *Lady Chatterley's Lover* in England in 1960.[14] Of greater significance was the invention—and subsequent mass availability—of the Birth Control Pill:

> More women—14 million in the United States and 60 million world-wide—use the pill than any other reversible method of contraception. The pill was the biggest break-through for giving women control of their reproductive lives of anything that came along until legalised abortion. . . . The sexual revolution [was] born on 9 May 1960 when the U.S. Food and Drug Administration approved the pill.[15]

Although the Pill was initially only available to married couples in New Zealand, a vigorous black market soon developed. Its availability had the effect of removing the threat of pregnancy for millions of women, thus giving them greater control over the consequences of their sexuality. This contributed to the loosening of traditional constraints on sexual relations and to the rise of what came to be known as the "permissive society." Although this liberalization was not as pervasive in New Zealand as overseas, its influence was exacerbated by the role of the media.

Whatever the perspective of the observer, the decade is viewed as a turning point. As Arthur Marwick puts it: ". . . left-centre and right [interpreters] do seem to agree that . . . *something* significant happened in the sixties. . . . What happened during this period transformed social and cultural developments for the rest of the century. . . . There has been nothing quite like it; nothing would be ever quite the same again."[16] The changing attitudes and reorientations of the 1960s had major implications for the ideas and ideals of succeeding decades, particularly in the nature of religious adherence and in the relation of church and society. It is to these issues that we now turn.

The Religious Crisis of the 1960s

The early 1960s represented a high-tide mark for mainstream churches in New Zealand. This followed the growth of the 1950s and the excitement generated by the Billy Graham Crusade in 1959. Christian adherence statistics stood at just under 90% of the population in both the 1956 and 1961 Censuses.[17] However, not all of these professed adherents were active members. Table 2 below compares the 1961–62 church attendance figures of the four largest Protestant denominations and shows that an average of just 14.92% of their members attended church even once a year. (As noted in chapter 5, church attendance in New Zealand has never exceeded 30% of the population. The peak church attendance figure of 29.8% was reached in 1896.)[18] In 1962, the Presbyterian Church had the largest numerical and percentage attendance; the Methodist Church had similar attendance percentages from a smaller base of adherents. The Anglican Church, although much larger, suffered from greater nominalism; only 10.50% of its membership attended Easter

Communion. Conversely, the Baptist Church was much smaller than the other three denominations, but had the largest active membership.

Church	Year	Census Adherents	Attendance/ Members	Percentage Active
Anglican	1961/62	835,434	87,710	10.50%
Presbyterian	1961	539,439	102,555	19.01%
Methodist	1961	173,878	31,674	18.22%
Baptist	1961/62	40,886	15,188	37.15%
Total		1,589,637	237,127	14.92%

Table 2: Comparative Church Statistics for 1961–62, for Anglican, Presbyterian, Methodist and Baptist Churches[19]

The 1960s also marked the beginnings of a decline in church adherence which has continued to the present day. This is demonstrated in the Religious Professions section of the quinquennial New Zealand Censuses from 1956 on; its impact is shown graphically in Figure 5 below.

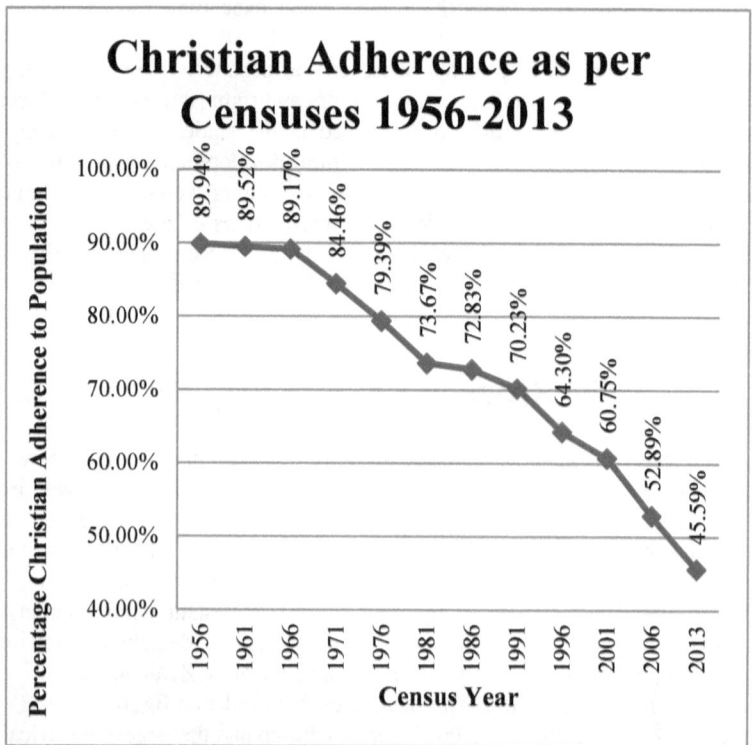

Figure 5: Christian Adherence as a percentage of the total population, 1956–2013. Derived from the Religious Professions section of the quinquennial New Zealand Censuses.[20]

This falling off in nominal adherence was paralleled by a major drop in actual church attendance (which was already at minority levels). This was part of a worldwide trend: the Religious Crisis of the 1960s was reflected in nearly every country in the western world. Indeed, British historian of religion Hugh McLeod argues that "in the religious history of the West these years may come to be seen as marking a rupture as profound as that brought about by the Reformation." During the 1960s, "Large numbers of people lost the habit of regular church-going.... There was a modest increase in the number of those professing other religion ... or stating that they had no religion. The main novelty here was that those who rejected Christianity were increasingly ready to say so loudly and openly."[21]

Several observations should be made about this decline as it occurred in New Zealand. Firstly, the initial signs of weakening in church attendance figures began amongst the youth of the churches. All mainstream churches had already begun to lose their younger members several years before their total membership figures began to decrease. This loss of young people is striking, given that the official statistics of the 1959 Billy Graham Crusade show that 7,981 (or 45.62%) of the 17,493 converts were aged between five to eighteen years.[22] The decline was particularly noticeable in the Anglican and Methodist Churches, with both Sunday School and Bible Class attendances showing marked falls from 1962 on, followed by a drop in communicants and membership by 1965–66. The church least affected by this process was the Baptist church, which was able to retain its young people until well into the late 1960s. Secondly, the religious crisis of the 1960s does not appear to be due directly to incidents such as the publication of *Honest to God* in 1963,[23] or the "God is Dead" controversy of the mid-1960s.[24] (This controversy was not confined to theological circles, since *Time* magazine had published an article on radical theology in October 1965 and its cover story for 8 April 1966 posed the question "Is God Dead?" The articles provoked a flood of correspondence.) These hurricane-like events both paralleled and reinforced the glacial changes of attitude and orientation that were already taking place. As has already been noted in chapter 1,[25] these gradual, subtle glacial changes are not necessarily attributable to any specific causative event or series of events. An example of the interaction between the hurricane and the glacier was the 1967 Geering heresy trial. This controversy, although appearing at the time to be an event impacting the Presbyterian Church with hurricane-like force, in fact represented the culmination of decades of glacial attitudinal change. Professor Lloyd Geering, Principal of the Presbyterian Knox Theological Hall, was charged with "disturbing the peace of the church" with his views questioning the resurrection of Jesus and the immortality of the soul. However, he was acquitted by the General Assembly of the Presbyterian Church of New Zealand.[26] It has been claimed that the heresy trial led to the loss of members from the Presbyterian Church of New Zealand.[27] In fact, this exodus had already been underway since 1960; the controversy simply accelerated this process.[28] While some of Geering's supporters made sweeping assertions that the trial had created a watershed in New Zealand religious history,[29] this claim seems somewhat overstated. What remained was a residual—and long-lasting—suspicion of Knox Theological Hall, which was seen by some as a coterie of extreme liberalism. (This perception did not match the reality, as the institution became more Evangelical and charismatic in the mid-1980s.) Nevertheless, the controversy did coincide with—and, in part, reflected—the beginnings of a shift towards Fundamentalism and Pentecostalism over the next fifteen years.[30]

In summary, then, New Zealand in the 1960s experienced the decline in religious adherence common to much of the Western world. Increasing numbers of people were prepared to state openly their lack of religious involvement, rather than to take refuge in nominal adherence. This decline could not be attributed to specific causative events, but was most marked—and occurred earlier—among young people. As will be seen, this facilitated the appeal of Evangelicalism and Pentecostalism in the later 1960s.

Out of the Ghetto?
Pentecostal Growth and Development in the 1960s

The religious decline of the 1960s, although pervasive, was not total. Parallel—and opposite—to this, a powerful movement of the Holy Spirit emerged in the early 1960s. In New Zealand, this spiritual impulse was initially located within independent Pentecostal groups—particularly the Latter Rain-inspired forerunners of the Indigenous Churches—later influencing the Assemblies of God and, after 1965, mainstream churches also. This marked the beginning of two decades of sustained Pentecostal growth that would transform the movement and extend its influence beyond its sectarian boundaries to become one of the strongest Pentecostal movements in the West.[31] This expansion would also change the ways in which the movement perceived—and was perceived by—the wider society, as well as its attitudes towards other churches and relationships within the movement itself. The rise of the Charismatic movement within the mainstream churches did much to change these attitudes and perceptions over the next two decades. By the end of the 1970s, the movement would be quite different in character from what it had been in previous decades.

Pentecostal Growth in the 1960s

There had been some Pentecostal growth in New Zealand during the 1950s, particularly in the latter half of the decade;[32] this gathered momentum as the 1960s began. The Ellerslie-Waiomio campaigns of Ray Bloomfield and Frank Houston, together with the Latter Rain evangelism of Rob Wheeler and his colleagues have been discussed in the previous chapter.[33] However, this evangelistic dynamism was not shared by all Pentecostal groups, most of whom remained church centered, rather than evangelism focused. For example, the Commonwealth Covenant Churches, despite being the third largest Pentecostal body in the 1961 Census, appear to have entered a period of decline over the next two decades as their British Israelism lost its relevance.[34] The National Revival Crusade—later renamed Christian Revival Crusade—also failed to build its constituency during the decade,[35] while the struggling Elim Church only had four congregations in 1960 and remained at this level until well into the 1970s.[36] A partial exception was the Church of Christ (New Zealand), which grew in numbers and extended its building several times in the 1960s and 1970s. However, this remained a single large congregation, rather than an association of churches.[37] Another, but limited, example of Pentecostal growth was the Apostolic Church, which undertook some evangelism in the 1960s,[38] although this was complicated by frustrations and tension over "unskilled national interference" in this work. These frustrations led to the secession of well-known Apostolic evangelists, brothers Norman and Gilbert White, from the movement in 1966.[39] This policy of national apostolic control reflected the stress on ecclesial centralism that characterized that Church in the 1960s and which hindered its charismatic ministry for some time to come.[40] The two Pentecostal groups that contributed the most to—and benefitted the most from—the evangelistic dynamism of the 1960s were the Indigenous Churches and the Assemblies of God.

The growth of the 1960s began through the activities of independent Pentecostal evangelists, particularly those who had been influenced by the Latter Rain movement and inspired by American examples such as Oral Roberts and Tommy Hicks.[41] Initially, there were only limited local pockets of evangelistic success, chiefly amongst Māori in isolated rural settlements, but this lack of results was about to change. The turning point came with the Worley Revival in Timaru in June and July 1960. A. S. Worley had come to New Zealand as an independent evangelist in late 1959[42] and his campaign in this religiously conservative city would become legendary in New Zealand Pentecostalism.[43] More than 600 conversions were recorded during the five weeks of the campaign and the healings that took place were given extensive and largely positive—newspaper coverage in the local newspaper, the *Timaru Herald*.[44] One unusual feature of this campaign was "teethfilling"; claims were made that people's teeth had been divinely filled in response to prayer. This particular sign received much publicity. Indeed, the Member of Parliament for Timaru, Rev. Clyde Carr, eventually raised the issue in Parliament, asking "could the Minister [of Health] or the Director of Dental Hygiene look into the matter?" He also requested the Minister to "take action to prevent the malpractices of quacks and unqualified people who assumed duties for which they were not equipped." Regrettably, the response of the Minister is not recorded in the *New Zealand Parliamentary Debates*.[45]

The success of the Worley campaign had several important implications for the future development of the Pentecostal movement in New Zealand. Firstly, the coverage of the campaign in the secular press increased public awareness of the ministry of healing and, ultimately, of Pentecostalism. As has been previously discussed, the link between Pentecostalism and healing was a strong one and examples of healing often led to the emergence and expansion of Pentecostal churches.[46] Indeed, Peter Morrow categorized the period between 1960 and 1962, during which Pentecostalism began its vigorous expansion, as a time of "healing revival" rather than a charismatic renewal.[47] This revivalism marked the beginnings of an increased public recognition of Pentecostalism, although there was also some strong opposition to the movement, particularly from mainstream churches. Secondly, the campaign sparked extensive independent Pentecostal evangelism, particularly in the South Island,[48] which complemented the effectiveness of the tent campaigns of Rob Wheeler and others in the North Island. This built upon a strong sense of opportunity and excitement. Ron Coady observed that these campaigns were not conducted on the basis of a planned strategy: "We [simply] went where we felt the Spirit would have us go, as we waited on the Lord and we felt God speak to us to go to a place."[49] At times there were invitations from people who had come across the campaigns in other towns. In rural Southland, the campaign in Tuatapere, for example, came about "because one family had attended the meetings in Invercargill and Gore . . . [and had asked] 'will you come to our town?'"[50] These results were significant and the growth exponential: Wheeler later remarked that "at one stage, between Ron Coady and myself, we were opening a new church every two weeks."[51] He also captured some of the sense of opportunity and energy that characterized this period in two editorials, written three months apart, in his magazine *Bible Deliverance* in 1961:

> 1960 was a wonderful year! More souls, healings, miracles, baptisms, exploits of faith, than any previous year. But 1960 is behind us, and now it is history. By God's grace, we shall make 1961 one hundred per cent greater.[52]

> Greetings from the South Island! It is harvest time. There is much work to be done in a short time. We are working from daylight until 1 and 2 in the morning with calls, meetings, writing and future plans. . . . Now we are in Dunedin ready to commence ten nights of meetings before going on to Invercargill. Brother Coady and Brother [Paul] Collins are campaigning in Gore. Brother [Everett] Johnson is in Timaru. Brother [Norman] White at Invercargill. Brother Hunt at Foxton and others are hard at the ingathering throughout the land in tents halls, churches and missions. . . . It is harvest time![53]

Figure 6: Rob Wheeler's tent campaign in Auckland, January 1962. Taken from the cover of *Bible Deliverance*, February 1962. Rob Wheeler, Auckland. Permission to reproduce requested 28 October 2013.

There was a strong sense of urgency to keep up with the opportunities that were opening up. This primary period of evangelism would last until 1965, by which time the churches generated by this expansion numbered more than sixty and were beginning to coalesce into a movement known as the "Indigenous Churches."

The Latter Rain orientation of many of these independent evangelists was significant. It gave them considerable freedom to conduct campaigns without the hindrance of denominational constraints and also shaped the character of the churches that resulted. Although these campaigners had initially focused purely on evangelism, they later came to adopt a church planting approach, with the intention of establishing independent local Pentecostal assemblies set up along Latter Rain lines.[54] The core value of these independent assemblies was the autonomy of the local church[55] and this is the sense in which the word "indigenous" came to be used, albeit erroneously. (Rob Wheeler's rationale for the term was that "the word 'indigenous' simply means 'native,' 'local,' 'belonging to the district,' and we prefer this word to 'independent,' for who can really be independent in the strictest sense and still follow the teachings of Paul on Church life?")[56] However, their collective identity was diffuse. As an early adherent put it, on looking back some twenty-five years later, "it was difficult to say exactly *what* we were back then. We were simply 'Christians'—not 'Pentecostals' or 'New Life Centre' people—we did not have any identifying 'tag'."[57] (The anachronistic reference to "New Life Centre" is to the name eventually adopted in the late 1980s.) None of this growth is reflected in the Census statistics during the 1960s, as the movement did not then have a corporate name and, indeed, resisted all attempts to impose a denominational title. Eventually these assemblies would become the Indigenous Churches of New Zealand and, two decades later, the New Life Churches of New Zealand. (The name "Indigenous Churches" was not popular, however; it was later facetiously said that the reason that it seldom appeared in the Censuses was that nobody knew how to spell "indigenous"!)[58] Nevertheless, there was an increasing degree of cohesion, and the movement's first National Conference, held in Richmond, Nelson at Easter 1965, attracted over 800 attendees. These loosely affiliated churches became a significant body over the next fifteen years and Peter Lineham describes them as "among the most dynamic forces in the religious life in New Zealand" in the 1970s.[59] He further attributes the breaking of the sectarian barriers which prevented the Pentecostal movement from impacting the mainstream churches to these independent Pentecostal groups.[60] As will be seen, some of these churches had a significant influence on the emergence of the Charismatic Renewal.

Their success formed the initial salient of Pentecostal evangelism in the early 1960s. This had immediate effects on other Pentecostal groups, particularly the Assemblies of God. Ian Clark recalls that as a consequence of these spectacular results, "a great cry went up [in the Assemblies of God] 'Why can't we do something like that too?'"[61] However, the phenomenal rise of these independent churches initially threatened the Assemblies of God in the same way as the Apostolic Church had done in the 1930s[62] and exacerbated tensions within its Executive. This led to the resignation of Frank Houston and Wallace Thompson in April 1961 in protest at the way some in the Assemblies of God were clinging to outmoded methods and attitudes.[63] (Houston commented some years later that this conservatism and legalism had been particularly acute among the British pastors on the Executive.[64] This was partly an issue of cultural identity: as Rob Wheeler put it, "the Assemblies were in the hands of British pastors, stiff and formal as could be."[65] The younger, New Zealand-born pastors wanted something that was their own and were attracted to the ideas of indigeneity and of power as distinct from inherited tradition.)[66] The resignations of Houston and Thompson forced the movement to take stock and led to the calling of an extraordinary Executive Council conference in June 1961 to address the crisis. After concerns for the future of the movement were vented, a prophetic intervention from Pastor John Wood of the Auckland Assembly steadied the gathering: "Hold fast! We have great truth and a great tradition. The Lord will help us if we faithfully go about his business. Our time will come!" (Clark comments that future events would prove that these were "prophetic words indeed.")[67] This led to a remarkable turn-around for the Assemblies of God. A new spirit of cooperation was engendered and the effectiveness of the movement's leadership structures was increased, leading Houston and Thompson to withdraw their resignations.

The immediate outcome was a new spirit of confidence and a willingness to develop more innovative and open ways of doing things. Much of this was due to the influence of Frank Houston and of Pastor Ralph Read.[68] Read had arrived in New Zealand from Australia in 1959 to take up the pastorate of the Sydenham Assembly of God. He was a skilled organizer and, as Chairman of the Executive, exercised strong and capable leadership over the Assemblies of God in the early 1960s.[69] Clark refers to his "disciplined and orderly hand" and the "forthright manner in which many problems were dealt with"; this resulted in a steady growth in the movement's morale and influence in the early 1960s.[70] Nevertheless, Read was also a conservative traditionalist and, as will be seen, strongly opposed both the Latter Rain movement and the then-emerging Charismatic movement. His conservatism later led to considerable divergence in the Australian Assemblies of God during his tenure as General Superintendent of that movement. This came to a head at its 1977 Conference, leading to him being voted out of office.[71] By contrast, Houston was an example of a new generation of New Zealand-born leadership emerging in the 1960s[72] and as Home Missions promoter for the movement after 1961 was in his element as an evangelist.[73] He lived and breathed for outreach. During his tenure, he conducted numerous successful campaigns and sought to release the Assemblies of God into greater evangelism. Clark observes that under Houston's ministry, "for the first time in decades the Assemblies of God developed a credible evangelistic outreach that gathered force in the following fifteen years [i.e., 1961–76]."[74] By contrast to Read and other conservatives in the movement, Houston had an open attitude to the new independent Pentecostal churches—including the Latter Rain-inspired groups—and maintained contact with them.[75] He became General Superintendent of the Assemblies of God in 1966, following Read's return to Australia at the end of the previous year. This marked a turning point for these churches, laying the foundations for their exponential expansion in the 1970s.

Frank Houston's appointment—which coincided with the appointment of several New Zealand-born pastors to the Executive Council—began a new era for the Assemblies of God. This marked the first time since the 1920s that the Council was composed solely of New Zealanders.[76] During Houston's twelve-year tenure, the movement grew from twenty-six churches in 1966 to eighty in 1977,[77] most of these planted through his dynamic influence or of those who had been trained under him. Much of this inspiration was due to "the modelling effect of his own faith, energetic leadership, boldness, evangelistic passion, pragmatism and reliance on the supernatural in ministry."[78] Other catalysts included the influence of Indigenous Church models of ministry and government,[79] the removal of the conservatism of overseas leadership in the Assemblies of God[80] and—especially—the role of the New Zealand National Training School, founded under Houston's leadership in 1968.[81] Australian Pentecostal Andrew MacFarlane notes that this school "was a profound model for church based ministry training which was to typify later megachurch institutions. Effectively, it aimed to replicate the particular style of the charismatic leader and multiply that ministry in other places"[82] and thus ensured that future Assemblies of God pastors would be modeled in Houston's image. By the end of the decade, these Bible School graduates were starting to move into pastoral work and to open new churches.[83] This laid the foundations for the exponential expansion of the Assemblies of God after 1970.

Another factor in the expansion of Pentecostalism was the growing ethnicization of the movement after 1965. This applied more to the Assemblies of God than to other Pentecostal churches, although the Apostolic Church built—and has since maintained—a substantial Māori membership.[84] This ethnic diversity—which would increase in the 1970s and beyond—was the result of increased immigration, particularly from the Pacific Islands. A large proportion of this was Samoan, since New Zealand had administered Western Samoa until its independence in 1962 and this had stimulated Samoan immigration into New Zealand. Samoan outreach began from the Mount Roskill Assembly of God and the first Samoan Assembly of God was affiliated in 1965. This wing of the movement grew exponentially over the next thirty-five years.[85]

Ian Clark suggests that the influx into the Assemblies of God over the next two decades built upon the 1960s in two ways. Firstly, he argues, Houston and his protégés were evangelistic in outlook and were not concerned with the maintenance of existing patterns or reinforcing the status quo, as some other Pentecostal groups were. Consequently, they were innovative and adaptable in their patterns of ministry; this fitted well with the ethos of the era. Secondly, most of these pastors were young men in their twenties and thirties, who had just come out of training and had nothing to lose and no traditional methods to protect. Their resourcefulness enabled them to do what the Indigenous Churches had done ten years before, namely, to reach out into all areas of society. In this way, "the Assemblies of God were ... transformed into an outward-looking Movement and lost the siege mentality and defensive attitudes they had maintained for so many years."[86] The same could also be said—although not to the same extent—of other Pentecostal groups in the 1960s.

By the end of the decade, New Zealand Pentecostalism had grown considerably and become more outward-looking. A dynamic new movement—the Indigenous Churches—had emerged from the sectarian obscurities of the 1950s, numbering sixty churches by 1965; this would constitute the largest Pentecostal group of churches by the beginning of the 1970s. The Assemblies of God were also expanding, from about twenty-five assemblies in 1960[87] to at least thirty-two in 1969.[88] In terms of Census statistics for the period—which are not complete, since they do not include the Indigenous Churches—they had surpassed the Apostolic Church to have the largest number of Pentecostal adherents by 1966.[89] Although the Apostolic Church was also growing steadily during the 1960s, this gap had widened further by 1971. This exponential growth, paralleled by the rise of the Charismatic movement in the mainstream churches, would accelerate in the 1970s.

Pentecostal Attitudes, Identity and Relationships in the 1960s

Pentecostal expansion in the 1960s was paralleled by changes in its attitudes, identity and relationships. These reflected shifts in the ways in which it was perceived by the wider society as well as in its adherents' views of themselves and other churches. As the decade began, it was generally seen as a strange fringe movement with weird ideas and practices. Cecily Worsfold—whose husband James was then the pastor of the Dunedin Apostolic Church—recalls "one Baptist family attending . . . in the early 1960s [who] were told that Pentecostals bit the pews, so when the congregation rose to sing a hymn the visitors felt along the top of the pew in front in order to find teeth marks."[90] Such erroneous characterizations reinforced their negative image. Consequently, there was a definite social stigma attached to any association with Pentecostal groups.[91] These misperceptions—and the stigma that accompanied them—persisted well into the 1960s. Furthermore, opposition to the Baptism of the Spirit was frequently voiced in the denominational churches. An Australian example from 1961 was New South Wales Baptist College Principal G. H. Morling's castigation of it as "unseemly behaviour," "extravagance" and "unhealthy emotionalism."[92] This opposition was reiterated in two articles by Allan Burrow, principal of the New Zealand Bible Training Institute, in its magazine *The Reaper* in 1963.[93] Opposition such as this created a sense of "us and them" in the movement and reinforced the boundaries of their sectarian identity.

While Pentecostals were viewed with distaste by some mainstream churches, the dislike was mutual. Reference was often made to the deadness of denominational churches and disbelief expressed that there could be any outpouring of the Spirit within such surroundings. One example of this was Rob Wheeler's editorial in *Bible Deliverance* for April 1965, which warned that "you cannot place new wine in old bottles. . . . You cannot keep the outpouring of the Holy Spirit within the confines of Historic Religion."[94] Another was Ralph Read's deep distrust of the ecumenical effect of the charismatic movement on Pentecostal churches in Australia at the end of the 1960s.[95] Many other Pentecostal groups were also closed and suspicious of other churches.[96] This was exemplified in the response when Rev. David Edmonds, one of the first Methodist charismatics, shared his testimony of being baptized in the Spirit with an Indigenous Pentecostal group about 1966. "The overall reaction of the congregation was one of *shock* that someone should have received the Spirit without having 'come out' of their church."[97] As will be seen in the next section, these attitudes began to change later in the decade.

However, the burgeoning expansion of Pentecostalism represented only one side of the story, since there were also significant divisions between Pentecostal churches in the 1960s. These disagreements were bitter and entrenched; the suspicion of other Pentecostal groups towards the Apostolic Church has already been remarked, as well as a general opposition to the proponents of the Bethel Temple doctrine of "the Name."[98] This antagonism appears to have intensified in the early 1960s, as is demonstrated by events following Rob Wheeler's Christchurch campaign at Easter 1961. Wheeler had been engaged by a group of Pentecostal churches—Apostolic, Elim and Assemblies of God—to conduct a combined campaign for them in the city.[99] He had carefully toned down his Latter Rain teachings in order to avoid offence in campaigns such as these. However, despite his caution and the positive results which accrued to the sponsoring Pentecostal churches, Wheeler was later confronted by the pastor chairing the campaign. This pastor charged him with teaching "Jesus Only" doctrines in his Tauranga Bible School and vehemently declared that "I have vowed to stamp these people out if it takes the last breath in my body!" Furthermore, if this was what Wheeler taught then he would be stamped out in the same way. Thus, in Wheeler's words, "we left on that kind of disinterested [*sic*] note."[100]

Although Wheeler does not identify this pastor, this was evidently Ralph Read, who was the pastor of the Sydenham Assembly of God, one of the churches sponsoring the campaign.[101] As we have already noted, Read was a conservative traditionalist and had a firm and forthright view of doctrine.[102] He was also strongly opposed to Latter Rain practices such as dancing in the Spirit. His antipathy to this movement may have stemmed from the loss of students from Pentecostal Church of Australia minister C. L. Greenwood's Bible College to "another college that had been established by a 'latter rain' church in Melbourne [i.e., the group associated with Ray Jackson]." Since Read was associated with Greenwood during his early ministry, this loss evidently colored his perceptions of the Latter Rain movement.[103] He was later to publish a booklet, under the auspices of the New Zealand Pentecostal Fellowship, against "the Name" teaching in 1966.[104] However, it is surprising that this issue should have emerged in the 1960s, since it was not one of Wheeler's major emphases and does not appear to have been previously linked to "Jesus Only" views.[105] There is, for example, no reference in the primary records of the original dissension over "the Name" in the 1940s and 1950s to any equation of this teaching with the Unitarian "Jesus Only" view. No condemnation of any deviant views on the Trinity appears in the various Minute Books of the Pentecostal Church of New Zealand,[106] or in the correspondence between the protagonists in the controversy. (This includes letters from Pastor Harry V. Roberts and other leaders of the Pentecostal Church.[107] Kevin Conner also reproduces the full text of a letter from Roberts to Stan Douglas—Conner's brother-in-law—setting out the development of the controversy. Although Roberts is highly critical of Jackson and his teaching, he nowhere equates this with

"Jesus Only" or Unitarian Pentecostalism.)[108] Further, none of the earlier published responses to "the Name" teaching make any reference to Unitarian tendencies.[109] This silence is significant, for if the doctrine had indeed been perceived as Unitarian, this would have been sufficient to irretrievably damn its proponents in the eyes of their Pentecostal colleagues. Nevertheless, Read insisted that it was Unitarian and therefore to be condemned. Other Pentecostal leaders, such as James Worsfold, followed his lead; Worsfold continued to maintain the identity of "the Name" teaching with "Jesus Only" doctrine to the end of his life.[110] For their part, the Indigenous Churches saw themselves as Trinitarian in doctrine and strongly resented this imputation of Unitarianism. It was not until the arrival of the United Pentecostal Church—a Unitarian Pentecostal, or "Jesus Only" group—in New Zealand in 1969 that attitudes began to soften towards them.[111] (This Unitarian Pentecostal group has never had contact with Trinitarian Pentecostals in New Zealand and many Pentecostals in this country would be unaware of its existence. According to Global Christianity researcher David Barrett, this group had established forty churches, with approximately 4,000 members by 1982.[112] However, Wheeler considers these statistics a "gross exaggeration"[113] and Census statistics place its membership at 258 adherents in 2013.)[114] Nevertheless, the opposition that the Indigenous Churches encountered reinforced their Latter Rain rejection of any church organization beyond the local assembly and they regarded the other Pentecostal churches as "Babylonian" because of their organizational structures. The result was fifteen years of mutual distrust and dislike, which persisted until 1975.[115] This had the effect of creating boundaries of identity in what had originally been a nonsectarian Pentecostal revival. Paradoxically, this conflict was beneficial, since, as Luther Gerlach and Virginia Hine note, perceptions of persecution are essential for the lift-off of a movement.[116] It is only from this point that the Indigenous Churches—the name later adopted by sections of the movement—can be identified as a distinct center of Pentecostal identity. The opposition, which continued throughout much of the 1960s, created a sense of "us and them" which reinforced the energy of the movement's evangelism.

This opposition to the Indigenous Churches took organizational form with the formation in 1966 of the New Zealand Pentecostal Fellowship.[117] While this was promoted as a vehicle for Pentecostal unity, this concord was somewhat circumscribed, since not all Pentecostal groups were represented. The Apostolic Church, the Assemblies of God and the Elim Church were all members of the New Zealand Pentecostal Fellowship, with the National Revival Crusade also being invited to join. The Indigenous Churches were, however, excluded; this policy of exclusion appears to have been directed against these churches as a movement, rather than against its adherents personally. Individual Indigenous Church adherents were "very welcome as individuals" to New Zealand Pentecostal Fellowship events, but the Indigenous Churches themselves were not permitted to be officially associated.[118] While their absence was, in part, a product of their independent stance and antipathy to other churches, it appears that the other Pentecostal churches had refused to allow them to join. Their anger at this exclusion reinforced their sectarian attitudes. This is evidenced by the report of an interview between the Committee of the New Zealand Pentecostal Fellowship and

Rob Wheeler and Ron Coady for the Indigenous Churches. Despite disclaimers on both sides, there was considerable mutual antagonism.[119] Ian Clark later observed that the New Zealand Pentecostal Fellowship "was really formed to keep the ... [Indigenous] Churches out; that's the bottom line.... In those days [i.e., the early 1960s] your greatest enemies were other Pentecostals. It was really quite tragic."[120] His perception is reinforced by the Statement of Faith issued by the Fellowship, which words the statement on Baptism in such a way as to exclude the formula used by the Indigenous Churches.[121] These divisions would not be fully healed until the 1970s.

Despite this institutional ecclesial distrust, there were a number of examples of Pentecostal cooperation during the 1960s which transcended organizational and doctrinal lines. Assemblies of God pastors Frank Houston and Bob Midgley were noted for their open attitude[122] and Apostolic evangelists Norman and Gilbert White frequently cooperated with Wheeler and other Indigenous Churches ministers.[123] In Christchurch, Peter Morrow was widely known for his love towards other Christians and this contributed to his wide acceptance amongst other churches there.[124] Furthermore, the converts of Pentecostal evangelism in the 1960s contributed to an increase in the number and size of Pentecostal congregations and consequently to a dilution of their sectarian attitudes. This changing social mix would be important in some of the developments in the 1970s and 1980s.

The Emergence of the Charismatic Movement

Another factor which contributed to the changing social and attitudinal shape of Pentecostalism in the 1960s was the rise of the Charismatic Movement within the mainstream churches. This movement was characterized by the experience of distinctively Pentecostal phenomena such as the Baptism of the Spirit, but outside a Pentecostal denominational or confessional framework. As such, its emergence in the mainstream churches represented a considerable enlargement of Pentecostalism's potential constituency. The Charismatic movement had been gaining ground in New Zealand since the 1950s,[125] although it did not attract public attention until the visits of South African Pentecostal David du Plessis,[126] American Episcopalian Dennis Bennett[127] and Anglican clergyman Michael Harper[128] in 1966 and 1967. The development of the movement can be divided into several stages. Anglican vicar Donald Battley defines these as "the period of the pioneers," extending from 1963 to about 1971, followed by "the time of ingathering" from 1971 to 1979 and "a time of depression" after 1979.[129] (An earlier stage—not mentioned by Battley—was the period before 1963, when the movement was largely an underground one.) Relations and interactions between the Pentecostal and Charismatic movements varied over time, roughly in line with this periodization. This section will address developments in the 1950s and 1960s; those relating to the 1970s and 1980s will be dealt with in Chapters 9 to 11.

A number of factors contributed to the rise of the Charismatic movement in the 1950s and 1960s, but there was neither a single source for, nor a unified manifestation of, this movement. An early participant observed that "God broke through from quite a number of different angles and different 'streams' almost simultaneously during the early [and] mid-1960s. . . . It's very difficult to attribute the development of the [Charismatic] movement to any one particular thing or church."[130] The catalysts that produced it varied from place to place; different churches experienced it in different ways and gave different responses to it. Although the movement emerged in the 1960s, its foundations were laid a decade earlier. A short-lived wave of interest in Pentecostal charismata occurred in Brethren assemblies between 1953 and 1956, when a number of Brethren had been filled with the Spirit, despite official opposition. Some of these had been brought into the Baptism of the Spirit through the influence of Ray Bloomfield—whose family had Brethren connections[131]—and would become influential in the Charismatic movement in the 1960s. Similarly, a number of Baptists also received the Spirit in the late 1950s, including Trevor Chandler, who would later become Frank Houston's copastor in the Lower Hutt Assembly of God.[132]

However, a key person in the emergence and development of the Charismatic movement was Bible teacher Campbell McAlpine, who arrived from South Africa in mid-1959 to work as an evangelist in New Zealand. He had great acceptability in the Brethren assemblies and also with Youth for Christ and was remembered as a dynamic speaker, with "a winning personality, and an aura of saintliness about him."[133] Consequently, he was frequently a featured speaker at Christmas camps and Conferences, as well as in evangelistic crusades and at the 1960 graduation of Bible Training Institute. However, his acceptability in Evangelical and Brethren circles declined when it became known that he had been filled with the Spirit and spoke in tongues in his private devotions. His ministry was thereafter limited to small house-groups where he was free to share his Charismatic testimony. Nevertheless, he made a strong impression on many of those who later became Charismatics. After leaving New Zealand in September 1963, he briefly returned the following year to assist, together with English revivalist Arthur Wallis and New Zealand Brethren Charismatic teacher Milton Smith, in the landmark Massey Conference. (Wallis' influence complemented that of McAlpine. During his time in New Zealand he helped to bring isolated Charismatics into contact with each other, thus laying the foundations of a Charismatic network and ultimately, of the Charismatic movement in this country.)[134] The Massey Conference represented the first gathering of this incipient movement, attracting Charismatic Christians as well as some Pentecostals, and is often seen as marking the beginnings of the Charismatic movement in New Zealand.[135] This perception is only partially correct since, as Peter Lineham demonstrates, the Charismatic Movement was already under way, although functioning largely as an underground movement in the mainstream churches. Nevertheless, it brought together three hundred participants from widely diverse mainstream church settings, as well as a number of Pentecostals who were having increasing personal input into the emerging movement. One Pentecostal pastor, reporting on the Conference, noted the attendance of leaders from most of the Pentecostal groups, almost half of whom had Latter Rain or independent Pentecostal connections. He further commented—with a degree of incredulity—on the

> gracious spirit of love and fellowship one towards the other as each one dropped their denominational tags. . .

> Believe it or not—as these ministers were all thrown in together, a spirit of love flowed between them and other denominational ministers.... Truly God was knitting hearts in a bond and fellowship between all His ministers.[136]

(The author of the article is not named, but may have been David Jackson, pastor of the Timaru Missionary Revival Centre, which was the publisher of the *Gospel Truth*. His expressions of incredulity—and his emphasis on the dropping of "denominational tags"—reflected his Latter Rain orientation. And, of the thirteen pastors named in the article, six were Latter Rain or independent Pentecostals.) The informal ecumenism exemplified by this early conference would be the most significant driving force behind the expansion of the Charismatic movement. Annual transdenominational conferences, patterned on the 1964 Massey Conference and featuring overseas and local participants in the Charismatic movement, became something of an established model for the movement over the next fifteen years. These conferences—particularly those conducted in the 1970s under the auspices of Christian Advance Ministries—continued to attract participants from all denominations as well as from Pentecostal churches. The waning of the Charismatic movement in the early 1980s can be attributed, at least in part, to the diminution of this informal ecumenism with the creation of in-house agencies for renewal within each denomination.

The impact of Charismatic visitors from overseas such as Campbell McAlpine and Arthur Wallis was reinforced by that of Charismatic publications. Assemblies of God evangelist David Wilkerson's book *The Cross and the Switchblade*[137] was by far the most influential of these, and was widely read in New Zealand.[138] An example of its influence is given in Anglican priest Father David Balfour's testimony in the first issue of *Logos* magazine.[139] His story is quite typical; an examination of the various testimonies published in *Logos*—which was effectively the voice of the New Zealand Charismatic movement from 1966 until 1970—shows that the role of literature was very important indeed in the spread of the movement. Other significant books included American author John Sherrill's *They Speak with Other Tongues*,[140] Michael Harper's *As at the Beginning*[141] and Dennis Bennett's *Nine O'Clock in the Morning*.[142]

A further catalytic factor, particularly in the early stages of the movement, was the personal—as distinct from organizational—influence of a number of Pentecostal leaders and individuals. Charismatic historian Allan Neil notes that almost all those experiencing charismatic renewal up to 1965 had done so through the influence of Pentecostal churches.[143] This influence took several different forms. The evangelistic campaigns of Latter Rain-oriented Rob Wheeler and Ron Coady, of Frank Houston and Trevor Chandler from the Assemblies of God and of the White brothers from the Apostolic Church, were all important catalysts. Several Pentecostal congregations also had significant input into the new movement, for example, Houston's Assembly of God church in Lower Hutt and Peter Morrow's Christchurch Revival Centre. It is significant that most of the Pentecostal influence on the Charismatic movement came from Pentecostal leaders who had been directly or indirectly influenced by the Latter Rain movement. Former charismatic Presbyterian elder—and later, a New Life pastor—Ken Wright sums up their influence thus:

There was no doubt at all that the nature of the ministries that we brought into the country at that time [he is probably referring to Dennis Bennett and Michael Harper], plus the ministries that [Assemblies of God pastor] Des Short was having ... with his major conferences [in Tauranga], had a tremendous influence overall on the whole move of the Spirit in the country, as well as, of course, the ongoing influence of the likes of Peter Morrow, Frank Houston, Rob Wheeler and [others] had a great, great, impact in these areas, to name just a few.[144]

There were, however, some reservations. The Apostolic Church had suspicions about the Charismatic movement, since the operation of spiritual gifts was not supervised by appointed apostolic and prophetic ministry. Nevertheless, it had a policy of allowing its ministers to belong to local Ministers' Fraternals, which "gave them an open door to ... share the truth of Pentecost, ... which had considerable impact because of their faithfulness and their obvious love and fellowship with ... vastly different ministers from totally contradictory theological backgrounds."[145]

Not all Pentecostal churches were as accepting of this. Wright contrasts this openness with the attitude of "a lot of other Pentecostal churches ... [who] were closed and suspicious" of other churches.[146] Thus, despite the support of some Pentecostal pastors and churches, little institutional encouragement was forthcoming. This institutional reticence was not limited to New Zealand. Pentecostal historian Edith Blumhofer notes the initial hesitations about the Charismatic movement in the American Assemblies of God, linking these with that church's inherent anti-ecumenism and anti-Catholicism in the 1960s.[147] In Australia, the distrust of Ralph Read towards the Charismatic movement has already been noted.[148] Nevertheless, the New Zealand Assemblies of God—under Houston's leadership—were quicker to embrace the new movement than were their more conservative Australian counterparts and this had positive consequences for their growth in the later 1960s and 1970s. Similarly, the less institutional character and greater charismatic freedom of churches influenced by the Latter Rain movement enabled them to contribute to—and benefit from—the Charismatic movement to a greater extent than other Pentecostal churches.[149]

Pentecostal support had several important consequences for the early Charismatic movement. In the 1960s, Pentecostal mentors provided a Biblical and conceptual framework for experiencing the Spirit.[150] This involved both praxis and hermeneutic. Charismatics adopted typically Pentecostal practices and worship patterns, including upraised hands, the use of glossolalia in worship, and exuberant praise.[151] These did not always fit well in a traditional church setting; as Donald Battley observes, "the early charismatics leaned heavily on pentecostal mentors and suffered much suspicion as a result."[152] Historian Elaine Bolitho notes that of the first eighteen Charismatic Methodist clergy, eleven eventually left New Zealand Methodist ministry. This is not surprising given the trenchant opposition from some official Methodist quarters—for example, Principal Eric Hames of Trinity Theological College who referred to Charismatics as "these theological misfits, who in the inscrutable wisdom of God are allowed to flourish." She does not reference the source of Hames' acidic comment.[153]

Furthermore, the charismatic experience was anchored in a Pentecostal Biblical hermeneutic and expressed in what Pentecostal scholar Stephen Land has called an "oral-narrative liturgy and theology"[154] of the experience of God. Such narrative liturgy and theology adhered closely to a literal reading of Scriptural models, with less attention being given either to critical analysis of these patterns or to their theological implications. The template of Pentecostal spirituality was also pervasive, with the Baptism of the Spirit being understood as an experience of the Spirit subsequent to salvation or baptism. This aspect of Pentecostal hermeneutics created a particular problem for Charismatics, since it implied a devaluation of all Christian experience prior to their reception of the Spirit. Anglican vicar Dale Williamson notes that "the term 'baptism in the Holy Spirit' ... carried the implication that the Holy Spirit was not present within a person until they had been baptised in the Holy Spirit. This did not sit well with the Anglican (or other mainstream churches') belief that the Holy Spirit is present at conversion, water baptism and confirmation."[155] Consequently, as the Charismatic movement began to distance itself from the Pentecostal movement over the next decade and to develop its own independent identity and theological justification, the terminology changed from "Charismatic movement" to "Charismatic Renewal." This terminology was particularly evident among Catholic Charismatics.[156] The change represented a theological shift towards acknowledging a previous work of the Spirit at conversion or baptism and a renewal—rather than an initial experience—of the Spirit as one was filled with the Spirit.

The Charismatic movement also had a significant influence on its Pentecostal counterpart. Initially, Pentecostal churches often provided safe havens for those Charismatics who were forced to leave their mainstream churches due to the unsympathetic attitudes of the denominations. History student Eric Hodgkinson, for example, notes that "people left denominational churches and joined Pentecostal churches because they could express their faith in a new setting without embarrassment" and "no longer had to struggle to bring change or renewal to their denominations."[157] This migration was reinforced later in the 1960s as other Charismatics fellowshipped with Pentecostal churches—while still remaining members of their own denomination—seeking settings where the gifts of the Spirit could be appropriated. This cross-pollination brought both growth and change. Pentecostal churches were no longer automatically viewed as extreme sects by those outside the movement and this new respectability would increase in the following decade. And, on the Pentecostal side, a number of churches all grew substantially through embracing the Charismatic Renewal. These included Frank Houston's Lower Hutt Assembly of God, Bob Midgley's Queen Street Assembly of God in Auckland, and Peter Morrow's Christchurch Revival Centre. By the 1970s, several of these congregations had attendance levels approaching one thousand people.[158] These large Pentecostal churches would become significant forces in the 1970s.

The influx of less radical and better educated Renewal participants into Pentecostal congregations helped to change both the social mix of these congregations and the attitudes and ideas that they held. Although many Pentecostal views remained unchanged—for example, the need for an experiential encounter with the Spirit, by contrast with "dead religion"—these were no longer as common or expressed with the same force. This led to the beginnings of a broadened worldview and a mellowing of Pentecostal attitudes. The influence of these wider Charismatic perspectives contributed to the alleviation of Pentecostal sectarianism and thus to the development of the Pentecostal movement over the next two decades. The patterns of Pentecostal polity also began to diversify in the 1970s. A number of Charismatics from Baptist and Brethren backgrounds became leaders of independent Pentecostal and Charismatic churches,[159] bringing new models of church polity with them. These would influence the ways in which some Pentecostal churches evolved during the 1970s and 1980s. These developments will be discussed in chapters 9 to 11. The contribution of the Charismatic movement to the development of the Pentecostal movement was therefore a significant one.

Conclusion

The 1960s were a time of opportunity and growth for Pentecostalism in New Zealand. The turbulence of the decade, reflected in increased individualism and in challenges to traditional institutions of authority, created contexts within which radical religious movements such as Pentecostalism could flourish. Thus the Religious Crisis of the 1960s, while impacting the mainstream churches adversely, served to advance Pentecostal forms of religious life; the experiential nature of Pentecostal spirituality meshed with the ethos of the era. The emergence of vigorous, noninstitutional Pentecostal movements such as the Indigenous Churches reflected the opportunities of this changing world. Some Pentecostal churches—particularly those influenced by the Latter Rain movement and also the Assemblies of God under Frank Houston's leadership—utilized these opportunities to the full.

The growth of the Pentecostal movement throughout the 1960s was substantial; by the end of the decade it had more than doubled in size from ten years previously.[160] This growth was paralleled by changes in its sectarian attitudes, particularly as the impact of the Charismatic movement intensified. The rise of this movement in the mainstream churches represented an enlargement of the Pentecostal constituency. This was reflected both in the sense that the experience of spiritual gifts was no longer peculiar to Pentecostals, as well as in a widening of their worldviews and perspectives. Thus, while Pentecostal support contributed to the emergence of the Charismatic movement, the reciprocal effect of this movement did much to change Pentecostal attitudes and laid a foundation for further expansion in the 1970s.

Notes

1. Arthur Marwick, *The Sixties: Cultural Revolution in Britain, France, Italy and the United States, c.1958-c.1974* (Oxford: Oxford University Press, 1998), 7, cited in Hugh McLeod, *The Religious Crisis of the 1960s* (Oxford: Oxford University Press, 2007), 1, and thence in Guy, *Shaping Godzone*, 19.

2. Robert Chapman, "From Labour to National," in Rice, *Oxford History of New Zealand*, 381.

3. Sinclair, *History of New Zealand*, 290.

4. National Government Minister of Labour, Tom Shand, cited in Simon Collins, "From guaranteed jobs for all to doleful days," *New Zealand Herald*, 14 October 2000, http://www.nzherald.co.nz/nz/news/article.cfm?c_id=1&objectid=155355 (accessed 14 April 2012).

5. Dunstall, "The Social Pattern," 451.

6. Michael King, *After the War: New Zealand Since 1945* (Auckland: Hodder and Stoughton, 1988), 91, cited in Guy, *Shaping Godzone*, 442.

7. Chapman, "From Labour to National," 382.

8. National Library of New Zealand—Te Puna Mātauranga o Aotearoa, "Television Arrives in New Zealand," http://www.natlib.govt.nz/collections/highlighted-items/television-arrives-in-new-zealand (accessed 16 April 2012). See also King, *Penguin History of New Zealand*, 452.

9. See "Today in History—9 October, The end of the 'six o'clock swill,'" History Group of the New Zealand Ministry for Culture and Heritage, *New Zealand History online—Nga korero a ipurangi o Aotearoa*, updated 20 December 2012 http://www.nzhistory.net.nz/the-end-of-the-six-oclock-swill (accessed 2 December 2013).

10. Clark, *Pentecost at the Ends of the Earth*, 94–95.

11. See King, *Penguin History of New Zealand*, 452–54; Sinclair, *History of New Zealand*, 307; and Guy, *Shaping Godzone*, 269–78.

12. BBC News, "In pictures: The Vietnam War," http://news.bbc.co.uk/2/shared/spl/hi/picture_gallery/05/in_pictures_the_vietnam_war_/html/6.stm (accessed 2 December 2013).

13. So, Guy, *Shaping Godzone*, 442–43.

14. John Capon, *. . . and there was light: The Story of the Nationwide Festival of Light* (London: Lutterworth Press, 1972), 88.

15. "Pill Remains Top Choice," *Timaru Herald*, 7 May 1990, 7.

16. Marwick, *The Sixties*, 4, 5, and 806. Emphasis as cited.

17. See Appendix A.

18. See above, 68.

19. Church statistics derived from the comparative tables given in "Appendix A: Church Statistics 1958–1971," in Knowles, "Some Aspects of the History of the New Life Churches of New Zealand 1960–1990," 381–82.

20. See Appendix A for an analysis of Censuses from 1901 to 2013.

21. McLeod, *The Religious Crisis of the 1960s*, 1.

22. Hutchinson and Wilson, *Let the People Rejoice*, 143. The converts came from the following age-groups: 5–11 years 966 (5.52% of the total); 12–14 years 2,892 (16.53%); 15–18 years 4,123 (23.57%); 19–29 years 4,171 (23.85%); 30–49 3,843 21.97%); and 50 years and above 1,498 (8.56%).

23. John A. T. Robinson, *Honest to God* (London: SCM Press, 1963).

24. For brief discussions of the "Death of God" question in the 1960s, see McGrath, *Christian Theology*, 254–56; and Patrick Gray, "'God is Dead' Controversy," *Religion: New Georgia Encyclopedia*, http://www.georgiaencyclopedia.org/nge/Article.jsp?id=h-861 (accessed 5 July 2012).

25. See above, 2.

26. Davidson, *Christianity in Aotearoa*, 167–70.

27. Laurie Barber, "Lloyd George Knows the Fathers: Professor Geering within the Tradition of Presbyterian Doctrinal Evolution," in *Religions and Change*. International Religious Studies Conference, 22–25 August 1983 at Central Institute of Technology, Heretaunga, New Zealand: to honour the retirement of Professor Lloyd Geering, and in

recognition of his contribution to religious studies, 61 (Wellington: Centre for Continuing Education, 1983), cited in Davidson, *Christianity in Aotearoa*, 170, endnote 25.

28. Davidson, *Christianity in Aotearoa*, 167–70.

29. So, James Veitch, "Lloyd Geering and the Great Debate: A Water-shed in New Zealand Religious History," in *Religions and Change*, 592, cited in Davidson, *Christianity in Aotearoa*, 170, endnote 23.

30. Ray Galvin, "Learning from the Sects," in Ker and Sharpe, *Towards an Authentic New Zealand Theology*, 99.

31. Lineham, "When the Roll is Called Up Yonder, Who'll be There?" in Pratt, *"Rescue the Perishing,"* 16.

32. See Appendix A.

33. See Chapter 6, 96–98.

34. Worsfold, *History of the Charismatic Movements in New Zealand*, 302–3.

35. Ibid, 296.

36. Ibid, 195–96.

37. Ibid, 308.

38. Ibid, 285, note 1.

39. Worsfold, *The Reverend Gilbert and Mrs Alice White*, 89.

40. Ibid, 88; Luke Worsfold, "Subsequence, Prophecy and Church Order," 207.

41. See above, 97.

42. For biographical accounts of Worley, see B. Knowles, "Worley, A. S.," in NIDPCM, 1217; and, more uncritically, Grice, *Apostle to the Nations*.

43. For eyewitness accounts of this campaign, see Knowles, *The History of a New Zealand Pentecostal Movement*, 73–83; Mary Henderson, *From Glory to Glory: A History of the Timaru New Life Centre 1960–1980* (Timaru: Dove Print, 1980), 2–8; and Murray, *Where to World 1977?* 24–29.

44. For example, "Parents say Prayer Transformed Boy's Twisted Foot: Now Walks Unaided," *Timaru Herald*, 6 July 1960, 12; "South Canterbury Dentists Offer Evangelist Facilities to Prove Claims," *Timaru Herald*, 2 September 1960, 12; "Editorial: Faith Healing Mission," *Timaru Herald*, 17 September 1960, 12.

45. *New Zealand Parliamentary Debates*, 324: 2544–45 (23 September 1960).

46. See above, Chapter 2 and Chapter 3.

47. Peter Morrow, Interview, Dunedin, 30 July 1990, cited in Knowles, *The History of a New Zealand Pentecostal Movement*, 89, footnote 17. The audio cassette of this interview is held in BKRP, MS-3530/030, Hocken Library, Dunedin.

48. Knowles, *The History of a New Zealand Pentecostal Movement*, 73–83.

49. Coady, Interview, cited in Knowles, *The History of a New Zealand Pentecostal Movement*, 111.

50. Ibid.

51. Wheeler, Interview, cited in Ibid, 116.

52. Rob and Beryl Wheeler, "Editorial," *Bible Deliverance*, January 1961, 2, cited in Knowles, *The History of a New Zealand Pentecostal Movement*, 91. For a full photostated set of *Bible Deliverance* from April 1959 to March 1966, see BKRP, MS-3530/002, Hocken Library, Dunedin.

53. Rob and Beryl Wheeler, "Editorial: A Call to Action!!!" *Bible Deliverance*, Easter 1961, 2, cited in Knowles, *The History of a New Zealand Pentecostal Movement*, 91.

54. Ibid, 116–17.

55. Knowles, *The History of a New Zealand Pentecostal Movement*, 40–41.

56. Rob Wheeler, "Indigenous Full Gospel Assemblies," *Church Bells*, July 1968, 32, cited in Knowles, *The History of a New Zealand Pentecostal Movement*, vi-vii. For a full photostated set of *Church Bells* from June 1966 to September 1968, see BKRP, MS-3530/003, Hocken Library, Dunedin.

57. Bill Hotter, comment to author, Christchurch, December 1989, cited in Knowles, *The History of a New Zealand Pentecostal Movement*, 119. Emphasis as cited.

58. Knowles, *The History of a New Zealand Pentecostal Movement*, vii.

59. Lineham, "Tongues Must Cease": 16.

60. Ibid: 15.

61. Clark, Interview, cited in Knowles, "Some Aspects of the History of the New Life Churches of New Zealand," 48, footnote 71.

62. Clark, *Pentecost at the Ends of the Earth*, 97.

63. Assemblies of God in New Zealand, "Our History," 6–7. http://www.agnz.org/history.htm (accessed 4 September 2007). See also Houston, *Being Frank*, 114–15.

64. Clark, *Pentecost at the Ends of the Earth*, 102 and note 5.

65. Rob Wheeler, cited in Hutchinson, "Wheeler, Rob," ADPCM.

66. Hutchinson, "Wheeler, Rob," ADPCM.

67. Clark, *Pentecost at the Ends of the Earth*, 103.

68. Ibid, 95.

69. Houston, *Being Frank*, 125. See also Worsfold, *History of the Charismatic Movements in New Zealand*, 216–17.

70. Clark, *Pentecost at the Ends of the Earth*, 106–7.

71. Shane Clifton, "The Apostolic Revolution and the Ecclesiology of the AoGA," *Australasian Pentecostal Studies*, no. 9 (March 2006), http://webjournals.alphacrucis.edu.au/journals/aps/issue-9/03-the-apostolic-revolution-and-the-ecclesiology-o/ (accessed 24 May 2012). See also Clifton, "An Analysis of the Developing Ecclesiology of the Assemblies of God in Australia" (PhD thesis in Theology, Australian Catholic University, 2005), 199, 205 and 208–9; and Clifton, *Pentecostal Churches in Transition: Analysing the Developing Ecclesiology of the Assemblies of God in Australia* (Leiden; Boston: Brill, 2009), 144–50.

72. Worsfold, *History of the Charismatic Movements in New Zealand*, 222.

73. Clark, *Pentecost at the Ends of the Earth*, 104.

74. Ibid.

75. For an example of this, see Knowles, *The History of a New Zealand Pentecostal Movement*, 107. See also Houston, *Being Frank*, 114–15.

76. Clark, *Pentecost at the Ends of the Earth*, 115–17.

77. Assemblies of God in New Zealand, "Our History," 6–7.

78. MacFarlane, "Houston, William Francis," ADPCM.

79. Clark, *Pentecost at the Ends of the Earth*, 97.

80. Carew and Troughton, "Māori Participation in the Assemblies of God," 104–5.

81. Clark, *Pentecost at the Ends of the Earth*, 122; Houston, *Being Frank*, 126; Worsfold, *History of the Charismatic Movements in New Zealand*, 216..

82. MacFarlane, "Houston, William Francis," ADPCM.

83. Clark, *Pentecost at the Ends of the Earth*, 115–17.

84. For discussions of Māori participation in the Assemblies of God, see Carew and Troughton, "Māori Participation in the Assemblies of God," 91–109; and for a more general approach, focusing on the Assemblies of God, ACTs Church (formerly the Apostolic Churches) and the Destiny Church, see Simon Moetara, "Māori and Pentecostal Christi-

anity in Aotearoa New Zealand," in Morrison et al., *Mana Māori and Christianity*, 73–90.

85. See below, 237.

86. Clark, *Pentecost at the Ends of the Earth*, 130.

87. This figure was obtained by taking the sixteen congregations listed as being in the movement in 1954 (Worsfold, *History of the Charismatic Movements in New Zealand*) and adding the new assemblies affiliated to the movement from 1954 up to 1960 (Clark, *Pentecost at the Ends of the Earth*, 82–90).

88. Clark, *Pentecost at the Ends of the Earth*, 127.

89. See Appendix A.

90. Cecily Worsfold, cited in Luke Worsfold, "Subsequence, Prophecy and Church Order," 9, footnote 28. Cecily Worsfold's husband James was the pastor of the Dunedin Apostolic Church at the time.

91. See, for example, Henderson, *From Glory to Glory*, 19; Murray, *Where to World 1977?* 25. See also Mrs. Dorothy Stewart, Interview, cited in Eric Hodgkinson, "The Independent Pentecostal Movement" (Research Essay in New Zealand Religious History, Massey University, 1989 (handwritten)), 3, BKRP, MS-3530/019, Hocken Library, Dunedin.

92. G. H. Morling, "Pentecostalism," *New Zealand Baptist* 77.80 (1961): 142–44, cited in Luke Worsfold, "Subsequence, Prophecy and Church Order," 44. For a biography of Morling, see E. R. Rogers, "Morling, George Henry (1891–1974)," *Australian Dictionary of Evangelical Biography* http://webjournals.ac.edu.au/journals/adeb/m_/morling-george-henry-1891-1974/ (accessed 12 October 2012).

93. A. L. Burrow, "The Tongues Movement," *The Reaper* 41.5 (1962): 176–80 and 252–55, cited in Luke Worsfold, "Subsequence, Prophecy and Church Order," 45. For a biography of Burrow, see Brian Dickey, "Burrow, Allan Lincoln John (1912–1976?)," *Australian Dictionary of Evangelical Biography* http://webjournals.ac.edu.au/journals/adeb/b_/burrow-allan-lincoln-john-1912-1976/ (accessed 12 October 2012).

94. Rob Wheeler, "Will God Revive the Historic Churches?" *Bible Deliverance*, April 1965, 13–15.

95. See below, 144.

96. Ken Wright, Taped Interview in response to Questionnaire, Palmerston North, April 1990, cited in Knowles, *The History of a New Zealand Pentecostal Movement*, 149–50. The audio cassette of this interview is held in BKRP, MS-3530/040, Hocken Library, Dunedin.

97. Knowles, *The History of a New Zealand Pentecostal Movement*, 176. Emphasis as cited.

98. See above, 56 and 73–74.

99. "Sunday Services," *Press*, 1 April 1961, 16.

100. Wheeler, Interview, cited in Knowles, *The History of a New Zealand Pentecostal Movement*, 105–6.

101. "Sunday Services," *Press*, 15 April 1961, 18; and 22 April 1961, 18.

102. See above, 118.

103. Clifton, "An Analysis of the Developing Ecclesiology of the Assemblies of God in Australia," 168 and footnote 584.

104. Ralph R. Read, *Water Baptism: The Formula and its Meaning. A Study of the Trinitarian Formula of Matthew 28 v.19 and the Formula of "Oneness" Teachers: A Guide and a*

Refutation ([Christchurch]: New Zealand Pentecostal Fellowship Publication, [1966]). Copy held in BKRP, MS-3530/022, Hocken Library, Dunedin.

105. See Knowles, *The History of a New Zealand Pentecostal Movement*, 17–26 for a coverage of the controversy.

106. Minute Book 1934–1951, Executive Council, Representing the Board of Elders of the Pentecostal Church of N.Z. (Inc.), Wellington; Minute Book 1934–1951, Board of Elders of the Pentecostal Church of N.Z. (Inc.), Wellington; and Minute Book 8 July 1942–3 December 1951, Wellington Pentecostal Evangelical Mission, Wellington.

107. Worsfold Research Papers, Wellington.

108. Roberts to Douglas, 27 May 1952, in Conner, *This is My Story*, 159–63.

109. Roberts, *Beware of the New Revelation on Water Baptism*, 24–31, cited in Worsfold, *History of the Charismatic Movements in New Zealand*, 184–90; Pennington, Pamphlet on "the Name" controversy, Worsfold Research Papers, Wellington, 1946.

110. Worsfold to Knowles, 14 January 1989, cited in Knowles, *The History of a New Zealand Pentecostal Movement*, 23, footnote 19.

111. Knowles, *The History of a New Zealand Pentecostal Movement*, 115.

112. Barrett, *World Christian Encyclopedia*, s.v. "New Zealand," Table 2.

113. Wheeler, Interview, cited in Knowles, *The History of a New Zealand Pentecostal Movement*, 24, footnote 24.

114. See Appendix A.

115. Clark, *Pentecost at the Ends of the Earth*, 102.

116. Gerlach and Hine, *People, Power, Change*, xvii.

117. Worsfold, *History of the Charismatic Movements in New Zealand*, 312–13; also Clark, *Pentecost at the Ends of the Earth*, 112.

118. Wheeler, Interview (quoting James Worsfold), cited in Knowles, *The History of a New Zealand Pentecostal Movement*, 250.

119. Clark, *Pentecost at the Ends of the Earth*, 113.

120. Clark, Interview, cited in Knowles, *The History of a New Zealand Pentecostal Movement*, 249.

121. Ibid, 25, 249–50.

122. Clifton, "An Analysis of the Developing Ecclesiology of the Assemblies of God in Australia," 201, footnote 689.

123. Knowles, *The History of a New Zealand Pentecostal Movement*, 61, 71, 90–92 and 115.

124. Elaine Bolitho, "With Hearts Strangely Warmed: The Charismatic Movement in the New Zealand Methodist Church," *Affirm* 5, no. 1 (Autumn 1997): 21.

125. The best account of this early period is Lineham, "Tongues must cease": 7–52. See also Knowles, *The History of a New Zealand Pentecostal Movement*, 143–51; and Hodgkinson, "The Independent Pentecostal Movement." For some examples of Methodist charismatics in the 1950s, see Bolitho, "With Hearts Strangely Warmed": 20.

126. Hodgkinson, "The Independent Pentecostal Movement," 13. For Du Plessis' autobiography, see David du Plessis, as told to Bob Slosser, *A Man Called Mr. Pentecost* (Plainfield, NJ: Logos International, 1977). Also see R. P. Spittler, "Du Plessis, David Johannes," in NIDPCM, 589–93.

127. For a brief biographical note on Bennett, see L. Christensen, "Bennett, Dennis Joseph, and Rita," in NIDPCM, 369–70.

128. For a brief biographical note on Harper, see P. D. Hocken, "Harper, Michael Claude," in NIDPCM, 689–90.

129. Donald Battley, "Charismatic Renewal: A View from the Inside," *Ecumenical Review*, no. 38 (1986): 49.
130. Wright, Interview, cited in Knowles, *The History of a New Zealand Pentecostal Movement*, 144–45.
131. Lineham, "Tongues must cease": 18–19.
132. Ibid: 22.
133. Ibid: 23. For a similar assessment of McAlpine, see Natalie Steel, *Milton Smith: A Man After God's Heart* (Auckland: Castle Publishing, 2003), 126–27.
134. Lineham, "Tongues must cease": 40; Steel, *Milton Smith*, 137–38.
135. Lineham, "Tongues must cease": 23–27 and 40–41.
136. "Most Unique Convention in History of New Zealand," *Gospel Truth*, August 1964, 6. For a full set of *Gospel Truth* from June 1964 to April 1965, see BKRP, MS-3530/004, Hocken Library, Dunedin. Most of this article was reprinted in Wheeler's *Bible Deliverance*, October 1964, 15. For a similar perception of the Conference, from a charismatic perspective, see Steel, *Milton Smith*, 138–39.
137. David Wilkerson, *The Cross and the Switchblade*, with John and Elizabeth Sherrill (1963; London: Hodder and Stoughton, 1967).
138. Lineham, "Tongues must cease": 20.
139. *Logos*, August 1966, 7.
140. John L. Sherrill, *They Speak with Other Tongues* (New York: McGraw Hill, [1964]).
141. Michael Harper, *As at the Beginning: The Twentieth Century Pentecostal Revival* (London: Hodder and Stoughton, 1965).
142. Dennis J. Bennett, *Nine O'Clock in the Morning* (Plainfield, NJ: Logos International, 1970).
143. Allan G. Neil, "Institutional Churches and the Charismatic Renewal: A Study of the Charismatic Renewal in the Anglican Church and the Roman Catholic Church in New Zealand" (STh Diploma in Church History, Joint Board of Theological Studies, 1974), 88.
144. Wright, Interview, cited in Knowles, *The History of a New Zealand Pentecostal Movement*, 147.
145. Wright, Interview, cited in Knowles, *The History of a New Zealand Pentecostal Movement*, 149.
146. Ibid.
147. Blumhofer, *The Assemblies of God*, 2:53 and 2:103–5.
148. See above, 118 and 120–21; See also 144.
149. Lineham, "Tongues must cease": 15.
150. Neil, "Institutional Churches and the Charismatic Renewal," 134 and 11–16.
151. Ibid, 106–7.
152. Battley, "Charismatic Renewal: A View from the Inside," 49.
153. Bolitho, "With Hearts Strangely Warmed": 21.
154. Stephen J. Land, "Pentecostal Spirituality: Living in the Spirit," in *Christian Spirituality: Post-Reformation and Modern*. World Spirituality: An Encyclopedic History of the Religious Quest, ed. Louis Dupré and Don E. Saliers, in collaboration with John Meyendorff, 18:485 (New York: Crossroad, 1989). See also Bradley Holt, "Spiritualities of the Twentieth Century," in *The Story of Christian Spirituality: Two Thousand Years, from East to West*, ed. Gordon Mursell, 313 (Oxford: Lion Publishing, 2001).

155. Dale Williamson, "An Uncomfortable Engagement: The Charismatic Movement in the New Zealand Anglican Church 1965–85" (PhD thesis in Church History, University of Otago, 2008), 18–19.

156. For an account of this, see T. P. Thigpen, "Catholic Charismatic Renewal," in NIDPCM, 460–67.

157. Hodgkinson, "The Independent Pentecostal Movement," 11.

158. For Houston's and Midgley's churches, see Clifton, "An Analysis of the Developing Ecclesiology of the Assemblies of God in Australia," 201 and footnote 688; for Morrow's church, see Knowles, *The History of a New Zealand Pentecostal Movement*, 161–69.

159. Kevin Ward, "The charismatic movement in New Zealand: Sovereign move of God or cultural captivity of the gospel?" (paper presented at University of Otago Seminar, Dunedin, 2010), 2. See also Knowles, "Some Aspects of the History of the New Life Churches of New Zealand," 117.

160. See Appendix A.

Chapter 8

Beyond the 1960s: Postmodernity, Secularization and the Relocation of Authority

What processes of historical change drove the transformations of the 1960s? While it is comparatively easy to describe "what happened," it is more difficult to explain "what was going on." The raw data of history involves both event and process. To capture these involves both observation and evaluation and their recording necessitates the techniques of narrative and analysis. The events of the 1960s have been described in chapter 7; this chapter focusses on their theoretical explanation. In particular, it critically examines the issues of postmodernity and secularization, before offering an alternative interpretation based on the increasing suspicion of institutions and the resultant relocation of authority.

The Rise of Postmodernity

As noted in the previous chapter, the pervasive effects of the Religious Crisis of the 1960s were experienced throughout the Western world.[1] The crisis was reflected in a profound change in religiosity—together with its corollary, an ongoing decline in church adherence—and is frequently interpreted as part of a paradigm shift from modernity to postmodernity. Although both of these terms are diffuse and ill-defined,[2] several features characterize this basic reorientation of social and cultural reality. French philosopher Jean-François Lyotard has famously defined the term "postmodern" as indicating "incredulity towards metanarratives" [*l'incrédulité à l'égard des métarécits*].[3] He uses the term "metanarrative" to indicate a legitimizing philosophy of history, an overarching progression of which historical trends and events are part and which they are said to exemplify.[4]

Numerous examples of metanarratives can be drawn from both sacred and secular history. Religious instances include the salvation-history of the Biblical accounts, Jesus' teaching regarding the both-here-and-coming Kingdom of God and Augustine of Hippo's theology of the eschatological City of God. Secular metanarratives have taken political, scientific and philosophical forms. An obvious political example is the Marxist idea of the inexorable dialectical advance of history, leading to the emancipating triumph of the revolutionary proletariat and the advent of the classless society. In the field of science, one instance is the process of evolution from lower to higher orders of organism; another is the idea of onward scientific progress which has characterized much of the modern era. In philosophy, the Enlightenment is viewed as a progression and liberation from oppressive dogmatism by the free and constructive use of reason to understand the world and thus as a movement from obscurity to light. A more extreme philosophical example is the idealistic Hegelian concept of the development and realization of Absolute Spirit, leading to the Kingdom of the Spirit as the goal of the entire process of history.[5]

All of these metanarratives contain the ideas of *progress* and *teleology*; postmodernism—as Jean-François Lyotard defines it—disallows these teleological frameworks, explicitly rejecting the proposition that the human race is following any particular course of development.[6] Since historiography—or the selection and interpretation of events and the allocation of significance to them—is a product of the historian's perspective, any unifying overarching metanarrative represents an imposed subjectivism and must be contested. (Hence social historian Professor E. H. Carr's famous admonition: "Before you study the history study the historian. . . . Before you study the historian, study his [sic] historical and social environment.")[7] History thus becomes atomized and relativized; the emphasis shifts from macrohistory to microhistory.[8] But one could also ask the question: might not the movement from modernity to postmodernity *itself* be construed as having elements of a metanarrative? If this is the case, then Lyotard's "incredulity towards metanarratives" surely becomes self-contradictory.

Another way of categorizing this paradigm shift is Polish sociologist Zygmunt Baumann's description of the new order as a "liquid" or "fluid" modernity. This contrasts with "solid" or "heavy" modernity, which was characterized by stable order and long-term commitment and by set norms and rules providing the illusion of mutual responsibility. In "liquid" modernity, social matrices such as gender, class, vocation and ethical orientation are invalidated as preservatives of identity; the norms of commitment and belonging become limited, flexible and temporary. Thus, traditional institutions of authority are dissolved and the construction of identity is individualized.[9] As several authors have noted, this liquescence has implications for the nature of the Christian Church. American theologian Leonard Sweet, for example, describes the postmodern era as "chaos, uncertainty, otherness, multiplicity and change," i.e., liquid "'wavescapes,' with the waters always changing and the surface never the same."[10] In this new world, he insists, the Church must adapt, becoming a fluid, flexible "aquachurch." Similarly, British theologian Pete Ward stresses the need to locate Christian identity outside the formal structures of "solid" Church institutions. He notes that these authoritarian and boundary-obsessed institutions demand "obedience, formalised association, hierarchy and defined limits" and extract "costly allegiance from [their] participants." By contrast, Christian identity in the Liquid Church is constructed outside formal structures and institutions, since it is centered on participation and flexibility rather than on obligation and commitment. Such a church represents a transition from authority to example and from refuge to network, reshaping itself around the worshippers as consumers, rather than as members.[11]

This contrast between authority and example highlights another feature of the postmodern era—the collapse of institutional authority. Since postmodernism abandons all absolutes, fixed certainties and foundations, it is characterized by relativism and pluralism. This, in turn, renders all truth statements limited, since these are made within a specific human perspective which must be recognized and deconstructed.[12] Their situatedness means that truth statements can be valid only within the context within which they are made; they cannot apply beyond this context. Institutions of authority therefore lose their public influence and claims to obedience; the churches—as traditional institutions of Christian authority—have been particularly hard hit in this regard. Consequently, theologians Edward Farley and Peter Hodgson argue, "the house of authority has collapsed, despite the fact that many people still try to live in it." (It should be noted, however, that they attribute this collapse to *modernity*, rather than to postmodernism.)[13] This statement, although extreme, is usually applied to the challenges of modern consciousness towards scriptural and traditional authorities, deriving from historical, sociophenomenological and theological criticism.[14] It could also be used as a convenient shorthand term for changing attitudes to institutional authority from the 1960s on. However, this should not be overstated since, although there was something of a legitimation crisis in the 1960s,[15] this challenge to authority did not necessarily imply a general anarchy. Indeed, in New Zealand "the underlying changes in the golden 1960s were social rather than political, ... individual rather than public. If they took a mass form they did so as protest movements, confronting or, at the most, working alongside the party structures."[16] Challenges to institutional authority were therefore modest and muted. What would emerge in the late 1960s were the beginnings of a suspicion of the institutions that had served as legitimators of social belonging and action. As will be argued later in this chapter, traditional standards of authority were deinstitutionalized and relocated during that decade, rather than rejected outright.

Secularization and the Decline of Church Adherence

One particular manifestation of postmodernity—and the usual suspect in investigations of declining Church adherence and attendance in New Zealand—is secularization. Sociologist Bryan Wilson has defined this as "the process whereby religious thinking, practice and institutions lose social significance."[17] He also notes that its effects may vary, depending on the teachings and characteristics of the sect or movement so affected and on the society, context and region within which the process takes place.[18] Despite this variety, a number of indicators enable the effects of secularization to be measured. These include declines in "religious attendance, commitment to orthodox belief, support for organized religion in terms of payments, membership, and respect, and ... the importance which religious activities such as festivals assume in social life."[19]

There is now a large body of literature by historians and sociologists that attempts to explain the religious crisis of the 1960s in terms of secularization.[20] Consequently, the period is fast becoming characterized as "the secularisation decade" in New Zealand and elsewhere.[21] In this country, much of this characterization is due to the strong emphasis placed on secularization by Lloyd Geering and his disciple, Religious Studies lecturer Jim Veitch, over the last forty years. Geering has been described as "the most significant scholar in . . . religious studies in New Zealand"[22] and as "the national prophet of our secularity."[23] His writing focus is on the role of Christianity in a secular world;[24] the titles of his numerous publications give an indication of this secularist emphasis. Some of the more important include *God in the New World* (1968), *Faith's New Age* (1980), *Tomorrow's God* (1994) and *Christianity without God* (2002).[25] Geering was a superbly articulate communicator and his books and articles made him a household name in New Zealand. Consequently, he and Veitch were usually the ones cited by the New Zealand media on religious subjects, a role labeled somewhat caustically "the darlings of the media" by sociologist of religion Kevin Ward.[26] This gave their views a dominant place in New Zealand religious discourse—to the exclusion of other viewpoints—and reinforced the supremacy of the secularization thesis as a preferred explanation for the changing status of Christianity. However, Emeritus Professor of Sociology David Martin has perceptively observed that proponents of this thesis tend to present it in prescriptive, rather than descriptive, terms; secularization is interpreted as what *should be* happening, rather than what *is* happening.[27] Similar criticisms of the secularist worldview have also been made by scholars such as theologian John Milbank and sociologist/philosopher Jürgen Habermas.[28]

The tide of secularization now appears to be turning, both within New Zealand and overseas and the ultimate secularity of society is much less assured. A comparison of two New Zealand academic conferences on Secularization—held twenty-six years apart—makes this point clearly. The papers from the first conference, held in 1976, all take secularization for granted; the majority of those from the 2002 conference question the inevitability of the secularization process to some extent.[29] It is increasingly being recognized that religion has not died out as the secularists had predicted and, indeed, that religious beliefs continue to be strongly held and spirituality to be strongly pursued. An examination of the "Religion" section of any bookstore will demonstrate a much greater range of religious titles on the shelves now than was the case in the supposedly more religious 1960s. The increasingly common practice of Māori *karakia* [prayers, incantations] and ceremonies such as the lifting of *tapu* [spiritual restrictions] at public functions is another example of religiosity "coming through the backdoor," somewhat to the secularists' dismay.[30] Furthermore, as Bruce Knox—former Executive Director of the Bible College of New Zealand—has shown, interest in theological education has grown in New Zealand. The number of students taking theological subjects at tertiary institutions in this country increased by 98% between 1988 and 1999—this at a time when church rolls were continuing to fall. Furthermore, more than two-thirds of these students were doing theological study for personal reasons; only 8.6% were studying in preparation for Christian ministry in the churches.[31] Knox concludes that this points to the continuing existence of active enquiry into Christian things and thus challenges the popular view that Christianity is in decline in New Zealand.[32]

It is therefore evident that spirituality has not died out. Indeed, as theologian Harvey Cox has noted, "today [in 1995] it is secularity, not spirituality, that may be headed for extinction."[33] (Cox's comment is a particularly telling one, given that his book *The Secular City*,[34] published thirty years earlier, was one of the "Bibles" of the secularists in the 1960s. Cox has since retreated from his earlier secularist views and now believes that the growth of Pentecostalism exemplifies this global religious renaissance.)[35] Other scholars also refer to the resacralizing of the world and to the Spirituality Revolution that now appears to be emerging.[36] Even among those scholars who insist that the secularization process is to some extent valid, there is a circumscription of its influence and effect. Thus, "instead of secularisation as an event 'after Christendom,' ... we have secularisation as a set of dynamics 'within Christendom.' ...Where religion has flourished in the west, ... it has done so by breaking out of the didactic mode of territorial Christendom. ... Decline does not mean death—the difference is important."[37] Secularization therefore represents a *reorientation*, rather than a *relinquishing*, of religious belief. This is manifest, not in the falling-off of spirituality and the death of Christianity, but in the decline of the institutions that have characterized it. This institutional diminution will be explored in the next section.

Less institutional forms of Christianity have both reflected and benefitted from these changes. The rise of the Pentecostal and charismatic movements has paralleled the decline of mainstream, institutional, Christianity worldwide. It is estimated that the global population of Pentecostals has increased from 72.2 million, or 5.84% of the Christian population, in 1970 to 523.8 million, or 26.19% of the Christian population, in 2000.[38] This Pentecostal expansion is particularly strong in Latin America; David Martin calls this growth "the largest global shift in the religious market place over the last 40 years [i.e., from 1960 to 2000]."[39] In New Zealand, Pentecostal groups grew 1,451.79% over the same period, from 4,333 adherents in 1961 to 67,239 in 2001.[40] This growth reflects, not a decline of Christian spirituality, but rather a deinstitutionalization of Christian participation. Profound changes *are* taking place in the institutional character of Christianity, but, as church historian Dominic Erdozain emphasizes, this does necessarily not mean its demise. As with American author Mark Twain, reports of Christianity's death have been greatly exaggerated.

Suspicion towards Institutions and the Relocation of Authority

Given the persistence of spirituality—despite the once-confident predictions of the secularists—and the liquescence of postmodernity, other explanations must be sought for the changing patterns of religiosity and adherence since the 1960s. These must account for both the declining participation in mainstream church life and the rise of Pentecostal and charismatic forms of spirituality. It is argued that one such interpretation—an increasing suspicion towards institutional forms of belonging and legitimation, with a concomitant relocation of authority—does much to explain these developments.

One factor that frequently is overlooked by proponents of the secularization theory is that the process of institutional decline is not limited to religious bodies. Suspicion towards institutions is manifest both in a dwindling core of committed membership and in a reluctance to accept institutional claims of authority. While this is most marked in the decline of church membership—which, in New Zealand, is voluntarist in nature—this phobia of commitment is reflected elsewhere also. In 2001, the International Year of the Volunteer, articles appeared in the secular press indicating the decline of all kinds of voluntary organizations and clubs in this country.[41] Furthermore, Kevin Ward has drawn an illuminating analogy from Rugby football, which has the status of a national religion in New Zealand. He observes that although membership of Rugby clubs in this country declined from 400,000 in 1970 to 120,000 by 2000, enthusiasm for the game remains widespread.[42] (The extent of this continuing interest was demonstrated by the excitement when New Zealand hosted and won the quadrennial Rugby World Cup tournament in 2011.) Ward finds the same phenomenon—i.e., of participation, but not membership—replicated in running clubs.[43] In other words, the decline in membership does not reflect a lack of interest, but rather a reluctance to commit to the institutions that service this interest. The suspicion of institutions and the reluctance to commit to membership in them therefore extends much further than religious groups.

The suspicion of organizational institutions is paralleled by a rejection of their bureaucratic modes of authority. Since current sociological theory views institutions as "comprising changing patterns of behavior based on relatively ... stable value systems,"[44] any diminution of this authority is reflected in their value systems. This contraction is mirrored in altered modes of behavior, particularly those based upon traditional forms of religious or church authority (for example, "no sex before marriage"). The churches are therefore fighting a losing battle to maintain traditional social mores, since their institutional authority is no longer universally accepted in the public arena. Jürgen Habermas categorizes this challenge as a "legitimation crisis," taking the revised Marxist view that "in the final analysis, [the] *class structure* is the source of the legitimation deficit."[45] It should be noted carefully, however, that this declining authority is not due to the process of secularization *per se*, but rather to the wider process of declining institutional—i.e., bureaucratic—authority. Nor is it limited to the churches, but is more pervasive, affecting all organizations and institutions of authority.

However, this rejection of authority—despite the reference of Edward Farley and Peter Hodgson to "the collapse of the house of authority"[46]—is neither total nor universally pervasive. The point at issue was the institution, not the authority. As I have argued elsewhere,[47] the suspicion of institutional forms of authority during the 1960s represents the *relocation*, rather than the *rejection*, of authority. In the later 1960s, particularly, the youth culture was marked by a resistance to collectively imposed forms of authority. This involved the rejection of traditional institutional standards of conduct, with the location of authority being both *personalized* and *internalized*: "do your own thing!" and "if it feels good, do it!"

This dependence on internal forms of authority was based on personal awareness and experience, either as an individual, or as part of a group. This was most evident in the drug culture. However, this shift should not be overemphasized, since elements of conventionality and continuity continued in the 1960s alongside these breakouts from conformity. The Youth Counterculture of the later 1960s was not as pronounced, militant, or oppositional in New Zealand as was the case overseas. Nevertheless, this marked the beginnings of a relocation of authority away from traditional, external institutions towards an internalized, autonomous authority. Or, to put it another way, a rejection of bureaucratic modes of power and a move towards personalized and individualized—i.e., charismatic—sources of authority.

The effect of this relocation was twofold. Firstly, it accelerated the decline of traditional institutions—such as the mainstream churches—and vitiated their ability to impose external norms of authority and behavior. Secondly, the focus on individualized authority, combined with a stress on values and things of the spirit, contributed to the emergence of a number of antimaterialist movements in the later 1960s. As Graeme Dunstall neatly puts it: "During the late 1960s a range of youthful voices articulated the problems of the spirit in a materialistic culture."[48] These voices included those of groups as diverse as the Values Party, the Hippie movement, the devotees of Hare Krishna and—especially—the Pentecostal and Charismatic movements. Even though the latter movements could be described as fundamentalist and hence holding to an authoritative external institution, i.e., the Bible, this was mediated in personalized and internalized ways. In the climate of the late 1960s, the individual's experience of spiritual reality was the crucial determinant. In contrast to the Billy Graham-type Evangelicalism of the late 1950s, "the Bible says" was now "the Bible says *to me*." External authorities, such as pastors and Bible teachers, were recognized and valued as charismatic authorities, but subordinated to the new criteria of internalized and personalized spiritual experience. The stress on a personal, charismatic experience of the Spirit, rather than on material, visible, bureaucratic institutions of authority aligned these new Pentecostal churches with the ethos of the era. The mainstream churches, because more institutional and organizational, were unable to respond in the same way.

It might seem ironic that the expansion of Pentecostalism in the 1960s should be linked so closely to this relocation of authority, given the reputation of the movement for strong, authoritative leadership. This leadership was, however, both personal, located in the person of the pastor or leader and charismatic, anchored in the empowering of the Holy Spirit, rather than bureaucratic and institutional. This led to the rapid evolution of the movement during the 1960s and 1970s. Mark Hutchinson has observed that the independent Latter Rain churches represented a significant deinstitutionalization in the changing ethos of Pentecostalism. "The emergence of the latter rain churches coincided with the postwar breakup of traditional relationships between mainline churches and the state, and so in a sense the emergence of [independent Latter Rain-influenced evangelist Rob] Wheeler and others in the New Zealand secular and religious media is a marker of the progress of de-instutionalisation [*sic*]."[49] This process gave the Latter Rain adherents considerable freedom and access to spiritual—i.e., charismatic—power. In this respect, social historian Robert Mapes Anderson's well-known "Vision of the

Disinherited" hypothesis is, to a limited extent, applicable.[50] However, the element of economic deprivation was absent, since the New Zealand Pentecostal movement expanded in the 1960s during a time of unparalleled national prosperity. This freedom of action and noninstitutional association was a key reason why the independent Latter Rain churches associated with Wheeler and his colleagues were at the forefront of Pentecostal expansion in the early 1960s. The open attitudes of Frank Houston and Bob Midgley also enabled the Assemblies of God to gain traction in the later 1960s.[51] By contrast other, more institutional, Pentecostal churches remained closed and suspicious until the end of the decade.[52]

However, the charismatic freedom of the Latter Rain churches became increasingly defined and circumscribed as the movement grew. For example, a common feature in the early 1960s was Body Ministry around the Communion table on Sunday morning. This practice had some similarity to Brethren patterns,[53] whereby any member of the local congregation [i.e., "the Body of Christ"] was free to preach, testify, or operate a spiritual gift as the Spirit moved them. The key criterion was that what was shared should fit in to the theme that the Holy Spirit was bringing out during the meeting. This sensitivity to the Spirit was highly developed and the way in which this Body Ministry flowed together was at times extraordinary. (The author was present on one occasion when a "spirit of prophecy" descended on the congregation and five or six people prophesied consecutively in one single prophetic utterance. Some of those prophesying would instantly pick up the flow of the prophecy in midsentence if another person hesitated or stopped speaking.) However, such freewheeling charismatic liberty became less common as the movement grew. Within five years, the freedom to preach was increasingly becoming limited to those who were recognized as having leadership potential and who could be trusted to discern and follow the theme of the Holy Spirit. This reflected the beginnings of a routinization of charisma, whereby recognition of ministry became the determining factor and charismatic freedom to minister increasingly dependent on this.[54] As with the Early Church, charismatic freedom continued, but increasingly became the province of charismatic leaders, rather than the whole People of God.

The freedom and deinstitutionalization brought by the Latter Rain movement in the 1960s also influenced the ways in which Pentecostal churches responded to the Charismatic movement. Early support came from the Latter Rain churches—by now becoming known as the Indigenous Churches of New Zealand—and from that section of the Assemblies of God associated with Frank Houston and Bob Midgley. Other sections of the Assemblies of God were less positive in their attitudes. In Australia, Ralph Read took issue with the doctrinal emphases of the Charismatic movement, publishing a warning in the Australian *Evangel* in 1969 against too close an association with it.[55] (Read's warning represents a good example of a bureaucratic form of Pentecostal leadership.) In the American context, Edith Blumhofer has castigated the Assemblies of God in her history of the movement for their attitudes to the Latter Rain and the emerging Charismatic movement.[56] However these cold shoulder approaches were not peculiar to the Assemblies of God, but were widespread amongst denominational Pentecostals. David du Plessis lamented "an apparent tendency to ignore the independent Pentecostals [this would have included the Latter Rain movement] in favor of organized movements such as the Assemblies of God, the Church of God, and the like." He sadly observed that although "there were dozens of pastors from independent Pentecostal churches [at the World Pentecostal Conference in Toronto in 1958], ... they were being ignored."[57] Some of this attitude was replicated in Australasia, but more so in Australia than in New Zealand.[58] The Apostolic Church remained cautious, despite their association with mainstream church ministers in local Ministers' Fraternals,[59] since they saw the operation of spiritual gifts as requiring the oversight of the apostles and prophets.[60] And, given the challenges by prophet Wilf Frater to the authority of the apostles in the Apostolic Church Council during the 1970s—which oversight he saw as repressing prophetic operation[61]—it is evident that this functioned as a means of bureaucratic control. Thus those independent Pentecostal churches which had been influenced by the Latter Rain movement were central in the development of receptivity to the Charismatic movement. Their deinstitutionalized, charismatic ethos enabled them to benefit from the suspicion of institutional authority that characterized the era.

Why, then, should these churches—as with other Pentecostal churches—move in a more authoritarian direction after the 1960s? The key lies in the nature of Pentecostal authority. This was both charismatic and personal, with the locus of power being the giftedness of the leader, rather than an organizational or denominational institution. This power did not vitiate the principle of the relocation of authority; rather it represented a concentration and recognition of that authority in the spiritually gifted leaders who had emerged from among the congregation. This was similar to the plight of the animals in novelist George Orwell's well-known *Animal Farm*: "All animals are equal" now became "All animals are equal, but some animals are more equal than others."[62] A further complicating factor was the growth of the individual churches in the movement. The typical Pentecostal leadership role of the charismatic sole pastor worked well in small congregations, where people were known and trust could be maintained. As the movement grew, these congregations became larger and more anonymous and—since organizational checks and balances had not yet been developed—this concentrated and intensified the power of the leader. The result was that Pentecostalism came to represent a small-church movement become large, with considerable dangers for the safety of both its leadership and its congregations. Many of the scandals that emerged in Pentecostal churches in later years had their roots in precisely this development.

Conclusion

Following the Religious Crisis of the 1960s, religiosity has changed and church adherence has decreased—in some cases precipitously—over the last four decades. A second, parallel trend has also appeared, namely, the rise of the Pentecostal and charismatic movements over the same period. Both the decline in church adherence and the growth of Pentecostalism are worldwide developments with particular implications for Christianity in the West. These facts are clear; their interpretation is much less so. The paradigm shifts that accompanied the rise of

Postmodernity have fostered the evolution of new, more "liquid" forms of social association. However, it is going too far to argue that these changes have resulted in the collapse of authority. Similarly, the process of secularization has been invoked to explain changing attitudes towards Christianity. This explanation appears valid only if the process is seen in terms of a reorientation, rather than the demise, of Christianity. Otherwise, it does not appear to match the facts of the continuing and changing forms of spiritual vitality.

The key element in these changes appears to be deinstitutionalization. This was reflected in an increasing suspicion of external institutions, together with an internalized, personal, relocation of authority. This shift was widespread in the social context and, although not peculiar to Christian and church institutions, does explain both the decline of institutional forms of Christianity and the rise of charismatic forms of spirituality. The charismatic freedom and internalized experiential authority espoused by the Pentecostal and Charismatic movements matched the ethos of the era, in a way that the institutional authority of denominational churches did not. Consequently, the one and the same process contributed to both the decline of mainstream Christianity and the rise of charismatic forms of spirituality.

However, this deinstitutionalized charismatic freedom—particularly that espoused by the Latter Rain movement—became more routinized and channeled into recognized ministry as the Pentecostal movement evolved. The initial spiritual freedom of the whole body of believers became the freedom of the charismatic leader, who embodied and exemplified the power of the Spirit. This power was personal and charismatic, rather than organizational and institutional. It therefore represented a different kind of authority from that of traditional institutions of legitimation. Eventually, the central role of the pastor in Pentecostal churches would grow into a position of considerable power, which, because not balanced by organizational checks and balances, would prove dangerous in some cases. Essentially, Pentecostalism had become a small-church movement grown large.

Notes

1. See above, 113.
2. McGrath, *Christian Theology*, 113–14.
3. Jean-François Lyotard, *The Postmodern Condition: A Report on Knowledge*, trans. Geoff Bennington and Brian Massumi, with foreword by Frederic Jameson (Manchester: Manchester University Press, 2004), xxiv. Original French text from Lyotard, *La Condition Postmoderne*. Collection Critique (Paris: Les Edition de Minuit, 1979), 7.
4. Ibid.
5. James C. Livingston, *Modern Christian Thought: From the Enlightenment to Vatican II* (New York: Macmillan, 1971), 155.
6. Willie Thompson, *Postmodernism and History* (Houndmills, Basingstoke: Palgrave Macmillan, 2004), 18.

7. E. H. Carr, *What is History? The George Macaulay Trevelyan Lectures Delivered in the University of Cambridge January–March 1961* (Harmondsworth: Penguin, 1986), 44.

8. Thompson, *Postmodernism and History*, 25.

9. Zygmunt Baumann, *Liquid Modernity* (Cambridge: Polity Press, 2000), discussed in Mike Riddell, "Beyond Ground Zero: Resourcing Faith in a Post-Christian Era," in *The Future of Christianity: Historical, Sociological, Political and Theological Perspectives from New Zealand*. ATF Series 11, ed. John Stenhouse and Brett Knowles, assisted by Antony Wood (Adelaide: ATF Press, 2004), 222–24.

10. Leonard Sweet, *Aquachurch: Essential Leadership Arts for Piloting Your Church in Today's Fluid Culture* (Loveland, CO: Group Publishing, 1999), 24, cited in Riddell, "Beyond Ground Zero," 222.

11. Draft manuscript of Pete Ward, *Liquid Church* (Carlisle: Paternoster Press, 2002), cited in Riddell, "Beyond Ground Zero," 223–24.

12. McGrath, *Christian Theology*, 114.

13. Edward Farley and Peter C. Hodgson, "Scripture and Tradition," in *Christian Theology: An Introduction to its Traditions and Tasks*, ed. Peter C. Hodgson and Robert H. King, 50 (London: SPCK, 1983).

14. Ibid, 46–51.

15. Jürgen Habermas, *Legitimation Crisis*, trans. Thomas McCarthy (Boston: Beacon Press, 1975), 73.

16. Chapman, "From Labour to National," 382.

17. Bryan Wilson, *Religion in Secular Society: A Sociological Comment* (London: C. A. Watts, 1966), xiv. This definition forms the basis of that adopted in Scott and Marshall, *A Dictionary of Sociology*, s.v. "Secularization, Secularization thesis."

18. Bryan R. Wilson, ed., *The Social Dimensions of Sectarianism: Sects and New Religious Movements in Contemporary Society* (Oxford: Clarendon, 1990), 122.

19. Scott and Marshall, *A Dictionary of Sociology*, s.v. "Secularization, Secularization thesis."

20. McLeod, *The Religious Crisis of the 1960s*, 6. For surveys of the literature and the current status of secularization theory, see David Martin, "Secularisation: Master Narrative or Several Stories?" in Stenhouse and Knowles, *Christianity in the Post Secular West*, 3–26; and Dominic Erdozain, "Review-Article: 'Cause is not Quite What it Used to Be': The Return of Secularisation," *English Historical Review* 127, no. 525 (March 2012): 377–400. I am grateful to Dr. Tim Cooper of the University of Otago for directing my attention to Dr. Erdozain's important review article.

21. Erdozain, "Cause is not Quite What it Used to Be": 392.

22. Majella Franzmann, "Australia, New Zealand and the Pacific Islands," in *Religious Studies: A Global View*, ed. Gregory D. Alles, 224 (Abingdon: Routledge, 2008).

23. Paul Morris, "Introduction," in *The Lloyd Geering Reader: Prophet of Modernity*, ed. Paul Morris and Mike Grimshaw, 14 (Wellington: Victoria University Press, 2007).

24. Franzmann, "Australia, New Zealand and the Pacific Islands," 224.

25. Lloyd Geering, *God in the New World* (London: Hodder and Stoughton, 1968); Geering, *Faith's New Age* (London: Collins, 1980); Geering, *Tomorrow's God* (Wellington: Bridget Williams, 1994); and Geering, *Christianity without God* (Wellington: Bridget Williams, 2002).

26. Kevin Ward, "Will We Find Church in a Future New Zealand?" in Stenhouse and Knowles, *Christianity in the Post Secular West*, 216.

27. Martin, "Secularisation: Master Narrative or Several Stories?" 9.

28. John Milbank, *Theology and Social Theory: Beyond Second Reason* (Oxford: Blackwell, 1993), 9; and Jürgen Habermas, "Religion in the Public Square," *European Journal of Philosophy* 14:1 (2006): 15; both cited in Jonathan Chaplin, "'Secularism': Three Concepts, Three Challenges" (paper presented at Centre for Theology and Public Issues Symposium on "Is New Zealand 'Secular' and Does it Matter?" St. Margaret's College, University of Otago, Dunedin, 19 August 2013).

29. "Secularisation of Religion in New Zealand," 1976 (held at the Department of University Extension, Victoria University of Wellington); and the 2002 "Future of Christianity in the West" Conference at the University of Otago, published in Stenhouse and Knowles, eds., *The Future of Christianity*; and Stenhouse and Knowles, eds., *Christianity in the Post Secular West*.

30. Erich Kolig, "Coming through the Backdoor? Secularisation in New Zealand and Māori Religiosity," in Stenhouse and Knowles, *The Future of Christianity*, 183–204.

31. Bruce Knox, "Christian Allegiance is Declining, Yet Theological Education is Booming," in Stenhouse and Knowles, *The Future of Christianity*, 73–87.

32. Ibid, 86.

33. Harvey Cox, *Fire From Heaven: The Rise of Pentecostal Spirituality and the Reshaping of Religion in the Twenty-First Century* (Reading, MA: Addison-Wesley, 1995), xv.

34. Harvey Cox, *The Secular City: Secularization and Urbanization in Theological Perspective* (London: SCM Press, 1966).

35. Cox, *Fire From Heaven*, 14–15.

36. William M. Johnston, "The Spirituality Revolution and the the Process of Reconfessionalisation in the West Today," in Stenhouse and Knowles, *Christianity in the Post Secular West*, 143–61.

37. Erdozain, "Cause is not Quite What it Used to Be," 398, 400.

38. Brett Knowles, "Pentecostalism and the Future of Christianity in the West: Reflections on a Conversation," in Stenhouse and Knowles, *Christianity in the Post Secular West*, 181–82.

39. David Martin, *Pentecostalism: The World Their Parish* (Oxford: Blackwell, 2002), xvii.

40. See Appendix A.

41. Sue Hoffart, "School Supermum: Robyn Crouth," in Jenny Chamberlain, "Secret Saviours," *North and South*, February 2001, 65–66; "Death of the Samaritan," *Sunday Star Times*, 3 March 2002, C5. See also John Bluck, "Being Church and Belonging: How Do Twenty-First Century New Zealanders Join the Church?" in *Thinking Outside the Square: Church in Middle Earth*, ed. Ree Boddé and Hugh Kempster (Auckland: St. Columba's Press & Journeyings, 2003), 17–18.

42. Kevin Ward, "Rugby and Church: Worlds in Conflict?" *Reality* 33 (October/November 2002): 26–30, cited in Ward, "'No Longer Believing'—or—'Believing without Belonging'," in Stenhouse and Knowles, *The Future of Christianity*, 63–64; and in Ward, "Will We Find Church in a Future New Zealand?" 213.

43. Ward, "Will We Find Church in a Future New Zealand?" 216.

44. Scott and Marshall, *A Dictionary of Sociology*, s.v. "Institution, Social Institution."

45. Habermas, *Legitimation Crisis*, 73. Emphasis as cited.

46. See above, 139.

47. Knowles, "Vision of the Disinherited?" 128–29.

48. Dunstall, "The Social Pattern," 452.

49. Hutchinson, "Wheeler, Rob (1931–)," ADPCM.

50. Anderson, *Vision of the Disinherited*.

51. Clifton, "An Analysis of the Developing Ecclesiology of the Assemblies of God in Australia," 201, footnote 689.

52. Knowles, *The History of a New Zealand Pentecostal Movement*, 149–50.

53. Peter L. Embley, "The Early Development of the Plymouth Brethren," in *Patterns of Sectarianism: Organization and Ideology in Social and Religious Movements*, ed. Bryan Wilson (London: Heinemann, 1967), 218.

54. Knowles, *The History of a New Zealand Pentecostal Movement*, 283–84.

55. Ralph Read, "The Ecumenical Spirit in the Church," *The Evangel*, 26.7 (August 1969): 4, cited in Clifton, "An Analysis of the Developing Ecclesiology of the Assemblies of God in Australia," 205. Read continued to hold these views into the mid-1970s.

56. Blumhofer, *The Assemblies of God*, 2:53, 103–5.

57. Du Plessis, *A Man Called Mr. Pentecost*, 191–92.

58. Clifton, "An Analysis of the Developing Ecclesiology of the Assemblies of God in Australia," 201, footnote 689.

59. Worsfold, *History of the Charismatic Movements in New Zealand*, 286.

60. Luke Worsfold, "Subsequence, Prophecy and Church Order," 114–17.

61. Ibid, 154–55.

62. George Orwell, *Animal Farm* (Fairfield, IA: 1st World Library Literary Society, 2005), 108.

Chapter 9

The 1970s: Part 1

The Turbulent Seventies:
Conservatism, Intensity and Polarization

The changes of the 1960s continued—and were extended—in the 1970s. The previous decade had been characterized by individual and social reorientations; the effects of these were reinforced by the political and economic shifts of the 1970s. The resulting turbulence had lasting effects on many aspects of New Zealand life, leading Keith Sinclair to dub the decade "the uncertain seventies" in the 1984 edition of his *History of New Zealand*.[1] The economic downturn following the two oil shocks of 1973 led to increasing inflation, higher public debt and ultimately to unemployment, industrial unrest and rising emigration. Since many of those who emigrated were educated young people in search of a better life overseas, this exodus was nicknamed the "brain drain." Economic decline was paralleled by social and political change, and the policies of the third Labour Government provided the catalyst for a period of political realignment—particularly in foreign affairs—from 1972 on. Developments within New Zealand tended to reflect the fluid international situation, as well as the political and economic trends of the era. One of the most significant events was Britain's entry into the European Economic Community in 1973 and the resulting loss of New Zealand's traditional core markets for its primary produce. Although the Labour Government had no control over the effects of many of these trends, the substantial electoral swing in the middle of the decade represented a backlash against this process of change.

The National Party attempted to turn this reaction to political advantage in the bitterly fought 1975 General Election and skillfully played on the fears of the average New Zealander. The most notorious example of this Machiavellian strategy was a National Party television advertisement which criticized the policies of their center-left Labour opponents. It showed a line of "dancing Cossack" cartoon figures across the screen, insinuating Labour's putative links with Moscow.[2] Robert Muldoon, the Leader of the Opposition, also sought to elicit support from the conservative element of the public, especially on what were perceived as "moral issues." Muldoon's abrasive public style[3] and harsh, intolerant and divisive attitude[4] set the tone for the ethos of the mid-1970s and for much of the controversy over public issues which characterized that era. In addition to controversies over specifically moralist concerns, other public issues in the 1970s and 1980s included the visits of nuclear warships from 1976 to 1984; the Bastion Point protest in 1977 and 1978; and the tour of New Zealand by the Springbok Rugby team in 1981, which sparked almost unprecedented scenes of militant social protest.

These public issues tended to have a private focus: historian W. H. Oliver notes that intimate issues, such as personal relationships and domesticity, became central during the decade.[5] This, he contends, contributed to "the altered character of the 1970s—a turning inwards to the private, the secluded and the self-contained" and to the "narrowing of horizons" that accompanied it.[6] However, personal relationships and domesticity were symptoms, rather than causes, of the changing attitudes of the decade. Conservatism, particularly in its religious form, rather than domesticity fuelled the engine of protest in the 1970s and 1980s. This lies behind the issues of personal morality, such as abortion and homosexuality, which attracted the most vociferous debate and which reached a climax with the opposition to the Homosexual Law Reform Bill in 1985. In all of these controversies, as well as in that which surrounded the Springbok Rugby Tour in 1981, the significant factor was the vehemence with which differences of opinion were expressed. This reflected "the heightened intensity of social concern" in the late 1970s and early 1980s and "the passionate need of alarmed people to convert others to their convictions."[7] The result was the polarization of New Zealand opinion and a shift towards conservatism which took political, social and theological forms in the late 1970s. Professor Colin Brown identifies the Charismatic Renewal as part of this move to the theological right.[8] As will be seen in chapter 11, the shift was also reflected in the laissez-faire economic conservatism of the mid-1980s, which reversed the regulatory controls that had characterized the interventionist Muldoon era from 1975 on.

The process of polarization was also increasingly evident in the churches. The breakdown of union negotiations between the Anglican and Methodist churches in England in 1969 had its counterpart in the rejection by New Zealand Anglicans of the *Plan for Union* in 1976. However, this failure, as well as that of the Presbyterians and Methodists to achieve church union in 1981, did not necessarily mark the end of ecumenical effort.[9] Nevertheless, it reflected the way in which differences between the churches were becoming more marked, echoing a trend towards something of an ecclesiastical tribalism and hence towards a polarization of opinion.[10] These attitudinal shifts also lay behind the attempts of Pentecostal groups to create clearly defined polities and kindled the vigor with which they pursued their own agenda, especially vis-à-vis the wider society. A shrinking of horizons was also reflected in the Charismatic movement in the early 1980s, as charismatic ecumenism diminished and a number of in-house agencies for renewal were established. These agencies included groups such as the Anglican Renewal Ministries, the Presbyterian Paraclete Trust, the Methodist Aldersgate Fellowship and Catholic Charismatic Renewal, giving a denominational, rather than an ecumenical, focuses to the Charismatic movement.[11]

This increasing polarization was paralleled by a shift towards conservatism within the churches. In general, liberal Christians focused on issues of social justice; conservative Christians stressed the moral responsibility of the individual.[12] Historian David Arrowsmith usefully sums up the conservative position as follows:

> the core of the Conservative Christian's beliefs is the necessity for individual salvation. From this core spring his [sic] attitudes to religion, society and the economy. He believes in a religion whose precepts are universally valid, but which demand individual commitment; he believes in a code of ethics whose rules apply equally to all men, but which demand individual moral responsibility; he extols a social and economic system which forces the individual to make his own way. The conservative Christian's ideology leads him to distrust the liberalizing and secularizing trends of contemporary culture; his moral absolutism leads him to oppose the permissive society; his economic individualism leads him to fear communism—and to preach the virtues of the free enterprise economy and the capitalist ethos.[13]

In 1972, Robert Muldoon, then the Minister of Finance, had noted the divergence of the conservative and liberal wings of the church on public issues and sought to utilize this to his own political ends. He recognized the political value of conservative Christian concern over public morality and assiduously courted the conservative churches during the 1975 Election campaign.[14] However, the Labour Party also had its advocates in the Clergy for Rowling activists who campaigned for Labour Prime Minister Wallace ("Bill") Rowling.[15] Muldoon claimed to be speaking for the "silent majority" of New Zealanders against the takeover of society by a vocal, permissive minority. He wrote in 1974—the year before he became Prime Minister—that: "The term 'silent majority' is one of the saddest of the many catchwords of our time. If the talkers really are the minority, and on many issues they are, then the majority are losing by default, and that is the worst kind of loss of all. ... If only there could be a crusade by the normal people which would match the crusading spirit of the subversive element."[16] Muldoon's advocacy of "a crusade by the normal people" against the "subversive element" echoed the views of conservative Christians who were alarmed over the inroads of the permissive society. These issues especially threatened their traditional model of the nuclear family; as sociologist Allanah Ryan notes, "the overall defining factor [in this conservative Christian response]... is concern with the family. This institution is constantly being invoked as being in a precarious position and therefore in desperate need of preservation and protection from the destabilising influences of 'permissive' society."[17]

A number of issues epitomized the permissive society for conservative Christians in the 1960s and 1970s.[18] The liberalization of attitudes to contraception in the early 1960s—in part stimulated by the availability of the Pill—had its counterpart in attitudes to abortion later in the decade. Pornography was also a highly visible—as well as visual—issue in the late 1960s and early 1970s. (Its increasing pervasiveness can be demonstrated from an analysis of submissions to the Indecent Publications Tribunal from 1964 to 1974. This Tribunal, set up in 1964, enabled a more consistent and unified approach to the issue of censorship than had previously been available in New Zealand. In the first year of its operation, it examined seven publications submitted to it, ruling three of these indecent and four not indecent. By 1970, this workload had grown to sixty-two submissions, forty-two of which were ruled indecent, nine restricted and eleven not indecent. The peak came in 1972, when 221 publications were submitted, nearly 91% of which were ruled indecent or placed under restriction.[19] Conservative Christians therefore had considerable justification for their concerns over the spread of pornography.) In the 1970s, opposition to abortion became more vehement,[20] with sex education in schools and the rise of second-wave feminism[21] also challenging ideas of parental authority, patriarchy and gender roles. Surprisingly, homosexuality appears to have had a lower profile and to have been a less important issue for conservative Christians in the 1960s. It would, however, expand into a highly divisive national issue in the 1980s.[22] Conservative Christian reactions to these issues will be examined next.

Conservative Christian Responses to "Permissiveness"

Missiologist Viv Grigg offers a succinct description of the Evangelical mind-set underlying conservative Christian responses to the permissive society. This includes "a perceived disempowerment, shock at the rapid breakdown of the social structure, a quiet rage at their sense of the loss of legitimacy and morality of the established church, then anger at the 'benign' governments of New Zealand."[23] Nevertheless, the progression from perceived disempowerment and shock to rage and anger took fifteen years to work through, coming to a peak with the groundswell of activism against the Homosexual Law Reform Bill in 1985. During this period, conservative responses to the permissive society took several different forms. The first stirrings of moralist protest began in 1970, when two single-issue groups were formed, the Society for the Protection of the Unborn Child [SPUC] and the Society for the Promotion of Community Standards [SPCS].[24] SPUC was launched in March 1970 to fight abortion; SPCS was formed eight months later to combat the spread of pornography. Allanah Ryan notes that these two organizations marked "the beginning of a moralist movement in New Zealand. While in the early seventies these two groups hardly represented a *movement* (in the sense that we have one in the late eighties), they were definitely a *new* kind of conservatism."[25] The impact of these early groups was reinforced and broadened by the 1972 Jesus Marches and by the formation of other conservative Christian activist groups in the 1970s and 1980s. Examples of these new groups include the Concerned Parents' Association—formed in 1974 to contest the introduction of sex education in schools[26]—and the Coalition of Concerned Citizens, which united opposition to the Homosexual Law Reform Bill in 1985.[27] Responses from Pentecostal churches included the establishment of new types of Christian schools, the Save Our Homes Campaign in 1977 and, in part, the formation of the Associated Pentecostal Churches of New Zealand in 1975. Some of these developments would have profound implications for the future orientation of New Zealand Pentecostalism.

This conservative Christian response to the permissive society formed part of a worldwide phenomenon, and laid the foundations for what became known as "the New Christian Right." Although this title refers specifically to the American context, it is also applicable to the development of similar moral activist movements elsewhere and Australian church historian John Evans, for example, uses it to describe the New Zealand phenomenon.[28] American scholars of religion Robert Liebman and Robert Wuthnow note that the rise of these movements was significant since it represented a change from "[political] abstinence . . . to political action, at least for a substantial segment of evangelicals," compelling the reexamination of sociopolitical theories.[29] The emergence of these moralist movements was the product of several shifts of focus in the early 1970s, when "The sharp line between the kingdom of God and the kingdom of Caesar began to blur. Unwilling to turn their backs on what appeared to be a deepening moral crisis . . . , evangelicals shifted their attention to the sphere of public life."[30]

The first of these shifts of focus was an eschatological one. Many conservative Evangelicals held premillennial views, believing that the world order was doomed to become progressively more degenerate, with the climax of evil coming just before the second coming of Christ. In the light of this pessimistic world view, there was little point in trying to change the world, since it was, by its very nature, doomed. In the case of Pentecostalism, "Pretribulational Premillennialism governed pentecostal thought on the Christian's role within society; with the end of the age just around the corner it meant that there was little interest expressed in social action or in otherwise affecting the community, especially in the political realm."[31] Various forms of premillennial belief remained prominent in the 1970s, the best-known although not altogether typical—exposition of this view being American writer Hal Lindsay's *The Late Great Planet Earth*.[32] This book achieved best-seller status among the Jesus People in the 1970s. Despite this prominence, Asian Pentecostal scholar Wonsuk Ma laments that "the message of the Lord's return began to disappear slowly, but steadily, from Pentecostal pulpits" in the 1960s. He attributes this to a growing focus on "worldly concerns such as blessing, [and] church growth" and to the rise of the Charismatic movement.[33] The rise of the new moral activist movements also implied a move away from this premillennial viewpoint. The assumption of the moralist participants that it was possible to change the world for the better—or at least to halt the process of decay—in reality was at variance with their premillennial theology. In New Zealand, as elsewhere, this shift was largely an unconscious one. Nevertheless, this conceptual shift both reflected and stimulated conservative Christian protest—exemplified by the Jesus Marches—and the beginnings of conservative Christian political pressure and the proliferation of lobbying groups.

The second shift of focus involved the conservative Christian response to secularization, which was then viewed as the key driving factor in the process of social change. (As has been demonstrated in chapter 8, the process of secularization is no longer espoused with the same degree of certainty in the twenty-first century. The author has argued in that chapter that increasing suspicion of traditional institutions and the consequent relocation of authority explain many of the processes formerly attributed to secularization.[34]

Nevertheless, perceptions of its validity—and hence of the toxic effects of secular humanism—were strong in the 1960s, 1970s and 1980s.) Because secularization was deemed to internalize religious authority, it effectively nullified religion as a source of influence in secular society. This abrogation of public religious authority thus led to morality, both public and private, becoming a matter of individual determination and choice. Secularization was therefore seen in the 1960s as a catalyst for the liberalization of moral standards; it was primarily the devaluation of religion implicit in this process that provoked the Christian moralists' reaction. In their eyes, society had departed from Christian principles and it was therefore necessary to return to traditional standards of morality. Since the activists' perception of morality was rooted in their Christian faith, this necessarily implied a return to traditional Christian belief. They therefore opposed this perceived secularization as much as the liberalization of moral standards that resulted from it; indeed, for some sections of the movement, secular humanism was the enemy *par excellence*. They demonized the term, projecting on to it all that was hostile to Christian values and attributing the spread of godlessness, moral relativism and permissiveness to its injurious influence.[35] In New Zealand, the Christchurch Integrity Centre was established in direct response to what were perceived as the inroads of secular humanism[36] and conservative Christians sought to reinstate Christianity as a legitimator of public morality.[37] In the 1970s, this reinstatement was seen as a matter of the adoption by society of Christian principles; by the late 1980s, the strategy had changed to placing conservative Christians into positions of power. Nevertheless, the enemy—i.e., secular humanism—remained the same. Indeed, Rob Wheeler's candidacy for the Mount Albert seat in the 1987 General Election was motivated by precisely this perception:

> A Satanic revival has touched New Zealand! Our nation has been converted to secular humanism, which is anti-Bible and anti-Christian! Satan has been at work at all levels, right up to the Government. ... When we can send Christians into Parliament ... we can effect a change in our nation that will touch the heart of every man and every woman. We need to be in every level of society.[38]

The third shift of focus was perhaps the most important one. Although the conservative Christian motivation was essentially a religious one, the accompanying moralist activism also represented a shift in attitude towards secular society. British Anglican Richard Russell has described this reorientation as a "growing crisis of the Evangelical world-view." He comments that, in the context of British Evangelicalism between 1963 and 1973, "there has been a considerable shift from setting up a choice between 'individual redemption' to 'social amelioration' to seeing their relation as conjunctive."[39] Furthermore, this represents a shift from a "Christ OR culture" to a "Christ AND culture" paradigm and parallels the movement towards a "social gospel" and the "secularisation of the Christian faith" in the early 1900s.[40] Russell may be correct in his insistence that the moralist movement represented a change in the Evangelical world view. In New Zealand, the new concern with moralist issues rather than with an individualistic faith marked a modification of the style of Evangelicalism that had prevailed in this country since the 1959 Billy Graham Crusade. To some extent, it also represented a revival of the conservative concern that had motivated the rise of the Temperance Movement in the 1880s.

Although moralist protest groups such as SPUC and SPCS represented only one element of conservative Christian concern over the changing moral values of society, in the 1970s, they tapped into a general sense of unease. A more public "grass-roots" response emerged in 1972 with the Jesus Marches, held in a number of centers across the country. These marches, which attracted between 70,000 and 85,000 participants, were important for future developments and—particularly—for the trajectory of New Zealand Pentecostalism in the 1970s. It is to these that we now turn.

The 1972 Jesus Marches and their Legacy

The motivation for the 1972 Jesus Marches[41] came from conservative Christian apprehension at the deteriorating moral standards of society and from their perception of the need to protest this decline. New Life pastor Rasik Ranchord, a participant in the Auckland march, described the Marches as being intended to bring about "an awareness of a need for righteousness in the country, and ... [to raise] up the profile of Christians; they needed to be more visible, and [to] let their convictions be *known* more widely.... to show that whilst [there was] decadence on one hand, ... there were lots of people that stood for righteousness."[42] Consequently, the scripture "Righteousness Exalts a Nation"[43] that appeared on placards carried by the marchers "was virtually the theme and heart of the Jesus Marches—a genuine concern for the moral state of the nation."[44]

In one respect, the Jesus Marches reflected the contagion of protest that had begun with demonstrations against the Vietnam War in 1965. As Michael King comments, there seemed to be "a super-abundance of causes that would bring people out into the streets" in protest during the late 1960s and early 1970s.[45] What *was* new, however, was the willingness of conservative Christians to take up such methods to make their convictions known. The Marches had a significant model to hand, being patterned on the Festival of Light held in Great Britain in September of the previous year.[46] Their indebtedness to the British event can be seen by comparing the Statements of their respective Executive Committees.[47] Some sections of these are identical, although there were also some striking differences. Prayer meetings for the marches in New Zealand seem to have been more fundamentalist and revivalistic—with calls for national repentance and revival—than those for the British Festival of Light. There were also similarities: both events, although planned as once-only rallies, led to frequent moral-crusade rallies after 1971. It is therefore evident that both the Festival of Light and the New Zealand Jesus Marches represented significant turning points, "ideas whose time had come." This explains why support for these events seemed to spread so rapidly.

The success of the first Jesus March in Auckland on Friday 5 May 1972 was reported by the *New Zealand Herald* on its front page under the headline "Jesus People Reign in Queen Street."[48] This led to spontaneously generated Jesus Marches in other parts of the country. A number of participants emphasize this spontaneity: Rasik Ranchord recalls that "other people got inspired, and ... many other cities took it up.... It almost seemed like a kind of 'spontaneous combustion.' People seemed to gravitate towards an idea like that and ... joined in."[49] However, this claim to spontaneity did not preclude the role of organization in the spread of the Jesus Marches from May to October 1972. The Māori evangelist Muri Thompson had done much to publicize the concept of the Jesus Marches throughout New Zealand in early 1972.[50] Furthermore, the establishment of a Board of Reference, comprising civic and religious leaders, provided an official focal point,[51] which was supplemented by local *ad hoc* committees in the various areas. These local "organising committees sprang up spontaneously, [each] consisting mainly of laymen in the 20 to 30 age group, with ministers often acting in advisory capacities."[52] Although these committee members represented many different churches, Evangelical, Pentecostal and Charismatic Christians were heavily involved, Indigenous Churches Pastor Rob Wheeler, for example, being Secretary of the Auckland Executive Committee.[53] This predominance is more marked in the Christchurch Committee, which included five Pentecostals, six Evangelicals and—so far as the author has been able to ascertain—at least three Charismatics among its twenty-one members. The Jesus Marches were essentially a lay movement as well as a young peoples' movement and owed much to the impetus generated by the Pentecostal and Charismatic movements. Blyth Harper, Administrator and Prayer Convener of the Auckland Jesus March, notes that "The main thrust, in terms of planning and initial participation, came from charismatic Christians, especially the Maori Evangelist, Mr. Muri Thompson."[54] Eventually more than a dozen marches were held throughout New Zealand: the first in Auckland in May 1972 and the final march at Parliament House in Wellington in October. Although estimates of the numbers varied, the Marches brought together between 70,000 and 85,000 people around the country in a concerted expression of concern over the moral decay of society.[55]

The organizational "spontaneity" of the Marches also extended to their character and to the participants in the events. Despite the Marches' focus on "Righteousness Exalts a Nation," they were somewhat equivocal in ethos, being an evangelistic proclamation and celebration of Jesus as well as a moralist protest. Consequently, it is not surprising that, on the night of the Auckland march, "what began as an idea of a formal protest march against the permissive society, ended with many of the 10,000 [participants] skipping and dancing their way down the street in the exuberance and joy of their love for Christ and oneness with one another."[56] This exuberance was, in fact, also a characteristic of the marches in other centers. Observers commented that "the original call to national righteousness, protesting against the moral landslide, tended to be swallowed up as the marches progressed, by a positive celebration of the Name, power and presence of Jesus."[57] This celebratory aspect owed much to the participation of the Jesus People, although this element should not be overstated. The street demonstrations of this movement of ex-hippies who had been converted to Christianity in the United States from 1969 on have been adduced as models for the New Zealand Jesus Marches. However, the Jesus People movement in New Zealand was different from that in America,[58] despite the shared symbolism (the One Way sign of an index finger pointing upwards, indicating that Jesus was the one way to God), slogans ("Jesus loves you") and music (such as "Jesus is a soul man"). The Jesus Marches in this country—to adapt the piquant phrase of David Martin—were not simply an example of "American countercultural radiation."[59] The organizer of the Wellington Jesus March noted in *Challenge Weekly* that "in New Zealand we have seen nothing of the [Jesus] movement in its natural setting or form. The Jesus Marches in New Zealand last year [1972] carried only the name 'Jesus People' but in most other respects, including the 'strong support of the establishment,' they were the antithesis of that which so suddenly and recently burst upon the American scene."[60] Rather, as a New Zealand observer commented, the New Zealand Jesus People movement was not "freakish" nor given to extremes, and was "unlikely to become a separate and organised church."[61] Nevertheless, many of the Jesus People eventually found a home in Pentecostal or charismatic churches.

Figure 7: The exultant crowd at Parliament grounds following the Jesus March through Wellington's streets, 9 October 1972. Photographer unidentified. Dominion Post Collection, Alexander Turnbull Library, Wellington, New Zealand. (PAColl-7327) Reference: EP/1972/4889A. Reproduced by permission from Alexander Turnbull Library.

How successful were the Jesus Marches? Despite the marchers' concern for national righteousness, little direct impact appears to have been made on the morality of the nation. Furthermore, the marches did not find favor with all sections of the Christian community. Several March committees failed to gain the necessary support from the local churches. The Dunedin Jesus March, for example, had to be cancelled due to lack of support. An Anglican member of the Dunedin *ad hoc* organizing committee commented that "the committee did not attract all the representatives it needed to ensure the march would be a success. The Pentecostal churches gave strong support to it, and there were representatives from the Otago University Evangelical Union, the Open Air Campaigners, and some others."[62] As well as this, other, more liberal, churches also opposed the emphasis of the Jesus Marches, as is evidenced by a critical editorial in the *New Zealand Methodist*, describing them as a narrowly defined "morality march" and as "limping for Jesus."[63] This caustic assessment, although possibly a valid criticism in terms of the original intentions for the Jesus March (as expressed in the publicity material for the March for Righteousness), was actually written before the march and proved, in the event, to be somewhat premature. The march in Auckland, as in other centers, took on a celebratory character, and this change in emphasis highlighted the prejudicial nature of the editorial. It consequently came under heavy attack in letters to the editor of the *New Zealand Methodist* for a number of weeks following the march.[64]

The significance of the 1972 Jesus Marches lay more in their indirect, rather than direct, effects. These were twofold, as befitted their equivocal nature as Jesus celebration and moralist protest. The Marches provided an example of the power of collective action and became a catalyst for increasing conservative Christian mobilization over the next fifteen years. Similar Jesus Festivals continued annually for some years, usually under the auspices of the Full Gospel Businessmen's Fellowship International,[65] in order to continue the momentum that had been generated. They also stimulated the beginnings of further specifically focused moralist campaigns, such as the Concerned Parents' Association—formed in 1974—and the Save our Homes Campaign, launched in 1977. However, with the emergence of lobbying groups such as these, the character of conservative Christian action changed. Whereas the Jesus Marches had represented a generalized protest, these groups—and others—helped to focus conservative Christian moral concern on specifically targeted moralist issues and to provoke and coordinate responses to these issues. In this way, the era of conservative Christian *protest* led into the era of conservative Christian *political pressure*.

The Jesus Marches also had other effects on the life of the Christian community. As Blyth Harper comments,

> the marches have quickened a home-grown Jesus movement among the young generation, working within and through the churches, many of which have experienced a new influx of life. . . . We have consciously not tried to establish a new movement. The whole Body of Christ, from Roman Catholic to Pentecostal, have participated according to their allegiance to Jesus, not according to denominations.[66]

It would appear that most of the Jesus People movement to which Harper refers was absorbed into the churches, and especially into those of Charismatic or Pentecostal persuasion. This reflected the general orientation of the Jesus People towards charismatic forms of Christianity, and was reinforced by subsequent developments. The effects of the Jesus Marches on the Pentecostal and Charismatic movements were therefore long-lasting. In particular, the sense of Christian unity, transcending denominational barriers,[67] was one of the marches' most powerful legacies: "The march also did something in that it brought together some elements of the Christian community which would normally be reticent about a public demonstration of love and loyalty to the Lord Jesus and a stand for righteousness. Unity was in evidence."[68] Since much of the impetus for the Jesus Marches came from Pentecostal and Charismatic Christians,[69] this sense of unity greatly strengthened the growth of these movements. Charismatic solidarity was further reinforced by the Christian Advance Ministries Charismatic Conference held in Palmerston North in January 1973. Pentecostal involvement in the Jesus Marches also did much to break down barriers between the various Pentecostal groups, although Ian Clark believes that the influence ran the other way. (As he puts it: "the Jesus Marches were a *fruit* of coming together rather than a catalyst to bring us together. I think that's really the order of events." He emphasizes the role of Canadian Bible teacher Ern Baxter's ministry in New Zealand in 1974 in bringing about Pentecostal unity.)[70] Certainly, the ministry of Baxter and others over the next two years reinforced this increasing Pentecostal openness, and led to the landmark Snell's Beach conference in March 1975 that would radically reconfigure New Zealand Pentecostalism. This will be discussed in chapter 11.

Towards Maturity:
The Development of the Charismatic Movement

The 1970s were a golden era of rapid and sustained growth for the Pentecostal and Charismatic movements in New Zealand. Census figures show that the number of Pentecostal adherents almost tripled between 1971 and 1981,[71] while the Charismatic movement had a greater impact in New Zealand during the decade than in any other English-speaking nation.[72] This expansion was paralleled by the ongoing evolution of the movements' character, manifest in their changing alliances, attitudes and orientations. Several events marked important turning points during the decade. The impact of the Jesus Marches of 1972 has already been noted. The formation of Christian Advance Ministries the same year and that of the Associated Pentecostal Churches of New Zealand in 1975 were also significant. The glacial changes of attitude and orientation that these hurricane events embodied had considerable impact on the development of the Pentecostal and Charismatic movements during the decade. By the end of the 1970s, each would have become a different kind of movement from what it had been in earlier years. The development of the Charismatic movement is discussed here; the evolution of the Pentecostal movement in the 1970s forms the subject of the next chapter.

In Donald Battley's three-part characterization of the Charismatic movement, the period from 1971 to 1979 is described as the Time of Ingathering, in contrast to the Period of the Pioneers up to 1971. The remainder of the 1970s was characterized by charismatic gatherings attracting four-figure attendances, the emergence of a renewal jet-set of very capable teachers, and the formation of new interdenominational agencies for renewal. These, he says, were "heady and exciting days."[73] Nevertheless, the Charismatic movement in the 1970s was rather different in character from what it had been in the previous decade. Firstly, it had previously been a largely Protestant phenomenon, although Catholic involvement became more overt after 1970. Peter Morrow led three Catholic Redemptorist priests—Fathers John McGill, Cecil Dennehy and Bruce McGill—into the Baptism of the Spirit in Christchurch in 1968. These three men were later to be very influential in the New Zealand Catholic Charismatic movement;[74] in this respect, Morrow was the "godfather" of that movement. Nevertheless, they were initially reluctant to identify themselves with it, only acknowledging their involvement after an American Catholic bishop had been baptized in the Spirit in 1970. This episcopal precedent gave them confidence to share their own experience and the Catholic Charismatic movement in New Zealand grew from there.[75] Another center of the movement also emerged in Auckland in 1970 as a result of the influence of overseas literature, particularly David Wilkerson's *Cross and the Switchblade* and Kevin Ranaghan's *Catholic Pentecostals*. Sociologists Vincent Reidy and James Richardson emphasize this Auckland wing, but overlook the earlier underground phase of the movement in Christchurch from 1968 to 1970.[76]

Secondly, as has been previously noted, Pentecostal input into the early Charismatic movement was very strong in the 1960s.[77] The Charismatic movement began to move away from a dependence on its Pentecostal mentors in the 1970s to establish an independent identity.[78] This brought about changes in theology and approach. The Life in the Spirit Seminars, published in 1971 by the Word of God community in Ann Arbor, Michigan, built upon a Catholic tradition of spiritual formation. This tradition was applied to the reception of the Holy Spirit.[79] This restatement of the theological and spiritual bases of the Baptism of the Spirit "gave [the Charismatic movement] tools that the Pentecostals had never developed," thus increasing its appeal to Christians in the mainstream churches.[80] Life in the Spirit seminars became a standard method of introducing Charismatic experience into denominational church congregations from then on. The impact of the Life in the Spirit seminars was reinforced by the formation in 1972 of Christian Advance Ministries.[81] This parachurch organization—and particularly its 1973 Summer School, which became the model for further annual transdenominational conferences—created a new sense of charismatic identity. People from all denominations attended these conferences; "nuns in 'habits' were not uncommon" among these attendees.[82] These summer schools contributed to a shift from a predominantly Pentecostal hermeneutic to a more theologically nuanced interpretation of Charismatic experience. Effectively, this marked a coming-of-age for the Charismatic Movement in New Zealand[83] and this new sense of identity was strengthened by the expansion of the renewal throughout the 1970s.

Despite this development of an independent identity, links between Pentecostals and Charismatics remained, with few exceptions,[84] warm and positive. These links were fostered by fellowship in parachurch groups such as Full Gospel Businessmen's Fellowship International,[85] Women's Aglow[86] and other interdenominational agencies. This informal ecumenism provided much of the dynamism that facilitated the growth of both the Charismatic and the Pentecostal movements in the 1970s. The best example of the shared sense of kinship comes from Peter Morrow's account of his fellowship with Catholic priest Cecil Dennehy, whom he led into the Baptism of the Spirit. Morrow often spent time at the Redemptorist monastery, talking to the priests there until midnight. He recalled

> leaving Cecil [Dennehy] at twelve o'clock (and he certainly had a very, very, wonderful love for God), and I remember him asking me "what do you think of ecumenicalism, Peter?" . . . I remember him lifting up his hand and saying "when the

Protestants lift up Jesus, and *they* see only Jesus, and the Catholics lift up Jesus, and *they* see only Jesus, we're going to come together in Jesus." And I said, "Cecil, that's *my* language; I think we're going to get on well together!"[87]

The warmth of this shared spirituality meant that there was an ongoing interaction between Pentecostals and Charismatics, even after the development of an independent Charismatic identity. The benefits of this were reinforced by more tolerant mainstream attitudes to the Charismatic movement throughout the 1970s and as people found that embracing the charismatic or Pentecostal dimension did not necessitate leaving their churches. Many churches—for example, the Presbyterian, Anglican and Baptist Churches—now produced broadly sympathetic official reports on the movement; these contrasted with the critical assessments of the previous decade.[88] The 1976 Anglican General Synod Report significantly noted that "between 40% and 50% of the clergy in the Auckland diocese were either participants in the renewal or open to the possibility of a charismatic experience."[89] (However, despite this Anglican participation, there were also some tensions—perhaps best summed up in the title of Dale Williamson's doctoral thesis, "An Uncomfortable Engagement"— over the "un-Anglican" nature of charismatic beliefs and practices.)[90] Although neither the Pentecostal or Charismatic movement had attracted media attention until the 1970s,[91] the increasing volume of published material on them from 1972 on drew attention to them and significantly increased their public profiles.[92] The movements also began to be the subjects of academic study[93] and of published books[94] and book chapters.[95] During the decade, nearly thirty articles, books and theses appeared on the two movements, compared with just seven over the quarter century from 1946 to 1970. This considerably raised their profile and increased their public acceptability. Colin Brown notes that Pentecostalism became more respectable during the 1970s,[96] although this was not simply an attempt by some Pentecostal leaders to change the movement's popular profile, as he claims. It also owed much to the changing attitudes to Pentecostalism and towards the Charismatic Movement, in part due to an increased public awareness.

The Charismatic Movement appears to have peaked by the end of the decade. During the 1970s, the movement was characterized by a recovery of faith, spellbinding preaching, a rediscovery of the Bible, a revival of music and many conversions. In all of these, there were experiences of spiritual "surprise" and "innocent enthusiasm."[97] However, Donald Battley calls the period after 1979 "a time of depression," noting that institutional responses to the movement were now hardening, pastoral damage was becoming more evident and, above all, burnout became widely evident amongst committed Charismatics. This, he says, led to the development of a siege mentality and to an exodus of Charismatics into independent Pentecostal churches and the more alive evangelical churches.[98] Nevertheless, the movement's legacy remained a positive one; in Elaine Bolitho's words, the charismatic movement can be seen as "providing continuity of God experience" in the midst of an era of discontinuity.[99] It continued to impact the churches in the 1980s: seven of the ten fastest-growing Presbyterian churches in that decade were charismatic in orientation.[100] The changes in the Charismatic movement in the 1980s will be discussed in chapter 11.

Notes

1. Sinclair, *History of New Zealand*, 308–22.
2. For a video clip of the advertisement, see Kate McMillan, "Media and politics—Journalists and politicians: an uneasy relationship," *Te Ara Encyclopedia of New Zealand*, updated 16 November 2012 http://www.TeAra.govt.nz/en/interactive/35759/dancing-cossacks-1975 (accessed 24 August 2013).
3. Sinclair, *History of New Zealand*, 315.
4. Keith Rowe, "Clergy for Rowling—the Almost Politicians," in *Dialogue on Religion: New Zealand Viewpoints 1977*, ed. Peter Davis and John Hinchcliff, 31 (Auckland: University of Auckland, 1977), cited in Davidson, *Christianity in Aotearoa*, 174.
5. W. H. Oliver, "The Awakening Imagination 1940–1980," in Rice, *Oxford History of New Zealand*, 565–66.
6. Ibid, 565, 567.
7. Ibid, 567.
8. Colin Brown, "Will the Charismatic Renewal Permanently Renew?" in *Religious Pluralism in New Zealand*, Article 3, 6 (Wellington: Department of University Extension Victoria University of Wellington, [1976]), typescript.
9. Davidson, *Christianity in Aotearoa*, 126.
10. Knowles, "Some Aspects of the History of the New Life Churches of New Zealand," 254–55.
11. Davidson, *Christianity in Aotearoa*, 171.
12. Guy, *Shaping Godzone*, 24.
13. David Arrowsmith, "Christian Attitudes towards Public Questions in New Zealand in 1975" (MA thesis in Political Studies, Auckland University, 1978), 116.
14. Knowles, *The History of a New Zealand Pentecostal Movement*, 213–14.
15. Rowe, "Clergy for Rowling—the Almost Politicians," 31–35.
16. R. D. Muldoon, *The Rise and Fall of a Young Turk* (Wellington: A. H. and A. W. Reed, 1974), 30–31.
17. Allanah Ryan, "'For God, Country and Family': Populist Moralism and the New Zealand Moral Right" (MA thesis in Education, Massey University, 1986), 6.
18. For a discussion of these issues and of conservative Christian responses to them, see Knowles, *The History of a New Zealand Pentecostal Movement*, 181–88.
19. Stuart Perry, *Indecent Publication Control in New Zealand* (Wellington: McCrae Publishers, 1975), cited in Knowles, "Some Aspects of the History of the New Life Churches of New Zealand," 139–43, and in Knowles, *The History of a New Zealand Pentecostal Movement*, 185–87.
20. So, Oliver, "The Awakening Imagination," 457.
21. See Knowles, "Some Aspects of the History of the New Life Churches of New Zealand," 193–200, and Knowles, *The History of a New Zealand Pentecostal Movement*, 223–24. For a systematic, but somewhat sketchy, account of the rise of the second-wave feminist movement in New Zealand, see Christine Dann, *Up From Under: Women and*

Liberation in New Zealand 1970–1985 (Wellington: Allen and Unwin/Port Nicholson Press, 1985).

22. Knowles, "Some Aspects of the History of the New Life Churches of New Zealand," 134–35, and Knowles, *The History of a New Zealand Pentecostal Movement*, 183.

23. Viv Grigg, *The Spirit of Christ and the Postmodern City* (Glen Eden, Auckland: Urban Leadership Foundation, 2009), 187.

24. Knowles, "Some Aspects of the History of the New Life Churches of New Zealand," 146; and Knowles, *The History of a New Zealand Pentecostal Movement*, 187–88.

25. Allanah Ryan, "Remoralising Politics," in *Revival of the Right: New Zealand Politics in the 1980s*, eds. Bruce Jesson, Allanah Ryan and Paul Spoonley, 57 (Auckland: Heinemann Reed, 1988). Emphasis as cited.

26. Knowles, *The History of a New Zealand Pentecostal Movement*, 182, 199 and 212–15; and Knowles, "Some Aspects of the History of the New Life Churches of New Zealand," 179–84.

27. Knowles, "Some Aspects of the History of the New Life Churches of New Zealand," 288, 299–308 and 342.

28. John Evans, "The New Christian Right in New Zealand," in Gilling, *"Be Ye Separate,"* 69–106.

29. Robert Liebman and Robert Wuthnow, "Introduction," in *The New Christian Right: Mobilization and Legitimation*, ed. Robert C. Liebman and Robert Wuthnow (New York: Aldine Publishing Company, 1983), 4.

30. Liebman, "The Making of the New Christian Right," in Ibid, 227.

31. Luke Worsfold, "Subsequence, Prophecy and Church Order," 71.

32. Hal Lindsay and C. C. Carlson, *The Late Great Planet Earth* (Grand Rapids, MI: Zondervan, 1976).

33. Wonsuk Ma, "Pentecostal Eschatology: What Happened When the Wave Hit the West End of the Ocean," in Hunter and Robeck, *The Azusa Street Revival and Its Legacy*, 232.

34. See above, 140–141.

35. Donald Heinz, "The Struggle to Define America," in Liebman and Wuthnow, *The New Christian Right*, 133–34.

36. Ryan, "Remoralising Politics," 59.

37. Knowles, *The History of a New Zealand Pentecostal Movement*, 203–4.

38. Stephen Stratford, "Christians Awake! Join the National Party, Save New Zealand," *Metro*, November 1986, 125.

39. Richard Russell, "The growing crisis of the Evangelical world-view and its resolutions" (MA thesis in Theology and Religious Studies, Bristol University, 1973), 98.

40. Ibid, 100. Capitalisation as cited.

41. See Knowles, *The History of a New Zealand Pentecostal Movement*, 189–99 for a discussion of the 1972 Jesus Marches.

42. Rasik Ranchord, Interview, Christchurch, 21 November 1989, cited in Knowles, *The History of a New Zealand Pentecostal Movement*, 190. Emphasis as cited. The audio cassettes of this interview are held in BKRP, MS-3530/032 and MS-3530/033, Hocken Library, Dunedin.

43. Proverbs 14:34.

44. Trevor Shaw, comp., *The Jesus Marchers 1972* (Auckland: Challenge Publishers, 1972), 7.

45. King, *Penguin History of New Zealand*, 453–54.

46. For a brief outline and analysis of the Festival of Light, see Roy Wallis and Richard Bland, "Purity in Danger: A survey of participants in a moral crusade rally," *British Journal of Sociology*, no. 30 (June 1979): 188. Fuller accounts are given in Flo Dobbie, *Land Aflame!* (London: Hodder and Stoughton, 1972); and Capon, . . . *and there was light*. See also Knowles, "Some Aspects of the History of the New Life Churches of New Zealand," 149–54.

47. The text of the Festival of Light's "Statement of Intent" is given in Capon, . . . *and there was light*, 20. That for New Zealand is given in Jesus March: March for Righteousness, Auckland, "Executive Committee Statement of Purpose" (Auckland, 1972), Ephemera Collection, Alexander Turnbull Library, Wellington (mimeographed).

48. "Jesus People Reign in Queen Street," *New Zealand Herald*, 6 May 1972, 1.

49. Ranchord, Interview, cited in Knowles, *The History of a New Zealand Pentecostal Movement*, 191.

50. For examples of Muri Thompson's promotion of the Marches, see "'Jesus Marches' plan for N.Z.," *Otago Daily Times*, 6 April 1972, 5; and "'March for Jesus' plan," *Press*, 13 April 1972, 11.

51. Jesus March, *Executive Committee Statement*, 2. This Board of Reference was extended for the later marches (*National Jesus Festival News No.1*, 1 August 1972).

52. Blyth Harper, cited in Shaw, *The Jesus Marchers*, p.27.

53. Jesus March, *Executive Committee Statement*, 2.

54. Blyth Harper, cited in Neil, "Institutional Churches and the Charismatic Renewal," 126, note 3.

55. *Challenge Weekly* cites 11 marches, and 85,000 participants (Blyth Harper, "85,000 publicly witness by Marching for Jesus," *Challenge Weekly*, 21 October 1972, 2). Trevor Shaw estimates the total participation at 70,000 people in 13 marches (Shaw, *The Jesus Marchers*, 7 and 16–17). Neil appears to cite Shaw, but lists only 12 marches, omitting the march in Tokoroa (Neil, "Institutional Churches and the Charismatic Renewal," 125).

56. "Unprecedented Event: 10,000 march for Jesus in Queen Street," *Challenge Weekly*, 13 May 1972, 1.

57. Harper, "85,000 publicly witness by Marching for Jesus," 2.

58. A point made by Robert Keyzer, "A Christian Revolutionary," *New Zealand Listener*, 13 November 1972, 10. For a contrary view, emphasising the countercultural elements of the "Jesus People," see Jill McCracken, "The God Squad," *New Zealand Listener*, 23 October 1972, 14–15.

59. Martin refers to "American cultural radiation" as a factor in the worldwide spread of Pentecostalism. Martin, *Pentecostalism: The World Their Parish*, 39 and 133.

60. "The Story of the Jesus People," review of *The Jesus People: Old-Time Religion in the Age of Aquarius*, ed. Ronald M. Enroth, Edward E. Ericson, Jr., and C. Breckinridge Peters, *Challenge Weekly*, 14 April 1973, 7.

61. Bernie Ogilvy, cited by McCracken, "The God Squad," 15.

62. "Jesus March Cancelled," *Otago Daily Times*, 18 July 1972, 1.

63. "Editorial: Limping for Jesus," *New Zealand Methodist*, 4 May 1972, 2. Much of this editorial was repeated in the "From the Churches" column in the *New Zealand Herald*, 8 May 1972, 16.

64. "Letters to the Editor," *New Zealand Methodist*, 18 May–15 June 1972.

65. As, for example, the "Jesus 75" campaign (John Bluck, "Jesus 75—a mixed blessing," *New Citizen*, 12 June 1975, 5).

66. Harper, "85,000 publicly witness by Marching for Jesus," 2.

67. A Canadian visitor to New Zealand noted that "everyone lost their denominational tags" in the marches (Paul Edmondson, reported in *Challenge Weekly*, 5 August 1972, 6).
68. *Challenge Weekly*, 27 May 1972, 1. The reference is to the Palmerston North Jesus March.
69. Neil, "Institutional Churches and the Charismatic Renewal," 126, note 3.
70. Clark, Interview, cited in Knowles, *The History of a New Zealand Pentecostal Movement*, 198 and footnote 47. Emphasis as cited.
71. See Appendix A.
72. Patrick J. St.G. Johnstone, *Operation World: A Handbook for World Intercession* (Bromley, Kent: STL Books, 1978), 318, cited in Ward, "The Charismatic Movement in New Zealand," 4, note 22.
73. Battley, "Charismatic Renewal: A View from the Inside," 49.
74. Gordon F. Copeland, *Faith That Works* (Lower Hutt: Barnabas Christian Trust, 1988), 36.
75. Knowles, *The History of a New Zealand Pentecostal Movement*, 164–67. Also Gaynor Loryman, "Growth of the Pentecostal Movement: 'A new relationship with Christ'," *Christchurch Star*, 27 October 1973, 7.
76. M. T. Vincent Reidy and James T. Richardson, "Roman Catholic Neo-Pentecostalism: The New Zealand Experience," *Australia and New Zealand Journal of Sociology*, no. 14 (1978): 222.
77. For examples of this input, see Knowles, *The History of a New Zealand Pentecostal Movement*, 173–74. Luke Worsfold, however, discounts this influence. Luke Worsfold, "Subsequence, Prophecy and Church Order," 191.
78. Neil, "Institutional Churches and the Charismatic Renewal," 131. See also Knowles, *The History of a New Zealand Pentecostal Movement*, 236.
79. P. D. Hocken, "Life in the Spirit Seminars," in NIDPCM, 840. For a brief discussion of the Seminars and of their impact in New Zealand, see Williamson, "An Uncomfortable Engagement," 194–99.
80. Battley, "Charismatic Renewal: A View from the Inside," 49.
81. Knowles, *The History of a New Zealand Pentecostal Movement*, 172–73. Also see Williamson, "An Uncomfortable Engagement," 150–205.
82. Hodgkinson, "The Independent Pentecostal Movement," 13.
83. Neil, "Institutional Churches and the Charismatic Renewal," 131.
84. For attitudes in the Australian Assemblies of God, see above, 118, 121 and 144. See also Benjamin Clark, "Averill, Thomas Lloyd Webster, (1913–)," ADPCM (accessed 12 April 2009).
85. Demos Shakarian, John and Elizabeth Sherrill, *The Happiest People on Earth* (Old Tappan, NJ: Spire Books, 1975); also see J. R. Zeigler, "Full Gospel Business Men's Fellowship International (FGBMFI)," in NIDPCM, 653–54.
86. See R. M. Griffith, "Womens Aglow Fellowship International," in NIDPCM, 1209–11.
87. Peter Morrow, Interview, Christchurch, 13 May 1988, cited in Knowles, *The History of a New Zealand Pentecostal Movement*, 167. Emphasis as cited. The audio cassette of this interview is held in BKRP, MS-3530/029, Hocken Library, Dunedin.
88. Brown, "The Charismatic Contribution," 105–8; cp. Davidson, *Christianity in Aotearoa*, 171.
89. Church of the Province of New Zealand, *Proceedings of the General Synod*, 1976 [Reports], 33, cited in Davidson, *Christianity in Aotearoa*, 171.
90. Williamson, "An Uncomfortable Engagement," ii.

91. The only published studies were several articles in the June 1966 issue of the Evangelical Anglican publication *Latimer* giving first impressions of the Charismatic Movement (Dale Oldham, "First Impressions," *Latimer*, no. 25 (June 1966): 14–18 and F. R. Entwhistle, "Baptism in the Spirit and Speaking in Tongues," *Latimer*, no. 25: 18–25); and New Zealand Broadcasting Corporation, *I Believe: A Series of Talks Broadcast over NZBC Stations in 1967* ([Wellington]: New Zealand Broadcasting Corporation, [1968], which included a radio talk by Rob Wheeler on the Indigenous Churches.

92. Early magazine and newspaper articles on the two movements include McCracken, "The God Squad," 14–15; and Loryman, "Growth of the Pentecostal Movement," 7.

93. For example, C. T. Waldegrave, "Social and Personality Correlates of Pentecostalism: A Review of the Literature and a Comparison of Pentecostal Christian Students with Non-Pentecostal Christian Students" (BPhil dissertation in Educational Psychology, University of Waikato, 1972); and Neil, "Institutional Churches and the Charismatic Renewal."

94. Two of the earliest books were Worsfold, *History of the Charismatic Movements in New Zealand*; and John Osborne, ed., *The Winds of the Spirit: An Introductory Study on the Charismatic Movement* (Auckland: Methodist Board of Publications, 1974); and N. F. H. Merritt, *To God Be The Glory: The First Ten and a Half Years of the Charismatic Movement at St. Paul's* (Auckland: St. Paul's Outreach Trust, 1981).

95. Colin Brown, "Pentecostalism, Neo-Pentecostalism and Naturalistic Explanation," in *The Religious Dimension: A Selection of Essays Presented at a Colloquium on Religious Studies Held at the University of Auckland, New Zealand in August 1975*, ed. J. Hinchcliff, 55–57 (Auckland: Rep Prep Ltd., 1975); and Brown, "Will the Charismatic Renewal Permanently Renew?"

96. Brown, "The Charismatic Contribution," 104. Not all articles were so positive: Geoff Chapple, "When the Spirit Moves," *New Zealand Listener*, 24 July 1976, 24–25 is somewhat condescending in tone, trying to explain the Charismatic movement from a psychological perspective.

97. Donald Battley, "The Renewal is over . . . is it?" *Affirm* 5.3 (Spring 1997): 17.

98. Battley, "Charismatic Renewal: A View from the Inside," 49.

99. Elaine Bolitho, *Meet the Baptists: Postwar personalities and perspectives* (Auckland: Christian Research Association of New Zealand, c.1993), 36, cited in Ward, "The Charismatic Movement in New Zealand," 4.

100. D. R. Strickland, "Church growth Analysis: the fastest growing and declining Presbyterian churches in New Zealand," Titirangi, 1985 (typescript).

Chapter 10

The 1970s: Part 2

"Heady and Exhausting Days": Pentecostal Growth in the 1970s

The 1970s were boom years for New Zealand Pentecostalism; almost all churches associated with the movement experienced sustained growth during the decade, in contrast to the decline in mainstream church attendances. Census statistics show that it almost trebled in size between 1971 and 1981,[1] becoming, as Peter Lineham notes, "one of the strongest Pentecostal movements in the West" in the 1970s.[2] However, its growth was actually greater than this, as many adherents preferred to identify themselves as "Christian" rather than as some variety of "Pentecostal." Consequently, Presbyterian minister Ray Galvin estimated that by 1982

> the total membership of Pentecostal churches [stood] at about 36,000 and their weekly adult attendance [at] above 40,000: hence, *the Pentecostal worshipping community is now approaching the size of the Presbyterian* and is certainly bigger than the Baptist or Methodist [churches]. . . . It is clear that *over the last fifteen years the centre of gravity of New Zealand Christianity has shifted somewhat in the direction of the Pentecostalist/Fundamentalist tradition.*[3]

This growth was reflected in the proliferation and expansion of Pentecostal churches throughout the country and was paralleled by the spread of the Charismatic movement in the mainstream churches. Even the increasingly independent identity of the Charismatic movement after 1973 did little to dampen Pentecostal optimism, which was reflected in increased exuberance and a profound sense of opportunity. The excitement of the period is captured in a Newsletter produced in early 1976 by one of the Indigenous Churches. This reported that "during 10 nights of recent meetings in Auckland, it is a conservative estimate that over 2000 people received the Baptism of the Holy Spirit. In one meeting alone, over 700 people recieved [*sic*] the Holy Ghost.

PRAISE THE LORD." The same newsletter noted that the Indigenous Churches were themselves experiencing vigorous growth:

> The Timaru Assembly has seen people come to Christ every Sunday night without fail since Christmas. Ashburton has seen 30 new people in the last 7 months. Motueka has 41 decisions last year, with new families being added again this year. They are planning another extension after their recent extension is completed.... Ivan Gutschlag has baptised over 20 people in Arrowtown since Christmas.[4]

The reference to baptisms is significant, since these churches practiced "believers' baptism," i.e., the baptism of converts by full immersion. These people therefore represented additions to the movement.

Other Pentecostal churches were also growing. The most spectacular increase was that of the Elim Church of New Zealand, which had been a moribund group up to the early 1970s, when it recorded just over 100 members in the 1971 Census. By 1981, this had grown to 1,257 adherents. The Blenheim Elim church, under Ian Bilby's leadership, headed this rapid growth, expanding from three members on his arrival there in 1972, to more than 400 adults in the congregation ten years later. In so doing, it became the largest Elim church in the country.[5] Pentecostal growth was particularly strong in the larger cities. In Auckland, the Queen Street Assembly of God had been experiencing a season of revival since 1970, growing at an unprecedented rate for the next fifteen years. Ian Clark notes that this church soon became the largest Pentecostal church in the country and exercised a huge influence on the Assemblies of God movement.[6] Its expansion necessitated a move to larger premises, with its meetings being relocated at the Auckland Town Hall from 1971 until 1985.[7] Similarly, the Sydenham Assembly of God in Christchurch also experienced revival—although this was more short-lived,[8] for reasons that will shortly be discussed[9]—with hundreds of hippies being saved and filled with the Spirit. This influx of Jesus People was the most significant visitation that the Sydenham church had experienced since Smith Wigglesworth's campaigns there fifty years previously.[10] The number of Assemblies of God congregations also grew, from forty at the 1971 Conference to eighty-five by 1979.[11] This increase was partly due to an influx of charismatic Christians from other denominations as the Charismatic movement made Pentecostalism more respectable and attractive.[12] Indeed, this expansion was so rapid by the mid-1970s that there was a real danger that the Assemblies of God Executive would be left behind by the growth of the movement.[13] The Indigenous Churches also enlarged significantly, with the Christchurch New Life Centre, for example, growing from 600 adherents in 1975 to more than 1,000 in 1979. As with the Assemblies of God, this increase was partly due to the transfer of Charismatic Christians.[14] These large churches represented the emergence of the new phenomenon of Pentecostal megachurches in New Zealand; these would become increasingly prominent over the next decade, particularly in Auckland.

The Changing Character of the Pentecostal Movement

The burgeoning growth of the movement, which peaked at the end of the 1970s, was accompanied by increasing diversity and complexity.[15] The composition of its congregations was changing, with an increasing predominance of young people.[16] Sociologist Michael Hill noted that there was an overrepresentation of younger age groups in the movement in relation to the population as a whole in the 1976 Census, and that the peak age of the churches in the Associated Pentecostal Churches of New Zealand was in the twenty-five to thirty year-old bracket.[17] This youthfulness had implications for the movement's attitudes and patterns of growth: Ian Clark notes that the growth of the Assemblies of God in the 1970s was largely due to a new generation of confident and adventurous young ministers, ably supported by Superintendent Frank Houston. This contributed to its transformation into an outward-looking movement and to the loss of the siege mentality and defensive attitudes that had characterized it for many years.[18]

This predominance of youth was paralleled by a transition into higher socio-economic levels.[19] The Auckland Assembly of God, for example, mutated markedly between 1970 and 1983, partly through social lift as the church became more middle class.[20] Clark noted that in comparison to earlier years, there were now people from many different professions in the movement.[21] This social lift was accompanied by greater affluence—particularly in the latter part of the decade—which increased the sociopolitical and economic resources of Pentecostal churches.[22] Feminist Sandra Coney ruefully lamented the financial power of the Christchurch New Life Centre in the context of its 1977 Save Our Homes campaign, noting that

> If [Pentecostal] power in numbers may be a carefully constructed fallacy [sic], their money is not. The Christchurch UWC [United Women's Convention] started its organising with $100 in the kitty. I've heard figures ranging up to $10,000 quoted to me in connection with "Save Our Homes." ... Where does the money come from? Not from a simple group of home-loving mothers, as Mrs. [Anne] Morrow, who just happens to be the wife of the "New Life Centre" pastor, would have us believe they were.[23]

This sense of power changed both the self-perceptions of the movement and the attitudes of society towards it.

The movement also became increasingly respectable as the public media began to take an interest in it. Examples of this new interest included an approach to Pastor Neville Johnson of the Auckland Assembly of God by Radio 1ZB in the early 1970s[24] and journalist Gaynor Loryman's positive article on the Pentecostal movement in the *Christchurch Star* in 1973.[25] This new respectability owed something to the influence of the Charismatic movement,[26] although Colin Brown mistakenly attributes it to deliberate attempts by Pentecostal pastors to improve their social standing and thus to facilitate growth.[27] (Brown overrelies on the example of James Worsfold, who stressed the connections of the Apostolic Church with Parliamentarians and other civic dignitaries.[28] This was a product of Worsfold's own enthusiasms and connections, since he lived close to Parliament Building in central Wellington and frequented its corridors as a self-appointed unofficial "chaplain"—complete with clerical collar—to the Members of Parliament.[29] The walls of Worsfold's study were covered with photographs of him taken with various Parliamentarians, ambassadors and other dignitaries.)

Another significant change in the 1970s was the increasing ethnicization of some sections of the movement. This ethnicization was most evident in the Assemblies of God and was particularly vigorous among the Samoan community; its effects were reinforced by the rise of churches catering for other ethnicities in the 1990s.[30] By contrast, Māori were not strongly represented in most Pentecostal churches. Philip Carew and Geoff Troughton observe that "Māori links with the Assemblies of God were tenuous" by the 1970s and that no sustained Māori work had ever been undertaken to that point.[31] Until the emergence of the Destiny Churches in the 1990s, the Apostolic Church was the only Pentecostal group with a significant Māori constituency.[32] This was despite the initial evangelistic expansion in the late 1950s of both the Assemblies of God and the Indigenous Churches having taken place amongst rural Māori.[33] That momentum was not sustained as the movements grew larger.

There was also an increasing diversity of origins, with pastors coming into Pentecostal churches from other movements, bringing different ideas and views with them. This influx created differences of approach from—and some tensions with—older, more traditional Pentecostals. Ian Clark refers to these younger pastors' "rather different views on how to respond to counsel and direction" from the Executive Council and to the "robust but positive exchanges" that resulted.[34] In the case of the Indigenous Churches, new pastors coming from Baptist and Brethren backgrounds took issue with its polity of the autonomy of the local church and sought greater structure and cooperation. This tension underlay some of the developments in that body in the 1980s.[35]

However, the most significant long-term development was the shift in Pentecostal perceptions of the pastor's role. The growth, socioeconomic lift and increasing diversity of the movement in the 1970s had implications for its traditional models of pastoral leadership.[36] In part, this was a product of a small-church movement becoming large; but it also reflected an attempt to move away from formal organizational controls to more charismatic forms of leadership. (This was an inevitable tension: Bryan Wilson has noted the conflicts in the pastoral role as a movement changes from revival to established church, basing his analysis on the Elim Foursquare Alliance of Great Britain.)[37] Many of the main Pentecostal groups in New Zealand were challenged in this regard, although not all in the same way. Even those groups—such as the Assemblies of God and the Apostolic Church—which had long-standing models of leadership had to reframe their polity in the 1970s. Others, such as the Indigenous Churches, had to work towards the development of new organizational frameworks. The Charismatic movement also had to define structures of accountability to counter extremism and autocracy. Not all of these changes were positive, nor were they fully resolved in the 1970s; many of the developments of the 1980s—in, for example, the Indigenous Churches—had begun in the previous decade.

The Apostolic Church appeared to have had the most clearly defined framework of ministry roles, with pastors and other local officers being appointed at prophetic direction and confirmed by apostolic oversight in the Council. James Worsfold notes that this centralized pattern was becoming dysfunctional by the 1970s and there was a trend towards greater local autonomy among the Apostolic churches.[38] His son Luke Worsfold asserts that the policy of centralism, whereby personnel were relocated to different pastorates around the country at the mandate of the Council "had the greatest potential for misuse and destroying the progress of both man and movement."[39] In some cases, individuals were prophesied into pastorates for which they were unsuited and, in other cases, despite their disinclination to relocate. He gives a striking example in the Council's arbitrary decision to relocate Pastor J. W. Keane from Rotorua to Otara, despite the latter's strong personal conviction against the move and his strenuous objections to it.[40] The issue came to a head with a particularly inept example in 1977, when James Worsfold—who was then General Secretary of the movement—was relocated at prophetic direction from Wellington to Auckland. This was despite his long service in Wellington and his national responsibilities there; it also involved considerable personal sacrifice for him, since he had to live alone in Auckland while his family remained in Wellington. This proved to be the last such forced relocation of a senior Apostolic minister and it is not surprising that tensions followed his return to Wellington several years later. As a result the attitude of the Apostolic Council towards such pastoral reappointments changed markedly in the 1980s with more weight being given to the views of the local pastor.[41]

The movement towards to an emphasis on pastoral authority was even more marked in the case of the Assemblies of God and the language used to describe this changed role is telling. A significant amendment resulted from a crisis in the Sydenham Assembly in 1973. This assembly followed the old system of congregational government that had been set up on its establishment in 1927, in which the members voted at regular intervals on the calling and continuance of their pastor. Although revival had taken place under Pastor Dennis Barton and hundreds of Jesus People had been added to the church, the core congregation voted not to renew his call at its Annual General Meeting. (Since the hundreds of new members did not yet have voting rights, this was effectively a coup by a minority of older, conservative members, who were unhappy at the changes that had taken place.) The outcome of this crisis was that he resigned to start a new work—unaffiliated with the Assemblies of God—elsewhere in Christchurch and took large numbers of the congregation with him. This debacle led to a long-overdue change in the Assemblies of God's congregational leadership polity, the Charismatic movement also contributing to this amendment, as well as current teaching on the "ascension gift ministries" of Eph.4:11. This change was highly significant: "Over the next ten years ... more and more assemblies abandoned traditional methods of congregational government in favor of rule by the pastor and an eldership appointed by him with congregational approval.... In this way the movement was largely transformed from democracy to theocracy at the local level."[42] An example of this process was the Lower Hutt Assembly of God, where

> Pastor Houston simply got up one morning and told the church he was not prepared to have to go through the reelection process every two years at the annual general meeting. . . . He then went on to state that he did not wish to work with a board chosen by members, but with men who clearly had the giftings of elders. He then proceeded to say who those would be and who would serve the church as a separate group of deacons. Few raised any objections, and the work of the church moved along without a pause.[43]

This theocratic pattern, based on recognized charismatic ministry gifting, became the norm, not only in the Assemblies of God, but also in other Pentecostal churches. It centralized local church leadership in the hands of the pastor and his council of elders. There were advantages in this pattern in that it gave the movement a focus for its charismatic authority. Its growth enabled it to speak with authority in its own right and this advanced the role of the pastor as the spokesman for that authority.[44] (The gender-specificity of the title "spokesman" is appropriate, since there were few female pastors in the movement at this time.) It therefore worked well in the majority of cases. However, there were also significant dangers in that it created space for an inherent authoritarianism to develop. And, while the elders, in theory, could exercise a moderating influence on pastoral extremes, their choice as elders was usually the pastor's prerogative and they consequently tended to act in confirmatory, rather than oppositional, roles. There were therefore few checks and balances in the theocratic system. The congregation, in particular, had little right of dissent, this being silenced with the use of scriptures such as Ps.105:15 "Touch not my anointed" (the pastor being "the anointed" and therefore above criticism). As will be seen in Chapter 11, events in the 1980s demonstrated the limitations and dangers of this polity.

There were also several attempts in the 1970s to impose some means of control on independent charismatics not subject to denominational or other authority as well as on undisciplined rogue pastors. The first of these was the emergence of the Discipleship movement (also known as the "Shepherding movement") in the United States and elsewhere.[45] This developed in response to the problem of the increasing number of wandering charismatics who were free from any system of accountability. It taught that every believer needed to submit to a "shepherd" or pastoral leader and that all pastors and leaders themselves needed to be personally submitted to another leader to foster accountability.[46] This idea was based on the teachings of Argentinian conference evangelist and speaker Juan Carlos Ortiz, which in turn drew inspiration from those of well-known Chinese Christian Watchman Nee. While the intention of the movement was no doubt a laudatory one, it could be applied in draconian ways and consequently created division and controversy in the Charismatic movement worldwide. Furthermore, it split congregations between those disciples who had submitted to leadership authority and those who had not; it also cut across denominational lines of authority.

Although Juan Carlos Ortiz and a number of other discipleship teachers were frequent visitors to New Zealand in the 1970s, their teachings did not take root here to the same degree as overseas.[47] In part, this was due to cultural and social factors, particularly the independence and egalitarianism that characterised New Zealand attitudes. As Rasik Ranchord comments, New Zealanders were not likely "to give that degree of control to another person.... We don't accept 'hierarchy' too well.... We like to be our own boss, and I don't think ... people would have taken too kindly [to that degree of authority]."[48] Nevertheless, the movement did reinforce ideas that were already beginning to emerge in this country. Its concerns were preempted by the "Covering" teaching of Indigenous Church pastor David Ellis, which expressed these ideas in a different way. Ellis taught that although charismatic ministry was of itself authoritative, since it was a manifestation of the Holy Spirit, it needed to be legitimated by submission to a "covering" or authority in the church. Local congregation members ministered under the covering of their pastor, while the pastors themselves were to be under the covering of a senior pastor in the movement. Given that the Indigenous Churches then had no authority structure beyond the local church, this provided a means of extralocal accountability in the movement, but also reinforced the authority of the local pastor over the congregation. This "Covering" teaching became quite pervasive in the next two decades and reinforced the trend towards pastoral theocracy.

Shifting Alliances and Relationships: Towards Rapprochement

The growth and changing character of the movement in the 1970s was paralleled by its shifting alliances and relationships. The distancing of the Charismatic movement from its Pentecostal counterpart, which has already been noted, enabled it to develop its own independent identity, although links of fellowship remained warm and genuine.[49] There were also attempts to restore previously severed connections, such as the South East Asia-Pacific Ministers Conference convened in Melbourne by Ray Jackson's Associated Mission Churches of Australasia in June 1973. This unsuccessfully attempted to renew associations between the Indigenous Churches and their Australian counterparts, both of which derived from the Latter Rain movement of the late 1940s and early 1950s.[50] The Conference sought to achieve commonality on this basis for the purpose of a missions thrust into Indonesia. However, nothing was achieved, since the New Zealand churches were rather different in ethos from their more sectarian Australian counterparts, having multiple founders and broader doctrinal emphases. Nevertheless, there was significant rapprochement between New Zealand Pentecostal churches throughout the decade.[51] The Jesus Marches had demonstrated the effectiveness of different churches working together for a common cause. Furthermore, the influence of the Charismatic movement had shown that it was possible to have genuine fellowship between Spirit-filled people of diverse church backgrounds. The most important factor, however, was the ministry of overseas speakers in the early 1970s—in particular, Ern Baxter—which stimulated this rapprochement. Ian Clark recalls that

> One of the major factors in Pentecostals flowing together was Ern Baxter. No question about Ern Baxter in my mind. He talked about things which no-one else was willing to talk about, and he opened the hearts and minds and understanding of people of their sinfulness in division in a way that hadn't been seen before. I was profoundly personally affected by Ern Baxter, and I still cherish to this day a vision of the united Pentecostal movement in this country.[52]

Clark does not explain what specific issues Baxter was addressing, but it would appear from the context of his comments that he was referring to division and disunity within the Pentecostal movement. Although Baxter's views were treated with extreme skepticism by Neville Johnson of the influential Queen Street Assembly of God in Auckland,[53] they also enjoyed wide acceptance in other New Zealand churches.

Baxter's call for Pentecostal unity was very much to the point, since, as has been previously noted, Pentecostalism has a long history of division in New Zealand.[54] (Even ostensibly ecumenical Pentecostal associations, such as the New Zealand Pentecostal Fellowship, perpetuated this division, since these were selective in their inclusiveness.)[55] As a result of the seed sown by Baxter, links between various Pentecostal groups began to develop around the country, particularly in Auckland. By 1974, an Auckland Pentecostal Ministers' Association had been set up, chaired by Indigenous pastor Shaun Kearney and Assemblies of God minister Don Dunn. This Association—which crossed denominational lines—met regularly for prayer and fellowship and, the following year, proposed a nationwide Unity Conference to be held at Snell's Beach in March 1975. This Conference, which attracted 160 pastors from all Pentecostal groups, represented a landmark in New Zealand Pentecostalism. It was the most widely representative Conference of its kind and was uniquely successful in inspiring Pentecostal unity.[56]

Several factors combined to produce this success. The rapport and confidence that had developed between different Pentecostal groups as a result of Baxter's ministry was a key factor, as also was a growing unity, particularly in the Auckland region. As well as this, delegates to the Conference were allocated to sleeping quarters with ministers from other Pentecostal groups rather than their own, thus ensuring across-the-board fellowship with new people, and the formation of lifelong friendships.[57] The most inspired decision, however, was the choice of Pastor Jack Hayford[58] from the well-known Church on the Way, Van Nuys, California, as the Conference speaker. Hayford was a superb communicator and deeply sensitive to the Holy Spirit. He also had the advantage of being able to speak into the New Zealand Pentecostal movement from a neutral standpoint, since Foursquare, his denomination, was not represented in New Zealand.[59] Rasik Ranchord notes that

> [Jack Hayford] was the right person to bring because of his ability to relate, particularly with the human aspect of things, and the way he shared his own heart, his struggles and his failures, . . . his type of ministry seemed to open people up. And

it certainly engendered a much more honest and open attitude towards people of other Pentecostal churches.... He showed the human face in ministry, not just his success side.... His openness before the brethren was an example to us, that we needed to be a bit more open towards one another.[60]

Hayford's openness and honesty produced a healing of relationships between the various Pentecostal churches and the generation of a new sense of Pentecostal unity. This was cemented at a meeting of Pentecostal leaders on the second day of the Convention. These included Mark (Marcus) Goulton and James Worsfold of the Apostolic Church; Frank Houston and Ian Clark of the Assemblies of God; Dudley Cooper of the Christian Revival Crusade; and Peter Morrow and Rob Wheeler of the Indigenous Churches. The only major Pentecostal group not represented at this meeting was the Elim Churches of New Zealand, since Gilbert Dunk, their General Secretary, did not attend the Convention. Clark recalls that:

> There were those who were all for pell-mell uniting all the Pentecostals into one body. And there were others who shrank back from that, if not in horror, [then] in trepidation, and in the finish, a compromise was reached. There were plenary sessions to begin with ..., but it became evident to the leadership of the various Pentecostal groupings that the plenary sessions wouldn't achieve [unity].... The key to the breakthrough was at a meeting down in the old farmhouse on the Snell's Beach property, when the leaders of all the groups ... sat together, and ... said "Yes, we want to flow together. Yes, we want to forget the past. Yes, we want to be brethren together. Yes, we do want to love one another. But we want to take it in stages, like a 'courtship' rather than [to] 'get married' straight away." We decided that I [as secretary of the about-to-be-formed APCNZ] would act as a "clearing house," that we would open our pulpits more to one another, and that we would make representations on social and moral issues, and I was appointed spokesman to do that. And we did it.[61]

This newfound unity took organizational form with the holding of annual conferences for the pastors of the movement and with the creation of a new "umbrella" body, the Associated Pentecostal Churches of New Zealand [APCNZ]. This was set up to speak on behalf of its member churches (the Apostolic Church, the Assemblies of God, the Christian Revival Crusade, the Elim Pentecostal Church and the Indigenous Churches of New Zealand). Despite not having attended the Snell's Beach Convention, Gilbert Dunk of the Elim Churches of New Zealand did take part in the later delegation to the Prime Minister and the Elim churches were affiliated to the APCNZ. Although this new body was also intended to facilitate representation to Government on social and moral issues, it did much to shape the development of the Pentecostal movement in the late 1970s and early 1980s.

The Associated Pentecostal Churches of New Zealand: Its Significance and Legacy

Initially, the new Association reinforced the rapprochement that was taking place[62] and Ian Clark notes the "steady erosion of separatist and elitist attitudes" that resulted.[63] Throughout the 1970s, these strongly attended annual APCNZ pastors' Conferences continued to strengthen the greater openness that was emerging and to facilitate "cross-pollination"—to use Clark's apt term—between the Pentecostal groups. However, his reference to "representations on social and moral issues" during his interview is significant, since moralist concerns were important stimuli in its formation. One of the first actions of the APCNZ was to send two delegations, one to the Prime Minister, Wallace ("Bill") Rowling and the other to the Leader of the Opposition, Robert Muldoon. Their stated purpose was to "discuss moral and social issues causing concern to the Pentecostal churches."[64] Most of the pastors interviewed during the author's doctoral research[65] linked the formation of the APCNZ with the sending of the two delegations, as did all references in documentary materials sighted by the author. It is therefore evident that moralist concerns provided the motivation, at least in part, for the setting up of the APCNZ.

Recollections of the Association's formation make significant references to the size and political strength of a united Pentecostal movement. Rasik Ranchord recalled that the APCNZ was formed so that "on ... moral issues, we could tell the Government that we were backed by at least 15,000 people."[66] Pentecostal consciousness of the need to have an effective political voice on moral issues to counter a perceived threat from the permissive society was one of the key factors in the formation of the APCNZ. As Auckland New Life pastor John Tiplady put it, "The [Pentecostal] churches were trying to do everything in an un-united [sic], uncoordinated, way, and ... really didn't have the strength of impact on Government that they could have if they united, so that was the reason for the delegations. It said 'Hey, we're united, and a significant force within New Zealand society.'"[67] This reference to a "significant force within New Zealand society" indicates that Pentecostal activism owed as much to an upward mobility as to a desire to influence social morality.

Although responses to the delegations were mixed, they were reported in the national press[68] and their members were interviewed several times on national radio. Both the Prime Minister and the Leader of the Opposition urged Christian involvement in the political arena. *Challenge Weekly* had previously reported the Prime Minister as making "a strong public statement approving and urging the involvement of Christians in politics"[69] and the Leader of the Opposition also encouraged Christian involvement in political issues.[70] There was evidently awareness, particularly by the Leader of the Opposition, of the depth of feeling over moral issues, and, it would seem, an attempt to use that concern to political advantage. Consequently, although both conservative and liberal Christian groups were courted by the politicians in the run-up to the 1975 election, conservative Christians were assiduously cultivated by the National Party. Muldoon, for example, took part in a Jesus 75 rally in Auckland in June[71] and, together with other

National Party MPs, addressed a service at the Christchurch New Life Centre in late September.[72]

The delegations achieved little, their effects being indirect, rather than direct. Nevertheless, there was a feeling in the Pentecostal movement of having arrived, believing that they had succeeded in gaining the ear of the Government where other churches had failed.[73] This perception was not entirely accurate, since other churches also sporadically lobbied the Government, particularly in the 1940s and 1950s, although less frequently in the 1960s and 1970s.[74] Nevertheless, it is an indicator of the sense of self-identity and political power that was developing in the movement in the mid-1970s. This somewhat triumphalist self-understanding was demonstrated in the antifeminist Save Our Homes campaign in 1977 and helped to reinforce the emerging moralist movement in the late 1970s and early 1980s.

This engagement with the political process represented a major shift in the attitude of Pentecostal churches and may reflect the way in which the concerns of mainstream churches were filtering through to the Pentecostal movement. This filtering process appears to have applied as much to the new Pentecostal ecumenism as to the concomitant political involvement over issues in the wider society. Not all the member churches of the APCNZ shared this change of attitude to the same extent, however. The Assemblies of God were extremely hesitant about political involvement, feeling that a linkage with any political party would be "quite fatal" for the movement.[75] By contrast, John Tiplady commented that the delegations marked the beginning of political awareness and involvement in the Indigenous Churches, especially in the Auckland region. From the perspective of these churches, the delegations "sparked off the thought that it wasn't 'ungodly' to get involved in the political arena. Up to that point, I think there was an influence that we were to be 'in the world but not of it' to the extent that we didn't have any input or . . . any concern for the political process. That [attitude] was changed."[76] This new attitude did not imply that the Pentecostal churches' conservative views on the problems of society had altered. Neither did their newfound involvement in politics lead necessarily to a liaison with the National Party, although they shared its conservative approach to the issues of the day.[77] Nevertheless, this informal convergence of views had hardened into some overt Pentecostal support for the National Party by the mid-1980s and the involvement of Pentecostals in the political process became more direct. By then, both the main political parties had recognized the potential benefits of this growing constituency and sought to encourage contacts with Pentecostal churches. The *Otago Daily Times* noted in 1985 that Labour leader David Lange had "urged his candidates, particularly rural ones, to make contact with Pentecostal churches. Diligent provincial members maintained a close awareness [of] and contact with these churches."[78] The reference to "rural" and "provincial" shows a keen awareness of the movement's spread beyond the main urban centers. However, members of Pentecostal churches tended to support the National Party rather than Labour. The most high-profile example of the new Pentecostal political involvement was Rob Wheeler's candidacy for the Mount Albert seat for National in the 1987 General Election.[79]

Throughout the remainder of the 1970s, the APCNZ continued to issue statements and to make submissions to Government on behalf of its member churches, as well as to work towards Pentecostal unity. Conventions were held on an annual basis until the early 1980s, when the format changed to a biennial one.[80] Nevertheless, Ian Clark believes that the APCNZ had begun to drift by the end of the decade: "With the departure of Frank [Houston] and me . . . , [APCNZ] lost a lot of its impetus. We'd had annual Conferences, and I think they were a *vital* thing. . . . The decision was made by the committee [in the 1980s] . . . to go to two-yearly meetings; that effectively took all the steam out of what God wanted to do. And, I think, we blew it. . . . [Since then] it's drifted."[81] Clark dates this loss of impetus to 1977, since Houston left for Australia that year. However, since Clark remained Secretary of the APCNZ until 1980,[82] the decline may have been more gradual. In part this drift was due to lack of leadership by the APCNZ, which, as a loose association of churches, existed at the will of—and had no real jurisdiction over— its member groups. This meant that, despite the theoretical goal of unity in the movement, there was no real convergence of perspective among the Pentecostal churches.[83] As well as this, some later Pentecostal leaders were not as enthusiastic about the APCNZ as its founders had been in the 1970s. Clark cites former Assemblies of God Superintendent Jim Williams, who became Chairman of the APCNZ Steering Committee[84] in 1985, as an example of this lack of enthusiasm.[85] Eventually the biennial Conventions ceased in 2000[86] and meetings of the Steering Committee several years later.

The APCNZ was significant as a focal point for Pentecostal unity and activism, particularly during its early years. The Pentecostal ecumenism that it fostered was one of the key driving forces behind the movement's expansion in the late 1970s and declining enthusiasm for the Association in the 1980s mirrored a narrowing of focus. There seems to be an inverse relationship between the size of a Pentecostal church and the degree of its conviction towards the APCNZ: megachurch congregations often appeared less committed towards Pentecostal ecumenism. This was because these large churches could generate their own resources without having to utilize outside assistance. As Clark put it in speaking of some Assemblies of God responses to the APCNZ's formation: "the [Assemblies of God] was booming, really, [so] why did they need the *APC[NZ]*?"[87] The shift to biennial Conferences in the 1980s reflected this declining enthusiasm and thus diminished a potent source of Pentecostal enrichment. Similarly, the creation of in-house denominational agencies for renewal in the early 1980s robbed the Charismatic movement of its key ecumenical dynamic.

Conclusion

The turbulent 1970s were a highly significant decade for New Zealand Pentecostalism. Reactions against social change—manifest in the rise of conservatism and in the intensity and polarization that accompanied responses to the permissive society—both contributed to, and were strengthened by, the movement's growth. This was not the only example of mutually reinforcing movements during the decade: the Jesus Marches—and the associated moralist movement—gained much of their support from the Pentecostal movement, but also enlarged the latter's constituency. Similarly, the Pentecostal and Charismatic movements each contributed to the other's development. The parallels between Pentecostal growth and conservative moralist activism continued into the 1980s, climaxing with the nationwide opposition to the Homosexual Law Reform Bill in the middle of that decade.

Another factor in the Pentecostal growth of the 1970s was the informal ecumenism that was one of the driving forces behind the movement's expansion. Although the Charismatic movement had developed its own identity after 1973, it continued to contribute to an enlargement of Pentecostal horizons and, in many cases, to the growth of the latter movement's churches. This contribution was both organizational and conceptual: as churches joined the Pentecostal movement and as Charismatics transferred their membership to it, traditional patterns of leadership were challenged, leading to changes of orientation and polity.

Two changes during the decade were particularly significant for the future of the movement. Firstly, standard Pentecostal leadership models were becoming less effective as their churches grew. Furthermore, the movement's changing character due to social lift and increasing respectability, together with the externalization of its focus as it became less sectarian and more outward-looking, transformed its leadership patterns. This was reflected in changing perceptions of the pastor's role, with a shift to more theocratic models of leadership (by contrast to democratic patterns in which the congregation had voting rights and input into decisions). This centralization of the pastor's role—together with attempts to curb independence and extremism through the application of discipleship and covering models—placed fresh emphasis on the pastor as the charismatic leader anointed by God. This shift enabled greater charismatic power through the authority of the pastor, but also brought about the loss of checks and balances and thus created the risk of this authority being abused. As well as this, it facilitated the growth of Pentecostal megachurches in the 1980s and beyond. This was also the case in Australia, where Pentecostal church historian Denise Austin observes that these megachurches were the product of a swing towards charismatic leadership in the 1970s. This produced a recentering away from traditional connexional frameworks, which had emphasized the movement as a united whole, toward larger autonomous local churches.[88]

The second change was the rapprochement between Pentecostal churches in the mid-1970s, which healed decades of distrust and suspicion. This reconciliation at the Snell's Beach Conference in March 1975 took organizational form in the creation of the Associated Pentecostal Churches of New Zealand. The new Association consolidated this newfound unity and allowed the movement to speak with a united voice on moralist issues. In so doing, it reflected a sense of self-confidence and power, laying the foundations for Pentecostal involvement in the political and social arenas for the remainder of the decade and into the 1980s. Although this political involvement was actually at variance with the movement's premillennial eschatology, it reflected awareness of its political influence and of the need to speak with a united Pentecostal voice on current issues. These perceptions continued into the 1980s, climaxing with the movement's strenuous opposition to the Homosexual Law Reform Bill in 1985 and 1986. These developments will be discussed in the next chapter.

Notes

1. See Appendix A.
2. Lineham, "When the Roll is Called Up Yonder, Who'll be There?" 16.
3. Galvin, "Learning from the Sects," 99. Emphasis as cited.
4. Kindah Greening, "From the Pastor's Desk," in Bethel Chapel, Invercargill, "Newsletter," Invercargill, [February 1976] (mimeographed). Cited in Knowles, *The History of a New Zealand Pentecostal Movement*, 277–78.
5. Yvonne Dasler, "Then they came to Elim . . . ," *New Zealand Listener*, 24 April 1982, 18.
6. Clark, *Pentecost at the Ends of the Earth*, 133.
7. Ibid, 134.
8. Assemblies of God in New Zealand, "Our History," 9.
9. See below, 173.
10. Clark, *Pentecost at the Ends of the Earth*, 143.
11. Ibid, 136 and 173, note 1.
12. Carew and Troughton, "Māori Participation in the Assemblies of God," 97.
13. Clark, *Pentecost at the Ends of the Earth*, 151.
14. Knowles, *The History of a New Zealand Pentecostal Movement*, 278.
15. Knowles, *The History of a New Zealand Pentecostal Movement*, 280–81 and 286; for the Charismatic movement, see Battley, "Charismatic Renewal: A View from the Inside," 49; and Battley, "The renewal is over . . . is it?": 17.
16. Worsfold, *History of the Charismatic Movements in New Zealand*, 289, note 1.
17. Michael Hill, "The Social Context of New Zealand Religion: 'Straight' or 'Narrow'"? in *Religion and New Zealand's Future*, ed. Kevin J. Sharpe (Palmerston North: Dunmore Press, 1982), 33, cited in Knowles, "Vision of the Disinherited?" 141, note 106.
18. Clark, *Pentecost at the Ends of the Earth*, 130. See also Carew and Troughton, "Māori Participation in the Assemblies of God," 97.
19. Knowles, *The History of a New Zealand Pentecostal Movement*, 284.
20. Laurie Guy, "'Spirit Possession' and 'Deliverance Ministry' in the Auckland Assembly of God, 1970–1983," in *Spirit Possession, Theology and Identity: A Pacific Exploration*, ed. Elaine M. Wainwright, General Editor, with Philip Cuthbertson and Susan Smith, 237 (Hindmarsh, SA: ATF Press, 2010).
21. See above, 95.
22. In the case of the Assemblies of God, see Clark, *Pentecost at the Ends of the Earth*, 171.
23. Sandra Coney, "Editorial," *Broadsheet*, May 1977, 11, cited in Knowles, *The History of a New Zealand Pentecostal Movement*, 233 and footnote 35.
24. Clark, *Pentecost at the Ends of the Earth*, 134.
25. Loryman, "Growth of the Pentecostal Movement," 7.
26. Carew and Troughton, "Māori Participation in the Assemblies of God," 97.

27. Brown, "The Charismatic Contribution," 104–5. See also Knowles, *The History of a New Zealand Pentecostal Movement*, 205.
28. Worsfold, *History of the Charismatic Movements in New Zealand*, 291.
29. See Luke Worsfold, "Subsequence, Prophecy and Church Order," 233 and note 63.
30. See above, 119.
31. Carew and Troughton, "Māori Participation in the Assemblies of God," 97.
32. Moetara, "Māori and Pentecostal Christianity in Aotearoa New Zealand," 79–83. See also Clark, *Pentecost at the Ends of the Earth*, 238.
33. See above, 96 and 98.
34. Clark, *Pentecost at the Ends of the Earth*, 149–50.
35. Knowles, *The History of a New Zealand Pentecostal Movement*, 269–70.
36. For the implications of this process within the Indigenous Churches, see Knowles, *The History of a New Zealand Pentecostal Movement*, 283–84.
37. B.R. Wilson, "The Pentecostalist Minister: Role Conflicts and Contradictions of Status," in Wilson, *Patterns of Sectarianism*, 138–57.
38. Worsfold, *History of the Charismatic Movements in New Zealand*, 287.
39. Luke Worsfold, "Subsequence, Prophecy and Church Order," 222.
40. Ibid, 225–27 and note 40.
41. Ibid, 231–36.
42. Clark, *Pentecost at the Ends of the Earth*, 143–44.
43. Ibid, 145.
44. Knowles, *The History of a New Zealand Pentecostal Movement*, 285.
45. For an account of this, see S. D. Moore, "Shepherding Movement," in NIDPCM, 1060–62.
46. Ibid, 1060.
47. For an account of the Discipleship/Shepherding movement in New Zealand, see Knowles, *The History of a New Zealand Pentecostal Movement*, 235–46.
48. Ranchord, Interview, cited in ibid, 244.
49. See above, 162–63.
50. Knowles, "Some Aspects of the History of the New Life Churches of New Zealand," 217–18. See also Knowles, *The History of a New Zealand Pentecostal Movement*, 49; and Chant, *Heart of Fire*, 201.
51. See Knowles, *The History of a New Zealand Pentecostal Movement*, 247–54.
52. Clark, Interview, cited in Knowles, *The History of a New Zealand Pentecostal Movement*, 248.
53. Clark, *Pentecost at the Ends of the Earth*, 149.
54. See above, 28, 55–56 and 73.
55. See above, 122–23.
56. Knowles, *The History of a New Zealand Pentecostal Movement*, 251–52; Clark, *Pentecost at the Ends of the Earth*, 152.
57. Clark, *Pentecost at the Ends of the Earth*, 152.
58. For a brief biography of Hayford, see S. D. Moore, "Hayford, Jack Williams Jr.," in NIDPCM, 692–93.
59. Clark, *Pentecost at the Ends of the Earth*, 152–53.
60. Ranchord, Interview, cited in Ibid, 252.
61. Clark, Interview, cited in Ibid, 253.
62. See Knowles, *The History of a New Zealand Pentecostal Movement*, 255–65.
63. Clark, *Pentecost at the Ends of the Earth*, 154.

64. "Rowling and Muldoon meet Pentecostals," *Challenge Weekly*, 16 August 1975, 1–2, cited in Knowles, *The History of a New Zealand Pentecostal Movement*, 255.

65. Published as Knowles, *The History of a New Zealand Pentecostal Movement*.

66. Rasik Ranchord to Howard Carter, 8 August 1975, Majestic House Correspondence Files [MHCF], Christchurch, cited in Knowles, *The History of a New Zealand Pentecostal Movement*, 255.

67. John Tiplady, Interview, Auckland, 2 March 1990, cited in Knowles, *The History of a New Zealand Pentecostal Movement*, 256. The audio cassette of this interview is held in BKRP, MS-3530/036, Hocken Library, Dunedin.

68. "Strong views on social, moral issues," *Evening Post*, 5 August 1975, 13.

69. "P.M. urges Christian involvement," *Challenge Weekly*, 3 May 1975, 1.

70. Reported in Rasik Ranchord to Don Capill, 6 October 1975, MHCF, cited in Knowles, *The History of a New Zealand Pentecostal Movement*, 257.

71. Reported in Bluck, "Jesus 75—a mixed blessing," 5.

72. Circular letter to Kath Shaw, 24 November 1975, MHCF, cited in Knowles, *The History of a New Zealand Pentecostal Movement*, 258.

73. Clark, Interview, cited in Knowles, *The History of a New Zealand Pentecostal Movement*, 258.

74. For example, see Colin Brown, *Forty Years On: A History of the National Council of Churches in New Zealand 1941–1981* (Christchurch: National Council of Churches, 1981), 145.

75. Clark, Interview, cited in Knowles, *The History of a New Zealand Pentecostal Movement*, 259.

76. Tiplady, Interview, cited in Knowles, *The History of a New Zealand Pentecostal Movement*, 259.

77. Knowles, *The History of a New Zealand Pentecostal Movement*, 259–60.

78. "Moral Coalition seen as political threat," *Otago Daily Times*, 14 September 1985, 4.

79. For articles on Wheeler's candidacy, see Brian Rudman, "For God and National," *New Zealand Listener*, 28 March 1987, 28–29; and Stratford, "Christians Awake!"

80. MHCF, cited in Knowles, *The History of a New Zealand Pentecostal Movement*, 263, note 32.

81. Clark, Interview, cited in Knowles, *The History of a New Zealand Pentecostal Movement*, 263. Emphasis as cited.

82. Clark, *Pentecost at the Ends of the Earth*, 175–76.

83. Clark, Interview, cited in Knowles, *The History of a New Zealand Pentecostal Movement*, 263.

84. Clark, *Pentecost at the Ends of the Earth*, 175–76.

85. Ibid, 153, note 13.

86. Ibid, 153.

87. Clark, Interview, cited in Knowles, *The History of a New Zealand Pentecostal Movement*, 259, note 16.

88. Denise A. Austin, *Our College: A History of the National College of Australian Christian Churches (Assemblies of God in Australia)*. Australian Pentecostal Studies Supplementary Series 5 (Sydney: Australian Pentecostal Studies, 2013), 135.

Chapter 11

The 1980s

Prelude to a Revolution

In the early 1980s, New Zealand continued the trend towards economic and social conservatism that had begun in the previous decade. This was most marked during the administration of National Prime Minister Robert Muldoon from 1975 to 1984. Although temperamentally aggressive and pugnacious, Muldoon was also a political conservative and he sought to retain the electoral middle ground by preserving individual economic security and by reinforcing the state's role as provider of support. This was a difficult task in the face of high inflation and increasing unemployment, large Budget and balance of payments deficits and the effects of the oil price rises of the 1970s. As conditions worsened, Muldoon followed an interventionist policy of controlling industrial relations, tightening controls on the economy and imposing strict freezes on wages and prices in 1982 and also, two years later, on interest rates. In addition, he attempted to reduce New Zealand's reliance on overseas sources of fuel by developing the country's natural gas and abundant hydroelectric energy potential. This policy, known as "Think Big," was reflected in the building of massive projects such as the Motunui methanol plant, the Marsden Point Oil refinery and the Clyde dam.[1] These expensive schemes were relatively unsuccessful; the reduction in oil prices that followed the initial oil shocks of 1973–75 made the Motunui and Marsden Point projects uneconomic and the expected financial benefits did not materialize.[2] Furthermore, the Clyde dam, one of the largest in New Zealand, was subsequently found to have been built right on top of an earthquake fault line in the Kawarau gorge.[3] These Think Big projects—and the increased overseas borrowing needed to finance them—put considerable long-term pressure on the New Zealand economy.

Financial constraints were paralleled by constricted social attitudes. The defensive negativism and narrowing of horizons that characterized the Muldoon era were accompanied by an increased intolerance of difference. Political commentator Colin James has commented that under Muldoon, "the New Zealand way of life became antagonistic, mean and grudging."[4] Nowhere was this intolerance more evident than in the turmoil that surrounded the 1981 Springbok Rugby Tour. New Zealand—along with other Commonwealth countries—had signed the Gleneagles Agreement in 1977, banning sporting contacts with South Africa because of its apartheid regime. However, the National Government was not prepared to enforce this ban, insisting that sport and politics did not mix and that its citizens had the freedom to hold their own stance. The country became deeply divided between those who supported the Government's view and those who insisted that the Springbok Tour represented a tacit approval of apartheid. Demonstrations and riots followed. In the first match of the Tour, against Waikato in Hamilton, several hundred demonstrators invaded the pitch before the game. This required police to physically remove them one by one, this taking considerable time and forcing the game to be abandoned, to the fury of those rugby supporters who had paid to see it.[5] This set the tone for the remainder of the Tour, with demonstrations and riots featuring around every match, together with levels of violence and disorder not seen in this country for more than fifty years. The Third Test, against the All Blacks at Eden Park in Auckland, was one of the most unusual in New Zealand rugby history. Streets around Eden Park were cordoned off and fighting in the streets continued throughout the match between police and protesters. The most memorable incident was a light aircraft flying over the field, dropping smoke flares and flour bombs on players and spectators alike. All Black front-row prop Gary Knight, an eighteen-test veteran, was felled by a direct hit from a flour bomb and the South African captain reportedly wondered whether or not New Zealand had an air force.[6]

The 1970s and 1980s also saw a growing emphasis on biculturalism, as Māori became more vocal about their status as *tangata whenua* [the indigenous people of the land]. Increasingly, Māori insisted that they "ought to be able to behave as Maori in wider New Zealand life rather than submerge their identity in favour of Pakeha [New Zealander of European descent] *mores* and values."[7] Māori status as *tangata whenua*—which implied *rangatiratanga* [sovereignty, chieftainship, right to exercise authority] over New Zealand's land—had been recognized by the Treaty of Waitangi in 1840; these promises had not, however, been kept. Anglican Bishop Whakahuihui Vercoe forcefully made this point in the presence of Queen Elizabeth II and other dignitaries at the Waitangi sesquicentennial celebrations in 1990 and his impromptu and controversial speech was widely reported. "Since the signing of that treaty 150 years ago I want to remind our partners that you have marginalised us. You have not honoured the treaty. We have not honoured each other in the promises we made on this sacred ground."[8] Vercoe's challenge to the Crown—in the person of her Majesty—was indicative of a growing sense of Māori self-confidence and assertiveness. Four events in the 1970s and 1980s exemplified this burgeoning Māori renaissance.

The first of these was the 1975 Māori Land March, headed by urban Māori women's leader Whina Cooper, who led a protest party on foot from Te Hapua in the far north to Parliament to protest land grievances.[9] The impact of this was reinforced in 1977–78 by an occupation of Bastion Point, a coastal piece of land in Orakei, Auckland, by several Māori groups. This seventeen-month occupation protested the Government's failure to return the land to Ngāti Whātua, the local Auckland *iwi* [tribe], after its seizure in World War 2 to build an emergency landing strip. The occupation was met with Governmental overkill, sparking the largest police operation seen in New Zealand to that time.[10] However, despite continuing conflicts over the ownership of land, changed cultural attitudes were beginning to emerge. One example of this was the response made by the education system to the declining use of the Māori language. Initiatives such as *kōhanga reo* [literally, "language nest," i.e., Māori-language preschools], *kura kaupapa Māori* [Māori-language cultural immersion schools] and *wānanga* [universities] were set up in the 1980s to revive the language.[11] The use of the Māori language is now becoming much more widespread, with dedicated Māori television channels and programs and an increasing use of Māori greetings and speeches on both formal and informal occasions. Another example was the highly successful Te Māori art exhibition, which toured the United States from 1984 onwards—and throughout New Zealand on its return home—presenting a new, united Māori front.[12] Traditionally, Māori identity was tribal. Since each *iwi* [tribe] hosted the Te Māori exhibition in turn, agreement needed to be reached between them over points of *tikanga* [custom] and *kawa* [protocol].[13] This reinforced the emergence of a new pan-Māori identity, which had its roots partly in Māori urbanization.[14] The fourth—and, in the long term, the most significant—event, was the extension, in 1985, of the Waitangi Tribunal's jurisdiction to cover retrospective land claims. This Tribunal had been established by the Rowling Labour Government in 1975 to address current Māori land claims; its extension now covered all land claims back to the signing of the Treaty of Waitangi in 1840. This meant that Māori could seek redress for historical—as well as current—wrongs, thus strengthening a sense of Māori history and identity. As a result, the number of land claims before the Tribunal had swelled from six in 1984 to almost 1,000 by 2000,[15] in the process creating what National Party leader Don Brash later called a "grievance industry."[16]

The pace of change would quicken in the middle of the decade. By 1984, New Zealand's economic plight had worsened and Prime Minister Muldoon called an early election in July that year. This proved to be an astonishing miscalculation on his part, since Labour won the election in a landslide. It led to an extraordinary constitutional crisis, as millions of dollars had flowed out of New Zealand in the month before the election, prompting calls for an urgent devaluation of the New Zealand dollar. Muldoon—who had been a prominent chartered cost accountant before entering politics and who was also Minister of Finance—had refused to do this, attempting instead to talk down the financial markets. In the interregnum between Election Night and the swearing in of the new Government—when the Labour Government was nominally in control, although Muldoon's administration still held the levers of power—the situation worsened. Eventually, Muldoon was persuaded to devalue the dollar by 20% and to remove the heavily interventionist financial controls on interest rates.[17] (As a result, these rates climbed from 11% to 15% in the first week following the removal of the controls; by 1987 they had reached the exceptional level of

21.5% on first mortgages.) It was therefore clear that New Zealand would experience "interesting times" throughout the remainder of the decade. This proved to be the case.

The election of the fourth Labour Government under David Lange in 1984 was the starting pistol for what Keith Sinclair has described as "a modern revolution"[18] in many areas of New Zealand life. In particular the free market monetarist policies of Roger Douglas, Minister of Finance—hence dubbed "Rogernomics"—sparked a process of radical economic restructuring over the next six years.[19] This was characterized by market-led restructuring and deregulation and the control of inflation through tight monetary policy, accompanied by a floating exchange rate and reductions in the fiscal deficit. These policies revolutionized New Zealand's economy, the contours of which were further altered by the stock market crash of October 1987. These economic changes were paralleled by political realignments. The prime example of the latter was New Zealand's exclusion from the ANZUS alliance with the United States and Australia following the banning of nuclear-powered or nuclear-armed ships from New Zealand territorial waters.[20] Despite considerable political pressure from the United States, the Government refused to change its position on the issue. Opinion polls showed that 56% of the New Zealand public opposed visits by nuclear ships, with only 29% in favor; the beginnings of this opposition can be traced back at least to 1976.[21] This had the effect of reinforcing this country's image as "clean, green and nuclear-free" and of strengthening New Zealand's identity in the eyes of the rest of the world.[22] This antinuclear stance was reinforced four months later from an unlikely source, when French secret service agents bombed and sunk the Greenpeace vessel *Rainbow Warrior*, killing a crew member, in Auckland harbor in July 1985. This terrorist attack was intended to prevent the *Rainbow Warrior* from sailing to Mururoa Atoll to protest French underground nuclear testing in the Pacific. Instead, it had the opposite effect of enlarging local and worldwide support for New Zealand's antinuclear stand.[23]

Defending Godzone: The Conservative Reaction

Following the 1984 election, the Labour Government sought to stimulate social change—the pace of which was often bewildering—and it is not surprising that there was a strong reaction from the forces of Christian conservatism. This had been building since the early 1970s, with perceptions of evangelical "disempowerment" and a "quiet rage" at the church's loss of legitimacy and morality, then anger at their sense of the government's benign apathy.[24] Consequently, "there was a strong sense that the conservative world was being overturned—dangerously so.... In the 1970s and 1980s, conservative Christians had increasingly 'had enough'—hence the strong conservative Christian voices in the abortion, homosexuality and feminism debates of that period."[25] This exasperation was not unique to New Zealand, since it reflected a worldwide conservative reaction to social change; this had emerged in the 1970s and became more militant and organized in the 1980s. The Moral Majority in the United States was the best-known example of this reaction, but it was not as formalized as this in New

Zealand.[26] A common feature in much of this response was an appeal to a largely mythical Christian past from which society was deemed to have fallen away. This perception was exemplified by the permissive society's abandonment of traditional standards of morality, i.e., its Christian heritage. In the 1970s the reinstatement of Christianity as a legitimator of public morality was viewed as a matter of the adoption by society of Christian principles. In the 1980s this had changed to become a strategy of placing conservative Christians into positions of power.[27] Christian political parties built upon this conservative mythology and the change of strategy; these lay behind the name of the "Christian Heritage Party," formed in 1989 to contest the 1990 General Election. Although that Party's founders were members of the conservative Dutch Reformed Church, its supporters were largely Evangelical and fundamentalist Christians, including Pentecostals, together with Roman Catholics.[28]

A key stimulus in this conservative reaction was the Labour Government's series of forums on the ratification of the United Nations Convention on the Elimination of All Forms of Discrimination Against Women in 1984. The predetermined nature of these forums, which followed a liberal feminist line, reinforced a view that the Labour Government was deliberately ignoring conservative concerns about social and political issues.[29] This perception was significant since, as journalist Bruce Ansley noted, "conservative women went to the [United Nations] forums and came away enraged. 'The forums rang an alarm bell . . . and people saw in the [Homosexual Law Reform] petition an opportunity to say something about the moral condition of our country.'"[30] However, these conservative responses tended to focus on issues of individual morality[31] and the preservation of the nuclear family; other issues were addressed only insofar as these impinged on these core concerns.[32] This was particularly so with Pentecostals, who viewed sex education in schools and the rise of feminism[33] as threatening the authority and integrity of the nuclear family[34] and homosexuality as a perversion of human sexuality.[35] They also opposed abortion and pornography, although these were viewed as a less direct threat to the Christian family.[36] By contrast, political issues such as the 1981 Springbok Tour were generally ignored by conservatives and—especially—by Pentecostals.[37]

This vehement and visceral moralist response reached a peak in 1985 with the conservative challenge to the Homosexual Law Reform Bill. This legislation sought to remove a legal anomaly, in that consensual sexual relations between homosexuals were unlawful in New Zealand while those between lesbians were not. Nevertheless, the issue was viewed by conservative sections of the community as "the apogee in the struggle over morality"[38] and was met with strenuous opposition, orchestrated by an umbrella organization, the Coalition of Concerned Citizens.[39] After months of crusading, the climax came with the presentation of an 815,000-signature Petition against the Bill to Parliament in September 1985.[40] This petition was, by far, the largest ever in New Zealand history,[41] representing nearly a quarter of the total population of New Zealand at the time. Indeed, Member of Parliament Graeme Lee lauded it as "the largest petition in the history of this Parliament—on a comparative [per capita] basis, the largest of any Parliament in the world."[42] Nevertheless, it was summarily rejected by the

Labour Government, which was determined to implement its program of social and economic change. For the conservative crusaders, this rejection represented a defeat of almost apocalyptic proportions, a moralist Armageddon in which the forces of righteousness had lost. As a result, conservative Christian public outspokenness faded after 1986[43] and the moralist focus began to shift from protest to political participation, with several Christian activists, including Pentecostals, standing as candidates in the 1987 General Election.[44] The launching of the Christian Heritage Party two years later, followed by that of the Christian Democrats in 1995, gave institutional form to this shift of focus.

Pentecostal Trends in the 1980s: From Charismatic Movement to Bureaucratic Institution?

Several trends are apparent in the development of Pentecostalism throughout the 1980s and beyond. The most important of these were the growth and diversification of the movement, the impact of new styles of leadership and the changing shape of Pentecostal spirituality.

Trend 1: The Growth and Diversification of the Movement

Much of the energy behind the moralist movement was generated by Pentecostals, although they tended to give support to movements of shared conservative concern generated by others, rather than to initiate action themselves. However, they could mobilize considerable support for such campaigns. This is demonstrated, in the case of the Homosexual Law Reform petition, by the minutes of an Indigenous Churches' "Regional Leaders' Meeting" in August 1985. These reported on the progress of the Petition and urged that "we do all we can to push for the 1,000,000 signatures wanted."[45] Despite their energy and activism, Pentecostals viewed the battle as primarily a spiritual one, rather than a social conflict. The erosion of traditional Christian morality was seen as having Satanic origins;[46] opposing this social decline therefore became part and parcel of spiritual warfare. It should be noted that this sense of conflict against principalities and powers is pervasive in Pentecostalism. Harvey Cox notes that "many Pentecostals ... are fascinated to the point of obsession with demonic spirits and powers of darkness."[47] Pentecostal spiritual warfare involved the confronting, naming and opposing of these spiritual forces.[48] A sense of aggressiveness and self-confidence accompanied this redirection of spiritual warfare and these attitudes were reflected in the songs of the movement during the mid-1980s.[49] By now,

> the Pentecostal movement in New Zealand was considerably larger and more self-confident tha[n] had been the case in the past. The militaristic emphasis of these songs clearly reflects both a sense of Pentecostal self-consciousness and assertiveness, and the context of moralist conflict within which they were composed. The changing character of these songs clearly indicates the ways in which Pentecostal attitudes and self-understandings were changing.[50]

Pentecostal self-confidence and assertiveness in the 1980s was largely based on the movement's self-perceptions of its growth and power. By the end of the 1980s, these churches had grown to become the largest Protestant body in New Zealand, with a combined attendance—as distinct from census adherence—of nearly 54,000 people. This was larger than that of the Presbyterian and Anglican churches, i.e., 52,780 and 45,225 people, respectively.[51] Their expansion had attracted the attention of both the National and Labour parties, whose leaders recognized the value of soliciting Pentecostal support.[52] (However, the politicians' cavalier dismissal of Pentecostals' conservative viewpoints on the Homosexual Law Reform Bill indicates that their valuation was a highly selective one.) The Assemblies of God and the Indigenous Churches were the two largest Pentecostal bodies, between them accounting for more than 58% of all New Zealand Pentecostals.[53] A comparison of the pastors listed in the Associated Pentecostal Churches of New Zealand Directories for the mid-1980s show that 74% of all Pentecostal pastors listed were affiliated to these two groups.[54] The greatest focus of this Pentecostal growth was Auckland,[55] where the Queen Street and Takapuna Assemblies of God attracted considerable media attention for their large congregations and expansive building projects.[56] A 1983 article noted that the Queen Street Assembly of God—"the church that's taking over Auckland"—was probably the largest church congregation of any denomination in New Zealand. It was then packing out the Auckland Town Hall three times each Sunday, while building a new 4,000-seat church at Beaumont Street in Freeman's Bay.[57] On the North Shore, the Takapuna Assembly of God was also building a 1,700-seat auditorium on prime real estate at the northern end of the Harbour Bridge and this was opened in 1984.[58] These large churches formed part of a global trend towards megachurches that was emerging in the 1980s.[59] At a denominational level, the Assemblies of God continued to grow throughout the 1980s; successive biennial conferences recorded increasing numbers of affiliated churches and credentialed ministers in the movement. There were ninety Assemblies of God churches and 181 ministers represented at its 1981 Conference; this had grown to 142 churches and 259 ministers eight years later.[60]

The Indigenous Churches also increased during the 1970s and early 1980s, although this growth is difficult to quantify, given that movement's reluctance to use a denominational label. Its adherents tended to describe themselves as "Christian" in Census returns; consequently, they were listed as having only 2,796 members in 1986, declining to 1,491 in 1991.[61] However, the DAWN Strategy Church surveys for 1986 and 1990 give figures for this group of 12,525 and 12,660 attendees, respectively. The Christchurch New Life Centre, the largest of the Indigenous Churches, had a congregation of more than a thousand by 1979.[62] However, the fastest rate of growth was recorded by the Elim Churches, which increased nearly twentyfold—from 121 to 2,352 members—between the 1971 and 1991 Censuses. Ian Bilby's Blenheim Elim Church led this rapid expansion, having grown from just four people in 1973 to become the largest Elim Church in the country—with a membership of more than four hundred—by 1982.[63] (Bilby relocated to Auckland in the mid-1980s, establishing the Auckland City Elim Church; this had grown to more than a thousand people and had become the "flagship" of the Elim Churches by 1991. He also became President of the Elim Church of New Zealand in 1981 and that denomination saw significant and sustained growth under his leadership for the next eighteen years.)[64]

The enlarged constituency of Pentecostalism, in part a product of the influx of new participants from the Charismatic movement, was accompanied by a rise in the socioeconomic and educational levels of its congregations. Ian Clark notes the growth in the size and prosperity of many local Assemblies of God, which contributed to a strengthening of that movement's national administration during the 1980s.[65] Similarly, church historian Laurie Guy commented that the Queen Street Auckland Assembly of God had "mutated markedly" in the 1970s "partly, at least, through social lift as the church became more middle class."[66] Other observers have also noted the increasingly respectable middle-class character of Pentecostal congregations.[67] Congregational members in the 1970s—and increasingly in the 1980s—included professional and semiprofessional people, as well as university graduates. Clark observed that, by contrast with the Pentecostalism of the 1950s, "you get people from many different professions in [the Pentecostal movement] today."[68] An unpublished sociological analysis of several New Life Churches in the late 1980s showed that their occupational mix was significantly higher than that of a representative sample taken from the population as a whole. It also showed that congregations in the larger cities had a higher socioeconomic level than those in smaller centers. (Strikingly, the Wellington congregation had a proportion of professional people three times higher than the national average; there did not appear to be any working class occupations represented in that congregation.)[69] These changes had their beginnings in the 1970s and became more overt in the 1980s, when "the Pentecostal movement appear[ed] to have ... become a 'yuppie' movement in many places, particularly in the Auckland area." The glossy periodicals and advertising circulars put out by various churches and parachurch agencies in the movement added weight to this perception.[70] As well as this, the movement was becoming more diverse, both ethnically and denominationally. Samoan Pentecostal churches, in particular, were growing strongly throughout the country.[71] There were also a number of other ethnically designated Pentecostal congregations, such as Tongan, Fijian and Indian, and new Pentecostal denominations were emerging, including Celebration Centres, Christian Outreach Churches, Destiny Churches and others.[72] By 1997, there would be at least eleven such denominations, compared with five at the end of the 1970s.[73]

Nevertheless, there were some worrying straws in the wind. Despite this continuing expansion and diversification, there were indications that the "boom period" of primary Pentecostal expansion that had characterized the previous two decades was over.[74] Growth rates for the 1980s were only half of what they had been in the 1960s and less than 30% of those in the 1970s. According to Census statistics, the movement grew by 110.66% between 1961 and 1971 and 188.68% between 1971 and 1981, but only by 55.84% between 1981 and 1991.[75] Furthermore, Pentecostal expansion in the 1980s was more intentional and directed, rather than the product of a sovereign move of the Holy Spirit; the steady growth of the Assemblies of God was a case in point. This was due in large measure to its institutional strategies. These included its regional Bible Schools, its adoption of church growth methods and its specifically targeted church planting program. Philip Carew and Geoff Troughton note that the Bible Schools were crucial in the movement's expansion from the 1970s on,[76] since they supplied trained ministers for the new churches that were opening up. The movement's church growth methods were modeled on those of Korean pastor Yonggi Cho, which Frank Houston had observed during a visit to Korea in 1977.[77] They also had wide circulation in New Zealand through the interdenominational Church Growth seminars run by Gordon Miller of World Vision in the 1980s and 1990s.[78] The Assemblies of God's church planting strategies were encapsulated in its Season of Harvest strategies, set up in the mid-1980s. These aimed at the establishing of 100 new churches, the releasing of 200 new ministers and the discipling of 20,000 new converts by the year 2000. These targets were largely achieved, since a report to the Assemblies of God Executive in 2001 showed that 123 new churches had been added to the movement, 314 new ministers had been accredited, and membership had grown by 13,500.[79] Other Pentecostal churches also became more strategic and intentional—and hence, more institutional—during the 1980s. In part, this was the product of the passing of the baton to a new generation of Pentecostal leadership, as well as of a decline in spiritual fervor and a redirection of the movement's energies. As will be seen, the movement became less charismatic and more managerial in character during the mid-1980s; this trend has largely continued since the 1980s to the present day.

There was also a shift of focus in the Charismatic movement during the decade. Donald Battley notes a decline after 1979[80] and elsewhere states that the revival was over by the mid-1980s, although it remained as a charismatic tradition within the church.[81] Viv Grigg places a later date on the primary end of the renewal, insisting that the nationwide movement halted in 1989 rather than 1979.[82] Nevertheless, charismatic renewal developed into a different kind of movement in the 1980s from what it had been in the previous decade, becoming more in-house and domesticated. In the case of the Anglican communion, it had changed in character from a spontaneous movement to an organized party in the church.[83] There were benefits and disadvantages to these changes. The domestication of the renewal ensured the continuation of its benefits to the churches—particularly to those of conservative and evangelical orientation— which grew as a result. (It has been observed that charismatic churches have tended to grow faster than noncharismatic ones.)[84] By 1990, Jim Veitch could note that "Charismatic Christianity ... has a strong hold and influence on mainline churches, and exerts tremendous influence on the leadership and on policy development" of these churches.[85] This was particularly so in the Baptist churches, 69% of which were charismatic by 1989.[86] On the negative side, the changed character of the renewal was paralleled by a waning of its spiritual power and by a narrowing of its horizons. This entrenchment was part of a wider process. The ecumenical movement had collapsed in the 1980s, following the rejection of the *Plan for Union* by the Anglicans in 1976 and the failure of the Presbyterians and Methodists to proceed with church union in 1981. The abandonment of formal ecumenical negotiations also had an impact on the Charismatic movement. Conversely, the ecclesiastical tribalism represented by the domestication of the renewal had the counterproductive effect of dampening down the informal ecumenism that had been one of its driving forces[87] in the 1970s.[88] The nature of the movement's leadership was also changing. Donald Battley astutely observed in 1986 that it was "still dominated by some of the first generation pioneers and by those of the second generation who have high vision and ability for spreading the renewal. They are popularizers rather than investigators."[89] This observation of the change in the nature of the movement's leadership as it transitioned from its pioneers to a new generation of charismatics in the mid-1980s is also applicable to Pentecostal churches.

Trend 2: The Impact of New Styles of Leadership

Despite the growth and diversification of the movement, some loss of spiritual impetus began to emerge in the early 1980s. Battley refers to a "time of depression" in the Charismatic movement after 1979.[90] Similarly, references to pastoral disillusionment, discouragement and stagnation begin to appear in the minutes of the Indigenous Churches' Regional Leaders' meetings and in its correspondence files from 1984 on.[91] These references are significant, given the place of these churches at the forefront of Pentecostal expansion in the 1960s. There was also disillusionment in the Assemblies of God, where considerable upheaval followed the dismissal of Neville Johnson, leader of the flagship Queen Street Assembly, for unspecified charges of "misuse of office, and immoral, improper, and deceitful conduct" in 1983. This led to the departure of many congregational members for other churches, with grave repercussions for that Assembly's massive building program. The incident also led to a weakening of trust and confidence in the movement's leadership and the emigration of a considerable number of its senior pastors to Australia over the next five years.[92] The Apostolic Church, for its part, was experiencing a decline in its prophetic ministry and the curtailment—and even the disappearance—of the travelling "apostle and prophet ministry" that had previously characterized its polity.[93] The Associated Pentecostal Churches of New Zealand also lost its momentum; its later leaders were not as enthusiastic as its founders had been and the annual pastors' conferences had declined to biennial gatherings by the early 1980s.[94]

This weakening of spiritual momentum was paralleled by changes in Pentecostal leadership styles. The character of the movement's polity underwent significant change as the decade progressed; this was evident in almost every Pentecostal group and was most clearly exhibited in their leadership models and styles. To some extent, this was the product of historical progression, as the pioneer generation was succeeded by a new generation of leaders who did not have the charismatic stature of their predecessors. Almost all of the main Pentecostal bodies had significant changes of leadership in the 1980s. In the Assemblies of God, the charismatic dynamism of the Frank Houston era continued for some time after his departure for Sydney in 1977 and the large Queen Street Assembly provided a similar model of church growth. Furthermore, Jim Williams, Houston's successor as Superintendent of the movement, was charismatic in personality and orientation, as Houston himself had been.[95] This ethos continued until 1985, when major organizational changes took place in the movement, in part due to the growth and increased prosperity which had enabled the modernization of its leadership structures.[96] This was manifest in a relocation of its headquarters office to Auckland[97] and—especially—in a complete change of personnel in its Executive Council. Williams had declined to stand for reelection as General Superintendent in 1985, feeling that it was time for a change of leadership; all of the Executive membership likewise had stood down.[98] Most of the new Executive members who replaced them were based in Auckland; this reflected a growing Auckland dominance in the movement. Ray Hughes, pastor of the large Takapuna Assembly of God on Auckland's North Shore, became the new Superintendent and would retain his position for the next eighteen years. His skills as a bureaucratic leader did much to change the character of the Assemblies of God over the next two decades. Ian Clark comments that

> In the following years of [Hughes'] long tenure of the General Superintendency there was a strong emphasis on order and management that became increasingly apparent as time went on. There is no doubt that the Movement profited greatly from the emphasis on decency and solidity which it certainly required at the time, but in later years a desire for a bit more of the fervour and excitement known in earlier years became increasingly evident.[99]

Hughes' tenure and the changes that accompanied it therefore represented both an increasing Auckland dominance and a bureaucratization of the Assemblies of God.

Other Pentecostal groups were also experiencing leadership transitions and changes of ethos in the 1980s. Luke Worsfold observes that the election of John Douglas as Superintendent of the Apostolic Church in 1986 brought "an influence that was far less Pentecostal,"[100] marking the beginnings of an ongoing process of restructuring.[101] He notes that Douglas' interests were primarily in education, but the Apostolic Church's national training school under his principalship "developed along lines that, to a large degree, ignored pentecostal teaching."[102] Other changes were more subtle, but equally significant. James Worsfold—Douglas' immediate predecessor—was the last apostolic president of the movement; future leaders would be identified as "superintendent" or "national leader." Furthermore, Douglas was voted in, rather than appointed by prophecy and apostolic confirmation as had been the pattern up to then.[103] Douglas' appointment therefore reflected

> a shift in the mode of leadership from a charismatic to a management style. In so doing the government of the church relied less on prophecy and more on discussion. . . . The infiltration of bureaucratic systems generated the notion that prophets were superfluous for gaining an understanding of God's plan hence the

prophets' role was reduced to endorsing or encouraging the decisions of the apostles.[104]

This modal shift became even more marked in 1988, when Ron Goulton was appointed General Superintendent, despite being an administrator with no previous pastoral experience. This was a major departure from previous practices. In Luke Worsfold's view, Goulton's leadership represented the "devolution of the presidential spiritual authority to a general secretarial administrative function."[105] He notes that "[in] the late 1980s . . . the movement was managed rather than led";[106] this process would continue in the 1990s under the national leadership of Pastor Phil Underwood. During Underwood's tenure, the tone of the Apostolic Church council meetings moved more towards an emphasis on debate than on prophetic revelation. Underwood was known to challenge the prophet to "explain himself" following a prophecy with which he could not find an appropriate level of agreement.[107] Pastor Brian Tamaki caustically refers to his experience, during his appointment by the council to the pastorate of the Rotorua Apostolic church, of the "manouevering and manipulation" that accompanied these bureaucratic decision-making processes in the 1990s.[108]

The Pentecostal group with the greatest change in leadership patterns in the 1980s was the Indigenous Churches. This movement stressed the autonomy of the local church, distrusting any attempts to introduce extralocal authorities that would compromise this independence.[109] However, several factors forced it in the direction of adopting national structures. The first was the growth of the movement, which numbered more than 12,000 adherents and at least 120 pastors by the mid-1980s, necessitating some form of central organization in order to maintain its cohesion. Furthermore, many of its younger pastors had come into the Indigenous Churches from the Charismatic movement and they exerted pressure for a closer and more defined structural format. There was also an urgent need for consistent patterns of discipline for dealing with pastors who had fallen into moral dereliction. There were several unfortunate instances of this in the 1980s and the discipline imposed on these offending pastors varied widely. It should be noted this was not solely an Indigenous Churches problem, as is evidenced by the dismissal of Neville Johnson[110] and by the discussion of such issues at an Associated Pentecostal Churches of New Zealand conference in 1987.[111] Tamaki also alludes to several such episodes in the local Apostolic church of which he had recently become the pastor.[112] Nor was it an exclusively Pentecostal one, although such cases in New Zealand and overseas attracted considerable public attention.[113] These incidents could be attributed, in part, to a generalized loss of spiritual fervor. Other contributing factors were the authoritarian role of the pastor over the congregation and the charismatic nature of Pentecostal ministry, which generated a personal power which could be exploited for unworthy ends.[114] Nevertheless, they produced a very real sense of pain at all levels of the Pentecostal movement and a loss of confidence in its ministry, resulting in congregational disenchantment and membership losses. The movement's prophetic ministry was also called into question for its failure to discern and address such moral failures.[115]

In the Indigenous Churches, the trend towards a national structure to facilitate dealing with issues such as this began with the formation of regional fellowships of pastors in the early 1980s.[116] By 1985, there were also pressures for senior leaders to be recognized as having a national responsibility within the movement. In the end, this took the form of an apostolic leadership and Rob Wheeler and Peter Morrow were recognized as such at the movement's 1987 Annual Pastors' Conference.[117] This change reflected a trend towards increasing professionalism in ministry, with an emphasis on charismatic office and position. A corollary of this was the stratification of leadership, with the emergence of an incipient hierarchy of pastors, senior pastors and apostolic leaders. Thus the Indigenous Churches became a different type of movement from what it had been in the 1960s, moving towards becoming the kind of routinized denomination that it professed to abhor.[118]

This new leadership structure was, in fact, short-lived. Both Wheeler and Morrow were replaced, due to ill-health, as the movement's leaders in 1989 by John Walton, a former Charismatic with an Exclusive Brethren background.[119] It is significant that Walton was "appointed," rather than "recognized" as the movement's leader and that he came from a Charismatic, rather than a Pentecostal, background.[120] His appointment marked both a transition to a second generation of leadership in the movement and a change from charismatic to bureaucratic methods of leadership selection. There were also other organizational changes. An official name—the "New Life Churches of New Zealand"—had been adopted in 1988 and pastors were issued with annually renewable accreditation cards in 1989. Job descriptions and guidelines for various positions in the movement's governance were issued in 1990. A bureaucratic framework was clearly emerging. However, the greatest departure from the emphases of the past was the formation of an official sickness insurance scheme for New Life pastors. For a movement that had begun its expansion in the early 1960s as a healing revival, this latter development indicated how greatly the New Life Churches had changed over the years.[121] Astonishingly, this telling shift of perception appears to have gone completely unnoticed.

What is the significance of these changes in the various Pentecostal groups? While these were to be expected as the movement grew and entered a second generation of leadership, the speed with which they took place is surprising. Viv Grigg sums up the consequences of this transition:

> The rapidity of institutionalisation into Pentecostalism in New Zealand very quickly diverted the revival from its motivation on release of the Spirit, to become driven by motivation to successful institutionalisation, (i.e., successful church growth in new congregations) perhaps largely because of the economic necessities of aspiring pastors for a sufficient membership base to sustain their own salary and the costs of institutional growth towards such a goal, perhaps because church growth was the clear goal of these denominations more than renewal.... The Pentecostal structuralist model of church growth replaced the model of freedom in the charismatic renewal. This has resulted positively in consolidation of the fruit of the renewal, but negatively it also has created a culture of power and control in many groups.[122]

This shift towards institutionalization reflected a change in perceptions of the pastoral role which, as many observers have noted, has led to the business model adopted by many Pentecostal churches in the 1980s.[123] Ian Clark notes that there was more emphasis on business in the General Council meetings of the Assemblies of God after 1987, in contrast to the charismatic style of Frank Houston and Jim Williams.[124] In one respect, this was a positive development, since some Pentecostal pastors demonstrated considerable entrepreneurial flair in setting up trusts and other business entities to facilitate the care of their congregations. New Life Pastor Bruce McDonald's Liberty Trust—a church-based cooperative established in 1989 to provide loan monies for church members struggling with high mortgage interest rates—is a good example of this.[125] Nevertheless, Pentecostal leadership models have tended to develop in the direction of the authoritarian, profit-driven corporate leadership style that characterized the 1980s.[126] This trend held considerable dangers: leadership trainer Simon Moetara notes, in the context of a discussion of Māori models of leadership, that

> Contemporary Pentecostal-Charismatic-Evangelical churches often emphasise "strong leadership," which can easily become strongly hierarchical. . . . Cults of personality can easily arise around strongly charismatic leaders, with followers being attracted to the individual leader rather than to the gospel of Christ. . . . [There are] some virtues to "benevolent autocratic rule."[127] . . . [However, the] absence of clear boundaries and accountability structures to pastoral power in the charismatic model of leadership can lead to the possibility of abuse and misuse.[128]

Viv Grigg also observes that

> the emphasis in the renewal moved from the confessional, healing, small group to the frontal, anointed pastor. More distinctive Pentecostal leadership styles replaced the grassroots, charismatic Spirit-led movement. Pentecostal pastoral enthusiasm for the rightness of their beliefs and sense of being anointed by God, plus the more directional leadership styles imported from US sources by many of these groups, added to general ignorance of what had been happening culturally in terms of diffusion of leadership under the Spirit in the indigenous renewal.[129]

The new styles of Pentecostal leadership that emerged during the 1980s therefore reflected, at least to some extent, an adoption of the cultural patterns of the surrounding culture, particularly of the business world. These hierarchical and authoritarian trends were detrimental to the egalitarian and inclusive spirituality of the movement.

Trend 3: The Changing Shape of Pentecostal Spirituality

In New Zealand Pentecostalism during the 1980s, the most difficult trend to identify was the way in which the contours of its spirituality were changing. This is because partly because the movement's emphasis on the immediacy of spiritual experience tended to preclude historical comparisons with previous patterns. For Pentecostals, what God is doing and saying *now* was the new normal; appeals to precedent or to tradition were simply irrelevant. Theologian Simon Chan notes that this is a general characteristic of the Pentecostal movement. He attributes this to a failure in traditioning that has resulted in a diluted Pentecostalism being passed on to the next generation, and to a lack of awareness by Pentecostals of being part of the wider Christian tradition.[130] This had a corollary in that there were few safeguards against the subversion of Pentecostal spirituality to the prevalent attitudes of the external culture. This assimilation was, to some degree, evident during the 1980s.

One of the characteristics of the period was the rise of the "'me' generation." This epithet is derived from an article by writer Tom Wolfe in *New York* magazine in 1976, in which he described the 1970s as the "'me' decade."[131] These attitudes became increasingly pervasive in the 1980s. An American study conducted in 2007 found that while only 12% of teenagers agreed with the statement "I am an important person" in the 1950s, this had risen to 80% by the late 1980s.[132] This growing trend in self-preoccupation was also evident in New Zealand.[133] It was manifest in a heightened self-centeredness, an increased consumerism and an emphasis on self-actualization. However, these attitudes also appeared to characterize much of the Pentecostal movement during the 1980s. The sense of self-confidence and assertiveness comes through in some of the songs sung in the movement. A study of the *Scripture in Song* series of music books—published in New Zealand between 1971 and 1987—demonstrates an increasing self-absorption in the lyrics of the songs.[134] This was manifest in a stronger emphasis on "*my* relationship with Christ"[135] but also in a detachment of one's "blessings" from dependence on God, since these benefits were produced by an exercise of one's faith.[136] The corollary of this disconnection from a reliance on divine abilities was a declining focus on prayer[137] and a shift to personal spiritual resources. This parallels Laurie Guy's observation that the Charismatic Renewal reinforced the privatization of religious experience, becoming focused on one's own spirituality, rather than on the needs of the surrounding society. Thus,

> Christian concern for many had shrunk to their private lives and their church worlds.... This privatised concern intensified through the influence of the charismatic movement of the 1970s and 1980s.... Charismatic Christian concern was often focused on its particular denomination, or its own congregation within that denomination, or even simply on personal spirituality.[138] ... While some parts of the movement became very politically activist, most parts turned their backs on the larger public world. Christianity essentially addressed the inner world and not the ordinary world of society.[139]

This privatization of spiritual experience was paralleled by a trend towards religious consumerism over the next two decades. A fresh Charismatic impulse emerged after 1983 with the arrival of the Third Wave movement, brought to New Zealand by teams from Anglican Bishop David Pytches' Chorleywood church in Britain and John Wimber's Vineyard Churches in the United States.[140] Although this brought about a restoration of confidence and vitality, Kevin

Ward is highly critical of this new energy. He sees it as a "recolonizing" of the New Zealand Charismatic movement by American forces and as "a captivity of the church by certain cultural trends which should have been more strongly resisted." He calls this process "Wimberisation"—after Wimber, the key figure in the Vineyard churches—arguing that it has produced a new "consumerism."[141] This was manifest in a consumerism of goods in the 1980s. i.e., the "Prosperity Gospel" and in a consumerism of experience in the 1990s, i.e., the "Toronto Blessing."[142] Ward's criticism has some validity and these trends were also reflected in Pentecostal churches. There was considerable resonance between the ethos of New Zealand Pentecostalism and the changing American Evangelical subculture which, as Martin Marty observed, had made more and more compromises with the larger culture.[143] American sociological writer Richard Quebedeaux's searching question "will success spoil the evangelicals?"[144] in the 1970s was equally applicable to the New Zealand Pentecostal movement in the 1980s. Despite the focus on a narrow moralism, its lifestyles and attitudes were becoming conformed to the prevailing culture and the movement was losing its prophetic edge. It was moving away from its countercultural stance and lowering its sectarian standards. This led to both a loss of spiritual depth and a diminution of spiritual power.

This shallowing of spiritual experience is demonstrated by a Pentecostal Alpha Course weekend camp in the 1990s, in which people were prayed for at the Saturday evening session to receive the Baptism of the Spirit. This prayer session was followed by a Camp Concert, in which everyone was expected to participate. Luke Worsfold laments that

> The depth of experience appears to have diminished, giving way instead to a less cataclysmic encounter, a swift and easy process.... By way of illustration, the depth of experience expected in the highly successful charismatically inclined Alpha course is evidenced by the manner in which being filled with the Spirit is accommodated. A weekend away in the latter part of the 10 week course included a Saturday evening prayer session where attendees would receive the Spirit, followed thirty minutes later by participation in a variety concert. Evidently, Alpha course organisers had little anticipation of participants being "drunk in the Spirit"; there seemed to be little thought of those receiving the Spirit being so affected by God's presence that they would neither want nor be capable of participation in entertainment of a secular nature.[145]

(Worsfold refers to the phenomenon of being "drunk in the Spirit." This occurs when a person is so overwhelmed by the Holy Spirit that he or she is unable to function in a normal manner until the anointing of the Spirit has lifted. The author recalls a young man at a youth camp in 1961 being so drunk in the Spirit that he was unable to speak English for three days.)

Luke Worsfold argues that this shallowing of charismatic experience produces "superficiality both in the experience of Spirit-baptism and in the accompanying expression of tongues."[146] Nevertheless, this diminution of spiritual power is difficult to define, being qualitative, rather than quantitative. The movement could justifiably claim considerable resources and energy; these were demonstrated, for example, in the moralist campaigns leading up to the Homosexual Law Reform

Petition in 1985. Furthermore, large congregations, the building of expansive Pentecostal churches and the increasing prominence of their pastors could be adduced as quantitative evidences of power; indeed, the assertiveness and self-confidence of the movement derives directly from this. However, this assessment is quantified by human yardsticks of size, prosperity and growth. What appeared to be diminishing *qualitatively* in the movement was the spiritual power that came from a dependence on the Holy Spirit, together with sensitivity to His leading. This is movingly articulated in a letter of resignation from Pastor David Shearer, who had left the Indigenous Churches in 1986 in protest at the way the movement was changing. His letter conveys a strong sense of spiritual loss:

> I have not sought to hide my growing concern at the direction in which we are moving. . . .
>
> It is my belief that our "stream" has lost its way in God and is now being led and directed by [the] human spirit rather than the Holy Spirit. . . . The pursuance of our present "stream" course is bringing us all further into the bondage of a growing denominational spirit. There seems to me to be less and less opportunity for the Holy Spirit to speak and be heard at our national conferences and regional leaders' meetings; while more and more we are being steered along a deceptive course designed to develop the *ICNZ* [Indigenous Churches of New Zealand] as a political force in the nation. . . .
>
> I have come to see . . . that, in our corporate times together, we no longer wait upon the anointing to lead and direct us. . . .
>
> We are no longer free to follow the pillar of cloud and fire by recognising the anointing of His Spirit, as it would come upon this one or that one. But we are being conditioned to follow personality and tradition. No longer free to catch the wind of God's Spirit and move forward under His anointed inspiration, we are now being propelled into the sea lanes of man's choosing and destination. The spontaneity and freedom of the Holy Spirit is being replaced by an increasing closing off and inflexibility towards anything new or different from the accepted ideas and doctrines of those steering the ship. . . .
>
> I must make my choice, as you must make yours. And I am convinced that I must not follow the direction in which our stream is being taken.[147]

Shearer's cry of pain was echoed by more than twenty other pastors who resigned from the Indigenous Churches following the recognition of Rob Wheeler and Peter Morrow as apostles in 1987. These seceding pastors formed a new fellowship of independent churches—the South Pacific Fellowship—to maintain the original Indigenous Churches principle of the autonomy of the local church and the charismatic freedom of the Spirit.[148] His anguished lament articulates the way in which the Pentecostal movement appeared to be turning from a God-dependence to a focus on human agency in the 1980s. It therefore serves as a fitting epitaph for the movement's diminishing depth of spiritual experience and for its declining reliance on and sensitivity to the Holy Spirit.

Conclusion

The 1980s were a period of far-reaching change as the narrowness and intolerance of the Muldoon era gave way to the process of revolutionary social, political and economic change that characterized the fourth Labour government. New Zealand Pentecostalism was also undergoing a revolution during the decade. The energy of the movement derived from its involvement in conservative moralist protest, its upward social mobility and in its growing size and diversity. Nevertheless, the picture was not entirely positive, since Pentecostal growth rates were beginning to decline and some degree of disillusionment was being felt in some sections of the movement. This was due both to a number of cases of pastoral immorality in several Pentecostal denominations and also to a perception that the movement had peaked at the beginning of the decade.

As the 1980s progressed, a new generation of leadership began to emerge. This represented a transition from the leadership patterns of the movement's charismatic pioneers to new, bureaucratic forms of governance. This process of institutionalization—which ran counter to the institutional suspicion of the 1960s which had stimulated Pentecostal growth[149]—affected almost all Pentecostal denominations and changed both the polity and the spirituality of the movement. These changes reflected both the influence of the wider context—i.e., the "me" generation—and the privatization of religious concerns. In effect, Pentecostals became religious consumers, focusing on their individual spirituality and following trends and emphases imported from America. This produced a lack of depth in its spiritual experience, a loss of sensitivity to the Holy Spirit and a diminution of its spiritual power. The Pentecostal impulse became much more a human impulse, with power usually vested in the anointed pastor or leader, rather than in the charismatic members of the congregation through whom the Holy Spirit spoke. This CEO business mentality reflected the ethos of the era, but would prove detrimental to the long-term spirituality of the Pentecostal movement in New Zealand. The process of institutionalization would continue in the 1990s.

Notes

1. Alan McRobie, "The Politics of Volatility, 1972–1991," in Rice, *Oxford History of New Zealand*, 395–96.

2. King, *Penguin History of New Zealand*, 489.

3. John E. Martin, "Hydroelectricity," *Te Ara Encyclopedia of New Zealand*, updated 9 November 2012 http://www.TeAra.govt.nz/en/hydroelectricity (accessed 2 March 2013).

4. Colin James, cited in King, *Penguin History of New Zealand*, 465.

5. For a blog discussing the deep division surrounding the 1981 Springbok Tour (including a photograph of the Hamilton pitch invasion), see Ben Schrader, "1981 Springbok Tour: Tom and my 'cold war'," *Te Ara Signposts*, posted 6 September 2011 http://blog.teara.govt.nz/2011/09/06/1981-springbok-tour-tom-and-my-cold-war/ (accessed 5 March 2013).

6. "Film: the third test—1981 Springbok tour," *New Zealand History online*, updated 20 December 2012 http://www.nzhistory.net.nz/media/video/the-third-test-auckland (accessed 5 March 2013).

7. King, *Penguin History of New Zealand*, 467–68.

8. Whakahuihui Vercoe, Bishop of Aotearoa, 6 February 1990, reported in the *New Zealand Herald*, 7 February 1990. Copy of speech in Sue Abel, *Shaping the News: Waitangi Day on Television* (Auckland: Auckland University Press, 1997), 213, Appendix 5.

9. Ranginui J. Walker, "Māori People since 1950," in Rice, *Oxford History of New Zealand*, 512–13.

10. Ibid, 513–14; King, *Penguin History of New Zealand*, 485–86.

11. Mark Derby, "Māori-Pākehā relations—Māori renaissance," *Te Ara Encyclopedia of New Zealand*, updated 13 July 2012 http://www.TeAra.govt.nz/en/maori-pakeha-relations/page-6 (accessed 5 March 2013).

12. Te Ahukaramū Charles Royal, "Māori—People and culture today," *Te Ara Encyclopedia of New Zealand*, updated 11 July 2013 http://www.TeAra.govt.nz/en/photograph/3831/te-maori-exhibition (accessed 2 December 2013).

13. King, *Penguin History of New Zealand*, 476.

14. Walker, "Māori people since 1950," 504.

15. King, *Penguin History of New Zealand*, 487 and 500.

16. "Don Brash: Nationhood," *New Zealand Herald*, 28 January 2004. http://www.nzherald.co.nz/treaty-of-waitangi/news/article.cfm?c_id=350&objectid=3545950 (accessed 13 May 2013).

17. McRobie, "The Politics of Volatility," in 402.

18. Sinclair, *History of New Zealand*, 323.

19. King, *Penguin History of New Zealand*, 490.

20. Ibid, 445.

21. George Bryant, *The Church on Trial* ([Whangarei]: Whau Publications, [1986]), 128–29.

22. Knowles, "Some Aspects of the History of the New Life Churches of New Zealand," 288.

23. King, *Penguin History of New Zealand*, 445; McRobie, "The Politics of Volatility," 404.

24. Grigg, *The Spirit of Christ and the Postmodern City*, 187.

25. Guy, *Shaping Godzone*, 25.

26. Knowles, "Some Aspects of the History of the New Life Churches of New Zealand," 289.

27. Knowles, *The History of a New Zealand Pentecostal Movement*, 203–4.

28. Knowles, "Some Aspects of the History of the New Life Churches of New Zealand," 289–90.

29. Ibid, 296–99.

30. Bruce Ansley, "The Growing Might of the Moral Right," *New Zealand Listener*, 26 October 1985, 17. The quotation is from Barry Reed, the Press officer for the Coalition of Concerned Citizens.

31. Arrowsmith has noted the conservative Christian focus on the individual. Arrowsmith, "Christian Attitudes towards Public Questions in New Zealand in 1975," ix. See above, 153.
32. Knowles, "Some Aspects of the History of the New Life Churches of New Zealand," 290.
33. For a discussion of Pentecostal attitudes to women, see Ibid, 200–206. Note the extended quotation from Ivanica Vodanovich, "Woman's place in God's World," *New Zealand Women's Studies Journal* 2 (August 1985): 68–79, in Knowles, "Some Aspects of the History of the New Life Churches of New Zealand," 204, footnote 129.
34. Ryan, "Remoralising Politics," 67, 71–73.
35. For examples of Pentecostal attitudes to homosexuality in the 1980s, see Jonathon Harper, "The Church that's taking over Auckland," *Metro*, November 1983, 125–26; and Stratford, "Christians Awake!" 130.
36. Knowles, "Some Aspects of the History of the New Life Churches of New Zealand," 293–94.
37. So, Brown, "The Charismatic Contribution," 104; and Bryant, *The Church on Trial*, 52.
38. Ryan, "Remoralising Politics," 76.
39. See Knowles, "Some Aspects of the History of the New Life Churches of New Zealand," 300–308, for a detailed discussion of this conservative opposition and of Pentecostal involvement in it. For a range of views, see also Ryan, "Remoralising Politics," 64 and 75–77; Ansley, "The Growing Might of the Moral Right," 16–18; Selwyn Dawson, "God's Bullies," *Auckland Metro*, September 1985, 170–76; Richard Gordon, "Fear and Loathing and the Moral Majority," *Metro*, December 1985, 121–41; and Bryant, *The Church on Trial*, 112–24.
40. Ansley, "The Growing Might of the Moral Right," 16–17.
41. "Day in the House," *Otago Daily Times*, 25 September 1985, 5.
42. *New Zealand Parliamentary Debates*, 466: 6978 (24 September 1985).
43. Peter Lineham, "Wanna be in my gang?" *Listener*, 11–17 September 2004, http://www.listener.co.nz/uncategorized/wanna-be-in-my-gang/ (accessed 4 December 2013).
44. Knowles, "Some Aspects of the History of the New Life Churches of New Zealand," 260; Guy, *Shaping Godzone*, 25; Knowles, "Wheeler, Rob," in NIDPCM, 1193–94; Rudman, "For God and National," 28–29; and—especially—Stratford, "Christians Awake!"
45. "Minutes of Leader's [sic] Conference of the Indigenous Churches of N.Z. held at Wallace [sic: Wallis] House, 15–16 August 1985," MHCF, cited in Knowles, "Some Aspects of the History of the New Life Churches of New Zealand," 305.
46. See, for example, Rob Wheeler's views, cited in Stratford, "Christians Awake!" 124.
47. Cox, *Fire From Heaven*, 281. For a discussion of deliverance ministry in the New Zealand context, see Guy, "'Spirit Possession' and 'Deliverance Ministry'," 209–40.
48. For a detailed "Third Wave" viewpoint on spiritual warfare, see C. H. Kraft, "Spiritual Warfare: A Neocharismatic Perspective," in NIDPCM, 1091–96.
49. Knowles, "From the Ends of the Earth We Hear Songs": 244–45, 247.
50. Ibid: 248.
51. Knowles, *The History of a New Zealand Pentecostal Movement*, 294.
52. See above, 179.
53. Wolfgang D. Fernández, *Institutional Analysis: Initial Findings* (Waikanae: DAWN Strategy New Zealand, [1987]), and DAWN Strategy New Zealand, *1990*

Church Survey Report (n.p.: DAWN Strategy New Zealand Committee, 1990), 12, both cited in Knowles, *The History of a New Zealand Pentecostal Movement*, 294. Both documents are held in BKRP, MS-3530/010, Hocken Library, Dunedin.

54. Associated Pentecostal Churches of New Zealand, "1983 Directory of Ministers" (Wellington: Associated Pentecostal Churches of New Zealand, 1983 (mimeographed)); and Associated Pentecostal Churches of New Zealand, "1986 Directory of Ministers" (Wellington: Associated Pentecostal Churches of New Zealand, 1986 (mimeographed)), both held in BKRP, MS-3530/008, Hocken Library, Dunedin; cited in Knowles, "Some Aspects of the History of the New Life Churches of New Zealand," 257–58.

55. For perceptive accounts of Auckland Pentecostal worship and congregational life, see Stratford, "Christians Awake!" 124–37; and Harper, "The Church that's taking over Auckland," 122–35.

56. Jack Leigh, "Getting Religion," *New Zealand Women's Weekly*, 8 July 1985, 59–62; for the growth of the Auckland Assemblies of God, see Harper, "The Church that's taking over Auckland," 122–25; and Tania Evans, "God Almighty," *New Outlook* (January/February 1985), 22–30.

57. Harper, "The Church that's taking over Auckland," 122–35; also Clark, *Pentecost at the Ends of the Earth*, 134.

58. Clark, *Pentecost at the Ends of the Earth*, 190–91.

59. Michael Frost, "Is there any movement away from dualism within New Zealand Pentecostal faith and praxis?" (CHTX480 Research Essay, University of Otago, 2010), 29.

60. Clark, *Pentecost at the Ends of the Earth*, 179 and 206.

61. See Appendix A.

62. Max Palmer to Chuck Lynch, 12 March 1979, MHCF, cited in Knowles, "Some Aspects of the History of the New Life Churches of New Zealand," 278. For an entertaining account of congregational life in this church from 1978 to 1984, see Neville Logan, *"Excuse Me, I Have to Shoot the Guitarist": The Amazing Adventures of a Kiwi Cartoonist* (Christchurch: Kotuku Foundation, 1997).

63. Dasler, "Then they came to Elim . . . ," 18–21; B. Knowles, "Bilby, Ian," in NIDPCM, 417.

64. Knowles, "Bilby, Ian," 417.

65. Clark, *Pentecost at the Ends of the Earth*, 193.

66. Guy, "'Spirit Possession' and 'Deliverance Ministry'," 237.

67. Stratford, "Christians Awake!" 126; Brown, "The Charismatic Contribution," 104.

68. Clark, Interview, cited in Knowles, *The History of a New Zealand Pentecostal Movement*, 47.

69. Brett Knowles, "'Vision of the Disinherited?' An examination of the expansion of the Neo-Pentecostal and Charismatic Movements in the 1960's and 1970's and a suggested hypothesis for the social causes of their growth" (paper presented at Post-Graduate Seminar, Department of History, University of Otago, Dunedin, 4 October 1989). Audio cassettes of seminar held in BKRP, MS-3530/042–043, Hocken Library, Dunedin.

70. Knowles, "Vision of the Disinherited?" 114..

71. Clark, *Pentecost at the Ends of the Earth*, 204.

72. Brett Knowles, "Is the Future of Western Christianity a Pentecostal One?" in Stenhouse and Knowles, *The Future of Christianity*, 40–41.

73. Knowles, "Clark, Ian George," in NIDPCM, 551–52.

74. Knowles, "Some Aspects of the History of the New Life Churches of New Zealand," 292.
75. See Appendix A.
76. Carew and Troughton, "Māori Participation in the Assemblies of God," 98.
77. MacFarlane, "Houston, William Francis," ADPCM.
78. Janet Marsh, comment to author, Dunedin, 8 December 2012. Used with permission.
79. Clark, *Pentecost at the Ends of the Earth*, 178, 202–3.
80. Battley, "Charismatic Renewal: A View from the Inside," 49..
81. Battley, "The renewal is over . . . is it?" *Affirm* 5, no. 3 (Spring 1997): 17.
82. Grigg, *The Spirit of Christ and the Postmodern City*, 144.
83. Battley, "Charismatic Renewal: A View from the Inside," 49.
84. Ward, "The Charismatic Movement in New Zealand," 3.
85. Jim Veitch, "Protestants since the 1960s," in *Religions of New Zealanders*, ed. Peter Donovan (Palmerston North: Dunmore Press, 1990), 96, cited in Ward, "The Charismatic Movement in New Zealand," 2–3.
86. Bolitho, *Meet the Baptists*, 37, cited in Ward, "The Charismatic Movement in New Zealand," 3.
87. For discussions of other processes that contributed to the Charismatic movement's success, see Ward, "The Charismatic Movement in New Zealand," 4; and Brown, "The Charismatic Contribution," 110–11.
88. Brown, "The Charismatic Contribution," 106–8; Davidson, *Christianity in Aotearoa*, 171.
89. Battley, "Charismatic Renewal: A View from the Inside," 52.
90. Ibid: 49.
91. For examples, see Knowles, "Some Aspects of the History of the New Life Churches of New Zealand," 279, footnote 86.
92. Clark, *Pentecost at the Ends of the Earth*, 184–86 and 196–97; for a perceptive account of its impact on the congregation, see Harper, "The Church that's taking over Auckland," 122–25.
93. For an important discussion of this decline in prophetic authority, see Luke Worsfold, "Subsequence, Prophecy and Church Order," 158–60.
94. Clark, *Pentecost at the Ends of the Earth*, 153; Knowles, *The History of a New Zealand Pentecostal Movement*, 262–63 and footnote 32.
95. Assemblies of God in New Zealand, "Our History," 9.
96. Clark, *Pentecost at the Ends of the Earth*, 193.
97. Ibid, 195.
98. Ibid, 192.
99. Ibid, 195.
100. Luke Worsfold, "Subsequence, Prophecy and Church Order," 158.
101. Ibid, 261.
102. Ibid, 158.
103. Ibid, 158 and 240.
104. Ibid, 167.
105. Ibid, 242.
106. Ibid, 207.
107. Ibid, 159.

108. Brian Tamaki, *Bishop Brian Tamaki: More than meets the eye* (Pakuranga, Auckland: Tamaki Publications, 2006), 122. For another perspective on this incident, see Lineham, *Destiny*, 46–47.
109. See above, 117.
110. See above, 194.
111. Luke Worsfold, "Subsequence, Prophecy and Church Order," 280.
112. Tamaki, *Bishop Brian Tamaki: More than meets the eye*, 125–26.
113. Knowles, "Some Aspects of the History of the New Life Churches of New Zealand," 280–81, and footnotes 91 and 92.
114. Ibid, 285–86.
115. Ibid, 281.
116. For a detailed account of these developments during the 1980s, see Ibid, 255–87 and 314–37.
117. Knowles, "Morrow, Peter and Anne," in NIDPCM, 908 and Knowles, "Wheeler, Rob," in NIDPCM, 1193–94.
118. Knowles, "Some Aspects of the History of the New Life Churches of New Zealand," 335–37.
119. Ibid, 328.
120. Ibid, 335.
121. Knowles, *The History of a New Zealand Pentecostal Movement*, 289.
122. Grigg, *The Spirit of Christ and the Postmodern City*, 159.
123. For example, Alan Jamieson, *A Churchless Faith: Faith journeys beyond evangelical, Pentecostal & charismatic churches* (Wellington: Philip Garside Publishing, 2001), 163, note 1.
124. Clark, *Pentecost at the Ends of the Earth*, 201.
125. Michael Frost, "McDonald, Bruce (1953–)," ADPCM (accessed 12 April 2009). Also Grigg, *The Spirit of Christ and the Postmodern City*, 81, figure 8.
126. Jamieson, *A Churchless Faith*, 154 and 163, note 1.
127. The phrase is from Donald E. Miller and Tetsunao Yamaguchi, *Global Pentecostalism: The New Face of Christian Social Engagement* (Berkeley: University of California Press, 2007), 187, cited in Moetara, "An exploration of notions of Māori leadership," 84.
128. Moetara, "An exploration of notions of Māori leadership," 83–84.
129. Grigg, *The Spirit of Christ and the Postmodern City*, 154.
130. Simon Chan, *Pentecostal Theology and the Christian Spiritual Tradition*, Journal of Pentecostal Theology Supplement Series 21, ed. John Christopher Thomas, Rickie D. Moore and Stephen J. Land (Sheffield: Sheffield Academic Press, 2000).
131. Tom Wolfe, "The 'Me' Decade and the Third Great Awakening," *New York*, 23 August 1976, http://nymag.com/news/features/45938/ (accessed 1 May 2013). Also discussed in Christopher Lasch, *The Culture of Narcissism: American Life in an Age of Diminishing Expectations* (New York: W. W. Norton, 1977), 5–7.
132. Mark Price, "Narcissists—those infatuated with self," *New Zealand Herald*, 25 July 2009, http://www.nzherald.co.nz/nz/news/article.cfm?c_id=1&objectid=10586451 (accessed 1 May 2013).
133. Dunedin psychologist Chris Skellett, cited in Ibid; and Marc Wilson, "Handing out reality checks," *New Zealand Listener*, 2–8 February 2013, http://www.listener.co.nz/lifestyle/psychology/handing-out-reality-checks/ (accessed 1 May 2013).
134. Knowles, "From the Ends of the Earth We Hear Songs," 227–49. See also Margaret Hall, "Today's Song for Tomorrow's Church: The Role Played by Contemporary

Popular Music in Attracting Young People to Church" (PhD thesis in Music, Griffith University: Queensland Conservatorium, 2006), 163.

135. Knowles, "From the Ends of the Earth We Hear Songs," 239.

136. Ibid, 242.

137. Ibid, 242–43.

138. Transcript of Interview of Angus McLeod by Laurie Guy, 11 December 2008, 9, cited in Guy, *Shaping Godzone*, 26.

139. Guy, *Shaping Godzone*, 26.

140. Battley, "Charismatic Renewal: A View from the Inside," 56; Battley, "The renewal is over . . . is it?": 17.

141. Ward, "The Charismatic Movement in New Zealand," 7.

142. Ibid, 7–8.

143. Martin Marty, cited in Richard Quebedeaux, *The Worldly Evangelicals* (San Francisco: Harper and Row, 1978), 12.

144. Ibid, 167–68.

145. Luke Worsfold, "Subsequence, Prophecy and Church Order," 104–5.

146. Ibid, 119.

147. [Pastor] David Shearer to All *ICNZ* [Indigenous Churches of New Zealand] Regional Representatives, 15 September 1986, cited in Knowles, "Some Aspects of the History of the New Life Churches of New Zealand," 332–33. Reproduced by permission from Pastor David Shearer.

148. Knowles, "Some Aspects of the History of the New Life Churches of New Zealand," 329–35.

149. See above, 141.

Chapter 12

The 1990s

Waitangi, "Ruthanasia," MMP and other Metamorphoses

The 1990s began in celebratory fashion with the opening of the Commonwealth Games in Auckland on 24 January 1990, followed a fortnight later by the 150th anniversary of the signing of the Treaty of Waitangi. The annual commemoration of the Treaty on 6 February had been instituted after the Second World War to emphasize the positive aspects of the Treaty relationship between Māori and Pākehā. In this sesquicentennial year, the celebrations were attended by Queen Elizabeth II and by Māori and Pākehā dignitaries of all kinds. However, they hid a deeper reality: although New Zealand's race relations were claimed to be among the best in the world, the actuality was rather different. Indeed, a Māori Methodist writer had noted at the centennial celebrations in 1940 that "the last 100 years is [sic] filled with the groans of the Maori."[1] It is therefore not surprising that the Waitangi celebrations should become the focus for protest as the Māori renaissance gathered momentum in the 1970s. Bishop Vercoe's forthright complaint to Queen Elizabeth at the 1990 event[2] was merely the most widely publicized example in a long litany of Māori grievance over the nonhonoring of the Treaty.

Nevertheless, some progress was being made on the redressing of past injustices. The work of the Waitangi Tribunal was gaining momentum, with a number of treaty claims being settled during the 1990s. The three largest of these—the "Sealords" settlement[3] and the claims of the Waikato-Tainui[4] and Ngāi Tahu[5] iwi [tribal groups]—were settled for the benchmark figure of $170 million each. The "Sealords" deal offered Māori twenty per cent of the nation's fishing quota, allocated among the various iwi by the Waitangi Fisheries Commission. The other claims were settled for a mixture of cash and Crown-owned land; that of Tainui was also accompanied by an unprecedented formal apology from the Crown, delivered in person by Queen Elizabeth during her visit to New Zealand in 1995. Nevertheless, the long-term outcomes of the settlements were not uniformly positive: Tainui lost a large proportion of its settlement monies as a result of leadership disputes, personality clashes and unwise decisions. (An example of the latter was its investment of $6.27 million in the Auckland Warriors Rugby League football team;[6] it later sold the nearly bankrupt club for just $1.) By contrast, Ngāi Tahu was led by capable leaders with a vision for the future: its *kaumātua* [elder] Sir Tipene O'Regan's stated aim in the late 1980s was to create a Māori middle class by the year 2015. Ngāi Tahu's shrewd husbanding of its capital has meant that the *iwi* is now well on the way to achieving this goal.

By April 2013, thirty-seven Waitangi Tribunal claims had been completed, with a total settlement of almost $1.16 billion. A further eighteen deeds of settlement had been signed and awaited legislative ratification; six more had reached the draft settlement stage; and fifteen were still under negotiation.[7] This was just over half of the total number of claims; the Government was aiming to complete the settlement, at least in principle, of the outstanding grievances by the end of 2014. There were also massive changes in policies relating to Māori. Many government services, such as health and welfare, which had previously been the responsibility of the Department of Māori Affairs were now devolved from the Public Service to *iwi* authorities.[8] In this way, Māori solutions could be sought in Māori ways for Māori problems.

Another theme of the early 1990s was the considerable levels of social and economic stress. The ongoing process of Rogernomics was now beginning to affect many New Zealanders, with the mantra from Wellington being "no pain, no gain." This move to a free market economy produced its greatest collateral damage in the rising levels of unemployment. At the time of the October 1987 Stock Market Crash, this stood at 4.1% of the workforce. By the end of the decade, this had grown to 8.8% and remained above this level for the next three years, reaching a high of 11.4% (or 194,000 unemployed) in the first quarter of 1992.[9] This social pain was exacerbated by the aggressive cost-cutting policies of the National government, which had succeeded Labour in the 1990 election, but continued many of its controversial economic policies. Indeed, Ruth Richardson, the new Minister of Finance, was even more monetarist in her approach than her predecessor, Roger Douglas, had been. Her policies of economic stringency came to be known as "Ruthanasia"—a combination of "Ruth" and "euthanasia."[10] At her urging, the National Party significantly reduced spending on social welfare, increased pharmaceutical charges and lifted the rentals on State Houses to market levels.[11] This burden was particularly heavily felt by Māori and Pacific Islanders, who often did not have the skills and educational levels of their Pākehā counterparts and who therefore were more reliant on welfare. Although there was an improvement in the unemployment level by the middle of the decade, this did not return to the pre-Stock Market Crash levels of 1987 until 2004.[12]

The economic pain of the early 1990s translated into increasing political suspicion of Government and its policies. New Zealand had had a two-party system of representation for many years, with either the conservative-centrist National Party or the center-left Labour Party occupying the Government benches. Third-party representation was infrequent and unusual, since these smaller parties could not generate the political momentum of the two larger parties. However, there appeared to be little difference between National and Labour, both of which had espoused policies of radical economic change. A poll taken in 1992 consequently showed that only 4% of the public trusted politicians; in 1975, this figure had been 32%.[13] There was therefore mounting pressure for electoral reform and a Royal Commission in 1993 recommended the implementation of a mixed-member proportional [MMP] system similar to that operating in Germany. This would enable a greater range of political views to be represented in Parliament. A national referendum endorsed this recommendation and the 1996 General Election was therefore conducted on an MMP format, rather than on the "first-past-the-post" model that had obtained in the past.

However, it quickly became evident that there would be a much greater level of political maneuvering under the new system. There were a number of defections prior to the 1996 Election as politicians left the main parties to form their own small groups. Since the MMP format necessitated the formation of a coalition Government, these minor parties came to hold the balance of power in Parliament. On Election night, National received forty-four seats and Labour thirty-seven, but neither party had gained sufficient to govern in its own right, which required sixty seats. Both parties therefore needed the support of MP Winston Peters' centrist New Zealand First party—which had gained seventeen MPs in Parliament—and began negotiations with it to form a Government. Peters thus enjoyed the position of kingmaker. He took eight weeks to make his decision, effectively holding the country to ransom, before committing to a coalition with National. This delay ensured that the coalition would be a fraught one and it was dissolved in 1998 after MP Jenny Shipley staged a coup in which she replaced Prime Minister Jim Bolger as the leader of the National Party. Shipley thus became New Zealand's first—although unelected—female Prime Minister.[14] Another disadvantage of MMP was the ease with which list MPs—who had entered Parliament on their party's list of appointees and did not owe allegiance to an electoral constituency—could change their affiliation once in Parliament. There were several egregious examples of this, which led to the eventual passage of the Electoral Integrity Act in 2001, requiring politicians elected from a party list to resign from Parliament if they left their party's parliamentary caucus.[15]

The National government remained in power for nine years until the end of the decade, when it was defeated in the 1999 Elections. During this decade, New Zealand continued its social, economic and demographic metamorphosis. Its ethnic composition was changing, with increasing immigration from nontraditional sources, particularly from Asia and the Pacific Islands. By 2001, New Zealand Asians numbered 6% of the population and Pacific Islanders 4.6%; small Middle Eastern and African communities were also growing.[16] This ethnic diversification was paralleled by the redirection of New Zealand's trading and defense relationships. While Britain had been New Zealand's major market in 1940, taking 87.4% of its exports, this proportion had fallen to just 6.2% in 2000. Exports to Australia had increased over the same period from 2.9% to 21.4% and other export markets, such as the United States, Canada, Japan and other Asian countries, were also expanding.[17] Similarly, New Zealand's expulsion from ANZUS over the nuclear ships issue had opened up increased defense participation with the United Nations, with New Zealand soldiers serving in Bosnia, East Timor and the Pacific.[18] All of these changes served to demonstrate that the composition and orientation of New Zealand society was changing considerably. This metamorphosis would accelerate in the next decade under the radical social engineering policies of the Helen Clark-led Labour Government from 1999 to 2008.

The Churches and the Challenges of the 1990s

The response of the churches to the challenges of the 1990s took several forms. The decade began with a conscious emphasis on evangelism, manifest in long-term commitments such as the Decade of Evangelism and in shorter-term ventures such as the 1990 Rise Up Together campaign.[19] Both derived from Pentecostal and charismatic precedents. The Rise Up Together campaign—to be discussed in the next section—was largely the product of a Pentecostal emphasis on aggressive evangelism. Conversely, the Decade of Evangelism, as Donald Battley notes, was one of the fruits of the Charismatic Renewal.[20] Although the Renewal was domesticated and internalized by the start of the decade, having become largely an assortment of denominational agencies for renewal, it continued to have an ongoing influence in the churches. Viv Grigg describes its legacies in theological, pastoral, structural and migrational terms. Theologically and pastorally, it fostered the creation of new theological paradigms and the development of small confessional groups such as the Life in the Spirit seminars. Structurally, it transformed leadership roles—particularly in the Baptist Church—and developed new socioeconomic and apostolic models of ministry and, in some cases, contributed to the restructuring of entire denominations. It also facilitated a migration from charismatic churches to institutional Pentecostalism[21] although, as will be argued in the next chapter, the direction of this exodus would be reversed in the 2000s.

In general, the mainstream churches placed a stress on social issues and—in particular—on biculturalism, social justice and the promotion of a Christian voice in the political arena. The bicultural impulse, which was founded on the honoring of the Treaty-based partnership between Māori and Pākehā, led to some ecclesial changes. The most far-reaching of these took place in the Anglican Church, which reformed its constitution in 1992, becoming three related but autonomous bodies or *tikanga* [social organizations, language, laws, principles and procedures] in partnership. These new *tikanga* represented the Māori, Pacific Island and Pākehā wings of the church, replacing the previous provincial and diocesan frameworks. They comprised *Te Rūnanga o te Pīhopatanga o Aotearoa* [The Council of the Diocese of New Zealand, i.e., the Māori Council], the Diocese of Polynesia and the Pākehā Diocesan Synods.[22] However, other churches were less committed to the issue of biculturalism: Pentecostals, in particular—with the honorable exception of the Apostolic Church[23]—largely ignored the issue until the latter part of the decade.[24] The Assemblies of God, for example, did not mention the sesquicentenary of the

Treaty of Waitangi in its official magazine *The Evangel* in 1990.[25] This cultural myopia was also evident in the New Life Churches, where the issue of biculturalism surfaced at its 1990 Pastors' Conference. A young Māori pastor made an impassioned plea during the business session asking why a *pōwhiri* [official welcome ceremony] by the *tangata whenua* [local tribes] had not been held at the opening of the Conference. (*Pōwhiri* were becoming an increasingly common practice in New Zealand life, especially where there was a Māori component to the gathering.) While his concerns received some sympathy, a discussion at the New Life Churches' Regional Leaders' Meeting two months later showed that exception had been taken to the way in which the issue had been raised. The minutes of that meeting showed that "some leaders were for [the continuation of the practice of a Māori greeting at the National Conference] and some against. Some ... felt that it wasn't so much the greeting, but the attitude of the person giving it that was the problem." Consequently, the motion was put and carried that "in reference to the Maori welcome, we see no reason for this practice to continue."[26] The movement's approach was largely behavioral, focusing on the young pastor's outburst, rather than on the cultural pain which had produced it. This negative attitude to Māori culture was also repeated in other Pentecostal churches (including the Apostolic and Elim churches).[27] It is therefore not surprising that Māori did not really feel part of the Pentecostal movement[28] and that, with the exception of the Apostolic Church, there was little Māori involvement in these churches.[29]

Churches also responded to the economic climate in several prophetic ways. The growth of food banks in the early 1990s, in part a direct result of National's benefit cuts, indicated that the problems of poverty and social justice were becoming more acute. The gap between rich and poor in New Zealand was then the fastest growing in the OECD and a social underclass was emerging as a result of high unemployment rates produced by Rogernomics and Ruthanasia. (This was demonstrated in a television program screened on TV1 on 25 August 1991—as part of a six-part documentary series entitled *Where to now?*—on the cycle of poverty and despair then prevalent among many New Zealanders. It highlighted some of the inequalities in New Zealand society, but suffered from the defect of the front man being a well-known and well-off Pākehā presenter speaking, in paternalistic fashion, on behalf of the underclass.)[30] These inequalities led to a significant response, the Churches' Social Justice Initiative of 1993, which directly challenged the Government's financial and social policies. Ten churches—the Apostolic, Anglican, Baptist, Catholic, Lutheran, Methodist and Presbyterian churches, the Associated Churches of Christ, the Religious Society of Friends (Quakers) and the Salvation Army[31]—combined in a cooperative project to promote the cause of social justice. They did this by issuing a Church Leaders' Statement of Intent in January 1993, followed six months later by a Church Leaders' Social Justice Statement. These two statements challenged the Government to consider the social cost of their policies, arguing *inter alia* that the test of any policy was whether it enhanced or threatened people's life and dignity. The statements generated lively public debate but were received with hostility by the National Government, although welcomed by the Labour and

Alliance Parties, which had more socialist leanings.[32] Interestingly, the most vigorous opposition came from MPs with church affiliations. Jenny Shipley, then Minister for Social Welfare and later to become Prime Minister, was particularly hostile: "I am disturbed personally—and I say this as an active member of the church—that some of the work that has been put in front of this nation that purports to be the position of the church, in fact comes out of some of the most left-wing thinking areas of New Zealand."[33] Professor of Public Policy Jonathan Boston describes the Social Justice Statements as the first occasion in New Zealand's history when the leaders of all major denominations put their names to documents dealing with matters of social and political theology.[34] Despite the vagueness of some of the Statements' language and their lack of concrete direction, they were nevertheless a prophetic stand for social justice and a direct challenge to government policies and priorities. This was reinforced by the *Hīkoi* of Hope, initiated by the Anglican General Synod in 1998.

The *Hīkoi* of Hope was modeled on the *hīkoi* [march] led by Whina Cooper to Parliament in 1975 protesting the alienation of Māori Land.[35] Two groups of marchers, starting from Cape Reinga in the north and Stewart Island in the south, marched the length of the country, converging on Parliament Buildings in Wellington to protest against poverty and inequality.[36] As the core group of about thirty marchers passed through each town, they were joined at its boundaries by people from local churches and conducted ecumenical rallies while in the area.[37] These rallies were sizeable: the one held in Dunedin had about 400 people in attendance from almost every church.[38] Pentecostals, however, were conspicuously absent. (There appeared to be only two Pentecostals present at the Dunedin *hīkoi*; the author—who was one of these—was frequently asked during the event, "Where are the Pentecostals?") The *hīkoi* attracted some media coverage, but this turned negative when the marchers' arrival in Blenheim coincided with the Anglican Church's increasing of the rentals on its housing in the town to market rates. This was castigated as Anglican hypocrisy and, since the Anglican Church had initiated the *hīkoi*, detracted from its message. The marchers' arrival in Wellington led to regular meetings between church leaders, government ministers and politicians where the churches' social concerns were raised. Nevertheless, Prime Minister David Lange was publicly scornful of the *hīkoi* on the *Holmes* program on prime-time national television[39] and little change eventuated from these consultations.[40]

The third change in the 1990s was the increasing promotion of a Christian voice in the political arena. Although Christianity had a role in many major political parties, it has never formed an explicit part of them, despite some MPs having strong Christian beliefs. To some extent, this reflected a separation of Church and State in New Zealand. The only exception to this general rule was the Rātana party, formed in 1928 by T. W. Rātana, the faith healer founder of the Rātana movement, to contest the "four quarters"—i.e., the four Māori seats—in Parliament.[41] This was achieved in 1943 and a strong alliance developed between the Rātana Church and the Labour Party, which lasted until the advent of MMP in 1996. However, the 1990s and the 2000s saw the emergence of several explicitly Christian political parties, largely in reaction to the failure of Christian moralist activism in the 1980s.

The first of these was the Christian Heritage Party, launched by businessman Bill van Rij and others in Christchurch in 1989. Van Rij came from a theologically conservative Dutch Reformed and Evangelical Presbyterian background and had also been involved in the Coalition of Concerned Citizens, formed in the mid-1980s to contest the Homosexual Law Reform Bill. This moralist controversy supplied the inspiration for the formation of the Party.[42] Models of a Christian or confessional party were also provided from van Rij's Dutch background and—more directly—from the Christian Heritage Party of Canada, with which he had been in contact.[43] Thus, many of the Party's founding members had connections with the Dutch Reformed Church, although membership was open to all evangelical Christians. This gave it a rigidly confessional base, which some religious conservatives found off putting and which diluted its Christian support base. Nevertheless, it achieved fifth place in the 1993 Election with 2.02% of the vote, making it the largest party outside Parliament. A second Christian party, the Christian Democrats, was formed in 1995 by Graeme Lee, a National MP who had defected from that party the previous year. This was less confessional and more value-based than Christian Heritage, allowing participation by anybody who shared its basic Christian moral outlook. The two parties contested the 1996 election as a single bloc—the Christian Coalition—achieving 4.33% of the vote, just below the 5% necessary to gain a seat in Parliament. Tensions between them led to the Coalition's dissolution in 1997; Christian Heritage continued its confessional approach, while the Christian Democrats rebranded themselves as Future New Zealand, contesting the 1999 Election under this name. Neither party was successful in that election. However, Future New Zealand later joined with MP Peter Dunne's centrist United Party to become the United Future New Zealand Party in 2000. Dunne retained his seat in the 2002 Elections and the party gained 6.7% of the vote, resulting in eight United Future New Zealand list MPs (including several former Christian Democrats) entering Parliament. Despite this overt Christian presence, the party was largely ineffective, having insufficient numbers to prevent the passage of controversial enactments such as the legalization of prostitution in 2003. For its part, Christian Heritage declined after 1997, undergoing a series of controversies and resignations. Its final demise came in 2005–6, following the conviction of its former party leader, Graham Capill, for historic rape and sexual abuse charges. A third, but short-lived, Christian political party, Destiny New Zealand, was formed in 2003, specifically to reflect the values of Brian Tamaki's Destiny Church; this will be discussed in the next chapter.

New Zealand Pentecostalism at the End of the Millennium

New Zealand Pentecostalism presented two different realities in the 1990s. From the perspective of an external observer, the movement seemed to be in good heart, being characterized by energy, extroversion and activity. However, there was also a hidden internal dissonance which reflected both a sense of loss and a search for the recovery of its charismatic power and relationships. Both of these realities continued throughout the 1990s and into the first decade of the twenty-first century.

External Vigor: Energy, Extroversion and Activity

The Rise Up Together campaign of 1990 reflected an energetic Pentecostal self-confidence, exemplified in the pounding beat of its theme song, "Rise up, You people of power, Stand up, across the land."[44] Despite the moralist defeats of the previous decade, there was still a strong sense of Pentecostal power and optimism, particularly in the larger urban centers.[45] The campaign—led by Auckland Christian businessman Trevor Yaxley—built upon this, seeking to systematically evangelize the country through evangelistic outreach, youth rallies and childrens' events.[46] This involved Action Training Camps, a practical training phase centered on outreach at the Auckland Commonwealth Games and a nationwide campaign by Rise Up Together teams from March to November 1990.[47] There was some success: by the end of June 1990, 147 towns and locations around the country had been visited by these teams and nearly 2,500 commitments to Christ had been recorded.[48] Nevertheless, the excitement was not sustained beyond the end of the campaign and Yaxley went on to found Lifeway Bible School and the Family Television Network. The latter evolved into Shine TV, which was launched on the Sky TV Network in 2001 and is still in operation. Other Pentecostal outreach projects in the 1990s included a Declaration of Unity in the Harvest, signed by the delegates to the 1991 APCNZ Conference, pledging their churches to work together in evangelism.[49] This may have been an extension of the Assemblies of God's Season of Harvest policy.[50]

Despite this energetic evangelism, the decadal growth rate of Pentecostal was slowing, decreasing to 36.27% for the ten years from 1991 to 2001, compared with 55.84% for the previous decade.[51] The Assemblies of God had the largest share of this expansion, growing from 181 churches in 1991 to 261 in 2002.[52] Much of its growth came from the expansion and diversification of ethnic churches. The number of European-culture Assemblies of God grew by 32% between 1987 and 1999, whereas that of its ethnic-culture churches grew by 262% over the same period.[53] This produced a demographic transformation in the movement, which became much more ethnically diverse in the 1990s.[54] (Indeed, European-culture Assemblies of God comprised only 49% of the total number of assemblies by 2003, although the ethnic congregations were generally smaller than their European counterparts.)[55] The Apostolic church was also placing a particular emphasis on its Māori work during the 1990s, in contrast to other Pentecostal groups.[56] The expansion of the decade owed much to the adoption of church growth policies by Pentecostal churches. However, this strategy also had a negative consequence, as Luke Worsfold points out in the case of the Apostolic Church:

> Since 1990 there has been a marked emphasis on church growth. ... The drive for church growth motivated younger members of the council to rely on natural talent rather than the spiritual exercises of prayer and waiting on God for prophetic revelation, As a result of the focus on expansion, some congregations grew but at the expense of depth of spirituality.[57]

As a result, the ethos of the Apostolic Church changed during the 1990s from an emphasis on the exercise of spiritual gifts to a focus on evangelism, church growth and church planting.[58] Similarly, the Assemblies of God were also stressing the planting of new churches.[59]

It is difficult to quantitatively assess the growth of individual Pentecostal bodies between 1991 and 2001, since a change in the Census methodology has rendered comparisons of data between 2001 and previous years invalid. Furthermore, the 2001 Census tended to lump a number of groups into the single category of "Pentecostal." This category increased 65.84% between 1991 and 2001; by contrast the increase of all Pentecostal groups—including those subsumed in this single category—over the decade was a more realistic 36.27%.[60] Some of this growth was a product of the emergence of large megachurches, particularly, but not exclusively, in Auckland. Viv Grigg notes that these large churches tended to emphasize the American-oriented Prosperity Gospel and drew in many from mainline and other Pentecostal churches in the 1990s.[61] They also tended to authoritarianism and to follow "seeker service" models of church, rather than to focus on experiential extremes.[62] In this latter respect, they were less Pentecostal in ethos than their earlier counterparts.

The most prominent example of this aggressive Pentecostal growth in the 1990s and 2000s was Brian Tamaki, who had begun his ministry as an Apostolic Church pastor in 1984. He was ordained as an apostle by the Apostolic Church in 1991, on the basis of his successful ministry in Te Awamutu and Rotorua.[63] However, he and his large Lake City Church in Rotorua left the Apostolic Church in 1994. Their departure was partly due to the 10% levy on church income that each local Apostolic congregation was required to pay to the Apostolic Church headquarters. In the case of Lake City Church, this levy amounted to a substantial $40,000 and Tamaki believed that these funds would be better employed in church planting projects, asking "what is our remittance used for?"[64] Another key factor in his resignation was a feeling of restriction, produced by the centralizing bureaucratic polities of the Apostolic Church.[65] Tamaki shifted to Auckland in 1998 with the intention of establishing "the largest Polynesian church in the world."[66] His aggressive style and ability to stir up controversy, together with his growing television ministry after 1999,[67] soon gained him a national reputation. They also led to the emergence of the Destiny Church movement as the most prominent example of New Zealand

Pentecostalism in the first decade of the twenty-first century.[68] Tamaki's growing influence will be discussed in the next chapter.

However, there were several events during the 1990s that enabled the public media to cast the Pentecostal movement in a bad light. The first of these was a prophecy made by Gerald Coates, a British Pentecostal leader from the House Church movement, who visited New Zealand in 1989 and again in 1990. During his first visit, Coates prophesied an impending volcanic eruption and earthquake, centered on Lake Taupo in the center of the North Island, which would take place in November 1991. This prophecy was reported by the leading Christian newspaper *Challenge Weekly* and endorsed by a number of prominent New Zealand Pentecostal leaders, including Elim Church leader Ian Bilby. Consequently, there was a substantial media backlash when the event failed to happen.[69] A similar issue—although in this case, caused by media misreportage—was the controversy that ensued over Brian Tamaki's imputed comments about women leaders in 2000. Tamaki had preached a sermon series entitled "A Fatherless Generation." In it, he focused on the responsibility of fathers to their children and on the increasing phenomenon of "runaway dads" who failed to undertake this role in the home and in society. This failure was manifest in an underrepresentation of men at the highest levels of power which, together with the "missing men" at home, was "the work of the devil."[70] Tamaki's focus was on the prevalent male abrogation of responsibility. However, several secular newspapers picked up his comments and reported them on their front pages as being a critique of female leadership, which was a misrepresentation of what he actually had said.[71] At the time, both the Prime Minister and the Leader of the Opposition were women (Helen Clark and Jenny Shipley). New Zealand also had a female Chief Justice (Sian Elias) and a female Attorney-General (Margaret Wilson) and would shortly have its second female Governor-General (Silvia Cartwright).[72] The Prime Minister took Tamaki's imputed comments personally, viewing them as an attack on her leadership. She recalled in 2004 that "four years ago ... he commented that having two New Zealand women leaders at the time was a sign that New Zealand was falling for the work of the devil."[73] Consequently, as Tamaki put it, "all hell broke loose!" and TVNZ pulled the plug on his television program, which was then just about to be launched. Tamaki thus became a controversial figure and future media coverage of him reinforced this negative perception.[74] His prominence in the first decade of the twenty-first century built upon this notoriety.

Internal Dissonance: Departures, Autonomy, Relationships and Power

While some Pentecostal churches in the 1990s were characterized by energy, extroversion and activity, there were also other trends that must be set against these positive attributes. These included the exodus of individuals and churches from Pentecostal denominations; the hunger for "fathering relationships" rather than bureaucratic authority; and the quest to recover the charismatic unpredictability, freedom and power of the earlier movement.

Although the exodus of people from the movement had always been something of an unacknowledged elephant in the room, this leave-taking seems to have increased during the 1990s. It went largely unnoticed, being balanced by the influx of transfer growth, but when it *was* remarked, it was attributed to backsliding and to younger people losing their faith and departing the church. However, sociologist Alan Jamieson has shown—in a highly significant study, based on interviews with more a hundred adult leavers from Evangelical, Pentecostal and Charismatic churches—that this was not the case. The average period of time Jamieson's respondents had spent in these churches was 15.8 years; 94% had been involved in some form of church leadership; and 36% had undertaken full-time or part-time theological study.[75] Jamieson uses theologian James W. Fowler's well-known six-part Stages of Faith model to explain this phenomenon, arguing that Pentecostal congregations tend to be loyalist "Stage 3," or synthetic-conventional, churches.[76] In these conformist groups, the maintenance of unanimity is central: one accepts the leadership of significant others and does not rock the boat. However, people advancing into the critical, questioning "Stage 4," or individuative-reflective, faith can often find themselves at variance with their "Stage 3" fellow believers and have to leave in order to develop their own individual spirituality. Jamieson found that few people had left the church because of loss of faith or "meta-grumbles"—i.e., questions about the deep-rooted foundations of the faith itself.[77] Instead, most leavers continued to maintain—at least in part—elements of Pentecostal faith that their erstwhile fellow believers considered that they had left behind.

The exodus of individuals was partly compounded by the secession of a number of Pentecostal churches from their parent bodies in the 1990s; this process would accelerate in the next decade. Reference has already been made to Brian Tamaki's defection from the Apostolic Church in 1994.[78] Other churches included the large West City Christian Centre, which left the Assemblies of God in 1997 without a detailed explanation, other than the movement's inability to facilitate the direction the church was now taking. More defections followed.[79] Another example of Pentecostal distancing was Paul de Jong—an Australian Assemblies of God minister, who had previously been Frank Houston's associate pastor in Sydney—who returned to New Zealand to set up the Auckland Christian Life Centre. It was a matter of continuing disappointment to the leadership of the Assemblies of God that Pastor de Jong did not apply for a New Zealand credential. Instead, he continued to remain aloof from the Assemblies of God in this country[80] and his Christian Life Centres became yet another Pentecostal denomination in New Zealand. There was also an increasing trend in the 1990s of local Assemblies of God identifying themselves by other titles, rather than by using the standard designation of "Assembly of God."[81] Ian Clark sees this as being symptomatic of a "loosening" in the corporate bonds of the movement, despite its growth in the 1990s.[82] However, it is significant that almost all of the seceding churches from the various Pentecostal denominations were large and vigorous churches, with strong, authoritative pastoral leadership. The secessions appear to be an attempt to maintain their freedom of charismatic action in the face of the increasing bureaucratization of the Pentecostal denominations. An example of this institutional focus is the list of appointments to official positions made by the Assemblies of God's Executive Council in 1996: these totaled thirteen separate categories of leadership![83] It is small wonder that there was a reaction to this on the part of some pastors. As Tamaki bluntly put it, with reference to the Apostolic Church: "What used to be a dynamic and cutting-edge movement was becoming increasingly caught up in the bureaucracy and politics of denominationalism and this dynamic was sucking the life out of some pastors like myself, who were forging new frontiers."[84] These sentiments would also have resonated with pastors in other Pentecostal denominations. However, there were other bureaucratic changes that went largely unnoticed. The New Life Churches, for example, issued a Handbook for Pastors in 1992 and set up superannuation and medical insurance schemes for its credentialed ministers.[85] These bureaucratic changes accelerated in the 1990s under John Walton, who became the National Leader of the New Life Churches after the resignations of Rob Wheeler and Peter Morrow.[86]

A second, related factor was a growing hunger for relational modes of pastoral association. While references to "relationship" and "fatherhood" were more prominent in some denominations than in others, it is significant that they were widely spread across the Pentecostal movement. This was a reaction to the increasing size and anonymity of Pentecostal denominations and also to the expanding bureaucracies that had emerged. The issue emerged at the Assemblies of God General Council as early as 1981, when a discussion took place as to whether the Executive of the movement was a "fathering" body or an administrative one. General Superintendent Jim Williams downplayed the issue, but later commented that those who felt the need of this "fathering" relationship should establish their own links with someone who could fulfill this role for them. (The issue came about because the rapid growth of the Assemblies of God in the 1970s meant that most pastors were only in their thirties and lacked senior role models to mentor and guide them. Regional gatherings of ministers did not provide a sufficient level of personal input.)[87] The possibility of a full-time "fathering" figure to mentor new works and their pastors was again raised at the General Council in 1985, but this did not eventuate.[88]

There were similar concerns in other Pentecostal groups also. "Fathering" was a major component in the debate over the evolving shape of the New Life Churches in the 1980s. The strongest proponent of this view was Pastor Ross Davies, who adamantly resisted the idea of an official structure and earnestly argued for "relationship rather than legislation." Davies stressed the responsibility of a father-pastor to train up young ministers, to launch them into their pastorates and to have a continuing relationship with them throughout the course of their ministries. He practiced what he preached, having a strong ongoing personal and pastoral relationship with his spiritual children in the ministry. In sociological terms, his approach was strongly charismatic in that the bonds of fellowship were personal and relational, rather than organizational. It was therefore at the opposite end of the sociological spectrum from the bureaucratic approach.[89] However, the New Life Churches eventually established an official, institutionalized model of leadership in 1987. As a consequence, Davies' followers resigned from the movement in protest and formed a new group—the South Pacific Fellowship—which followed his relationship model of collective identity.[90] Davies himself had resigned from the New Life Churches the previous year.

However, the ideas of "fathering" and "relationship" were widespread. Church historian Nigel Scotland notes that the standard question in the late 1980s in the British House Church movement was no longer "which apostle are you under?" but "who do you relate to?" This represented a shift from hierarchical to relational modes of association.[91] This restructuring gained momentum in the 1990s, with the Apostolic Church developing relations-based networks instead of the centralized bureaucracy that had previously characterized its polity. Pastor Bruce Monk, who became the movement's Apostolic Leader in 2001, was a key figure in this change of focus and his Equipper's Network signaled the beginnings of a separate stream within the Apostolic Church.[92] However, these changes did not happen quickly enough for some: the lack of "fathering" in the Apostolic Church was one of Brian Tamaki's stated reasons for his secession from that movement in 1994.[93] Tamaki believed that two of the key dynamics of a successful church were "spiritual fathering" and "the development of spiritual sons and daughters" and saw the authority of the church as being based upon this.[94] This emphasis on personal relationship accounts for the strong charismatic influence that Tamaki was able to exercise in the Destiny Church and also for his ability to mobilize his members in aggressive moralist protest. However, Luke Worsfold notes that there were disadvantages to these alternative personal, charismatic networks. They effectively enable "supervisors with a particular emphasis [to] attract the allegiance of those who resonate with their philosophy and praxis so creating a network of churches who exhibit the same characteristics. The denomination then becomes an affiliation of churches who no longer share a common distinctive."[95] Furthermore, as Simon Moetara notes, relational networks surrounding a charismatic leader could easily become hierarchical. In such cases, "cults of personality can easily arise around strongly charismatic leaders, with followers being attracted to the individual leader rather than to the gospel of Christ." This, he observes, is particularly true of movements in which Māori were strongly represented.[96]

A third factor in the quest for the recovery of charismatic power was the emergence of the Toronto Blessing in January 1994.[97] This eruption of phenomena such as laughter, crying, shaking, spiritual drunkenness, falling under the Spirit and other physical manifestations began at the Toronto Airport Vineyard Church and quickly spread worldwide from there. American sociologist Margaret Poloma sees this as a recovery from the "charismatic drought" of the 1980s and early 1990s, basing this view upon a survey conducted with nearly 1,000 participants in the Toronto Blessing in 1995. These respondents reported a spiritual refreshing from feelings of spiritual dryness and discouragement.[98] While a number of evangelists, such as South African Rodney Howard-Browne,[99] brought the new phenomena to New Zealand, the more usual method of transmission was for people to visit Toronto for themselves.[100] Over the next four years, thousands did so, sparking a Pentecostal pilgrimage industry.[101] A related outbreak in 1995 at the Brownsville Assembly of God in Pensacola, Florida[102] created another locus of spiritual pilgrimage. However, the Toronto Blessing was controversial because of some of the bizarre physical manifestations that accompanied it. Kevin Ward, for example, castigates the Church for focusing on "faddisms" such as the Toronto Blessing, citing British Baptist charismatic leader Douglas McBain to the effect that "the Church of the 1990s is spiritually poorer through overdosing on the spectacular."[103] Such episodes challenged stereotypes of charismatic experience and punctured Pentecostal respectability. Consequently it was not acceptable to all Pentecostal groups, although some influential churches—such as the Auckland Assembly of God—and several Pentecostal denominations strongly supported it. While these phenomena were not new, their reemergence "pointed to the continuing hunger in New Zealand for the revival spirit of the 1970's, which was now only a pleasant memory."[104] By accommodating them, Pentecostal churches were acknowledging their dryness and seeking a recovery of charismatic unpredictability, freedom and power.

To summarize: to an outside observer, the Pentecostal movement in the 1990s appeared to be in good health, being characterized by energy, extroversion and activity. Nevertheless, there were some indications of internal dissonance, reflected in the quest for a renewal of charismatic freedom and power, in contrast to the bureaucratic modes of polity in many Pentecostal denominations. The exodus of individuals from Pentecostal churches and the secession of churches from Pentecostal denominations represented, in part, an attempt to achieve charismatic autonomy and greater spiritual power. Desire for "fathering relationships" among the movement's pastors similarly indicated a rejection of bureaucratic modes of authority. Finally, the openness of a number of Pentecostal churches to the Toronto Blessing derived from a hunger to recover the charismatic unpredictability and freedom of the earlier movement. All of these trends represented a reaction to the ongoing sociological progression from charismatic to bureaucratic modes of Pentecostal organization that was taking place during the 1980s and 1990s.

Conclusion

If the 1980s had been a revolutionary decade, these processes of social transformation continued and intensified in the 1990s. The accelerating Māori renaissance—most evident in the growing number of compensation cases before the Waitangi Tribunal—and the deepening socioeconomic impact of Rogernomics were the two major trends throughout the decade. Economic pain gave rise to political suspicion and to mounting pressure for electoral reform; this led to the adoption of the MMP model of parliamentary representation in 1996. Its introduction resulted in increased fragmentation and diversification in New Zealand political life. The Churches also changed throughout the 1990s, implementing new ecclesial structures and placing an increasing emphasis on social justice in the light of the socioeconomic distress of the decade. However, their protests had little impact on Government policies and the focus changed to Christian political participation as the decade progressed.

Pentecostal churches were largely isolated and insulated from these issues. Laurie Guy has attributed this to the privatization of Christian concern, which, for many, "had shrunk to their private lives and their church worlds."[105]

Certainly there was little Pentecostal interest in biculturalism and social justice, although this began to change in some churches towards the end of the decade. As the Rise Up Together campaign demonstrated in 1990, Pentecostals tended to focus on evangelism, rather than on prophetic challenges to socioeconomic evils. Such movements as did emerge focused on the charismatic gifts of the Spirit and the prophetic office within the church, such as the Prophetic Movement, which arrived in New Zealand in the 1990s. Assemblies of God pastor and historian Paul Harrison refers to several School of the Prophets seminars and conferences that took place in Auckland in the 1990s.[106] These movements, based on the model of the Kansas City Prophets,[107] tended to reinforce the inward-looking orientation of Pentecostal churches, rather than to prophetically challenge the surrounding society.

Thus, despite the apparent health and vitality of New Zealand Pentecostalism, there were some worrying indications of dissonance and malaise. These were reflected in the exodus of individuals and churches from Pentecostal denominations and the proliferation of new Pentecostal groups. Large megachurches emerged with authoritative, charismatic leadership; but their rise was often accompanied by the decline of other Pentecostal churches. This trend was reinforced by the hunger for relationship-based church structures, in which senior "fathers" in the movement personally mentored younger ministers. This was a reaction to the anonymous, bureaucratic model of polity that increasingly characterized Pentecostal denominations. The quest for a recovery of charismatic unpredictability and power also found expression in the Toronto Blessing and in other eruptions of revivalist phenomena. In all of these changes, the compelling motivation was a desire to reverse the trend that had begun in the 1980s from charismatic to bureaucratic modes of Pentecostal organization.

Notes

1. The Methodist Church of New Zealand, *Minutes of the Annual Conference, 1940*, 150–51, cited in Allan Davidson, "Churches and the Treaty: A History," in National Council of Churches in New Zealand, Church and Society Commission, *The Pakeha and the Treaty: Signposts*, 35 (Auckland: National Council of Churches, 1986).

2. See above, 186.

3. King, *Penguin History of New Zealand*, 501. Enacted by the Treaty of Waitangi (Fisheries Claims) Settlement Act 1992. http://www.legislation.govt.nz/act/public/1992/0121/latest/whole.html (accessed 13 May 2013).

4. Enacted by the Waikato Raupatu Claims Settlement Act 1995. http://www.legislation.govt.nz/act/public/1995/0058/latest/DLM369893.html?src=qs (accessed 13 May 2013).

5. Enacted by the Ngāi Tahu Claims Settlement Act 1998. http://www.legislation.govt.nz/act/public/1998/0097/latest/DLM429090.html?src=qs (accessed 13 May 2013).

6. Paul Yandall, "Rough tackles in Warriors' hardest game," *New Zealand Herald*, 25 September 2000, http://www.nzherald.co.nz/nz/news/article.cfm?c_id=1&objectid=152646 (accessed 15 May 2013).

7. Office of Treaty Settlements: Te Tari Whakatau Take e pa ana ki te Tiriti o Waitangi, "Settlement Progress: Claims Progress," updated 8 April 2013 http://www.ots.govt.nz/ (accessed 13 May 2013).

8. King, *Penguin History of New Zealand*, 499–500.

9. Statistics New Zealand (Tatauranga Aotearoa): *Infoshare*, "Labour Force Status by Sex by Age Group (Qrtly-Mar/Jun/Sep/Dec)," http://www.stats.govt.nz/infoshare/ViewTable.aspx?pxID=adbb94b9-f930-4a8a-8d17-cee68290292 (accessed 10 May 2013).

10. Patrick Allen, "'Bankrupt' Western Governments Need 'Ruthanasia'," CNBC, Europe: Economy, 8 September 2010, http://www.cnbc.com/id/39054360 (accessed 31 August 2010).

11. King, *Penguin History of New Zealand*, 493.

12. Statistics New Zealand (Tatauranga Aotearoa): *Infoshare*, "Labour Force Status by Sex by Age Group (Qrtly-Mar/Jun/Sep/Dec)."

13. Cited in King, *Penguin History of New Zealand*, 493.

14. Ibid, 493–95.

15. John E. Martin, "Parliament—Impact of MMP," *Te Ara Encyclopedia of New Zealand*, updated 13 July 2012 http://www.TeAra.govt.nz/en/parliament/page-9 (accessed 14 May 2013).

16. King, *Penguin History of New Zealand*, 498–99..

17. Ibid, 498.

18. Ibid, 497.

19. Davidson, *Christianity in Aotearoa*, 183, 185.

20. Battley, "The renewal is over . . . is it?": 28.

21. Grigg, *The Spirit of Christ and the Postmodern City*, 142–44.

22. Davidson, *Christianity in Aotearoa* [1997], 185.

23. Moetara, "Māori and Pentecostal Christianity in Aotearoa New Zealand," 81–82; Moetara, "An exploration of notions of Māori leadership," 49.

24. Moetara compares the engagement of three Pentecostal churches (Apostolic, Assemblies of God and Destiny) with Māori up to 2009. Moetara, "Māori and Pentecostal Christianity in Aotearoa New Zealand," 73–90.

25. Carew and Troughton, "Māori Participation in the Assemblies of God," 99.

26. Otago/Southland New Life Churches, "Minutes of the Regional Pastors' Meeting," 27 February 1991, paragraph 4, "Issue of Maori Greeting at the National Conference," reporting on discussion of the issue at the Regional Leaders' Meeting in November 1990, cited in Knowles, "Some Aspects of the History of the New Life Churches of New Zealand," 291–92.

27. Moetara, "Māori and Pentecostal Christianity in Aotearoa New Zealand," 78.

28. See the comments cited in Knowles, "Some Aspects of the History of the New Life Churches of New Zealand," 292, footnote 13. See also Lloyd Martin, *One Faith, Two Peoples: Communicating Across Cultures Within the Church*, 3rd ed. (Paraparaumu: Salt Company Publishers, 2001).

29. Clark, *Pentecost at the Ends of the Earth*, 238; Moetara, "Māori and Pentecostal Christianity in Aotearoa New Zealand," 80; Moetara, "An exploration of notions of Māori leadership," 49; Carew and Troughton, "Māori Participation in the Assemblies of God," 92.

30. Gordon Dryden, "Episode 1: The Vicious Cycle," in *Where To Now?* TV1, 25 August 1991 (Auckland: Tiger Films for the Pacific Foundation, 1991).
31. Jonathan Boston, "Christianity in the Public Square: The Churches and Social Justice," in *Voices for Justice: Church, Law and State in New Zealand*, ed. Jonathan Boston and Alan Cameron, 12 (Palmerston North: Dunmore Press, 1994).
32. Ibid, 13.
33. Jenny Shipley, cited in the *Dominion*, 22 July 1993, and thence in Boston and Cameron, *Voices for Justice*, 21–22.
34. Boston and Cameron, *Voices for Justice*, 13.
35. "Today in History: 13 October—1975 Whina Cooper leads land march to Parliament," *New Zealand History online*, updated 15 November 2013 http://www.nzhistory.net.nz/whina-cooper-led-land-march-te-ropu-o-te-matakite-reaches-parliament (accessed 2 December 2013).
36. For a video of the *hīkoi*, see Allan K. Davidson, "Anglican Church—Church debate and dissent," *Te Ara Encyclopedia of New Zealand*, updated 20 June 2013 http://www.TeAra.govt.nz/en/video/27683/hikoi-of-hope-1998. For a discussion of its aims and objectives, see Dorothy [sic], "The Hikoi of Hope," *NZine*, 16 October 1998, http://www.nzine.co.nz/hot/hikoi.html (both accessed 17 May 2013).
37. Vivienne Paterson, "Hikoi Sweeps into Otago," *Otago Daily Times*, 8 September 1998, 1; "Hikoi highlights Dunedin's poverty," *Otago Daily Times*, 11 September 1998, 5; and "Mayor Joins March against Poverty," *Otago Daily Times*, 12 September 1998, 5.
38. Tracie Barrett, "March Swells," *Otago Daily Times*, 14 September 1998, 5.
39. Dorothy, "Hikoi of Hope," *NZine*.
40. Susan St. John, "Ten Years on from the Hikoi of Hope," Child Poverty Action Group, 21 September 2008, http://www.cpag.org.nz/resources/presentations/10-years-on-from-the-hikoi-of-hope/ (accessed 17 May 2013).
41. For a brief—but comprehensive—coverage of the religious and cultural issues underlying the development of the Rātana movement, see Keith Newman, "Rātana, the Prophet: Mā te wā—the Sign of the Broken Watch," in Morrison et al., *Mana Māori and Christianity*, 243–63.
42. "Message from the President," Christian Heritage Party of New Zealand, [1989], 2, cited in Knowles, "Some Aspects of the History of the New Life Churches of New Zealand, 1960–1990," 308, footnote 83.
43. OVGuide, "Bill Van Rij Video—Interviews," http://www.ovguide.com/bill-van-rij-9202a8c04000641f80000000006b160e# (accessed 17 May 2013).
44. Lyrics of Phil Pringle, "Rise Up (You People of Power)," Wesley Methodist Church Klang, http://www.klangwesley.com/songs.php?songID=288 (accessed 22 May 2013).
45. See Rudman, "For God and National," 28–29; and Philip Matthews, "True Believers," *New Zealand Listener*, 15 July 2000, 15–21.
46. Davidson, *Christianity in Aotearoa*, 183; Grigg, *The Spirit of Christ and the Postmodern City*, 238.
47. *Rise Up Together New Zealand*, "Strategy Report" (January/March 1990), 8–9.
48. *Rise Up Together New Zealand*, "Report" (July/September 1990), 9.
49. Clark, *Pentecost at the Ends of the Earth*, 214.
50. Ibid, 213.
51. See Appendix A. See also Knowles, *The History of a New Zealand Pentecostal Movement*, 292.

52. Clark, *Pentecost at the Ends of the Earth*, 215; Associated Pentecostal Churches of New Zealand, "Pastors Directory 2001/2002" (mimeographed, Associated Pentecostal Churches of New Zealand, Christchurch, [2001]), BKRP, MS-3530/008, Hocken Library, Dunedin.

53. Clark, *Pentecost at the Ends of the Earth*, 254.

54. Carew and Troughton, "Māori Participation in the Assemblies of God," 92. See also Clark, *Pentecost at the Ends of the Earth*, 218.

55. Clark, *Pentecost at the Ends of the Earth*, 254.

56. Moetara, "Māori and Pentecostal Christianity in Aotearoa New Zealand," 81–82.

57. Luke Worsfold, "Subsequence, Prophecy and Church Order," 159.

58. Ibid, 72 and note 106, and 211.

59. Clark, *Pentecost at the Ends of the Earth*, 230.

60. See Appendix A.

61. Grigg, *The Spirit of Christ and the Postmodern City*, 161–62.

62. Frost, "Is there any movement away from dualism within New Zealand Pentecostal faith and praxis?" 29.

63. Tamaki, *Bishop Brian Tamaki: More than meets the eye*, 131; Lineham, *Destiny*, 48–49.

64. Luke Worsfold, "Subsequence, Prophecy and Church Order," 220.

65. Tamaki, *Bishop Brian Tamaki: More than meets the eye*, 151–55; Moetara, "An exploration of notions of Māori leadership," 52; Lineham, *Destiny*, 48–52.

66. Tamaki, *Bishop Brian Tamaki: More than meets the eye*, 175–82; Moetara, "Māori and Pentecostal Christianity in Aotearoa New Zealand," 82; Lineham, *Destiny*, 57–59.

67. Tamaki, *Bishop Brian Tamaki: More than meets the eye*, 176, 183–86 and 191–96; Lineham, *Destiny*, 75–78 and 82–89.

68. For a comprehensive critical analysis of the Destiny movement and its founder, see Lineham, *Destiny*. Lineham had previously written about Destiny in Lineham, "Wanna be in my gang?" and in Lineham, "The Rise and Significance of the Destiny Church," in Morrison et al., *Mana Māori and Christianity*, 111–37.

69. Paul Harrison, "Prophetic Ministry within Movements of the Modern-Day Church" (CHTX480 Research Essay, University of Otago, 2003), 50–51; Clark, *Pentecost at the Ends of the Earth*, 216.

70. Tamaki, *Bishop Brian Tamaki: More than meets the eye*, 188; Lineham, *Destiny*, 84–85.

71. For example, Alan Samson, "Female Leaders 'sign of Devil'," *Dominion Post*, 14 February 2000, 1 and 7; and "Leaders sign of devil: TV preacher," *New Zealand Herald*, 14 February 2000, 1.

72. King, *Penguin History of New Zealand*, 463.

73. Helen Clark, cited in Kevin List, "PM's Presser: Enough, Polls, Iran & NZ Troops, Prime Minister's Press Conference, 24 August 2004," Scoop: *Independent News*, 24 August 2004, http://www.scoop.co.nz/stories/HL0408/S00247.htm (accessed 26 May 2013).

74. Tamaki, *Bishop Brian Tamaki: More than meets the eye*, 187–90; Lineham, *Destiny*, 76–80.

75. Jamieson, *A Churchless Faith*, 16–18.

76. Derived from James W. Fowler, *Stages of Faith: The Psychology of Human Development and the Quest for Meaning* (San Francisco: Harper, 1981; 1995).

77. Jamieson, *A Churchless Faith*, 69.

78. See above, 217.

79. Philip D. Carew, "Māori, Biculturalism and the Assemblies of God in New Zealand, 1970–2008" (MA thesis in Religious Studies, Victoria University of Wellington, 2009), 28–29. See also Clark, *Pentecost at the Ends of the Earth*, 235.

80. Clark, *Pentecost at the Ends of the Earth*, 232–33.

81. Ibid, 216–17.

82. Ibid, 238.

83. Ibid, 227.

84. Tamaki, *Bishop Brian Tamaki: More than meets the eye*, 151.

85. Knowles, *The History of a New Zealand Pentecostal Movement*, 289. See above, 197.

86. For biographies of Walton, see B. Knowles, "Walton, John," in NIDPCM, 1184; and John Walton, *The Walton Story: John Walton's Memoirs*. 3rd ed. (Palmerston North: John Walton, 2012), Kindle Edition. See also M. Toomer, "National Church Leader 'walks with his people'," *Challenge Weekly*, 8 May 1996.

87. Clark, *Pentecost at the Ends of the Earth*, 180.

88. Ibid, 191.

89. Knowles, "Some Aspects of the History of the New Life Churches of New Zealand," 268–69.

90. Ibid, 329–35.

91. Nigel Scotland, *Charismatics in the New Millennium* (Surrey: Inter Publishing Service, 2000), 301, cited in Harrison, "Prophetic Ministry within Movements of the Modern-Day Church," 52, note 149.

92. Luke Worsfold, "Subsequence, Prophecy and Church Order," 244–45.

93. Ibid, 220–21; Tamaki, *Bishop Brian Tamaki: More than meets the eye*, 151–55.

94. Tamaki, *Bishop Brian Tamaki: More than meets the eye*, 151.

95. Luke Worsfold, "Subsequence, Prophecy and Church Order," 246.

96. Moetara, "An exploration of notions of Māori leadership," 83–84.

97. For a critical sociological analysis of the phenomenon, see M. M. Poloma, "Toronto Blessing," in NIDPCM, 1149–52.

98. Ibid, 1150, 1152.

99. For a brief biographical note on Howard-Browne, see R. M. Riss, "Howard-Browne, Rodney M.," in NIDPCM, 774.

100. Clark, *Pentecost at the Ends of the Earth*, 224.

101. Jamieson, *A Churchless Faith*, 67, note 2.

102. For a descriptive account, see W. H. Barnes, "Brownsville Revival," in NIDPCM, 445–47.

103. Douglas McBain, *Fire Over the Waters: Renewal Among Baptists and Others from the 1960s to the 1990s* (London: Darton, Longman, Todd, 1997), cited in Ward, "The Charismatic Movement in New Zealand," 8. Ward does not provide a page number for this citation from McBain.

104. Clark, *Pentecost at the Ends of the Earth*, 232.

105. Guy, *Shaping Godzone*, 26.

106. Harrison, "Prophetic Ministry within Movements of the Modern-Day Church," 72; 76 and note 228; 85 and note 265.

107. For a brief account, see G. W. Gohr, "Kansas City Prophets," in NIDPCM, 816–17.

Chapter 13

The 2000s

Brave New World?

Any optimism that might have accompanied the beginning of a new millennium collapsed abruptly as a result of the terrorist attack on the New York World Trade Centre on 11 September 2001. This was indeed a hurricane event; the changed attitudes and perceptions that resulted were, for once, products of a single catalytic incident, as well as of a cumulative, glacial series of changes. The subsequent War against Terrorism—which took military form with the invasions of Iraq and Afghanistan—reshaped attitudes and perspectives and introduced a new reality, which was all the more terrifying for being unforeseen. As the tensions that followed the attack indicated, the world was no longer the same. Nevertheless, contemporaneous broader changes, unrelated to acts of terrorism, were also taking place. China's progress towards becoming the second economic superpower after the United States indicated that the twenty-first century might well be a Chinese century, as the twentieth century had been an American one. The problems of the West were further exacerbated towards the end of the decade by the banking crises of 2008, from which the world has still not fully emerged. It is evident that humanity has entered, if not a brave new world, then certainly a frightening new one.

    This reshaping of the world has had profound implications for Christianity. In America, these events have reinforced religion's place as the bulwark of a civic faith and given fresh emphasis to the traditional motto of "in God we trust." On the other hand, the secularism of Europe has also continued, with the vacuum becoming increasingly filled by Islam, as immigration and increasing Moslem birthrates extend its influence. Alarmed commentators have suggested that Europe is fast becoming "Eurabia," a claim that is not, however, backed up by demographic evidence.[1] On the other hand, the rise of Christianity—and of its imputed offspring, capitalism—in China is an indication that the Christian world is relocating, rather than relinquishing, its constituency.[2] Effectively, it is becoming a religion of the Third World, rather than of the West.

New Zealand was also experiencing several significant changes in the first decade of the twenty-first century. Its changing demographic mix, as it steadily became a more multicultural society, has already been noted.[3] The number of Māori land claims before the Waitangi Tribunal was increasing, although these generally tended to be smaller in scale than those settled previously. There had been twelve claims totaling $540 million between 1991 and 2000, an average of $45.04 million per claim; by contrast, there were eighteen claims totaling $546 million between 2001 and 2010, an average of $30.34 million per claim.[4] As well as this, the latter half of the 1990s and most of the following decade were positive years for the New Zealand economy, with the benefits of the Rogernomics era at last beginning to emerge. The New Zealand Government achieved Budget surpluses from 1994 to 2009—in contrast to years of deficits prior to this[5]—and the decline in unemployment was continuing. Although this had already fallen to below 7% of the workforce as the Fifth Labour Government took office in 1999, it fell still further, by 2004 reaching 3.8%, the lowest rate for eighteen years.[6] It remained within a percentage point of this low level throughout the remainder of Labour's nine-year term in office.

The most significant stimuli for change, however, were the policies of the new Labour Government. This Government, under the commanding presence of its leader Helen Clark, quickly established a solid minority coalition partnership with the left-leaning Alliance Party, aided by support from the Greens.[7] Labour was a socialist party and a number of its early policies—such as the increase in the minimum wage and the introduction of a Working for Families welfare package for low-income families—reflected this. Employment law was changed to favor the trade unions and collective bargaining; affirmative action strategies were introduced to assist disadvantaged groups—such as Māori—and Air New Zealand and the national rail network were renationalized. However, the most significant social change came during Labour's second term from 2002 to 2005. The extent and scope of the policies passed in this term enabled the Government's critics to charge it with social engineering.[8] It broke traditional links with Britain by establishing a Supreme Court, thus ending the role of the British Privy Council as the final court of legal appeal. It also abolished the traditional Honors system—such as knighthoods—based on British precedents, although these were reinstated by the National Government in 2009. These policies were the product of an increasing political independence, which was reflected in New Zealand's military service in the war in Afghanistan—although not in Iraq—and in peace-keeping duties in East Timor and elsewhere. The rationale behind this differentiation of international involvement was that New Zealand had been asked by the United Nations to send combat troops to Afghanistan and East Timor. Conversely, the request to participate in the Iraq war had come from the United States, not from the United Nations. In the view of the Labour Government the latter request represented a partisan, rather than a global, approach.

A number of the policies of the Labour Government were socially provocative. It alienated Māori support by introducing a Foreshore and Seabed Bill which preempted the discussion in the Māori Land Court of Māori claims to the foreshore and seabed, vesting title of these in the Crown.[9] This led to the May 2004 defection of Tariana Turia, then Minister for the Community and Voluntary Sector, to form a Māori Party specifically to contest this issue. None of the major parties contested the by-election that followed and Mrs. Turia easily regained her seat, receiving 92.74% of the votes cast. However, the most controversial changes of Labour's second term related to public morality. These included the Prostitution Reform Act of 2003 legalizing prostitution and the Civil Union Act of 2004 enabling same-sex couples to cohabit in a civil union.[10] Another was the 2002 amendment of the Property (Relationships) Act of 1976, which treated *de facto* couples in the same way as legally married couples in the event of a marriage breakup. The 2007 repeal of Section 59 of the Crimes Act removed the rights of parents to use "reasonable force" (i.e., smacking) in the discipline of their children. Changes such as these flew in the face of traditional codes of morality and attracted conservative opposition, particularly from Brian Tamaki's Destiny Church. (Tamaki provocatively described this legislation—and the gay agenda that he believed it represented—as "terrorism of a political kind.")[11] Nevertheless, this opposition seemed powerless to reverse the course of social and political change.

The Destiny Phenomenon

The inability of churches to influence public issues reflected both their declining institutional authority and the continuing fall in church adherence. The 2013 Census showed that only 45.59% of New Zealanders claimed any church adherence[12] with the largest category of responses being "No Religion" (i.e., 1,653,348, or 38.55% of the population). New Zealand was steadily moving towards becoming a non-Christian country. Furthermore, Allan Davidson has observed that the collapse of church union and of the umbrella Conference of Churches in Aotearoa New Zealand in September 2005 represented "the last gasp of Christendom" in New Zealand.[13] This reflected the ongoing effects of the Religious Crisis of the 1960s and the concomitant suspicion of institutions, both of which were discussed in Chapter 8.

Nevertheless, significant new centers of Christian energy were emerging. Opposition to changing public morality culminated in the Enough is Enough march in August 2004, when approximately 5,000 Destiny Church supporters marched on Parliament to protest the Civil Union legislation.[14] This march, featuring a 300-strong black-shirted *haka* group, attracted considerable public attention and criticism. (A *haka* was a ritual Māori dance of challenge and defiance, with actions and rhythmically shouted words.) Tamaki later admitted that the regimented lines of the *haka* group, together with the spontaneous chant of "Enough is Enough" and the anger displayed in the march did give it an overly militant look.[15] This perception was, to some extent, justified. Christian commentator Mick Duncan observed that the fury expressed in the *haka* represented a "public display of outrage" at the "national rape" of New Zealand's moral standards by the gay and lesbian communities.[16] Conversely, these communities and their supporters castigated the black-shirted marchers as a new kind of Nazism. (Ironically, the "Nazi" epithet had originated from MP David Benson-Pope, who was later temporarily suspended from Cabinet over allegations of aggressive bullying during his earlier career as a teacher.)[17] The "Nazi" label was also used by Georgina Beyer, New Zealand's first transsexual member of Parliament, who was almost apoplectic with rage at the march, likening it to the Nuremburg rallies of the 1930s.[18] Her reaction was prominently featured in the national news and reinforced the media's adverse perception of Tamaki and his movement.[19] The march had mixed results: Tamaki claimed that it raised awareness of the issues among Christians. His assertion was reinforced by the results of a poll—on whether gay relationships should be recognized—conducted on TV One's *Close-up* program. This attracted 17,463 responses: 13,147 of these (or 75.28% of the total) responded "no."[20] However, the media response was almost uniformly negative. TVNZ terminated Destiny's television broadcasting contract two weeks later, ostensibly to make way for expanded children's programming.[21] Nevertheless, the "Enough is Enough" march gave Tamaki national prominence, representing "a new style of Pentecostalism emerging.... Destiny looks to be a new kind of player on the New Zealand political and religious scene." While other conservative churches had expressed concern over the Civil Union Bill, "only Destiny was willing to take it to the streets."[22] Although Tamaki's stance was supported by several large Auckland megachurches, for example, Pastor Peter Mortlock's City Impact Church,[23] few other Pentecostal churches were as aggressive in their approach to social and political issues.[24] In part, this reflected a sense of disillusionment following the rejection of the Homosexual Law Reform Petition in 1986 and Tamaki was critical of the political apathy and indifference that he perceived within the Christian community.[25] However, the criticism was mutual: other Pentecostal pastors, as Tamaki himself wryly notes, also had "an issue with Brian."[26]

The aggressiveness of Destiny Church ensured its continuing prominence throughout the remainder of the decade. This built upon negative media perceptions of its leader, which had resulted from the controversy surrounding his reported remarks on female leadership at the end of the previous decade.[27] His lavish lifestyle and perceived cult of personality attracted particular criticism,[28] as did his ordination as "Bishop" Brian Tamaki in 2005.[29] This was reinforced by reports of his Sonship Covenant, initiated at a Labour Weekend Destiny Church Conference in 2009 and issued the following month. This set out "covenant protocols" between Tamaki as a spiritual father and his disciples (i.e., his "spiritual sons") and also between the members of his discipleship corps (i.e., "the brotherhood").[30] His followers were required, among other things, to give Bishop Tamaki obedience, honor and loyalty and to imitate his faith.[31] The Covenant included detailed instructions for public conduct and behavior towards him, as well as guidelines for etiquette and protocol, both in the presence of the Bishop and also in church services.[32] While there was much public criticism of these practices, they represented *tikanga* [custom] and *kawa* [protocol] based upon Māori understandings of prophethood. Indeed, Peter Lineham sees Tamaki as the latest in a long tradition of charismatic Māori leaders, such as Te Kooti, Te Whiti, Rua Kenana, T. W. Rātana and Wiremu Tamihana. As he puts it,

> [Tamaki] offers hope and love to the disaffected and the poor. ... The followers believe in him. ... Brian Tamaki is the symbol of their success, he's what they can be, he's kind of their hope. ... Ratana said he would attract the Morehu, the

nobodies, and he would put them together and he would give them a sense of purpose and a voice and a meaning. That's very much what Brian Tamaki's doing, so there is a very long tradition.³³

Similarly, Tamaki's ordination as Bishop represented a functionalist view of the office, rather than a hierarchical one. In the New Testament sense, *episkopos* [bishop] simply meant "overseer" and this represented precisely Tamaki's role in relation to the (then) eighteen churches in the Destiny movement. However, critics of the title tended to see it in non-New Testament—i.e., hierarchical—terms and therefore chided Tamaki for assuming an implied superiority of status.

Figure 8: Bishop Brian Tamaki, speaking at a Destiny Church conference in Auckland, 22 October 2006. William Jackson, public domain. http://en.wikipedia.org/wiki/File:Bishop-Tamaki-Auckland-2006.jpg (accessed 10 April 2013).

Much of the significance of the Destiny Church lies in its identity as a Māori movement. This was atypical of New Zealand Pentecostalism, since most other Pentecostal groups—with the honorable exception of the Apostolic Church—had done little to incorporate Māori culture or to engage with Māori as equals.³⁴ In part, this was due to a focus on multiculturalism and ethnic diversity, rather than on a biculturalism that treated Māori as equal partners as had been guaranteed by the Treaty of Waitangi.³⁵ Biculturalism, in Pākehā [non-Māori] eyes, was seen as preferential treatment of Māori, rather than as an equality that had been promised, but not delivered, to them.[36] However, Philip Carew and Geoff Troughton argue that Pentecostal rejection of biculturalism was a symptom, rather than a cause, deriving from a "disconnection with Māori."[37] As a long-standing Māori member of the Apostolic Church commented, "the classical Pentecostal denominations have abrogated their responsibility to Māori, which has . . . contributed to the success of Destiny."[38] By contrast, most of Tamaki's followers are Māori[39] and, in particular, the urban, nontribalized Māori who comprise 81% of the total Māori population of New Zealand.[40] His strong, authoritative leadership represents a Māori way of doing things. One of his pastors comments that "[Māori] look for those strong character traits we see in the likes of Brian Tamaki, a strong leader who's charismatic, and is able to speak at the highest of levels and whose name is out there. . . . Māori are attracted to that."[41] Another observer notes that Māori are overrepresented in secular groups characterized by strong leadership, such as gangs, the army and sports teams. He comments that "maybe [Māori] people want to feel like they're under the discipline of someone . . . they're things that are quite highly structured, high expectations, high discipline."[42] As such, Tamaki's strong moral stance represents a new authoritative urban Māori alternative to tribalism, offering a voice and a sense of purpose and meaning to those who have been alienated and disadvantaged by the circumstances of life. In this respect, he resembles T. W. Rātana, the Māori healer of the 1920s, who addressed his appeal to the *Mōrehu* [remnant], giving them a new sense of identity and self-worth.[43]

Tamaki has also had political goals. Several members of his church had stood as United-Future candidates in the 2002 Election; one (Kelly Chal) entered Parliament on its party list, but was later disqualified since she was not a New Zealand citizen. Tamaki subsequently became disillusioned with Peter Dunne, the leader of the United-Future party, since he voted with Labour on confidence and supply matters, despite the "Future" wing of the party being a conservative Christian bloc. However, the dislike was mutual: while Tamaki saw the United-Future Party as compromising with Labour, Dunne likened the Destiny Party, in pejorative terms, to the Taliban.[44] Tamaki therefore saw the environment as conducive to the entry of a new Christian party that would oppose the liberalism of the present government, particularly on gay issues.[45] Consequently, he launched the Destiny Party, led by his protégé Richard Lewis, in 2003 to contest the 2005 General Election.[46] As was to be expected, the Destiny Party had a conservative agenda and rapidly developed a strong voice on Māori issues—in particular, on the Treaty of Waitangi. Destiny Church was unique among New Zealand Pentecostal churches in having a high view of the Treaty. Tamaki saw it as a covenant between Māori and the Crown, with God as the third party.[47] He also insisted that it could not fulfill its purpose until all parties are faithful to God: "until we as a nation will humble ourselves before the One True Living God, the true spirit of Te Tiriti O Waitangi [the Treaty of Waitangi] will not be restored. This process must start with the church and the Crown."[48] This emphasis on Māori issues led to Tamaki receiving an official invitation to join the Waitangi Day Celebrations in 2005, where a photograph of him sitting with politician Don Brash and Māori activist Tame Iti made front-page news.[49] He was also invited by the Māori Queen, Dame Te

Atairangikaahu to celebrations for the thirty-ninth and fortieth anniversaries of her coronation. The latter celebration was particularly satisfying for him, since the Queen asked him to sit at her left side in the official welcoming party, which meant that the Prime Minister and Cabinet all had to *hongi* [to press noses together in greeting] Tamaki before greeting the Queen. Prime Minister Helen Clark, who detested him, was particularly flustered by this, much to his delight.[50]

This increased prominence did not, however, lead to electoral success for the Destiny Party. In the 2005 Elections, the Party received only 14,120 votes (0.62% of the national total). Other Christian parties also lost ground, the Christian Heritage Party receiving only 0.12% of the vote and United-Future—which was represented in Parliament, since its leader Peter Dunne won his electorate seat—2.67% of the vote. The total Christian vote was therefore only 3.4%.[51] Brian Tamaki attributes at least part of Destiny's lack of success to the formation of the Māori Party, which he says "effectively took 90% of the wind out of our sails."[52] The Destiny Party therefore disbanded in 2007, joining with some ex-United Future MPs to form the Family Party. In recent years, Destiny seems, in the words of Peter Lineham, to have "lost its mojo."[53] The movement experienced some schism and financial decline after 2006 although it should not be assumed from this that it is in retreat.[54] It later gained legal recognition as an Urban Māori Authority, which gave it access to government funding and contracts for the operation of their support services among disadvantaged urban Māori.[55] The most recent of Tamaki's goals is the building of a City of God in the economically depressed South Auckland area.[56] This would provide accommodation and employment—centered on a new worship center—for his followers, and contribute to the alleviation of social and economic distress. Some Auckland city councilors have come out in favor of his proposal, seeing it as beneficial for South Auckland, one of the most economically depressed urban areas in the country. However, few people have noted the association with a similar proposal a century earlier, i.e., John Alexander Dowie's Zion City in Illinois.[57] The history of this earlier venture might provide cautionary examples for the Destiny project.

New Zealand Pentecostalism in the Twenty-First Century

Was Destiny Church Typical of New Zealand Pentecostalism?

The vigor of churches such as Destiny, together with increasing numbers of Pentecostals in the Census statistics up to 2006, might indicate a positive trajectory for the movement. But how typical was Destiny and what was the situation of Pentecostalism in Aotearoa-New Zealand in the first decade of the new century?[58] The data is ambiguous. The latest Census figures—from the 2013 Census—identifies the movement as the fifth largest denominational grouping, on a Census adherence basis, in New Zealand. (The higher nominalism of the larger denominations means that the ratio of Pentecostal participation—as distinct from adherence—is greater, making it the largest Protestant body in New Zealand, second only to the Catholic Church. This trend was discernible as early as 1990.)[59] However, comparisons should not be drawn too sharply, since methodological changes to the Census questionnaire in 1986 and 2001 make it difficult to determine long-term trends in New Zealand religiosity.[60] Certainly, Pentecostalism is highly visible in this country, with at least four large New Zealand Pentecostal churches broadcasting on national television. There are a number of Pentecostal megachurches,[61] particularly in Auckland, as well as many smaller churches in regional and provincial centers. Nevertheless, it is noteworthy that the number of Pentecostal respondents dropped by 6.51% (from 79,635 to 74,439 adherents) between the 2006 and 2013 Censuses. Although the combined returns for the "Pentecostal: not further defined" and "Pentecostal: not elsewhere classified" categories increased by 14.21% from 42,066 to 48,042 adherents, those for each specified Pentecostal denominations decreased over the seven-year period. In total, this figure fell from 37,569 to 26,397 (a decline of 29.74%).[62] This might indicate that institutional forms of Pentecostalism are weakening. The significance of this will be explored further in the next section.

The energy exemplified by the large Auckland churches was also quite localized, both geographically and socially. Viv Grigg has noted that, in Auckland, Pentecostal weekly attendance had grown from 1% to 2.3% of the population by 2001. He further observed that the charismatic-Evangelical-Pentecostal cluster of churches had grown from 4.5% to almost 6% of the Auckland population in the fifteen years from 1986 to 2001.[63] In his words, "the Auckland church is not in decline, it is bursting its seams."[64] Much of this vigor was due to the expansion of ethnic—particularly Samoan—churches in Auckland. However, this dynamism was not uniform throughout the country and Grigg foresees another probable phase of national decline outside of Auckland.[65] He attributes this waning of charismatic vitality to "too rapid institutionalization, lack of sustained theological development, failure to develop leadership training and breakdown of information flow from core leaders as [the movement] became denominationalised."[66] (Conversely, Donald Battley insists that the decline of the renewal was due to its playing down of the charismatic gifts in the 1980s, considering this to be a "great mistake.")[67] While Grigg and Battley are primarily referring to the Charismatic movement, this diminution of vigor also affected Pentecostal churches, many of which had become more settled and mainstream, in contrast to their vigorous sectarian beginnings. Their mainstream status was indicated by the way in which the funeral of prominent New Life pastor Peter Morrow in 2001 was reported not only in the local newspaper, but also on prime-time television news.[68] However, it is also noteworthy that Peter Lineham now includes the New Life Centres, along with the Brethren and the Salvation Army, as examples of "older, more laid-back conservative churches" which were not booming in 2004.[69] This was in marked contrast to the 1960s and 1970s, when they had been "among the most dynamic forces in the religious life in New Zealand."[70] This loss of Pentecostal energy was paralleled by a loss of constituency. As will be seen in the remainder of the chapter, many Pentecostal groups, particularly those outside the main population centers, suffered significant declines in the first decade of the twenty-first century.

"Things fall apart; the centre cannot hold . . ."

Pentecostals have always placed an emphasis on the individual's experience of the Spirit. The corollary of this, as Simon Chan notes, is that they also tend to have a weak sociological view of the church. "The church," he says, "tends to be seen as essentially a service provider catering to the needs of individual Christians. . . . The church [is seen] as a community brought about by people united for a common purpose, so that the koinonia is not primarily the creation by the Spirit of God but by a kindred human spirit."[71] This locates the primary identity of the church in the associated individuals that comprise it, rather than these individuals being identified by their membership of the church. This weak ecclesiology facilitates easy transfers of allegiance and belonging—also known as the "circulation of the saints"[72]—and exemplifies the changing contours of New Zealand Pentecostalism in the first decade of the twenty-first century.

Despite the continuing vibrancy of Auckland churches such as Destiny, Pentecostal churches in New Zealand have suffered from both decline and division in the last fifteen years. This reflected a diminishing cohesiveness in the movement, in which—to use Irish poet W.B. Yeats' words—"Things fall apart; the centre cannot hold..."[73] One significant example of this increasing disintegration is the Associated Pentecostal Churches of New Zealand, which had been one of the key examples of Pentecostal unity in the 1970s. After dwindling for years, its biennial conventions were reduced in format to meetings of Pentecostal leaders in 2000 and eventually wound up in 2003. This reflected a gradual decline in enthusiasm over time, combined with a change of leadership in the Association about 1998.[74] There were also defections of a number of large flagship Pentecostal churches from their parent denominations in the 1990s and 2000s. In the case of the Assemblies of God, these included large European-culture churches such as the Auckland Victory Christian Centre and the West City Christian Centre. Ian Clark ascribes their departure to the development of independent trajectories, with the larger churches in the movement not being tied in the Assemblies of God's goals and vision.[75] Their departure increased the influence of ethnic—particularly Samoan—Assemblies of God and the most significant demographic in the movement became Samoan. These Samoan churches had always engaged in aggressive evangelism from their inception and had grown to over eighty churches by 2003, one-quarter of the total number of Assemblies of God.[76] (Of the 108 ethnically designated Pentecostal churches listed in the 2001/2002 Associated Pentecostal Churches of New Zealand Directory, ninety-nine were Assemblies of God; three-quarters of the ethnic churches in the listing were Samoan. Most were located in Auckland and Wellington.)[77] Other ethnic churches—for example, Tongan, Fijian, Indian and Korean Assemblies of God—also became increasingly prominent, reflecting the increasing multiculturalism of New Zealand society.[78] There were other issues also: Gateway Church in Hamilton left the Assemblies of God in 2000 over the movement's handling of a sexual impropriety case against its pastor. This episode seems to have impacted on other assemblies in the Waikato also.[79] Further problems continued in 2002, with more churches leaving, a split in the main Christchurch assembly and other problems in Assemblies of God church leadership, requiring the intervention of the Executive.[80]

The appointment of Pastor Ken Harrison as Superintendent in 2003 provided the decisive leadership needed to steady the movement and the Assemblies of God recovered its equilibrium to some degree.[81] However, a major schism occurred in 2005, with about thirty Samoan Assemblies of God seceding from their parent body to form their own independent Samoan group, resulting in continuing legal and constitutional conflict.[82]

Other Pentecostal groups also suffered division and decline between 2000 and 2010. The large Majestic House church in Christchurch, the flagship of the New Life Churches, left that movement later in the decade to pursue its own vision. However, the greatest decline was suffered by the Apostolic Church, which lost a number of its churches to the Destiny Church in 2001 and 2003.[83] This transfer was partly explained by the fact that Brian Tamaki, the leader of the Destiny Church, had formerly been an apostle in the Apostolic Church before leaving that movement in 1994. The loss was particularly acute among Māori: the percentage of Māori adherents in the Apostolic Church in 2009 was little over half of what it had been in 2001.[84] Given that the Apostolic Church was already becoming more bureaucratic in its ethos and praxis, it is not surprising that these seceding churches should seek a more charismatic form of leadership, such as that represented by Tamaki. The Apostolic Church's increasing bureaucratization was evidenced in the appointment of Church Health Consultants in 2001–2,[85] the declining role of prophetic input into the National Leadership Team[86] and the increasing use of secular counseling. With regard to the latter, Luke Worsfold acidly comments that "The profiling of secular counselling in the Apostolic Church lends credence to the observation that the denominational distinctives are fading from preeminence, members from yesteryear viewing the utilisation of a christianised psychological counselling model as inferior to prayer, confession or a trip to the altar."[87] It is therefore not surprising that the number of Apostolic churches dropped from ninety-nine to fifty-five congregations—a 45% decrease—between 2002 and 2012.

Quantitative evidence of this decline comes from a comparison of denominational listings utilizing the last Pastors' Directory issued by the Associated Pentecostal Churches of New Zealand in 2001–2 and website listings as at 2012 for the various New Zealand Pentecostal churches. This is summarized in Table 10 in Appendix B.[88] On analysis of this data, several trends immediately become apparent. The number of churches had declined in the majority of Pentecostal denominations between 2002 and 2012, in some cases precipitously so. Overall, the decline was just over 8.5%—from 701 to 641 churches—over the ten years. In general, the larger denominations were hardest hit: the four largest Pentecostal groups—which comprised 75% of the total number of Pentecostal churches—declined 19.89% from 528 to 423 churches. Two denominations—the Apostolic Church and the Christian Outreach Centres—declined more than 40%, while there were three others with decreases of between 30% and 40%. Some Pentecostal groups did appear to have increased during the decade, but this data was not as positive as it seemed. The Samoan Assemblies of God were locked in a vigorous legal battle for control of church assets with their former parent body, the Assemblies of God.[89] The Destiny Church had grown from five to ten churches, but this included a secession of nine churches from the Apostolic Church in 2003;

evidently not all of these churches had survived the transfer to Destiny. The Christian Life Centres increased from one church to six by 2012; but this merely reflected the suburbanization of a large central city church. Furthermore, some of the new groups that emerged appear to have done so as secessions from other Pentecostal bodies. These changes appear to indicate that New Zealand Pentecostal growth was more a product of the "circulation of the saints"[90] than of evangelism. This characteristic, combined with the exodus of long-term participants from Pentecostal churches, represent worrying straws in the wind for New Zealand Pentecostalism. In addition, the trend noted by Alan Jamieson in the 1990s—i.e., of Evangelicals, Pentecostals and Charismatics leaving their churches—continued, many of these ending up in networks of small informal house-fellowship groups. Peter Lineham estimates that there are up to 600 of these groups in Auckland alone and that they constitute a major change in the shape of New Zealand church life.[91]

Where Have All the "Penties" Gone?

So, to paraphrase a pop song from the 1960s, where have all the "Penties" gone? Firstly, the growth of urban Pentecostal megachurches could indicate that members of smaller churches have been absorbed into these larger bodies. (An example of this occurred in the early 1990s, when an Elim pastor moved to Christchurch to open a large "city church." The immediate result was the closure of six suburban Elim churches in Christchurch as their members transferred to the new church.) This process of consolidation reflected a global trend: sociologist Mark Chaves has demonstrated that approximately 45% of worshippers in America attend the largest 10% of churches, most of which tended to preach the prosperity gospel.[92] However, an analysis of Pentecostal belonging in each provincial area reveals significant geographical differences. The number of Pentecostal churches in Auckland, the location of many of these large megachurches, had declined by only 6.44% between 2002 and 2012. (These figures exclude the effect of the Samoan Assemblies of God, since figures for this group were unreliable and the location of its churches could not be verified.) In other urban centers of more than 100,000 people—Hamilton, Tauranga, Napier/Hastings, Wellington, Christchurch and Dunedin—the decline increased to 8.94%. In the provincial towns of less than 100,000 people, which were less likely to have megachurches, this reduction was greater still: 23.75% overall. Six of the sixteen provincial areas—Northland, Waikato, Bay of Plenty, Gisborne, Tasman and the Chatham Islands—had drops of more than 30% in the number of Pentecostal churches. The falloffs in these more sparsely populated provincial areas, where few megachurches are located, were therefore unlikely to be due to Pentecostal gravitational accretion to larger churches.

A second factor is the trend towards informal house-fellowship groups—which has already been noted—and the emergence of "firefly" churches, which appear out of nowhere, attract followers for a short time and then disappear. In part, this appears to reflect a rejection of Pentecostal institutionalism and an attempt to return to the less structured models of the 1960s and 1970s. This is indicative of a wider trend in New Zealand society, particularly with regards to institutional belonging. A third significant trend is the Pentecostal leavening of mainstream churches. This appears to reverse the exodus of the 1960s and 1970s, when people left mainstream churches for Pentecostal groups. A survey of four mainstream churches in Dunedin in 2013 asked congregational respondents if they had ever been a member of, or participant in, a Pentecostal church, and if so, for how long. (Catholic and Brethren churches were also approached, but did not take part in the survey.)[93] The following results were obtained:

Church	Number of previous Pentecostal members	% of previous Pentecostal members in respondents	Weighted average length of participation in Pentecostal movement (in years)
Presbyterian (n. = 82)	42	51.22%	6.92
Baptist (n. = 163)	81	49.69%	7.15
Anglican (n. = 27)	5	18.52%	12.70
Methodist (n. = 14)	2	14.29%	1.75
Average (n. = 71.5)	32.5	45.45%	7.21

Table 3: Previous Pentecostal involvement of current mainstream church members

This data shows that, on the average, more than forty-five per cent of these churches' present congregations had previously been members of, or participants in, Pentecostal churches. This proportion was higher in the larger churches—i.e., Presbyterian and Baptist—in the survey. The average length of previous participation in Pentecostal churches was 7.21 years—rather less than the 15.8-year average claimed by Alan Jamieson[94]—and a number of respondents had been in the movement for more than twenty years. Several of these had held pastoral offices—in one case, the responsibility for national ministry training in a Pentecostal denomination. It is therefore clear that there has been a noticeable exodus from Pentecostal to mainstream churches over the last two decades and that these ex-Pentecostals have enriched the life of the receiving churches. The effect of this has been to reinforce the impact of the Charismatic movement and to pentecostalize aspects of mainstream church life, particularly in the areas of music and worship styles.

Towards the future

Given these developments, what might the future face of New Zealand Pentecostalism look like? Although the current religious scene is characterized by change and fluidity, four elements are apparent. Firstly, there is a trend towards "believing, but not belonging." This reflects a movement towards a privatization of belief without a concomitant belonging to institutions that service that belief, combined with a decline in institutional forms of authority. The analogy of declining membership of rugby football clubs in New Zealand, despite a continuing intense interest in the game, was discussed in chapter 8.[95] This was not a trend unique to Pentecostalism, nor indeed to New Zealand. Historian John Stenhouse quotes American sociologist of religion Peter Berger as saying that "Overseas sociological studies suggest that many of the growing group professing 'no religion' should be understood not as doctrinaire secularists or atheists but as 'floaters' who, embracing eclectic 'pick-and-mix' beliefs derived from various spiritual traditions, identify with no particular denomination or brand of religion."[96] "Believing without belonging" is evidently a worldwide trend and it remains the dominant religious pattern in twenty-first century Pākehā New Zealand.[97]

Secondly, there is a strong trend towards ethnicization in the New Zealand church generally, including Pentecostal churches. This is largely, but not entirely, due to increasing immigration and the diversifying of New Zealand society and is most evident in the larger population centers, especially Auckland and Wellington. Simon Moetara notes Peter Lineham's prediction that "ethnicity will be the dominant mode of social organization in New Zealand churches in the future, having seen it already in the Assemblies of God Movement and the three[-]tikanga structure of the Anglican Church." Lineham adds that this does not necessarily imply ethnic denominations: "the congregations could be ethnic, but the denominations don't need to be ... a structure whereby, there's a mixture of leaders but, as a local area, effective evangelization could well be in ethnic streams."[98] There are strengths to this approach, since cultural patterns are not a hindrance to Pentecostal worship and practice. However, there are also weaknesses and, as the Samoan Assemblies of God schism indicates, dangers of degeneration into a Pentecostal tribalism.

The third trajectory is that of a rising "cottage Christianity" which replaces the traditionally structured church for its participants. This represents a shift from "mega" to "micro" forms of Christianity and has sometimes been called a "house church movement." However, it is probably too much to say that it is a movement, since it has no networked interconnections, nor is it a homogenous association of house groups. Although numbers are difficult to ascertain, it is estimated that there are between three hundred to six hundred such house-group churches meeting in Auckland alone.[99] A variant of this format is the cafe-group, in which small groups meet for prayer and discussion of theology and scripture, over early morning coffee in a local coffee bar. These house- and coffee-groups resist a collective label and tend to make up their procedures as they go along. Lineham sees this, together with ethnicization, as one of the key features of the future church.[100]

A fourth trend, diametrically opposite to that of the house church, is the rise of city megachurches in the larger population centers. There is little love lost between the two extremes. House-church leaders decry the anonymity of the large megachurch; on the other hand, megachurch pastors insist that the house-churches have no covering—i.e., authoritative control—and are therefore subject to error.[101] The trend from church to megachurch has been picturesquely likened to a move from corner general store churches to niche market and market-driven, competitive supermarket churches.[102] The analogy is apt, given the variety, resources and money associated with both supermarkets and megachurches.

A number of independent Pentecostal megachurches are emerging in New Zealand, such as Paul de Jong's Life Church, Brian Tamaki's Destiny Church and Peter Mortlock's City Impact Church. These churches tend to be both traditional and up-market, preaching a simple, clear, traditional message using traditional Biblical forms, but wrapping the message in modern channels of expression and communication. Their message tends to be a prosperity gospel, in which wealth is seen as good, so long as it is shared. Giving therefore comprises a major part of the megachurches' message. The emphasis on money makes these churches an object of media interest and financial issues frequently feature in articles about them in newspapers, magazines and other media.[103]

The megachurch has sometimes been claimed as the wave of the future and large Pentecostal churches such as Yonggi Cho's Yoido Full Gospel Church in Seoul, Korea and Pastor Brian Houston's Hillsong Church in Sydney are often held up as exemplars for others.[104] While it is true that churches such as these have considerable power and influence, there are also dangers. Firstly, these churches tend to be

> competitive, highly controlled and structured. The prophets have been replaced by systems men. Church growth methods, television programmes and commercial strategies have been employed to promote their churches. It has become "religion as entertainment." The churches are private ventures, helping people to achieve personal fulfillment and success, a tool to individual significance and identity, a kind of therapeutic movement.[105]

Furthermore, the strong leadership needed to run such churches can breed cults of personality and—as historian Lord Acton famously observed—"power tends to corrupt, and absolute power corrupts absolutely."[106] The absence of boundaries and accountability structures can lead to possibilities of abuse and misuse.[107] Finally, the issue of succession in these churches is fraught with difficulty, since the strong mantle of the charismatic lead pastor may not be transferable to his successor, resulting in a more bureaucratic form of leadership and reducing the vitality and effectiveness of the megachurch.

Although it is difficult to predict the trajectory of New Zealand Pentecostalism into the remainder of the twenty-first century, there are some positive indications for the future. In the wider community, there is a recovery of some of the youth idealism that had characterized the 1960s and which contributed to Pentecostal expansion in that decade. A Dunedin high school principal recently commented to the author that many pupils at her school are heavily involved in community and service projects. She observed that this is a school-wide phenomenon and is not limited to Pentecostal or Christian young people.[108] Nevertheless, there are specific Christian manifestations of this reemerging commitment, with young people becoming involved in service agencies such as Servants and living and working in Asian urban slums.[109] Others are participating in new communal lifestyles such as Urban Monasticism and in social assistance projects in their local communities. One group of Dunedin Christians has purchased a discontinued primary school campus and plan to build a community of low-cost family "cohouses,"[110] using the main school buildings as a community center.¹¹¹ These local examples reflect a wider trend of engagement in community-based social ministries and a holistic understanding of the Christian gospel.¹¹² Although these developments are not limited to Pentecostalism, they do reflect changing perceptions of the Holy Spirit's work in the world. These idealistic young people are often highly educated—in some cases, holding doctoral degrees—and are fully committed to following the Holy Spirit both within and beyond their churches. If the future of institutional Pentecostalism seems difficult to project, one is reminded of the metaphor of the Spirit as the wind that blows where it will, both inside and outside organizational boundaries. Perhaps this fluidity of action and response is the key to the movement's future. It seems fitting, therefore, to end with a poem from New Zealand's foremost poet, James K. Baxter:

Lord, Holy Spirit,
You blow like the wind in a thousand paddocks,
Inside and outside the fences,
You blow where you wish to blow.

Lord, Holy Spirit,
You are the sun who shines on the little plant,
You warm him gently, you give him life,
You raise him up to become a tree with many leaves.

Lord, Holy Spirit,
You are the mother eagle with her young,
Holding them in peace under your feathers.
On the highest mountain you have built your nest,
Above the valley, above the storms of the world,
Where no hunter ever comes.

Lord, Holy Spirit,
You are the bright cloud in whom we hide,
In whom we know already that the battle has been won.
You bring us to our Brother Jesus
To rest our heads upon his shoulder.

Lord, Holy Spirit,
You are the kind fire who does not cease to burn,
Consuming us with flames of love and peace,
Driving us out like sparks to set the world on fire.

Lord, Holy Spirit,
In the love of friends you are building a new house,
Heaven is with us when you are with us.
You are singing your song in the hearts of the poor.
Guide us, wound us, heal us. Bring us to the Father.¹¹³

Notes

1. The Pew Research Center, "The Future of the Global Muslim Population: Projections for 2010–2030," *Forum on Religion and Public Life*, January 2011, http://www.pewforum.org/The-Future-of-the-Global-Muslim-Population.aspx (accessed 1 June 2013). For a discussion of the "Eurabia" controversy, see Tom Heneghan, "Will Pew Muslim birth rate study finally silence the 'Eurabia' claim?" *Reuters Faithworld Blog*, posted 27 January 2011, http://blogs.reuters.com/faithworld/2011/01/27/will-pew-muslim-birth-rate-study-finally-silence-the-eurabia-claim/ (accessed 1 June 2013).

2. Niall Ferguson, "Episode 6: Work," in *Civilization: Is the West History?* Prime TV, 28 May 2013.

3. See above, 211; also see Grigg, *The Spirit of Christ and the Postmodern City*, 127.

4. Office of Treaty Settlements, "Settlement Progress: Claims Progress."

5. Trading Economics, "New Zealand Government Budget," January 1990–June 2013, http://www.tradingeconomics.com/new-zealand/government-budget (accessed 5 June 2013).

6. Statistics New Zealand (Tatauranga Aotearoa): *Infoshare*, "Labour Force Status by Sex by Age Group (Qrtly-Mar/Jun/Sep/Dec)."

7. King, *Penguin History of New Zealand*, 495.

8. Grigg, *The Spirit of Christ and the Postmodern City*, 189.

9. Mark Hickford, "Law of the foreshore and seabed," *Te Ara Encyclopedia of New Zealand*, updated 9 November 2012 http://www.TeAra.govt.nz/en/law-of-the-foreshore-and-seabed (accessed 5 June 2013).

10. For Pentecostal views on this Bill, see Clark, *Pentecost at the Ends of the Earth*, 255; and Tamaki, *Bishop Brian Tamaki: More than meets the eye*, 292–93.

11. Tamaki, *Bishop Brian Tamaki: More than meets the eye*, 220.

12. See Appendix A.

13. Allan K. Davidson, "History Changes: Critical reflections on New Zealand and Pacific History [online]," *Stimulus: The New Zealand Journal of Christian Thought and Practice* 19, no. 2 (July 2012): [16]–25, http://search.informit.com.au/ document Summary;dn=645230770933960;res=IELHSS>ISSN:2230-5963 (accessed 14 February 2013).

14. Ben Schrader, "Parades and protest marches: Protest marches, 1980s to 2000s," *Te Ara Encyclopedia of New Zealand*, updated 13 July 2012 http://www.TeAra.govt.nz/en/photograph/21123/enough-is-enough-march (accessed 2 December 2013). See also Lineham, Destiny, 12–22; and Tamaki, *Bishop Brian Tamaki: More than meets the eye*, 258–91.

15. Tamaki, *Bishop Brian Tamaki: More than meets the eye*, 262.

16. Michael Duncan, "Destiny March: Public Display of Outrage," *Baptist* 121 (April 2005): 13–14, cited in Grigg, *The Spirit of Christ and the Postmodern City*, 192.

17. "Minister Fires on Destiny Church," *New Zealand Herald*, 17 August 2004, http:// www.nzherald.co.nz/nz/news/article.cfm?c_id=1&objectid=3584811; and TVNZ, "Timeline: Benson-Pope Career Controversy," *One News*, 27 July 2007, http://tvnz.co.nz/view/page/411368/1256078 (both accessed 4 September 2013).

18. Leah Haines, "Destiny Church black shirts spark anger," *Dominion Post*, 24 August 2004, http://groups.yahoo.com/group/foresightissues/message/314 (accessed 3 August 2013).

19. For a moderate lesbian response to the "Enough is Enough" rally (including numerous photographs of the event), see Beautiful Monsters: random rants and ravings, "Enough is enough," posted 24 August 2004, http://stonesoup.co.nz/ecoqueer/archives/003699.html (accessed 19 July 2013). This blog attracted a considerable number of comments, both for and against the Destiny position.

20. *CloseUp@7*, TVNZ, 2 December 2004, cited in Tamaki, *Bishop Brian Tamaki: More than meets the eye*, 292.

21. Tamaki, *Bishop Brian Tamaki: More than meets the eye*, 197–98.

22. Lineham, "Wanna be in my gang?"

23. Lineham, *Destiny*, 135.

24. Ibid, 150 and 167; also (with regard to Destiny's lack of support from other churches), Ibid, 151 and 157.

25. Tamaki, *Bishop Brian Tamaki: More than meets the eye*, 258.

26. Ibid, 257.

27. See above, 218.

28. Moetara, "Māori and Pentecostal Christianity in Aotearoa New Zealand," 83; Lineham, *Destiny*, 222–28.

29. Tamaki, *Bishop Brian Tamaki: More than meets the eye*, 354–62; Lineham, *Destiny*, 111–14.

30. Lineham, *Destiny*, 255–57; and Destiny Church, "Protocols & Requirements Between Spiritual Father & His Spiritual Sons," [29 November 2009]. I am grateful to Professor Peter Lineham for a copy of this document.

31. Destiny Church, "Protocols & Requirements," 7.

32. Ibid, 8–10.

33. Peter Lineham, cited in Catherine Masters, "Destiny Latest in a Long Line," *New Zealand Herald*, 28 August 2004. http://www.nzherald.co.nz/section/1/story.cfm?c_id=1&objectid=3587622 (accessed 17 July 2008) and thence cited in Moetara, "An exploration of notions of Māori leadership," 52–53; See also Lineham, *Destiny*, 171–83.

34. For significant articles analysing the place of Māori in New Zealand Pentecostalism, see Moetara, "Māori and Pentecostal Christianity in Aotearoa New Zealand," 73–90; and Carew and Troughton, "Māori Participation in the Assemblies of God," 91–109. Moetara, "An exploration of notions of Māori leadership" also provides a useful discussion of this issue.

35. See Moetara, "An exploration of notions of Māori leadership," 49–50; Moetara, "Māori and Pentecostal Christianity in Aotearoa New Zealand," 49–50; and—especially—Carew and Troughton, "Māori Participation in the Assemblies of God," 100, 102–7.

36. Carew and Troughton, "Māori Participation in the Assemblies of God," 100.

37. Ibid, 107.

38. Glen Tupuhi, Interview, 30 October 2008, cited in Moetara, "Māori and Pentecostal Christianity in Aotearoa New Zealand," 82.

39. Lineham, *Destiny*, 171–83; Tamaki, *Bishop Brian Tamaki: More than meets the eye*, 331.

40. King, *Penguin History of New Zealand*, 473. See also Moetara, "Māori and Pentecostal Christianity in Aotearoa New Zealand," 76 and 82.

41. Pastor James Roberts, Interview, 9 April 2008, cited in Moetara, "An exploration of notions of Māori leadership," 52.

42. Lloyd Martin, Interview, [no date], cited in Moetara, "An exploration of notions of Māori leadership," 84.

43. See above, 232–33.
44. Tamaki, *Bishop Brian Tamaki: More than meets the eye*, 253; see also Lineham, *Destiny*, 146–47.
45. Tamaki, *Bishop Brian Tamaki: More than meets the eye*, 215–16, 221; Lineham, *Destiny*, 147–50.
46. Tamaki, *Bishop Brian Tamaki: More than meets the eye*, 215–16, 221 and 223–26. The Party's policies are set out in full at Ibid, 231–47. See also Grigg, *The Spirit of Christ and the Postmodern City*, 197.
47. Moetara, "Māori and Pentecostal Christianity in Aotearoa New Zealand," 83. See also Lineham, *Destiny*, 178–79.
48. Tamaki, *Bishop Brian Tamaki: More than meets the eye*, 339; Moetara, "An exploration of notions of Māori leadership," 52.
49. Jonathan Milne and Amanda Spratt, "Strange Bedfellows," *Herald on Sunday*/APN, 6 February 2005; Ian Stewart, "Three's a Crowd at Waitangi," *Sunday News*, 6 February 2005; and Ruth Berry, "Political Musical Chairs at Te Tii ceremonies," *New Zealand Herald*/APN 7 February 2005. See Tamaki, *Bishop Brian Tamaki: More than meets the eye*, 331–38; and Lineham, *Destiny*, 79 and 178–79.
50. Tamaki, *Bishop Brian Tamaki: More than meets the eye*, 340–45; Lineham, *Destiny*, 176–78.
51. Tamaki, *Bishop Brian Tamaki: More than meets the eye*, 320. For an analysis of the Destiny Party results, see Lineham, *Destiny*, 155–58.
52. Tamaki, *Bishop Brian Tamaki: More than meets the eye*, 331; Lineham, *Destiny*, 150–51.
53. Lineham, *Destiny*, 127.
54. Ibid, 105–8, 236–39 and 263.
55. TVNZ, "Destiny could receive govt funding," *One News*, 19 October 2008, http://tvnz.co.nz/view/page/423466/2214759 (accessed 30 October 2008), cited in Moetara, "An exploration of notions of Māori leadership," 51. See also Lineham, *Destiny*, 212–17.
56. Lineham, *Destiny*, 257–62.
57. Blumhofer, "Dowie, John Alexander," in NIDPCM, 586–87.
58. Much of the following material was presented as Brett Knowles, "Transforming Pentecostalism: The Changing Shape of Pentecostalism in Aotearoa-New Zealand," (paper presented at the Empowered21 Global Scholars' Consultation, Alpha Crucis College, Parramatta, Sydney, 8–10 July 2013).
59. DAWN Strategy New Zealand, *1990 Church Survey Report*, 12, cited in Knowles, *The History of a New Zealand Pentecostal Movement*, 294.
60. See Appendix A for a discussion of these changes.
61. For a discussion of megachurches in New Zealand, see Lineham, *Destiny*, 60–62 and 165–66. See also Lineham, "Three Types of Church," in Boddé and Kempster, *Thinking Outside the Square*, especially 204–6 and 216–19; and Philip Matthews, "Gimme that big-time religion," *New Zealand Listener*, 23 November 2002, 28–30.
62. See Appendix A.
63. Grigg, *The Spirit of Christ and the Postmodern City*, 52–53.
64. Ibid, 48.
65. Ibid, 56–57.
66. Ibid, 199–200.
67. Battley, "The renewal is over . . . is it?": 28.
68. Knowles, "Is the Future of Western Christianity a Pentecostal One?" 41.
69. Lineham, "Wanna be in my gang?"

70. Lineham, "Tongues must cease": 16.
71. Chan, *Pentecostal Theology and The Christian Spiritual Tradition*, 98. Chan discusses the nature of Pentecostal ecclesiology in chapter 4 of this study.
72. Reginald W. Bibby and Merlin B. Brinkerhof, "The Circulation of the Saints: A Study of People Who Join Conservative Churches," *Journal for the Scientific Study of Religion*, no. 12 (1973): 273–83.
73. William Butler Yeats, "The Second Coming," in *Michael Robartes and the Dancer, by William Butler Yeats* (Churchtown, Dundrum, Ireland: Cuala Press, 1920), 19–20.
74. Clark, *Pentecost at the Ends of the Earth*, 153 and 231; Knowles, *The History of a New Zealand Pentecostal Movement*, 263.
75. Clark, *Pentecost at the Ends of the Earth* 254–55; see also Carew, "Māori, Biculturalism and the Assemblies of God," 28.
76. Clark, *Pentecost at the Ends of the Earth*, 119. See above, 119.
77. Associated Pentecostal Churches of New Zealand, "Pastors Directory 2001/2002"; see also Carew and Troughton, "Māori Participation in the Assemblies of God," 93.
78. Carew and Troughton, "Māori Participation in the Assemblies of God," 92–93.
79. Clark, *Pentecost at the Ends of the Earth*, 246.
80. Ibid, 248.
81. Ibid, 254.
82. Carew and Troughton, "Māori Participation in the Assemblies of God," 93.
83. Luke Worsfold, "Subsequence, Prophecy and Church Order," 247–48, 271.
84. Moetara, "Māori and Pentecostal Christianity in Aotearoa New Zealand," 82.
85. Luke Worsfold, "Subsequence, Prophecy and Church Order," 249–50.
86. Ibid, 156.
87. Ibid, 263.
88. See below, 259–260.
89. Louisa Cleave, "Churches' call divides flock," *New Zealand Herald*, 7 August 2007, http://www.nzherald.co.nz/nz/news/article.cfm?c_id=1&objectid=10456213 (accessed 22 February 2013).
90. Bibby and Brinkerhof, "The Circulation of the Saints": 273–83.
91. Lineham, cited in Darryl Hutchinson, "Rethinking Religion," in *The Nation*, TV3, 3 April 2010.
92. Mark Chaves, *Congregations in America* (Cambridge, MA: Harvard University Press, 2004), 17–21, cited in Catherine Bowler, "Blessed: A History of the American Prosperity Gospel" (PhD thesis in Religion, Duke University, 2010), 14, http://dukespace.lib.duke.edu/dspace/bitstream/handle/10161/2297/D_Bowler_Catherine_a_20 1005.pdf?sequence=1 (accessed 22 June 2013). I am grateful to Professor Peter Lineham for this reference.
93. Brett Knowles, Research Project on New Zealand Pentecostalism, 3 March 2013.
94. Jamieson, *A Churchless Faith*, 20.
95. See above, 142.
96. Peter Berger, "Reflections on the Sociology of Religion Today," *Sociology of Religion* 62.4 (2001): 443–55), cited in John Stenhouse, "God's Own Silence: Secular Nationalism, Christianity and the Writing of New Zealand History," *New Zealand Journal of History* 38, no. 1 (2004): 57.
97. Stenhouse, "God's Own Silence": 57.

98. Peter Lineham, Interview, 18 August 2008, cited in Moetara, "An exploration of notions of Māori leadership," 11 and footnote 23. See also Moetara, "Māori and Pentecostal Christianity in Aotearoa New Zealand," 86.

99. See above, 239.

100. Lineham, cited in Hutchinson, "Rethinking Religion."

101. So, Mortlock, cited in Hutchinson, "Rethinking Religion."

102. Lineham, "Three Types of Church," 199–224.

103. Hutchinson, "Rethinking Religion."

104. For example, Mun-hong Choi, "Korean Pentecostalism: A Case Study of Reverend Youngsan Yonggi Cho"; and Shane Clifton, "Australian Pentecostalism: Origins, Developments, and Trends" (both papers presented at the Empowered21 Global Scholars' Consultation, Alpha Crucis College, Parramatta, Sydney, 8–10 July 2013).

105. Lineham, *Destiny*, 162.

106. Lord Acton, letter to Bishop Mandell Creighton, 3 April 1887, in [Louise Creighton], *Life and Letters of Mandell Creighton*, 2 vols. (London: Longmans, Green and Co., 1904), 1: chapter 13, cited in Knowles, *Oxford Dictionary of Quotations*, http://www.oxfordreference.com/browse?t1=ORO:GEN00170 (accessed 8 August 2013).

107. Moetara, "An exploration of notions of Māori leadership," 83–84.

108. Principal Judith Forbes, comment to author, Dunedin, 27 October 2013. Used with permission.

109. Also known as "Servants to Asia's Urban Poor." http://servantsasia.org/ (accessed 27 October 2013).

110. See The Cohousing Association of the United States, "Cohousing: What is cohousing?" http://www.cohousing.org/what_is_cohousing (accessed 27 October 2013).

111. Dan Hutchinson, "Housing plan for school site," *The Star*, 3 October 2013, 1.

112. Donald E. Miller, "Pentecostalism and Social Transformation," in Hunter and Robeck, *The Azusa Street Revival and Its Legacy*, 335.

113. James K. Baxter, "Song to the Holy Spirit," in *Collected Poems: James K. Baxter*, ed. J. E. Weir (Oxford: Oxford University Press, 1981), 572. Copyright. Reproduced by permission from the James K. Baxter Trust.

Appendix A

Census figures for Pentecostal Adherence

Some indication of the size and growth of the Pentecostal movement can be ascertained from the returns for "Religious Adherence" in the quinquennial Census of Population conducted by the New Zealand Department of Statistics.[1] The tables below show the development of the various groups comprising the movement from 1901 to 2013. However, several qualifications must be made.

Firstly, "religious adherence" is a self-nominating classification in the Census. Adherence (as per the Census figures) is not necessarily reflected in participation in the life of the group so nominated. Historian Ali Clarke, for example, has estimated—citing the *Year Book of the Diocese of Christchurch* for 2007—that just over 13% of those declaring themselves Anglican in the Canterbury region in the 2006 Census actually attended worship. She also notes that attendance at Christmas communion—when larger congregations might be expected—amounted to only 15% of Canterbury's Anglican population.[2] Other sources place religious participation at an even lower level: Kevin Ward notes that the usual weekly attendance figure cited for New Zealand churches was in the vicinity of 10% of the population in 2000.[3] Secondly, changes in the Census categories render the comparison between quinquennial figures sometimes less than accurate. Until 1981, the religious affiliation question required one's affiliation to be written in; in 1986, this was changed to a tick-box method for the five main denominations (together with "object to state" and "no religion") and a write-in box to specify these other denominations, thus skewing the data in favor of the main denominations.[4] Furthermore, in the 2001 and 2006 Censuses, "Up to four responses were coded . . . , whereas, in 1996, only one response was coded. This makes it difficult to compare the 1996 and 2006 data, and the 1996 and 2001 data."[5] It also results in the combined total of all adherents exceeding the total population by 52,563 in 2001, by 139,758 in 2006 and by 101,733 in 2013. The Censuses from 1991 to 2001 also contained a different mix of categories from preceding and following Censuses. Subsidiary categories such as "uncertain," "not specified," etc. were included in the "Other Returns" figures in other years; these categories were not given between 1991 and 2001.

Thirdly, not all Pentecostal denominations had a clear sense of their own identity. The main example here is the group known originally as the "Indigenous

Churches of New Zealand" and after 1988 as the "New Life Churches of New Zealand." Adherents of this group eschewed denominational names, preferring to return "Christian" in response to the religious adherence question. Consequently, the name "Indigenous Churches" does not appear in the Census until 1976, although by then the movement was already one of the two largest Pentecostal groups in the country. This was exacerbated by the categorization processes of the Department of Statistics: after 1991, responses were often accumulated into summary categories such as "Pentecostal." This was particularly noticeable in the 1991 Census, when the category "New Life Churches" did not appear, although the "Pentecostal" category increased markedly. Given that the New Life Churches were then the second largest Pentecostal group in New Zealand, this was a significant omission. Another aspect of this was the ephemeral nature of some Pentecostal classifications. Pentecostal and Quasi-Pentecostal groups such as these which appeared after 1926 were subsumed in a category labeled "Ephemeral Groups" in the Tables. Finally, it should be noted that no Censuses were conducted in the years 1931, 1941 and 1946. The 1931 Census was not taken because of the Depression; the 1941 Census was deferred until after the end of World War Two and the 1946 Census combined with the 1945 Census.

As a general rule, data in the Table for each Census are taken from the comparative figures in the succeeding Census, where these are given (i.e., those for 1991 and 1996 are taken from the corrected figures given in the 2001 Census). This ensures that classification errors are minimized, since these are usually corrected in following Censuses. Where no comparative figures were given in the Censuses, the data pertaining to that year are used. This is the case with the data from 1901 to 1916, 1991 and from 2001 to 2013.

Appendix A 251

Religious Body	1901	1906	1911	1916	1921	1926	1936
Apostolic Church		5*	13*	20*		12*	390
Assemblies of God					4*		389
British Israelite (Quasi-Pentecostal)	34	24	19			43	704
Catholic Apostolic (Quasi-Pentecostal)	326	381	336	341	380	280	347
Christian Fellowships							
Christian Outreach							
Church of Christ (New Zealand)							
Commonwealth Covenant Church							
Elim Church							
Full Gospel						4	
Independent Pentecostal							
Indigenous Pentecostal/New Life							
Latter Rain							
New Covenant/National Revival Church/ Christian Revival Crusade							
Pentecostal (Assembly/Mission, etc.)				6		726	490
Revival Centres							
United Pentecostal							
Vineyard Churches							
Ephemeral (Pentecostal)			4				5
Ephemeral (Quasi-Pentecostal)		1	13	26	4		3
Total Pentecostals		5	13	26	4	742	1,274
Total Quasi-Pentecostals	360	406	359	341	380	323	1,054

Table 4: Comparative Census Returns for Pentecostal and Quasi-Pentecostal adherents, 1901 to 2013 (part 1)

Religious Body	1945	1951	1956	1961	1966	1971	1976
Apostolic Church	707	756	969	1,399	1,841	2,361	2,682
Assemblies of God	362	475	747	1,060	2,029	3,649	5,547
British Israel/ite (Quasi-Pentecostal)	181	102	56	69	61	18	
Catholic Apostolic (Quasi-Pentecostal)	137	74	65	34	11		
Christian Fellowships					122	72	87
Christian Outreach							
Church of Christ (New Zealand)				599	610	1,085	819
Commonwealth Covenant Church	835	659	813	875	506	385	360
Elim Church			2	219	172	121	335
Full Gospel	1		32	334	1,185	1,333	703
Independent Pentecostal							50
Indigenous Pentecostal/New Life					23	12	824
Latter Rain		21					
New Covenant/National Revival Church/ Christian Revival Crusade	46	57	61	63	296	75	75
Pentecostal (Assembly/Mission, etc.)	443	477	567	659	1,115	1,859	4,830
Revival Centres		1			11	19	50
United Pentecostal							
Vineyard Churches							
Ephemeral (Pentecostal)		3	3		5		
Ephemeral (Quasi-Pentecostal)	4	6	5	1	9		
Total Pentecostals	2,394	2,449	3,194	5,208	7,915	10,971	16,362
Total Quasi-Pentecostals	322	182	126	104	81	18	

Table 5: Comparative Census Returns for Pentecostal and Quasi-Pentecostal adherents, 1901 to 2013 (part 2)

Religious Body	1981	1986	1991	1996	2001	2006	2013
Apostolic Church	4,497	4,194	6,804	8,913	8,109	8,328	6,120
Assemblies of God	12,465	14,925	17,226	17,520	16,023	15,300	13,806
British Israelite (Quasi-Pentecostal)							
Catholic Apostolic (Quasi-Pentecostal)							
Christian Fellowships	240	1,074	1,344				
Christian Outreach				300	225	123	78
Church of Christ (New Zealand)	678	486					
Commonwealth Covenant Church	327	261	297	165	18	18	6
Elim Church	1,257	2,157	2,352	3,018	2,607	2,214	1,494
Full Gospel	432	348		483	849	1,092	1,074
Independent Pentecostal	66				228	237	141
Indigenous Pentecostal/New Life	5,280	2,796	1,491	3,918	5,862	7,941	2,157
Latter Rain							
New Covenant/National Revival Church/ Christian Revival Crusade		426		132	135	99	51
Pentecostal (Assembly/Mission, etc.)	6,369	15,717	19,083	33,987	31,647	42,066	48,042
Revival Centres	60		756	273	252	243	195
United Pentecostal				408	528	369	258
Vineyard Churches				342	774	1,605	1,017
Ephemeral (Pentecostal)							
Ephemeral (Quasi-Pentecostal)				3			
Total Pentecostals	31,671	42,384	49,353	69,459	67,257	79,635	74,439
Total Quasi-Pentecostals				3			

Table 6: Comparative Census Returns for Pentecostal and Quasi-Pentecostal adherents, 1901 to 2013 (part 3)

A comparison of these Pentecostal figures with those from other significant categories puts them in perspective. Although the movement is continuing to expand, it remains at less than 4% of the total Christian population in 2013 (which is itself less than half of the total population).

Year	1901	1906	1911	1916	1921	1926	1936
Pentecostals	0	5	13	26	4	742	1,274
Total Christian	744,083	851,982	954,171	1,048,479	1,162,840	1,262,629	1,389,296
Object to State	18,295	24,325	35,905	25,577	38,591	62,585	71,302
No Religion	910	1,229	4,474	4,184	3,919	2,838	4,292
Other Religion	5,061	5,207	6,535	12,060	9,941	7,644	8,938
Other Returns	4,370	5,835	7,383	9,149	3,622	9,073	17,831
Total Population	772,719	888,578	1,008,468	1,099,449	1,218,913	1,344,769	1,491,659
% Pentecostals/ Christians	0.00%	0.00%	0.00%	0.00%	0.00%	0.06%	0.09%
% Christians/ Population	96.29%	95.88%	94.62%	95.36%	95.40%	93.89%	93.14%

Table 7: Comparative Census Returns for General Population, 1901 to 2013 (part 1)

Year	1945	1951	1956	1961	1966	1971	1976
Pentecostals	2,394	2,449	3,194	5,208	7,915	10,971	16,362
Total Christian	1,530,912	1,761,056	1,955,719	2,161,786	2,387,058	2,417,645	2,463,654
Object to State	133,431	137,597	173,569	204,056	210,851	247,019	434,898
No Religion	11,313	11,475	12,651	17,486	32,780	57,485	100,398
Other Religion	10,769	11,149	11,259	11,364	16,132	17,824	39,636
Other Returns	15,953	18,376	21,220	20,292	30,098	122,658	64,677
Total Population	1,702,378	1,939,653	2,174,418	2,414,984	2,676,919	2,862,631	3,103,263
% Pentecostals/ Christians	0.16%	0.14%	0.16%	0.24%	0.33%	0.45%	0.66%
% Christians/ Population	89.93%	90.79%	89.94%	89.52%	89.17%	84.46%	79.39%

Table 8: Comparative Census Returns for General Population, 1901 to 2013 (part 2)

Year	1981	1986	1991	1996	2001	2006	2013
Pentecostals	31,671	42,384	49,353	69,459	67,257	79,635	74,439
Total Christian	2,315,736	2,376,645	2,328,762	2,189,445	2,107,437	2,130,315	1,933,851
Object to State	468,573	244,731	251,709	256,593	239,244	242,610	173,034
No Religion	166,014	533,766	670,455	867,264	1,028,052	1,297,104	1,635,348
Other Religion	41,073	46,053	65,079	91,998	146,643	204,624	254,208
Other Returns	151,878	62,079	0	0	0	293,052	347,340
Total Population	3,143,274	3,263,274	3,316,005	3,405,300	3,468,813	4,027,947	4,242,048
% Pentecostals/ Christians	1.37%	1.78%	2.13%	3.17%	3.19%	3.74%	3.85%
% Christians/ Population	73.67%	72.83%	70.23%	64.30%	60.75%	52.89%	45.59%

Table 9: Comparative Census Returns for General Population, 1901 to 2013 (part 3)

Notes

1. Office of the Registrar-General, *Results of a Census of the Colony of New Zealand taken for the night of the 31st March, 1901* (Wellington: Government Printer, 1902), "Census Tables, 1901: Part II.—Religions of the People," 85–87; Office of the Registrar-

General, *Results of a Census of the Colony of New Zealand taken for the night of the 29th April, 1906* (Wellington: Government Printer, 1907), "Census Tables, 1906: Part II.—Religions of the People," 95–96; Office of the Registrar-General, *Results of a Census of the Dominion of New Zealand taken for the night of the 2nd April, 1911* (Wellington: Government Printer, 1912), "Census Tables, 1911: Part II.—Religions of the People," 102–3; Census and Statistics Office, *Results of a Census of the Dominion of New Zealand taken for the night of 15th October, 1916* (Wellington: Government Printer, 1920), "Census Tables, 1916: Part IV.—Religions," 4–5; Census and Statistics Office, *Results of a Census of the Dominion of New Zealand taken for the night of the 17th April, 1921* (Wellington: Government Printer, 1922), "Part VII.—Religions: Statistical Tables," 17–18; Dominion of New Zealand, *Dominion of New Zealand Population Census, 1926* (Wellington: Government Printer, 1928), "Vol. VIII.—Religious Professions of the Population," 8–10; Census and Statistics Department, *Dominion of New Zealand Population Census, 1936*, "Vol. VI.—Religious Professions," 3–4; Census and Statistics Department, *New Zealand Population Census, 1945* (Wellington: Census and Statistics Department, 1952), "Vol. VI.—Religious Professions," 3–4; Census and Statistics Department, *New Zealand Population Census, 1951* (Wellington: Government Printer, 1953), "Vol. III—Religious Professions," 9–12; Department of Statistics, *New Zealand Population Census 1956* (Wellington: Government Printer, 1958), "Volume III— Religious Professions," 13–17; Department of Statistics, *New Zealand Population Census 1961* (Wellington: Government Printer, 1964), "Vol. 3—Religious Professions," 8–10; Department of Statistics, *New Zealand Census of Population and Dwellings, 1966* (Wellington: Department of Statistics, 1968), "Volume 3—Religious Professions," 9–11; Department of Statistics, *New Zealand Census of Population and Dwellings, 1971* (Wellington: Department of Statistics, 1974), "Volume 3—Religious Professions," 11–13; Department of Statistics, *New Zealand Census of Population and Dwellings, 1976* (Wellington: Department of Statistics, 1980), "Volume 3—Religious Professions," 14–15; Department of Statistics, *New Zealand Census of Population and Dwellings, 1981* (Wellington: Department of Statistics, 1983), "Volume 3—Religious Professions," 8–9; Department of Statistics, *1986 New Zealand Census of Population and Dwellings* (Wellington: Department of Statistics, 1988), "Series C, Report 14—Religious Professions," 14–15; Statistics New Zealand—Te Tari Tatau, *2001 Census of Population and Dwellings: National Summary* (Wellington: Statistics New Zealand—Te Tari Tatau, 2002), "Table 16: Religious Affiliation (Total Responses) and Sex for the Census Usually Resident Population Count, 1991, 1996 and 2001," 174–78, www.stats.govt.nz/Census/2001-census-data/2001-census-national-summary.aspx (acces-sed 11 December 2003); Statistics New Zealand—Tatauranga Aotearoa, *2006 Census of Population and Dwellings: National Summary* (Wellington: Statistics New Zealand—Tatauranga Aotearoa, 2006), "Table 31: Religious Affiliation (Total Responses) for the Census Usually Resident Population Count, 2006," http://www.stats.govt.nz/Census/2006CensusHomePage/classification-counts-tables/about-people/religious-affili-ation.aspx (accessed 11 December 2013); Statistics New Zealand—Tatauranga Aotearoa, *2013 Census totals by topic* (Wellington: Statistics New Zealand—Tatauranga Aotearoa, 2013), http://www.stats.govt.nz/Census/2013-census/data-tables/total-by-topic.aspx (ac-cessed 11 December 2013).

2. Ali Clarke, Draft research paper, Hocken Library, Dunedin, 2012. I am grateful to Dr. Clarke for permission to use these data.

3. Kevin Ward, *The Church in Post-Sixties New Zealand: Decline, Growth and Change*. Archer Studies in Pacific Christianity (Auckland: Archer Press, 2013), 7 and 11. Ward analyses these low attendance figures in greater detail in Ward, "Towards 2015:

The future of mainline Protestantism in New Zealand," *Journal of Beliefs and Values* 27, no. 1 (April 2006), 13–23.

4. Statistics New Zealand—Tatauranga Aotearoa, "2006 Census: Definitions and Questionnaires. Forms: Individual and dwelling forms, historical." 1981 Personal Questionnaire and 1986 Personal Questionnaire, http://www.stats.govt.nz/Census/about-2006-census/2006-census-definitions-questionnaires/forms.aspx (accessed 20 February 2013).

5. Statistics New Zealand—Tatauranga Aotearoa, "Information by Variable: Religious affiliation." Comparability with 1996 and 2001 Census data, http://www.stats.govt.nz/Census/about-2006-census/information-by-variable/religious-affilia-tion.aspx (accessed 20 February 2013).

Appendix B

Summary of Pentecostal Church Affiliations, 2002–12

A comparison of denominational listings utilizing the last Associated Pentecostal Churches of New Zealand Pastors Directory (from 2001–2)[1] and current websites for the various New Zealand Pentecostal churches[2] yields evidence of a substantial decline between 2002 and 2012. This is summarized in Table 10 below.

Pentecostal Body	Number of Churches				Comment
	2002	2012	Change	%	
Assemblies of God	261	233	-28	-10.73%	Schism of about 30 Samoan Assemblies of God churches in 2005
New Life Churches of New Zealand	108	93	-15	-13.89%	
Apostolic Churches (renamed ACTs Churches)	99	56	-43	-43.43%	Schism of 9 churches to Destiny in 2003
Elim Churches	60	41	-19	-31.67%	
Other churches (not specified)	33	30	-3	-9.09%	
Vineyard Churches	26	16	-10	-38.46%	
International Convention of Faith Ministries	19	18	-1	-5.26%	
Christian Revival Crusade Churches	12	8	-4	-33.33%	
Christian Outreach Centres	11	6	-5	-45.45%	
Millennium Ministries	7		-7	-100.00%	No data available for 2012
Christian Covenant Churches	5	0	-5	-100.00%	Closed; churches transferred to other groups
Associated Fellowships	3		-3	-100.00%	No data available for 2012

Rhema Churches	0	0	0		Previously closed?
Network of Christian Ministries	25	29	4	16.00%	
LinkNZ	15	19	4	26.67%	
Christian City Churches	9	16	7	77.78%	
Destiny Churches	5	10	5	100.00%	
Celebration Centres	2	7	5	250.00%	
Christian Life Churches	1	6	5	500.00%	
Samoan Assemblies of God in New Zealand	0	45[3]	45		About 30 of these churches had split from the Assemblies of God in 2005
City Impact Church	0	5	5		New group (split off from New Life Churches)
New Frontiers Churches	0	3	3		New group
Total	701	641	-60	-8.56%	

Table 10: Comparison of Pentecostal Churches 2002–12 (categorized into growing and declining churches and sorted in order of size at 2002)

Notes

1. Associated Pentecostal Churches of New Zealand, "Pastors Directory 2001/2002."

2. Apostolic/Acts Churches, http://www.apostolic.org.nz/churches/ (accessed 21 March 2012); Assemblies of God Churches, http://www.agnz.org/about/findachurch/62/345/ (accessed 21 March 2012); Christian City Churches (C3 Churches), http://www.c3churchglobal.com/church/5/25 (accessed 24 March 2012); Celebration Centres Churches, http://www.celebrationcentre.com/celebration_centre/movement/ (accessed 21 March 2012); Christian Life Churches, http://lifenz.org/church/locations/ (accessed 21 March 2012); Christian Outreach Centres Churches (data advised by Bruce Currie, Dunedin, 25 April 2012); Christian Revival Crusade Churches, http://www.crcnz.org/ (accessed 21 March 2012); Destiny Churches, http://www.destinychurch.org.nz/ (accessed 21 March 2012); Elim Churches, http://www.elim.org.nz/about/church_locator.aspx (accessed 21 March 2012); City Impact Church, http://www.cityimpactchurch.com/locations (accessed 21 March 2012); International Convention of Faith Ministries, http://www.icfm.org/cgi-bin/gx.cgi/AppLogic+FTContentServer?pagename=FaithHighway/10000/1000/199/international_06#NewZealand (accessed 21 March 2012); Network of Christian Ministries Churches, http://www.thenetwork.org.nz/thenetwork/Members.html (accessed 21 March 2012); New Frontiers Churches, http://www.newfrontierstogether.org/Groups/103229/Newfrontiers/Worldwide/New_Zealand/New_Zealand.aspx (accessed 21 March 2012); New Life Churches of New Zealand, http://newlife.org.nz/churches/ (ac-

cessed 21 March 2012); Samoan Assemblies of God Churches in New Zealand, http://en.wikipedia.org/wiki/Samoan_Assemblies_of_God_churches_in_New_Zealand (accessed 21 February 2013); Vineyard Churches, http://www.vineyard.org.nz/styled/page5.html (accessed 21 March 2012).

3. The Samoan Assemblies of God in New Zealand claimed 135 churches on their Wikipedia website in 2013 (Samoan Assemblies of God Churches in New Zealand, http://en.wikipedia.org/wiki/Samoan_Assemblies_of_God_churches_in_New_Zealand). However, this figure should be viewed with extreme suspicion, since more than forty of the churches in this listing are also listed under identical or similar names on the Assemblies of God website; others appear to exist only on paper. There were also legal and constitutional issues over which organisational authority these churches came under. It is unlikely that all the churches claimed by the Samoan Assemblies of God in New Zealand actually existed or were affiliated with it. See Cleave, "Churches' call divides flock." This article refers to eighty-five Samoan Assemblies of God churches in New Zealand, of which forty were linked to the parent Assemblies of God; this gives a figure of forty-five Samoan churches aligned with the breakaway group as at 2007. This number has been taken as a safer estimate than the 135 claimed in the Wikipedia website.

Appendix C

Tables of New Zealand Pentecostal Churches

The following tables set out the origins of, the relationships between and the trajectories of the various groups in the New Zealand Pentecostal movement.

Body	Date emerged	Originated	Still active?	Notes
Catholic Apostolic Church (Quasi-Pentecostal)	1860s		No	Active until 1930s; last census reference 1966.
British Israel Movement (Quasi-Pentecostal)	1880s		No	Last Census reference 1971. Diffuse movement, rather than formal institution, but several Pentecostal British Israel churches emerged from 1933 on.
Pentecostal Church of New Zealand [PCNZ]	1924	Smith Wigglesworth Campaigns, 1922 and 1923–24	No	Wound up 1952: Remnant of PCNZ amalgamated with Elim Church (Great Britain) to form Elim (NZ) Church.
Assemblies of God [AoG]	1927	Import from USA; Based on secession from PCNZ	Yes	
Revival Fire Mission	1930	Dallimore mission	No	Closed 1968.

Table 11: Dates, Origins and Trajectories of Pentecostal Denominations (part 1)

Body	Date emerged	Originated	Still active?	Notes
Apostolic Church	1934	Import from Britain; Secessions from PCNZ and AoG	Yes	
Christian Fellowships	1939?		No	Last Census reference 1991.
Commonwealth Covenant Church	1939	British Israel connections	Yes	Began as independent Pentecostal congregation. Changed name to New Covenant Assembly (1941), then to National Revival Crusade (1944) and to Christian Revival Crusade (c.1958).
Christian Revival Crusade Churches	1939	Some British Israel connections	Yes	
Church of Christ (New Zealand)	1946	Some British Israel connections	Yes	Now a largely Chinese culture church.
New Life Churches of New Zealand	1946	Secession from PCNZ	Yes	Latter Rain influence 1948 on; sometimes known as "Full Gospel" in late 1950s; "Indigenous Churches" increasingly used after 1965; official name of "New Life Churches" adopted 1988.
Elim Church (New Zealand)	1952	Remnants of PCNZ	Yes	Amalgamation of Elim Church of Great Britain with PCNZ.
Revival Centres	1958	Secession from Christian Revival Crusade	Yes	
United Pentecostal Church	1969	Import from USA	Yes	Unitarian ("Jesus Only") Pentecostals.
Vineyard Churches	After 1983	Import from USA	Yes	First census returns 1996.

Table 12: Dates, Origins and Trajectories of Pentecostal Denominations (part 2)

Appendix C 265

Body	Date emerged	Originated	Still active?	Notes
Christian Outreach Centres	Mid-1980s?	Import from Australia	Yes	First census returns 1996.
Christian City Churches	Late 1980s?	Import from Australia	Yes	
South Pacific Churches	1987	Secession from New Life Churches	Yes	
Christian Life Centres	1996	Founded by former Australian AoG minister	Yes	
New Frontiers	1997?	Import from Britain	Yes	
Network of Christian Ministries	1997		Yes	
Destiny Church	1998?	Secessions from Apostolic Church	Yes	Founder Brian Tamaki left Apostolic Church 1994; Destiny Church emerges about 1998.
International Convention of Faith Ministries	2001		Yes	No information: in 2001/2 APCNZ Pastors Directory.
Celebration Centres	2001		Yes	No information: in 2001/2 APCNZ Pastors Directory.
City Impact Church	After 2001	Secession from New Life Churches?	Yes	Church founder Peter Mortlock still in 2001/2 APCNZ Pastors Directory as New Life Churches pastor.
Samoan Assemblies of God	2005	Major secession from AoG	Yes	Number of churches not accurately known.

Table 13: Dates, Origins and Trajectories of Pentecostal Denominations (part 3)

Bibliography

Databases and Manuscript Collections

Australian Dictionary of Evangelical Biography. http://webjournals.ac.edu.au/journals/adeb/.
Australian Dictionary of Pentecostal and Charismatic Movements. http://webjournals.ac.edu.au/journals/ADPCM/.
Brett Knowles Research Papers [BKRP]. MS-3530/001-044. Hocken Library, Dunedin.
History Group of the New Zealand Ministry for Culture and Heritage, *New Zealand History online—Nga korero a ipurangi o Aotearoa.* http://www.nzhistory.net.nz/.
James Worsfold Research Papers. Private collection. Wellington.
National Library of New Zealand—Te Puna Mātauranga o Aotearoa, "Collections." http://www.natlib.govt.nz/collections/.
———, "Papers Past." http://paperspast.natlib.govt.nz/cgi-bin/paperspast/.
Statistics New Zealand (Tatauranga Aotearoa). http://www.stats.govt.nz/.
Te Ara Encyclopedia of New Zealand. http://www.teara.govt.nz/en/.

Other Resources

Abel, Sue. *Shaping the News: Waitangi Day on Television.* Auckland: Auckland University Press, 1997.
Adams, John A. D. "The Scriptural Statement Concerning the Baptism with the Holy Spirit, Chapters XIII–XVI." *Good News*, 1 May 1928, 3–7. http://webjournals.alphacrucis.edu.au/journals/GN/gn-vol19-no5-may-1928/03-scriptural-statement-concerning-bapt-XIII-XVI/ (accessed 7 March 2012).
———. *The Church as Revealed in Scripture.* Dayton, OH: John J. Scruby, [1906]. Pamphlets 156/21, Hocken Library, Dunedin.
Ahlstrom, Sydney E. *A Religious History of the American People.* New Haven: Yale University Press, 1973.
Allen, Patrick. "'Bankrupt' Western Governments Need 'Ruthanasia'." CNBC, Europe: Economy, 8 September 2010. http://www.cnbc.com/id/39054360 (accessed 31 August 2010).

Anderson, Robert Mapes. *Vision of the Disinherited: The Making of American Pentecostalism.* New York: Oxford University Press, 1979.

Ansley, Bruce. "The Growing Might of the Moral Right." *New Zealand Listener*, 26 October 1985, 16–18.

Apostolic/Acts Churches. http://www.apostolic.org.nz/churches/ (accessed 21 March 2012).

Arrowsmith, David. "Christian Attitudes towards Public Questions in New Zealand in 1975." MA thesis in Political Studies, Auckland University, 1978.

Assemblies of God Churches. http://www.agnz.org/about/findachurch/62/345/ (accessed 21 March 2012).

Assemblies of God in New Zealand. "Our History." http://www.agnz.org/history.htm (accessed 4 September 2007).

Associated Pentecostal Churches of New Zealand. "Pastors Directory 2001/2002." Mimeographed, Associated Pentecostal Churches of New Zealand, Christchurch, [2001]. BKRP, MS-3530/008. Hocken Library, Dunedin.

Auckland Council of Christian Congregations. *The Dallimore campaign exposed: the full report of the joint clerical medical, and professional committee of inquiry into the faith healing mission conducted by Mr. A.H. Dallimore, 1932.* Auckland: Wilson and Horton, 1932.

Austin, Denise A. *Our College: A History of the National College of Australian Christian Churches (Assemblies of God in Australia).* Australian Pentecostal Studies Supplementary Series 5. Sydney: Australian Pentecostal Studies, 2013.

Baer, Jonathan R. "Redeemed Bodies: The Functions of Divine Healing in Incipient Pentecostalism." *Church History: Studies in Christianity and Culture* 70, no. 4 (December 2001): 735–72.

Balmer, Randall. *Mine Eyes Have Seen the Glory: A Journey into the Evangelical Subculture in America.* New York: Oxford University, Press, 1989.

Barrett, David B., ed. *World Christian Encyclopedia: A Comparative Study of Churches and Religions in the Modern World, AD 1900–2000.* Nairobi: Oxford University Press, 1982.

Bartleman, Frank. *Another Wave Rolls In! [formerly What really happened at "Azusa Street?"].* Ed. John Walker; rev. and enlarged ed., ed. John G. Myers. [1925]; Northridge, CA: Voice Publications, 1970. Reproduced http://www.arlev.co.uk/azusa/ (accessed 16 November 2011).

Battley, Donald. "Charismatic Renewal: A View from the Inside." *Ecumenical Review*, no. 38 (1986): 48–56.

———. "The Renewal is over . . . is it?" *Affirm* 5, no. 3 (Spring 1997): 17, 28.

Baxter, James K. "Song to the Holy Spirit." In *Collected Poems: James K. Baxter*, ed. J. E. Weir, 572. Oxford: Oxford University Press, 1981.

BBC News. "In pictures: The Vietnam War." http://news.bbc.co.uk/2/shared/spl/hi/picture_gallery/05/in_pictures_the_vietnam_war_/html/6.stm (accessed 2 December 2013).

Beautiful Monsters: random rants and ravings. "Enough is enough." Posted 24 August 2004. http://stonesoup.co.nz/ecoqueer/archives/003699.html (accessed 19 July 2013).
Bennett, Dennis J. *Nine O'Clock in the Morning*. Plainfield, NJ: Logos International, 1970.
Best, Elsdon. *Maori Religion and Mythology: Being an Account of the Cosmogony, Anthropogony, Religious Beliefs and Rites, Magic and Folk Lore of the Maori Folk of New Zealand, Part 1*. Wellington: Government Printer, 1976.
Bibby, Reginald W., and Merlin B. Brinkerhof. "The Circulation of the Saints: A Study of People Who Join Conservative Churches." *Journal for the Scientific Study of Religion*, no. 12 (1973): 273–83.
Bible Deliverance, April 1959–March 1966. BKRP, MS-3530/002. Hocken Library, Dunedin.
"Biography of Brother Mandus." http:brothermandus.wwwhubs.com/ (accessed 18 March 2009).
Bluck, John. "Being Church and Belonging: How Do Twenty-First Century New Zealanders Join the Church?" In Boddé and Kempster, *Thinking Outside the Square: Church in Middle Earth*, 13–29.

———. "Jesus 75—a mixed blessing." *New Citizen*, 12 June 1975, 5.

Blumhofer, Edith L. *The Assemblies of God: A Chapter in the Story of American Pentecostalism*. 2 vols. Springfield, MS: Gospel Publishing House, 1989.
Board of Elders of the Pentecostal Church of N.Z. (Inc.). Minute Book 1934–1951. Wellington. Held by Wellington City Elim Church.
Boddé, Ree, and Hugh Kempster, eds. *Thinking Outside the Square: Church in Middle Earth*. Auckland: St. Columba's Press & Journeyings, 2003.
Bolitho, Elaine. "With Hearts Strangely Warmed: The Charismatic Movement in the New Zealand Methodist Church." *Affirm* 5, no. 1 (Autumn 1997): 20–23.
Bosch, David J. *Transforming Mission: Paradigm Shifts in the Theology of Mission*. American Society of Missiology Series 16. Maryknoll, NY: Orbis Books, 1991, 1995.
Boston, Jonathan. "Christianity in the Public Square: The Churches and Social Justice." In *Voices for Justice: Church, Law and State in New Zealand*, ed. Jonathan Boston and Alan Cameron, 11–35. Palmerston North: Dunmore Press, 1994.
Bowler, Catherine. "Blessed: A History of the American Prosperity Gospel." PhD thesis in Religion, Duke University, 2010. http://dukespace.lib.duke.edu/dspace/bitstream/handle/10161/2297/D_Bowler_Catherine_a_201005.pdf?sequence=1 (accessed 22 June 2013).
Breward, Ian. *A History of the Churches in Australasia*. Oxford History of the Christian Church, ed. Henry and Owen Chadwick. Oxford: Oxford University Press, 2011.
Brooking, Tom, and Paul Enright. *Milestones: Turning Points in New Zealand History*. With picture research by Harry Mills. Lower Hutt: Mills Publications, 1999.

Brown, Colin. "Pentecostalism, Neo-Pentecostalism and Naturalistic Explanation." In *The Religious Dimension: A Selection of Essays Presented at a Colloquium on Religious Studies Held at the University of Auckland, New Zealand in August 1975*, ed. J. Hinchcliff, 55–57. Auckland: Rep Prep Ltd., 1975.

———. "The Charismatic Contribution: How significant is the Charismatic Movement?" In Colless and Donovan, *Religion in New Zealand Society*, 99–118.

———. "Will the Charismatic Renewal Permanently Renew?" In *Religious Pluralism in New Zealand*, Article 3, 6. Wellington: Department of University Extension Victoria University of Wellington, [1976]. Typescript.

———. *Forty Years On: A History of the National Council of Churches in New Zealand 1941–1981*. Christchurch: National Council of Churches, 1981.

Bryant, George. *The Church on Trial*. [Whangarei]: Whau Publications, [1986].

Burgess, Stanley M., and Eduard M. van der Maas, eds. *New International Dictionary of Pentecostal and Charismatic Movements*. Grand Rapids, MI: Zondervan, 2002.

Capon, John. *. . . and there was light: The Story of the Nationwide Festival of Light*. London: Lutterworth Press, 1972.

Carew, Philip D. "Māori, Biculturalism and the Assemblies of God in New Zealand, 1970–2008." MA thesis in Religious Studies, Victoria University of Wellington, 2009.

———, and Geoff Troughton. "Māori Participation in the Assemblies of God." In Morrison et al., *Mana Māori and Christianity*, 91–109.

Carr, E. H. *What is History? The George Macaulay Trevelyan Lectures Delivered in the University of Cambridge January–March 1961*. Harmondsworth: Penguin, 1986.

Celebration Centres Churches. http://www.celebrationcentre.com/celebration_centre/movement/ (accessed 21 March 2012).

Census and Statistics Department. *Dominion of New Zealand Population Census, 1936*. Wellington: Government Printer, 1940.

———. *New Zealand Population Census, 1945*. Wellington: Census and Statistics Department, 1952.

———. *New Zealand Population Census, 1951*. Wellington: Government Printer, 1953.

Census and Statistics Office. *Results of a Census of the Dominion of New Zealand taken for the night of 15th October, 1916*. Wellington: Government Printer, 1920.

———. *Results of a Census of the Dominion of New Zealand taken for the night of the 17th April, 1921*. Wellington: Government Printer, 1922.

Challenge Weekly, "P.M. urges Christian involvement," 3 May 1975, 1.

———, "Unprecedented Event: 10,000 march for Jesus in Queen Street," 13 May 1972, 1.

———. "The Story of the Jesus People." Review of *The Jesus People: Old-Time Religion in the Age of Aquarius*, eds. Ronald M. Enroth, Edward E. Ericson, Jr., and C. Breckinridge Peters. 14 April 1973, 7.

Chamberlain, Jenny. "Secret Saviours." *North and South*, February 2001, 65–66.
Chambers, J. B. *To God be the Glory*. Christchurch: Presbyterian Bookroom, 1965.
Chan, Simon. *Pentecostal Theology and the Christian Spiritual Tradition*. Journal of Pentecostal Theology Supplement Series 21. Eds. John Christopher Thomas, Rickie D. Moore and Stephen J. Land. Sheffield: Sheffield Academic Press, 2000.
Chant, Barry. "The Nineteenth and Early Twentieth Century Origins of the Australian Pentecostal Movement." In Hutchinson and Piggin, *Reviving Australia*, 97–122.
———. *Heart of Fire: The Story of Australian Pentecostalism*. Rev. ed. Plympton, South Australia: Tabor Publications, 1997.
———. *The Spirit of Pentecost: The Origins and Development of the Pentecostal Movement in Australia 1870–1939*. Asbury Theological Seminary Series in World Christian Revitalization Movements in Pentecostal/Charismatic Studies 5. Lexington, KY: Emeth Press, 2011.
Chaplin, Jonathan. "'Secularism': Three Concepts, Three Challenges." Paper presented at Centre for Theology and Public Issues Symposium on "Is New Zealand 'Secular' and Does it Matter?" St. Margaret's College, University of Otago, Dunedin, 19 August 2013.
Chapman, Robert, "From Labour to National." In Rice, *Oxford History of New Zealand*, 351–84.
Chapple, Geoff. "When the Spirit Moves." *New Zealand Listener*, 24 July 1976, 24–25.
Choi, Mun-hong. "Korean Pentecostalism: A Case Study of Reverend Youngsan Yonggi Cho." Paper presented at the Empowered21 Global Scholars' Consultation, Alpha Crucis College, Parramatta, Sydney, 8–10 July 2013.
Christian City Churches (C3 Churches). http://www.c3churchglobal.com/church/5/25 (accessed 24 March 2012).
Christian Life Churches. http://lifenz.org/church/locations/ (accessed 21 March 2012).
Christian Revival Crusade Churches. http://www.crcnz.org/ (accessed 21 March 2012).
Church Bells, June 1966–September 1968. BKRP, MS-3530/003. Hocken Library, Dunedin.
Church of Christ New Zealand. http://www.chinese.ccnz.org.nz/ (accessed 3 February 2012).
City Impact Church. http://www.cityimpactchurch.com/locations (accessed 21 March 2012).
Clark, Ian G. *Pentecost at the Ends of the Earth: The History of the Assemblies of God in New Zealand (1927–2003)*. Blenheim: Christian Road Ministries, 2007.
Clarke, Ali. Draft research paper. Hocken Library, Dunedin, 2012.
Clements, Kevin. "The Religious Variable: Dependent, Independent or Interdependent?" In *A Sociological Handbook of Religion in Britain*, ed. Michael Hill, IV: 36–45. London: SCM Press, 1971.

Clifton, Shane. "An Analysis of the Developing Ecclesiology of the Assemblies of God in Australia." PhD thesis in Theology, Australian Catholic University, 2005.

———. "Australian Pentecostalism: Origins, Developments, and Trends." Paper presented at the Empowered21 Global Scholars' Consultation, Alpha Crucis College, Parramatta, Sydney, 8–10 July 2013.

———. "The Apostolic Revolution and the Ecclesiology of the AoGA." *Australasian Pentecostal Studies*, no. 9 (March 2006), http://webjournals.alphacrucis.edu.au/journals/aps/issue-9/03-the-apostolic-revolution-and-the-ecclesiology-o/ (accessed 24 May 2012).

———. *Pentecostal Churches in Transition: Analysing the Developing Ecclesiology of the Assemblies of God in Australia.* Leiden; Boston: Brill, 2009.

Cohousing Association of the United States. "Cohousing: What is cohousing?" http://www.cohousing.org/what_is_cohousing (accessed 27 October 2013).

Colless, Brian, and Peter Donovan, eds. *Religion in New Zealand Society*, 2nd ed. Palmerston North: Dunmore Press, 1985.

Conner, Kevin J. *The Name of God.* Portland, OR: Conner Publications, 1975.

———. *This is My Story: With Lessons I've Learnt Along the Way.* Vermont, Vic.: Published by author, 2007.

Copeland, Gordon F. *Faith That Works.* Lower Hutt: Barnabas Christian Trust, 1988.

Cox, Harvey. *Fire From Heaven: The Rise of Pentecostal Spirituality and the Reshaping of Religion in the Twenty-First Century.* Reading, MA: Addison-Wesley, 1995.

———. *The Secular City: Secularization and Urbanization in Theological Perspective.* London: SCM Press, 1966.

Crawford, John, ed. *Kia Kaha: New Zealand in the Second World War.* Auckland: Oxford University Press, 2000.

Dallimore, A. H. *Britain-Israel: Chats about our Empire, our People and our Origin*, 2nd ed. Auckland: n.p., 1932?

———. *Healing by Faith: including many Testimonies of healing received by people in New Zealand.* 2nd ed. Auckland: n.p., 1932?

Dann, Christine. *Up From Under: Women and Liberation in New Zealand 1970–1985.* Wellington: Allen and Unwin/Port Nicholson Press, 1985.

Darroch, Murray. *Everything you ever wanted to know about Protestants but never knew who to ask.* New Zealand ed. Wellington: Catholic Supplies, 1984.

Dasler, Yvonne. "Then they came to Elim . . . ." *New Zealand Listener*, 24 April 1982, 18–21.

Davidson, Allan K. "History Changes: Critical reflections on New Zealand and Pacific History [online]." *Stimulus: The New Zealand Journal of Christian Thought and Practice* 19, no. 2 (July 2012): [16]–25. http://search.informit.com.au/documentSummary;dn=645230770933960;res=IELHSS>ISSN:2230-5963 (accessed 14 February 2013).

———. *Christianity in Aotearoa: A History of Church and Society in New Zealand.* Wellington: Education for Ministry, 1991.

———. "Churches and the Treaty: A History." In *The Pakeha and the Treaty: Signposts,* ed. National Council of Churches in New Zealand, Church and Society Commission, 31–37. Auckland: National Council of Churches, 1986.

———, and Peter J. Lineham, eds. *Transplanted Christianity: Documents Illustrating Aspects of New Zealand Church History.* 2nd ed. Palmerston North: Dunmore Press, 1988.

Dawson, Selwyn. "God's Bullies." *Auckland Metro,* September 1985, 170–76.

Dayton, Donald W. *Theological Roots of Pentecostalism.* Studies in Evangelicalism 5. Metuchen, NJ; London: Scarecrow Press, 1987.

Department of Statistics. *1986 New Zealand Census of Population and Dwellings.* Wellington: Department of Statistics, 1988.

———. *New Zealand Census of Population and Dwellings, 1966.* Wellington: Department of Statistics, 1968.

———. *New Zealand Census of Population and Dwellings, 1971.* Wellington: Department of Statistics, 1974.

———. *New Zealand Census of Population and Dwellings, 1976.* Wellington: Department of Statistics, 1980.

———. *New Zealand Census of Population and Dwellings, 1981.* Wellington: Department of Statistics, 1983.

———. *New Zealand Population Census 1956.* Wellington: Government Printer, 1958.

———. *New Zealand Population Census 1961.* Wellington: Government Printer, 1964.

Destiny Church. "Protocols & Requirements Between Spiritual Father & His Spiritual Sons." [29 November 2009].

Destiny Churches. http://www.destinychurch.org.nz/ (accessed 21 March 2012).

Dirks, Tim. "Filmsite Movie Review: Little Caesar (1930)." http://www.filmsite.org/littc.html (accessed 14 June 2009).

Dobbie, Flo. *Land Aflame!* London: Hodder and Stoughton, 1972.

Dominion of New Zealand. *Dominion of New Zealand Population Census, 1926.* Wellington: Government Printer, 1928.

Dorothy [sic]. "The Hikoi of Hope." *NZine,* 16 October 1998. http://www.nzine.co.nz/hot/hikoi.html (accessed 17 May 2013).

Drummond, Andrew Landale. *Edward Irving and his circle; including some consideration of the "Tongues" Movement in the light of modern psychology.* London: James Clarke and Co., [1934].

Dryden, Gordon. "Episode 1: The Vicious Cycle." In *Where To Now?* Auckland: Tiger Films for the Pacific Foundation, 1991. TV1, 25 August 1991.

Du Plessis, David. *A Man Called Mr. Pentecost.* As told to Bob Slosser. Plainfield, NJ: Logos International, 1977.

Duhigg, Charles. "The Nation: Depression, You Say? Check Those Safety Nets." *New York Times,* 23 March 2008. www.nytimes.com/2008/03/23/weekinreview/23duhigg.html?pagewanted=all&_r=0 (accessed 14 August 2013).

Dunstall, Graeme. "The Social Pattern." In Rice, *Oxford History of New Zealand*, 451–81.

Edgar, S. L. *A Handful of Grain: The Centenary History of the Baptist Union of New Zealand*. Vol. 1, 1945–1982. Wellington: New Zealand Baptist Historical Society, 1982.

Elim Churches. http://www.elim.org.nz/about/church_locator.aspx (accessed 21 March 2012).

Elliott, Peter. "Nineteenth-Century Australian Charismata: Edward Irving's Legacy." *Pneuma: The Journal of the Society for Pentecostal Studies* 34, no. 1 (2012): 26–36.

Elsmore, Bronwyn. *Like Them That Dream: The Maori and the Old Testament*. Tauranga: Tauranga Moana Press, 1985.

———. *Mana from Heaven: A Century of Maori Prophets in New Zealand*. Tauranga: Moana Press, 1989.

Embley, Peter L. "The Early Development of the Plymouth Brethren," in Wilson, *Patterns of Sectarianism*, 213–43.

Entwhistle, F. R. "Baptism in the Spirit and Speaking in Tongues." *Latimer*, no. 25 (June 1966): 18–27.

Erdozain, Dominic. "Review-Article: 'Cause is not Quite What it Used to Be': The Return of Secularisation." *English Historical Review* 127, no. 525 (March 2012): 377–400.

Espinosa, Gastón. "Ordinary Prophet: William J. Seymour and the Azusa Street Revival." In Hunter and Robeck, *The Azusa Street Revival and Its Legacy*, 29–60.

Evans, John. "The New Christian Right in New Zealand." In Gilling, *"Be Ye Separate,"* 69–106.

Evans, Robert, and Roy McKenzie. *Evangelical Revivals in New Zealand: A History of Evangelical Revivals in New Zealand and an Outline of Some Basic Principles of Revivals*. Paihia: Colcom Press, 1999.

Evans, Tania. "God Almighty." *New Outlook*, January/February 1985, 22–30.

Executive Council, Representing the Board of Elders of the Pentecostal Church of N.Z. (Inc.). Minute Book 1934–1951. Wellington. Held by Wellington City Elim Church.

Farley, Edward and Peter C. Hodgson. "Scripture and Tradition." In *Christian Theology: An Introduction to its Traditions and Tasks*, eds. Peter C. Hodgson and Robert H. King, 2nd rev. and enlarged ed., 35–61. Philadelphia: Fortress Press, 1985.

Ferguson, Niall. "Episode 6: Work." In *Civilization: Is the West History?* Prime TV, 28 May 2013.

Ferris, A. J. *Armageddon is at the Doors*. Lower Hutt: Lower Hutt Branch of the British-Israel World Federation, [1934].

———. *British-Israel teaching Concerning the signs of the approaching end of the age*. Wellington: British-Israel World Federation, 1934.

———. *Why the British are Israel: Nine conclusive facts proving that the Anglo-Saxons represent the House of Israel of Scripture*. Lower Hutt: British-Israel World Federation, 1934.

Fowler, James W. *Stages of Faith: The Psychology of Human Development and the Quest for Meaning*. 1981; San Francisco: Harper, 1995.
Franzmann, Majella. "Australia, New Zealand and the Pacific Islands." In *Religious Studies: A Global View*, ed. Gregory D. Alles, 218–41. Abingdon: Routledge, 2008.
Frappell, Samantha. "Post-War Revivalism in Australia: the Mission to the Nation, 1953–1957." In Hutchinson and Piggin, *Reviving Australia*, 249–61.
Frost, Michael. "Is there any movement away from dualism within New Zealand Pentecostal faith and praxis?" CHTX480 Research Essay, University of Otago, 2010.
Fullerton, Douglas. "How Christianity came to South Yunnan." http://www.dofu.dk/pages/1a.%20How%20Christianity%20came%20to%20South%20Yunnan.pdf (accessed 29 July 2009; site now discontinued).
Galvin, Ray. "Learning from the Sects." In Ker and Sharpe, *Towards an Authentic New Zealand Theology*, 99–103.
Geering, Lloyd. *Christianity without God*. Wellington: Bridget Williams, 2002.
———. *Faith's New Age*. London: Collins, 1980.
———. *God in the New World*. London: Hodder and Stoughton, 1968.
———. *Tomorrow's God*. Wellington: Bridget Williams, 1994.
Gerlach, Luther P., and Virginia H. Hine. *People, Power, Change: Movements of Social Transformation*. Indianapolis: Bobbs-Merrill, 1970.
Gibbons, P. J. "The Climate of Opinion." In Rice, *Oxford History of New Zealand*, 308–36.
Gilling, Bryan D. "Retelling the Old, Old Story: A Study of Six Mass Evangelistic Missions in Twentieth-Century New Zealand." DPhil thesis in History, University of Waikato, 1990.
———. "Convinced Christians convincing convinced Christians? A Study of Attenders at a Luis Palau Crusade Meeting." In Pratt, *"Rescue the Perishing,"* 77–95.
———. "Mass Evangelism in Mid-Twentieth-Century New Zealand." In Pratt, *"Rescue the Perishing,"* 43–56.
———, ed. *"Be Ye Separate": Fundamentalism and the New Zealand Experience*. Waikato Studies in Religion 3. Hamilton: University of Waikato and Colcom Press, 1992.
Gordon, Richard. "Fear and Loathing and the Moral Majority." *Metro*, December 1985, 121–41.
Gospel Truth, June 1964–April 1965. BKRP, MS-3530/004. Hocken Library, Dunedin.
Gould, John. *The Rake's Progress? The New Zealand Economy Since 1945*. Auckland: Hodder and Stoughton, 1982.
Gray, Patrick. "'God is Dead' Controversy." *Religion: New Georgia Encyclopedia*. http://www.georgiaencyclopedia.org/nge/Article.jsp?id=h-861 (accessed 5 July 2012).
Grice, Robert E. *Apostle to the Nations: An Authorized Biography of A. S. Worley, a Man of Faith and Miracles*. Walhalla, SC: Faith Training Center, n.d.

Grigg, Viv. *The Spirit of Christ and the Postmodern City.* Glen Eden, Auckland: Urban Leadership Foundation, 2009.

Guy, Laurie. "'Spirit Possession' and 'Deliverance Ministry'" in the Auckland Assembly of God, 1970–1983." In *Spirit Possession, Theology and Identity: A Pacific Exploration*, ed. Elaine M. Wainwright, General Editor, with Philip Cuthbertson and Susan Smith, 209–40. Hindmarsh, SA: ATF Press, 2010.

———. "Miracles, Messiahs and the Media: The Ministry of A. H. Dallimore in Auckland in the 1930s." In *Signs, Wonders, Miracles: Representations of Divine Power in the Life of the Church.* Studies in Church History 41, eds. K. Cooper and J. Gregory, 453–63. Woodbridge: Ecclesiastical History Society, 2005.

———. "One of a Kind? The Auckland Ministry of A. H. Dallimore." *Australasian Pentecostal Studies*, no. 8 (July 2004), http://webjournals.ac.edu.au/journals/aps/issue-8/06-one-of-a-kind-the-auckland-ministry-of-a-h-dall/ (accessed 9 November 2011).

———. *Shaping Godzone: Public Issues and Church Voices in New Zealand 1840–2000.* Wellington: Victoria University Press, 2011.

Habermas, Jürgen. *Legitimation Crisis.* Translated by Thomas McCarthy. Boston: Beacon Press, 1975.

Hall, Margaret. "Today's Song for Tomorrow's Church: The Role Played by Contemporary Popular Music in Attracting Young People to Church." PhD thesis in Music, Griffith University: Queensland Conservatorium, 2006.

Harper, Blyth. "85,000 publicly witness by Marching for Jesus." *Challenge Weekly*, 21 October 1972, 2.

Harper, Jonathon. "The Church that's taking over Auckland." *Metro*, November 1983, 122–35.

Harper, Michael. *As at the Beginning: The Twentieth Century Pentecostal Revival.* London: Hodder and Stoughton, 1965.

Harrell, David Edwin, Jr. *All Things are Possible: The Healing and Charismatic Revivals in Modern America.* Bloomington, IN: Indiana University Press, 1975.

———. *Oral Roberts: An American Life.* Bloomington, IN: Indiana University Press, 1975.

Harrison, Paul. "Prophetic Ministry within Movements of the Modern-Day Church." CHTX480 Research Essay, University of Otago, 2003.

Heinz, Donald. "The Struggle to Define America." In Liebman and Wuthnow, *The New Christian Right*, 133–48.

Henderson, J. M. *Ratana: The Man, The Church, and the Political Movement.* Memoirs of the Polynesian Society, 36. 2nd ed., 36. Wellington: A. H. and A. W. Reed in association with the Polynesian Society, 1972.

Henderson, Mary. *From Glory to Glory: A History of the Timaru New Life Centre 1960–1980.* Timaru: Dove Print, 1980.

Heneghan, Tom. "Will Pew Muslim birth rate study finally silence the 'Eurabia' claim?" *Reuters Faithworld Blog.* Posted 27 January 2011. http://blogs. reuters.com/faithworld/2011/01/27/will-pew-muslim-birth-rate-study-finally-silence-the-eurabia-claim/ (accessed 1 June 2013).

Hill, Michael. "The Sectarian Contribution: The Decline of Church-based Spirituality and the Rise of Sectarianism." In Colless and Donovan, *Religion in New Zealand Society*, 119–42.

Hodgkinson, Eric. "The Independent Pentecostal Movement." Research Essay in New Zealand Religious History, Massey University, 1989 (handwritten). BKRP, MS-3530/019, Hocken Library, Dunedin.

Hollenweger, Walter J. *The Pentecostals*. Translated by R. A. Wilson. London: SCM Press, 1972.

Holt, Bradley. "Spiritualities of the Twentieth Century." In *The Story of Christian Spirituality: Two Thousand Years, from East to West*, ed. Gordon Mursell, 305–65. Oxford: Lion Publishing, 2001.

Houston, Hazel. *Being Frank: The Frank Houston Story*. London: Marshall Pickering, 1989.

Hudson, Winthrop S. *Religion in America*. New York: Charles Scribner's Sons, 1965.

Hunter, Harold D., and Cecil M. Robeck, Jr., eds. *The Azusa Street Revival and Its Legacy*. Cleveland, TN: Pathway Press, 2006.

Hutchinson, Darryl. "Rethinking Religion." In *The Nation*, TV3, 3 April 2010.

Hutchinson, Mark. "'Second Founder': A C Valdez Sr and Australian Pentecostalism." *Australasian Pentecostal Studies*, no. 11 (January 2009), http://webjournals.alphacrucis.edu.au/journals/aps/issue-11/02-second-founder-a-c-valdez-sr-and-australian-pen/ (accessed 2 June 2010).

———. "Edward Irving's Antipodean Shadow." *e:Oikonomia: The Sydney College of Divinity e-journal of theology, ministry and the arts* 3, no. 1 (April 2008), http://oikon.webjournals.org/articles/1/04/2008/7063.htm?id={756C09C7-58E5-41DC-9B5B-0F6C94A7EE79} (accessed 13 April 2009).

———, and Stewart Piggin, eds. *Reviving Australia: Essays on the History and Experience of Revival and Revivalism in Australian Christianity*. Studies in Australian Christianity 3. Sydney: Centre for the Study of Australian Christianity, 1994.

Hutchinson, Warner, and Cliff Wilson. *Let the People Rejoice*. Wellington: Crusader Bookroom Society, 1959.

IMDb. "Heavenly Creatures." http://www.imdb.com/title/tt0110005/ (accessed 20 August 2013).

———. "Rebel Without a Cause." http://www.imdb.com/title/tt0048545/ (accessed 20 August 2013).

International Convention of Faith Ministries. http://www.icfm.org/cgi-bin/gx.cgi/AppLogic+FTContentServer?pagename=FaithHighway/10000/1000/199/international_06#NewZealand (accessed 21 March 2012).

Ireton, Douglas B. "'O Lord How Long?': A Revival Movement in New Zealand 1920–1933." MA thesis in History, Massey University, 1986.

———. "A Time to Heal: The Appeal of Smith Wigglesworth in New Zealand 1922–24." BA (Hons.) dissertation in History, Massey University, 1984.

Jackson, H. R. *Churches and People in Australia and New Zealand 1860–1930.* Wellington: Allen and Unwin/Port Nicholson Press, 1987.

Jamieson, Alan. *A Churchless Faith: Faith journeys beyond evangelical, Pentecostal & charismatic churches.* Wellington: Philip Garside Publishing, 2001.

Jesus March: March for Righteousness, Auckland. "Executive Committee Statement of Purpose." Auckland, 1972, Ephemera Collection, Alexander Turnbull Library, Wellington. Mimeographed.

Johnston, William M. "The Spirituality Revolution and the the Process of Reconfessionalisation in the West Today." In Stenhouse and Knowles, *Christianity in the Post Secular West*, 143–61.

Jull, David. "The Knapdale Revival (1881): Social Context and Religious Conviction in 19th Century New Zealand." *Australasian Pentecostal Studies*, no. 7 (March 2003), http://webjournals.ac.edu.au/journals/aps/issue-7/02-the-knapdale-revival-1881-social-context-and-re/ (accessed 10 November 2011).

Kemp, Rev. Joseph. *How I was healed, or, A New Zealand miracle: An autobiographical sketch of Miss Fannie Lammas, Nelson, New Zealand.* Auckland: Book Room, [Baptist] Tabernacle, [1923].

Ker, John M., and Kevin J. Sharpe, eds. *Towards an Authentic New Zealand Theology.* Auckland: University of Auckland Chaplaincy Publishing Trust, 1984.

Keyzer, Robert. "A Christian Revolutionary." *New Zealand Listener*, 13 November 1972, 10–11.

King, Michael. "Between Two Worlds." In Rice, *Oxford History of New Zealand*, 285–307.

———. *The Penguin History of New Zealand.* Albany: Penguin, 2003.

King, Paul L. "Healing." In *The Encyclopedia of Christian Civilization. Volume II: E-L*, ed. George Thomas Kurian, 1099–1106. Oxford: Wiley-Blackwell, 2011.

Kirkup, James. "World facing worst financial crisis in history, Bank of England Governor says." *Telegraph*, 6 October 2011. http://www.telegraph.co.uk/finance/financialcrisis/8812260/World-facing-worst-financial-crisis-in-history-Bank-of-England-Governor-says.html (accessed 11 October 2011).

Knowles, Brett. "'From the Ends of the Earth We Hear Songs': Music as an Indicator of New Zealand Pentecostal Theology and Spirituality." *The Spirit and Church* 3, no. 2 (November 2001): 227–49.

———. "'From the Ends of the Earth We Hear Songs': Music as an Indicator of New Zealand Pentecostal Theology and Spirituality." *Australasian Pentecostal Studies*, no. 5–6 (April 2002), http://aps.webjournals.org/Issues.asp?index=9&id={CE149387-42E6-48C3-801C-7ED675022C60} (accessed 27 May 2005).

———. "'Vision of the Disinherited?' An examination of the expansion of the Neo-Pentecostal and Charismatic Movements in the 1960's and 1970's and a suggested hypothesis for the social causes of their growth." Paper presented at Post-Graduate Seminar, Department of History, University of Otago, Dunedin, 4 October 1989.

———. "Is the Future of Western Christianity a Pentecostal One? A Conversation with Harvey Cox." In Stenhouse and Knowles, *The Future of Christianity*, 39–59.

———. "Pentecostalism and the Future of Christianity in the West: Reflections on a Conversation." In Stenhouse and Knowles, *Christianity in the Post Secular West*, 177–207.

———. "Some Aspects of the History of the New Life Churches of New Zealand 1960–1990." PhD thesis in Church History, University of Otago, 1994.

———. "Transforming Pentecostalism: The Changing Shape of Pentecostalism in Aotearoa-New Zealand." Paper presented at the Empowered21 Global Scholars' Consultation, Alpha Crucis College, Parramatta, Sydney, 8–10 July 2013.

———. "Vision of the Disinherited? The Growth of the Pentecostal Movement in the 1960s, with particular reference to the New Life Churches of New Zealand." In Gilling, *"Be Ye Separate,"* 107–41.

———. Research Project on New Zealand Pentecostalism, 3 March 2013.

———. *The History of a New Zealand Pentecostal Movement: The New Life Churches of New Zealand from 1946 to 1979*. Studies in Religion and Society 45. Lewiston, NY: Edwin Mellen Press, 2000.

Knox, Bruce. "Christian Allegiance is Declining, Yet Theological Education is Booming." In Stenhouse and Knowles, *The Future of Christianity*, 73–87.

Kolig, Erich. "Coming through the Backdoor? Secularisation in New Zealand and Māori Religiosity." In Stenhouse and Knowles, *The Future of Christianity*, 183–204.

Land, Stephen J. "Pentecostal Spirituality: Living in the Spirit." In *Christian Spirituality: Post-Reformation and Modern*. World Spirituality: An Encyclopedic History of the Religious Quest, eds. Louis Dupré and Don E. Saliers, in collaboration with John Meyendorff, 18:479–99. New York: Crossroad, 1989.

Lasch, Christopher. *The Culture of Narcissism: American Life in an Age of Diminishing Expectations*. New York: W. W. Norton, 1977.

Leigh, Jack. "Getting Religion." *New Zealand Women's Weekly*, 8 July 1985, 59–62.

Liebman, Robert. "The Making of the New Christian Right." In Liebman and Wuthnow, *The New Christian Right*, 227–38.

———, and Robert Wuthnow. *The New Christian Right: Mobilization and Legitimation*. New York: Aldine Publishing Company, 1983.

Liebman, Robert, and Robert Wuthnow. "Introduction." In Liebman and Wuthnow, *The New Christian Right*, 1–9.

Life, "Photographic Essay, 'The third force in Christendom: gospel-singing, doomsday-preaching sects emerge as a mighty movement in world religion,' photographed for Life by Carl Mydans," 9 June 1958, 113–21.

Lindsay, Hal, and C. C. Carlson. *The Late Great Planet Earth*. Grand Rapids, MI: Zondervan, 1976.

Lineham, Peter J. "Brethren Revivalism: A Second Look at New Zealand." In *Growth of the Brethren Movement: National and International Experiences*.

Essays in Honour of Harold H. Rowdon, eds. Neil T. R. Dickson and Tim Grass, 154–75. Carlisle: Paternoster, 2006.

———. "Tongues must cease: The Brethren and the Charismatic Movement in New Zealand." *Christian Brethren Research Journal*, no. 34 (November 1983): 7–52.

———. "New Zealand Religious History, a Bibliography: Section Q-R-S." S.v. "Revivalism." http://www.massey.ac.nz/~plineham/RelhistNZ.htm (accessed 29 August 2012).

———. "The Rise and Significance of the Destiny Church." In Morrison et al., *Mana Māori and Christianity*, 111–37.

———. "Three Types of Church." In *Thinking Outside the Square*, eds. Ree Boddé and Hugh Kempster, 199–224. Auckland: St. Columba's Press & Journeyings, 2003.

———. "Wanna be in my gang?" *Listener*, 11–17 September 2004. http://www.listener.co.nz/uncategorized/wanna-be-in-my-gang/ (accessed 4 December 2013).

———. "When the Roll is Called Up Yonder, Who'll be There?" In Pratt, *"Rescue the Perishing,"* 1–22.

———. *Destiny: The Life and Times of a Self-Made Apostle*. Auckland: Penguin, 2013.

———. Review of *The History of a New Zealand Pentecostal Movement*, by Brett Knowles. *Stimulus* 10:1 (February 2002): 65.

Livingston, James C. *Modern Christian Thought: From the Enlightenment to Vatican II*. New York: Macmillan, 1971.

Logan, Neville. *"Excuse Me, I Have to Shoot the Guitarist": The Amazing Adventures of a Kiwi Cartoonist*. Christchurch: Kotuku Foundation, 1997.

Logos, August 1966.

Loryman, Gaynor. "Growth of the Pentecostal Movement: 'A new relationship with Christ'." *Christchurch Star*, 27 October 1973, 7.

Lyotard, Jean-François. *The Postmodern Condition: A Report on Knowledge*. Translated by Geoff Bennington and Brian Massumi, with foreword by Frederic Jameson. Manchester: Manchester University Press, 2004.

Ma, Wonsuk. "Pentecostal Eschatology: What Happened When the Wave Hit the West End of the Ocean." In Hunter and Robeck, *The Azusa Street Revival and Its Legacy*, 227–42.

Marquand, I. G. "The New Zealand Presbyterian New Life Movement: A Case Study in Church Growth." MTh thesis in Church History, University of Otago, 1977.

Martin, David. "Secularisation: Master Narrative or Several Stories?" In Stenhouse and Knowles, *Christianity in the Post Secular West*, 3–26.

———. *Pentecostalism: The World Their Parish*. Oxford: Blackwell, 2002.

Martin, Lloyd. *One Faith, Two Peoples: Communicating Across Cultures Within the Church*. 3rd ed. Paraparaumu: Salt Company Publishers, 2001.

Marty, Martin E. "Introduction: Religion in America 1935–1985." In *Altered Landscapes: Christianity in America 1935–1985*, eds. David W. Lotz, Donald

W. Shriver, Jr., and John F. Wilson, 1–16. Grand Rapids, MI: Eerdmans Publishing Company, 1989.
Marwick, Arthur. *The Sixties: Cultural Revolution in Britain, France, Italy and the United States, c.1958-c.1974*. Oxford: Oxford University Press, 1998.
Mason, Bruce. *The end of the golden weather: A voyage into a New Zealand childhood*. Wellington: Price Milburn, [1962].
Mathew, Thomson K., and Kimberly Ervin Alexander. "The Future of Healing Ministries." In Synan, *Spirit-Empowered Christianity in the 21st Century*, 313–36.
Matthews, Philip. "Gimme that big-time religion." *New Zealand Listener*, 23 November 2002, 28–30.
———. "True Believers." *New Zealand Listener*, 15 July 2000, 15–21.
Max Weber: On Charisma and Institution Building. Selected Papers. Edited and with an introduction by S.N. Eisenstadt. Chicago: University of Chicago Press, 1968.
Maxwell, David. "'Networks and Niches': The Worldwide Transmission of the Azusa Street Revival." In Hunter and Robeck, *The Azusa Street Revival and Its Legacy*, 127–39.
McCracken, Jill. "The God Squad." *New Zealand Listener*, 23 October 1972, 14–15.
McEldowney, Dennis, ed. *Presbyterians in Aotearoa 1840–1990*. Wellington: The Presbyterian Church of New Zealand, 1990.
McGrath, Alister E. *Christian Theology*. 2nd ed. Oxford: Blackwell, 1999.
McGregor, Fay. *My Testimony*. Auckland: Fayth Russell, 2006.
McIntyre, W. David. "From Dual Dependency to Nuclear Free." In Rice, *Oxford History of New Zealand*, 520–38.
McLeod, Hugh. *The Religious Crisis of the 1960s*. Oxford: Oxford University Press, 2007.
McRobie, Alan. "The Politics of Volatility, 1972–1991." In Rice, *Oxford History of New Zealand*, 385–411.
Merritt, N. F. H. *To God Be The Glory: The First Ten and a Half Years of the Charismatic Movement at St. Paul's*. Auckland: St. Paul's Outreach Trust, 1981.
Mews, Stuart. "The Revival of Spiritual Healing in the Church of England 1920–26." In Shiels, *The Church and Healing*, 299–331.
Millard, Edward C. *The Same Lord: An Account of the Mission Tour of the Rev. George C. Grubb in Australia, Tasmania and New Zealand From April 3rd 1891, to July 7th, 1892*. London: E. Marlborough, 1893.
———. *What God Hath Wrought: An Account of the Mission Tour of the Rev G. C. Grubb, M.A. (1889–1890) Chiefly From the Diary Kept by E. C. Millard One of His Companions, in Ceylon, South Africa, Australia, New Zealand, Cape Colony*. London: E. Marlborough, 1891.
Miller, Donald E. "Pentecostalism and Social Transformation." In Hunter and Robeck, *The Azusa Street Revival and Its Legacy*, 335–48.
Miller, Edward. *Thy God Reigneth: The Story of the Revival in Argentina*. Burbank, CA: World Missionary Assistance Plan, 1968.

Moetara, Simon. "An exploration of notions of Māori leadership and a consideration of their contribution for Christian leadership in the Church of Aotearoa-New Zealand today." MTh dissertation in Theology, Laidlaw College/Tyndale Graduate School of Theology, 2009.

———. "Māori and Pentecostal Christianity in Aotearoa New Zealand." In Morrison et al., *Mana Māori and Christianity*, 73–90.

Morris, Paul. "Introduction." In *The Lloyd Geering Reader: Prophet of Modernity*, eds. Paul Morris and Mike Grimshaw, 8–22. Wellington: Victoria University Press, 2007.

Morrison, Hugh, Lachy Paterson, Brett Knowles and Murray Rae, eds. *Mana Māori and Christianity*. Wellington: Huia Publishing, 2012.

Muldoon, R. D. *The Rise and Fall of a Young Turk.* Wellington: A. H. and A. W. Reed, 1974.

Murray, Laurie. *Where to World 1977?* Palmerston North: By the author, 1977.

National Jesus Festival News No.1, 1 August 1972.

Neil, Allan G. "Institutional Churches and the Charismatic Renewal: A Study of the Charismatic Renewal in the Anglican Church and the Roman Catholic Church in New Zealand." STh Diploma in Church History, Joint Board of Theological Studies, 1974.

Network of Christian Ministries Churches. http://www.thenetwork.org.nz/thenetwork/Members.html (accessed 21 March 2012).

New Frontiers Churches. http://www.newfrontierstogether.org/Groups/103229/Newfrontiers/Worldwide/New_Zealand/New_Zealand.aspx (accessed 21 March 2012).

New Life Churches of New Zealand. http://newlife.org.nz/churches/ (accessed 21 March 2012).

New Zealand Broadcasting Corporation. *I Believe: A Series of Talks Broadcast over NZBC Stations in 1967.* [Wellington]: New Zealand Broadcasting Corporation, [1968].

New Zealand Evangel, 6 June 1924–[December 1972]. Microfiche. Hocken Library, Dunedin.

New Zealand Methodist, "Editorial: Limping for Jesus," 4 May 1972, 2.

———, "Letters to the Editor," 18 May–15 June 1972.

New Zealand Parliamentary Debates. vol. 324 (September 1960).

———. vol. 466 (September 1985).

Newman, Keith. "Rātana, the Prophet: Mā te wā—the Sign of the Broken Watch." In Morrison et al., *Mana Māori and Christianity*, 243–63.

———. *Ratana Revisited: An Unfinished Legacy*. Auckland: Reed, 2006.

———. *Rātana: The Prophet*. North Shore: Penguin, 2009.

Ng, Sik Hung. *The Social Psychology of Power*. European Monographs in Social Psychology 21. London: Academic Press, 1980.

Nichol, John Thomas. *The Pentecostals [formerly Pentecostalism]*. Plainfield, NJ: Logos International, 1966.

Niebuhr, H. Richard. *The Social Sources of Denominationalism*. 1929; New York: Meridian Books, 1959.

Office of the Registrar-General. *Results of a Census of the Colony of New Zealand taken for the night of the 31st March, 1901.* Wellington: Government Printer, 1902.

———. *Results of a Census of the Colony of New Zealand taken for the night of the 29th April, 1906.* Wellington: Government Printer, 1907.

———. *Results of a Census of the Dominion of New Zealand taken for the night of the 2nd April, 1911.* Wellington: Government Printer, 1912.

Office of Treaty Settlements: Te Tari Whakatau Take e pa ana ki te Tiriti o Waitangi. "Settlement Progress: Claims Progress." http://www.ots.govt.nz/ (accessed 13 May 2013).

Offiler, W. H. *God and His Bible or the Harmonies of Divine Revelation.* Seattle, WA: Bethel Temple, Inc., 1946.

———. *God, and His Name.* Seattle, WA: Temple Publishing House, [1932].

Offiler, W. H. *The Majesty of the Symbol, or Bible Astronomy.* Seattle, WA: By the Author, 1933.

Oldham, Dale. "First Impressions." *Latimer*, no. 25 (June 1966): 14–18.

Oliver, W. H. "The Awakening Imagination 1940–1980." In Rice, *Oxford History of New Zealand*, 539–70.

Orwell, George. *Animal Farm.* Fairfield, IA: 1st World Library Literary Society, 2005.

Osborne, John, ed. *The Winds of the Spirit: An Introductory Study on the Charismatic Movement.* Auckland: Methodist Board of Publications, 1974.

OVGuide. "Bill Van Rij Video—Interviews." http://www.ovguide.com/bill-van-rij-9202a8c04000641f80000000006b160e# (accessed 17 May 2013).

Paproth, Darrell. "Revivalism in Melbourne from Federation to World War I: the Torrey-Alexander-Chapman Campaigns." In Hutchinson and Piggin, *Reviving Australia*, 143–69.

Pentecostal Messenger, December 1943. BKRP, MS-3530/006. Hocken Library, Dunedin.

Perry, Stuart. *Indecent Publication Control in New Zealand.* Wellington: McCrae Publishers, 1975.

Pew Research Center. "The Future of the Global Muslim Population: Projections for 2010–2030." *Forum on Religion and Public Life*, January 2011. http://www.pewforum.org/The-Future-of-the-Global-Muslim-Population.aspx (accessed 1 June 2013).

Pierard, Richard V. "Civil Religion: Parallel Development or Replacement for Traditional Christianity in the West." In Stenhouse and Knowles, *Christianity in the Post Secular West*, 163–76.

Pilgrim, David. "The Golliwog Caricature." Jim Crow Museum of Racist Memorabilia, Ferris State University, MI. http://www.ferris.edu/news/jimcrow/golliwog/ (accessed 1 September 2011).

Pollock, John. *Billy Graham: The Authorised Biography.* London: Hodder and Stoughton, 1966.

Pratt, Douglas, ed. *"Rescue the Perishing": Comparative Perspectives on Evangelicalism and Revivalism.* Waikato Studies in Religion 1. Auckland: College Communications, 1989.

Pringle, Phil. "Rise Up (You People of Power)." Lyrics at Wesley Methodist Church Klang. http://www.klangwesley.com/songs.php?songID=288 (accessed 22 May 2013).

Quebedeaux, Richard. *The Worldly Evangelicals*. San Francisco: Harper and Row, 1978.

Read, Ralph R. *Water Baptism: The Formula and its Meaning. A Study of the Trinitarian Formula of Matthew 28 v.19 and the Formula of "Oneness" Teachers: A Guide and a Refutation*. [Christchurch]: New Zealand Pentecostal Fellowship Publication, [1966]. Copy held in BKRP, MS-3530/022. Hocken Library, Dunedin.

Reed Essential Māori Dictionary [Te Papakupu Taketake a Reed]: Māori-English/English-Māori. Auckland: Reed Publishing, 1999.

Reidy, M. T. Vincent, and James T. Richardson. "Roman Catholic Neo-Pentecostalism: The New Zealand Experience." *Australia and New Zealand Journal of Sociology*, no. 14 (1978): 222–30.

Revival News, March 1962–December 1966. BKRP, MS-3530/001. Hocken Library, Dunedin.

Rice, Geoffrey W., ed. *Oxford History of New Zealand*. 2nd ed. Auckland: Oxford University Press, 1996.

Richmann, Christopher J. "Prophecy and Politics: British-Israelism in American Pentecostalism." *Cyberjournal for Pentecostal Research*, no. 22 (January 2013), http://www.pctii.org/cyberj/cyberj22/richmann.html (accessed 14 August 2013).

Riddell, Mike. "Beyond Ground Zero: Resourcing Faith in a Post-Christian Era." In Stenhouse and Knowles, *The Future of Christianity*, 215–30.

Rise Up Together New Zealand, "Report," July/September 1990, 9.

———, "Strategy Report," January/March 1990, 8–9.

Riss, Richard M. *Latter Rain: The Latter Rain Movement of 1948 and the Mid-Twentieth Century Evangelical Awakening*. Etobicoke, ON, Canada: Honeycomb Visual Productions, 1987.

Roberts, H. V. *New Zealand's Greatest Revival*. Auckland: New Zealand Pelorus Press, 1951. Copy held in BKRP, MS-3530/005. Hocken Library, Dunedin.

Roberts, Oral. *If you need Healing, Do these Things*. Tulsa, OK: Healing Waters, 1947.

Robinson, John A. T. *Honest to God*. London: SCM Press, 1963.

Rogers, Owen. "The New Zealand Presbyterian New Life Movement." BD dissertation in Church History, University of Otago, 1990.

Rowe, Keith. "Clergy for Rowling—the Almost Politicians." In *Dialogue on Religion: New Zealand Viewpoints 1977*, eds. Peter Davis and John Hinchcliff, 31–35. Auckland: University of Auckland, 1977.

Rudman, Brian. "For God and National." *New Zealand Listener*, 28 March 1987, 28–29.

Russell, Richard. "The growing crisis of the Evangelical world-view and its resolutions." MA thesis in Theology and Religious Studies, Bristol University, 1973.

Ryan, Allanah. "'For God, Country and Family': Populist Moralism and the New Zealand Moral Right." MA thesis in Education, Massey University, 1986.
———. "Remoralising Politics." In *Revival of the Right: New Zealand Politics in the 1980s*, eds. Bruce Jesson, Allanah Ryan and Paul Spoonley, 56–85. Auckland: Heinemann Reed, 1988.
Samoan Assemblies of God Churches in New Zealand. http://en.wikipedia.org/wiki/Samoan_Assemblies_of_God_churches_in_New_Zealand (accessed 21 February 2013).
Sanford, Agnes. *The Healing Light*. 8th ed. St. Paul, MN: Macalester Park Publishing Co., [1949].
Schrader, Ben. "1981 Springbok Tour: Tom and my 'cold war'." *Te Ara Signposts*. Posted 6 September 2011. http://blog.teara.govt.nz/2011/09/06/1981-springbok-tour-tom-and-my-cold-war/ (accessed 5 March 2013).
Scott, John, and Marshall, Gordon, eds. *A Dictionary of Sociology*. 3rd rev. ed. New York: Oxford University Press, 2009.
Shakarian, Demos, and John and Elizabeth Sherrill. *The Happiest People on Earth*. Old Tappan, NJ: Spire Books, 1975.
Shaw, Trevor, comp. *The Jesus Marchers 1972*. Auckland: Challenge Publishers, 1972.
Sherrill, John L. *They Speak with Other Tongues*. New York: McGraw Hill, [1964].
Shiels, W.J., ed. *The Church and Healing: Papers read at the twentieth Summer meeting and the twenty-first Winter meeting of the Ecclesiastical History Society*. Studies in Church History 19. Oxford: Basil Blackwell, 1982.
Shirres, Michael P. *Te Tangata: The Human Person*. Auckland: Accent Publications, 1997.
Shortland, Edward. *Maori Religion and Mythology*. London: Longmans, Green and Co., 1882.
Simpson, Tony. *The Sugarbag Years: An Oral History of the 1930s Depression in New Zealand*. 2nd ed. Auckland: Hodder and Stoughton, 1984.
Sinclair, Keith. *A History of New Zealand*. Rev. ed. Harmondsworth: Penguin, 1984.
Soltau, George. *The Inquiry Room: Hints for Dealing with the Anxious*. London: Morgan and Scott, 1884. http://www.inquiryroom.com/the_inquiry_room_by_george_soltau.htm (accessed 31 August 2013).
———. *The Person and Work of the Holy Spirit*. London: Jas. Nisbet, [1920?].
———. *The Person and Work of the Holy Spirit*. The "Bible-Talk" Series 1. London: John F. Shaw and Co., [1886].
St. John, Susan. "Ten Years on from the Hikoi of Hope." Child Poverty Action Group, 21 September 2008. http://www.cpag.org.nz/resources/presentations/10-years-on-from-the-hikoi-of-hope/ (accessed 17 May 2013).
Statistics New Zealand—Tatauranga Aotearoa. *2006 Census of Population and Dwellings: National Summary*. Wellington: Statistics New Zealand—Tatauranga Aotearoa, 2006. http://www.stats.govt.nz/Census/_2006Census HomePage/classification-counts-tables/about-people/religious-affiliation.aspx (accessed 11 December 2013).

———. *2013 Census totals by topic.* Wellington: Statistics New Zealand—Tatauranga Aotearoa, 2013. http://www.stats.govt.nz/Census/2013-census/data-tables/total-by-topic.aspx (accessed 11 December 2013).

Statistics New Zealand—Te Tari Tatau. *2001 Census of Population and Dwellings: National Summary.* Wellington: Statistics New Zealand—Te Tari Tatau, 2002. www.stats.govt.nz/Census/2001-census-data/2001-census-national-summary.aspx (accessed 11 December 2003).

Steel, Natalie. *Milton Smith: A Man After God's Heart.* Auckland: Castle Publishing, 2003.

Stenhouse, John. "God's Own Silence: Secular Nationalism, Christianity and the Writing of New Zealand History." *New Zealand Journal of History* 38, no. 1 (2004): 52–71.

———, and Brett Knowles, eds. *Christianity in the Post Secular West.* Hindmash, SA: ATF Press, 2007.

Stenhouse, John, and Brett Knowles, eds. *The Future of Christianity: Historical, Sociological, Political and Theological Perspectives from New Zealand.* ATF Series 11. Assisted by Antony Wood. Adelaide: ATF Press, 2004.

Stern, Fritz, ed. *The Varieties of History From Voltaire to the Present.* New York: Meridian Books, 1956.

Stormont, George. *Smith Wigglesworth: A Man Who Walked with God.* Chichester: Sovereign World, 1990.

Strachan, C. Gordon. *The Pentecostal Theology of Edward Irving.* London: Darton, Longman and Todd, 1973.

Stratford, Stephen. "Christians Awake! Join the National Party, Save New Zealand." *Metro,* November 1986, 124–37.

Strickland, D. R. "Church growth Analysis: the fastest growing and declining Presbyterian churches in New Zealand." Typescript, Titirangi, 1985.

Synan, Vinson. "The Charismatic Renewal After Fifty Years." In Synan, *Spirit-Empowered Christianity in the 21st Century,* 7–24.

———. *The Holiness-Pentecostal Tradition: Charismatic Movements in the Twentieth Century.* 2nd ed. Grand Rapids, MI: William B. Eerdmans, 1997.

———, ed. *Spirit-Empowered Christianity in the 21st Century.* Lake Mary, FL: Charisma House, 2011.

Szakolczai, Arpad. "Charisma." In *Encyclopedia of Social Theory,* eds. Austin Harrington, Barbara I. Marshall and Hans-Peter Müller, 52–54. London and New York: Routledge, 2006.

Tamaki, Brian. *Bishop Brian Tamaki: More than meets the eye.* Pakuranga, Auckland: Tamaki Publications, 2006.

Taylor, Nancy M. *Official History of New Zealand in the Second World War, 1939–45. The New Zealand People at War: The Home Front, Volume II.* Wellington: Historical Publications Branch, Department of Internal Affairs 1986.

Te Aka Māori-English, English-Māori Dictionary and Index. http://www.maoridictionary.co.nz/ (accessed 10 September 2013).

The Special Committee on Moral Delinquency in Children and Adolescents. *Report of the Special Committee on Moral Delinquency in Children and*

Adolescents. Appendix to the Journals of the House of Representatives of New Zealand; H.47. Wellington: Government Printer, 1954.
Thompson, R. J. "Sects in New Zealand." In Ker and Sharpe, *Towards an Authentic New Zealand Theology*, 89–97.
Thompson, Willie. *Postmodernism and History*. Houndmills, Basingstoke, Hants.: Palgrave Macmillan, 2004.
3 *News*, "Big Boi's NZ Golliwog Encounter," 26 August 2011. http://www.3news.co.nz/Big-Bois-NZ-Golliwog-encounter/tabid/418/ articleID/223634/ Default.aspx (accessed 1 September 2011).
Toomer, M. "National Church Leader 'walks with his people'." *Challenge Weekly*, 8 May 1996.
Trading Economics. "New Zealand Government Budget." January 1990–June 2013. http://www.tradingeconomics.com/new-zealand/government-budget (accessed 5 June 2013).
Troughton, Geoffrey M. "Christianity and Community: Aspects of Religious Life and Attitudes in the W[h]anganui-Manawatu Region, 1870–1885." MA thesis in History, Massey University, 1995.
Van Dusen, Henry P. "Force's Lessons for Others." *Life*, 9 June 1958, 122–24.
Vineyard Churches. http://www.vineyard.org.nz/styled/page5.html (accessed 21 March 2012).
Waldegrave, C. T. "Social and Personality Correlates of Pentecostalism: A Review of the Literature and a Comparison of Pentecostal Christian Students with Non-Pentecostal Christian Students." BPhil dissertation in Educational Psychology, University of Waikato, 1972.
Walker, Ranginui J. "Māori People since 1950." In Rice, *Oxford History of New Zealand*, 498–519.
Wallis, Roy, and Richard Bland. "Purity in Danger: A survey of participants in a moral crusade rally." *British Journal of Sociology*, no. 30 (June 1979): 188–205.
Walton, John. *The Walton Story: John Walton's Memoirs*. 3rd ed. Palmerson North: John Walton, 2012. Kindle Edition.
Ward, Kevin. "'No Longer Believing'—or—'Believing without Belonging'." In Stenhouse and Knowles, *The Future of Christianity*, 60–72.
———. "The charismatic movement in New Zealand: Sovereign move of God or cultural captivity of the gospel?" Paper presented at University of Otago Seminar, Dunedin, 2010.
———. "Towards 2015: the future of mainline Protestantism in New Zealand." *Journal of Beliefs and Values* 27, no. 1 (April 2006): 13–23.
———. "Will We Find Church in a Future New Zealand?" In Stenhouse and Knowles, *Christianity in the Post Secular West*, 209–38.
———. *The Church in Post-Sixties New Zealand: Decline, Growth and Change*. Archer Studies in Pacific Christianity. Auckland: Archer Press, 2013.
Weber, Max. "The Nature of Charismatic Domination." In *Max Weber: Selections in Translation*, ed. W. G. Runciman. Translated by E. Matthews, 226–50. Cambridge: Cambridge University Press, 1978.

Wellington Pentecostal Evangelical Mission. Minute Book 8 July 1942–3 December 1951. Wellington. Held by Wellington City Elim Church.

Whitley, H. C. *Blinded Eagle: An Introduction to the Life and Teaching of Edward Irving*. London: SCM Press, 1955.

Whittaker, Colin C. *Seven Pentecostal Pioneers*. Basingstoke, Hants: Marshall, Morgan and Scott, 1983.

Wilkerson, David. *The Cross and the Switchblade*. With John and Elizabeth Sherrill. 1963; London: Hodder and Stoughton, 1967.

William Branham Home Page. "The Pillar of Fire Photographed." http://www.williambranhamhomepage.org/lhoust.htm (accessed 26 November 2013).

Williamson, Dale. "An Uncomfortable Engagement: The Charismatic Movement in the New Zealand Anglican Church 1965–85." PhD thesis in Church History, University of Otago, 2008.

Wilson, Bryan. *Religion in Secular Society: A Sociological Comment*. London: C. A. Watts, 1966.

———. "The Pentecostalist Minister: Role Conflicts and Contradictions of Status." In Wilson, *Patterns of Sectarianism*, 138–57.

———, ed. *The Social Dimensions of Sectarianism: Sects and New Religious Movements in Contemporary Society*. Oxford: Clarendon, 1990.

———, ed. *Patterns of Sectarianism: Organization and Ideology in Social and Religious Movements*. London: Heinemann, 1967.

Wilson, Marc. "Handing out reality checks." *New Zealand Listener*, 2–8 February 2013. http://www.listener.co.nz/lifestyle/psychology/handing-out-reality-checks/ (accessed 1 May 2013).

———. *You can't go home again*. Harmondsworth: Penguin, c.1940.

Wolfe, Tom. "The 'Me' Decade and the Third Great Awakening." *New York*, 23 August 1976. http://nymag.com/news/features/45938/ (accessed 1 May 2013).

Woodard, Christopher. *A Doctor Heals by Faith*. London: Max Parrish, 1953.

———. *A Doctor's Faith Holds Fast*. London: Max Parrish, 1955.

Worsfold, James E. *A History of the Charismatic Movements in New Zealand, including a Pentecostal Perspective and a Breviate of the Catholic Apostolic Church in Great Britain*. Bradford: Julian Literature Trust, 1974.

———. *The Reverend and Mrs Edward and Eily Weston*. New Zealand Apostolic Pioneer Breviate Series 1. Wellington: Julian Literature Trust, 1994.

———. *The Reverend Gilbert and Mrs Alice White*. New Zealand Apostolic Pioneer Breviate Series 2. Wellington: Julian Literature Trust, 1995.

Worsfold, W. Luke. "Subsequence, Prophecy and Church Order in the Apostolic Church, New Zealand." DPhil thesis in Religious Studies, Victoria University of Wellington, 2004.

Yeats, William Butler. "The Second Coming." In *Michael Robartes and the Dancer, by William Butler Yeats*, 19–20. Churchtown, Dundrum, Ireland: Cuala Press, 1920.

Yska, Redmer. *All Shook Up: The Flash Bodgie and the Rise of the New Zealand Teenager in the Fifties*. Auckland: Penguin, 1993.

Name Index

Acton, Lord 242
Adams, John A.D. .... xvii, 8–12, 22, 23, 43
Ahlstrom, Sydney 74
Alexander, Charles M. 22
Alexander, Kimberley 76
Allen, A. A. 76
Anderson, Robert Mapes 143
Ansley, Bruce 189
Arnold, R. Louis 93
Arrowsmith, David 153
Augustine of Hippo 137
Austin, Denise 181
Bailey, Mr. and Mrs. 11
Balfour, David 125
Banks, John 72, 79
Barrett, David 122
Bartleman, Frank 29, 34, 48
Barton, Dennis 173
Battley, Donald 123, 126, 161, 163, 193, 194, 212, 236
Baumann, Zygmunt 138
Baxter, Ern 161, 176
Baxter, James K. .... xix, 243
Bennett, Dennis 123, 125, 126
Bensley, Mike 97
Benson-Pope, David 231
Berendsen, Carl 67
Berger, Peter 241
Beyer, Georgina 232
Bilby, Ian 8, 170, 191, 218
Blair, Colin and Lyn xix
Bloomfield, Ray 96, 97, 100, 101, 114, 124
Blumhofer, Edith 126, 144

Boddy, A. A. 19
Bolger, Jim 211
Bolitho, Elaine 126, 163
Booth, Herbert 9, 20
Bosch, David 3
Boston, Jonathan 214
Bosworth, F. F. 10, 11
Braddock, Henry 18
Branham, William 72, 75, 76, 97, 101
Brash, Don 187, 234
Brown, Colin 152, 163, 171
Brown, Vin 51, 71, 72, 97
Bruce, Hugh H. 28, 43
Buchanan, W. A. 20
Burrow, Allan 120
Capill, Graham 215
Capone, Al 17
Carew, Philip 96, 172, 193, 234
Carr, Clyde 115
Carr, E. H. 138
Cartwright, Sylvia 218
Cathcart, William 49, 54
Chal, Kelly 234
Chambers, Jim 100
Chan, Simon 199, 237
Chandler, Trevor 124, 125
Chant, Barry 9, 10, 43, 48, 71
Chapman, J. Wilbur 22
Chapman, Robert 109, 110
Chaves, Mark 239
Cho, David (Paul) Yonggi 193, 242
Churchill, Winston 66
Clark, Helen 212, 218, 230, 235

Clark, Ian 6, 20, 26, 29, 30, 33, 52, 55, 56, 70, 93, 95, 96, 110, 117–19, 123, 161, 170–72, 176–78, 180, 192, 195, 198, 219, 237
Clarke, Ali .... xviii, xix, 249
Coady, Ron 74, 95, 97, 98, 116, 123, 125
Coates, Gerald 218
Cobb, A. J. 28
Coe, Jack 76
Collins, Paul 116
Coney, Sandra 171
Conner, Kevin 95, 121
Cookson, J. E. 69, 70
Cooper, Dudley 177
Cooper, Tim xviii
Cooper, Whina .... xv, 186, 214
Cox, Harvey 141, 190
Cullen, Ivor 93
Currie, Bruce and Lesley xix
Cutten, E. C. 46, 47
Dallimore, A. H. 45–47, 49, 51, 52, 56, 70, 97, 263
Darroch, Murray 51
Davidson, Allan 90, 231
Davies, Ross 220, 221
Dayton, Donald 7
de Bres, Joris 1
de Jong, Paul 219, 242
Dennehy, Cecil 161, 162
Diana, Princess of Wales 87
Dickson, A. S. 54
Douglas, John 195
Douglas, Roger 188, 210
Douglas, Stan 121
Dowie, John Alexander 7, 8, 10, 45, 235
Drummond, Henry 8
du Plessis, David 123, 144
Duff, Oliver 68
Duncan, Mick 231
Dunk, Gilbert T. S. 94, 177
Dunn, Don 176
Dunne, Peter 215, 234, 235
Dunstall, Graeme 66, 143
Edinburgh, Duke of 87

Edmonds, David 120
Edmondson, Al 72, 73
Edward VIII, King 47
Eisenhower, Dwight D. 75
Elias, Sian 218
Elizabeth II, Queen 186, 209
Ellis, David 175
Ellis, J. 10
Erdozain, Dominic 141
Eusebius of Caesarea xviii
Evans, John 155
Farley, Edward 139, 142
Faupel, D. William xviii
Ferrell, Harvey 97
Ferris, A. J. 51
Finch, Benny 97
Flett, Miss 54
Forbes, George 42
Forbes, Judith xix
Fowler, James W. 219
Frater, Wilf 145
Fullerton, John 19, 20
Fullerton, Martha 19, 20
Galvin, Ray 169
Gee, Donald 33, 75
Geering, Lloyd 113, 140
Gerlach, Luther 47, 122
Gilling, Bryan 91
Glover, Kelso 27, 30
Gould, John 87
Goulton, Mark (Marcus) 177
Goulton, Ron 196
Graham, Billy 75, 90–92, 95, 100, 111, 113, 143, 157
Greenway, A. L. 52, 55
Greenwood, C. L. 121
Grigg, Viv 154, 193, 197, 198, 212, 217, 236
Grubb, George 6
Gutschlag, Ivan 170
Guy, Laurie 192, 199, 222
Habermas, Jürgen 140, 142
Hames, Eric 126
Harper, Blyth 158, 160
Harper, Michael 123, 125, 126
Harrell, David Edwin, Jnr. 75

Harris, Leo 51, 72, 93
Harrison, Ken 238
Harrison, Paul 223
Hayford, Jack 176, 177
Hegel, Georg W. F. 138
Hewitt, Isaac 54
Hewitt, John H. 54, 55
Hezmalhalch, Tom 10, 11
Hicks, Tommy 97, 98, 101, 115
Hickson, James Moore 18, 25
Hill, Michael 171
Hine, Virginia 47, 122
Hodgkinson, Eric 127
Hodgson, Peter 139, 142
Hollenweger, Walter 73, 76
Holmes, Cecil 68, 88
Holyoake, Keith 42, 109
Houston, Brian 242
Houston, Frank 96, 97, 100, 101, 114, 117–19, 123–28, 144, 171, 174, 177, 180, 193–95, 198, 219
Houston, Hazel 95
Howard-Browne, Rodney 221
Hudson, Winthrop 74
Hughes, Ray 195
Hugo, Victor 2
Hulme, Juliet 88, 89
Humbard, Rex 76
Hunt, Ian 97, 99, 116
Hunt, Mavis 99
Hutchinson, Mark .... xvii, 7, 10, 26, 143
Ireton, Douglas B. 17, 18
Irving, Edward 5–7, 10
Iti, Tame 234
Jackson, David 95, 125
Jackson, Hugh 17, 18
Jackson, Peter 88
Jackson, Ray 72–74, 79, 94, 121, 175
Jacobson, Miss 11
James, Colin 185
Jamieson, Alan 219, 239, 240
Jeffreys, Stephen 33
Johnson, Everett 116
Johnson, Neville 171, 176, 194, 196
Jones, Len J. 31, 55, 77
Jull, Sandi xix
Keane, J. W. 173
Kearney, Shaun 176
Kemp, Joseph 18
Kenana, Rua 232
King, Michael 67, 109, 157
Knight, Gary 186
Knowles, Adrienne .... xix, 303
Knox, Bruce 140
Kuhlman, Kathryn 76
Lake, John G. 10, 11, 45, 47, 51
Lammas, Fannie 18
Lancaster, Sarah Jane 20, 26, 27, 48, 49
Land, Stephen 126
Lange, David 179, 188, 214
Lawrence, D. H. 111
Lee, Graeme 189, 215
Leonard, Mrs. 11
Lewis, Richard 234
Liebman, Robert 155
Lind, Abraham 12, 23, 24
Lindsay, Gordon 76
Lindsay, Hal 155
Lineham, Peter ..... xvii, xviii, 7, 95, 117, 124, 169, 232, 235, 236, 239, 241
Loryman, Gaynor 171
Lovatt, C. J. 28
Lyotard, Jean-François 137, 138
Ma, Wonsuk 155
MacFarlane, Andrew 119
Mandus, Brother 100
Marsh, Janet xix
Marshall, Cecil 100
Marshall, Joseph 9
Martin, David 140, 141, 159
Marty, Martin 2, 200
Marwick, Arthur 109, 111
Marx, Karl 138, 142
Mason, Bruce 87
Massey, William Ferguson 50
Mathew, Thomson 76
Maxwell, David 12

Mazengarb, Oswald, QC 88, 89
McAlpine, Campbell 124, 125
McBain, Douglas 222
McCabe, Joshua 54, 55
McCarthy, Joseph 68, 74
McDonald, Bruce 198
McGill, Bruce 161
McGill, John 161
McGregor, Bruce 98
McGregor, Fay 98
McLeod, Hugh 113
McPherson, Aimee Semple 23, 45
Midgley, Robert (Bob) 93, 123, 127, 144
Milbank, John 140
Miller, Gordon 193
Moetara, Simon 198, 221, 241
Monk, Bruce 221
Moody, Dwight L. 8
Morling, G. H. 120
Morrow, Anne 171
Morrow, Peter 95, 115, 123, 125–27, 161, 162, 177, 197, 201, 220, 236
Mortlock, Peter 232, 242, 265
Muldoon, Robert 151–53, 178, 185, 187, 202
Müller, George 7
Murray, Laurie 95
Mussolini, Benito 48
Mustapha Kemal, Pasha 48
Nee, Watchman 174
Neil, Allan 125
Niebuhr, H. Richard 2
North, Dr J. J. 21, 22
Offiler, W. H. 73, 74
Oliver, W. H. 152
O'Regan, Sir Tipene 210
Ortiz, Juan Carlos 174, 175
Orwell, George 145
Osborn, T. L. 76, 77, 97, 101
Parham, Charles Fox 6, 9, 29, 51
Parker, Honora 88
Parker, Pauline 88, 89

Pennington, E.E. 24, 29, 73
Perón, Juan 97
Peters, Winston 211
Phillips, Jock 65, 79, 88
Pollock, John 92
Poloma, Margaret 221
Price, Charles S. 45, 75
Pytches, David 199
Quebedeaux, Richard 200
Ranaghan, Kevin 162
Ranchord, Rasik 157, 158, 175, 176, 178
Rātana, Tahupōtiki Wiremu ..... xv, 18, 215, 232, 234
Read, Ralph 118, 120–22, 126, 144
Reid, Andrew 11, 21
Reidy, M. T. Vincent 162
Richardson, James 162
Richardson, Ruth 210
Roberts, H. V. 8, 20, 21, 23, 24, 27, 29, 34, 73, 121
Roberts, Henry 8, 9, 20–22, 24, 25
Roberts, Oral 75–77, 98–101, 115
Rogerson, Freddie 97
Rowling, Wallace ("Bill") 153, 178, 187
Russell, Richard 156
Ryan, Allanah 153, 154
Salaman-Simpson, Kwong 99
Sanford, Agnes 100
Sankey, Ira D. 8
Savage, Michael Joseph 42, 46
Scadden, Cecil C. H. 33, 43, 44, 57
Scotland, Nigel 221
Seymour, William J. ... xvii, 10, 11, 29
Shand, Tom 109
Shearer, David .... xix, 201
Sherrill, John 125
Shipley, Jenny 211, 214, 218
Short, Des 126
Simpson, Tony 41

Sinclair, Sir Keith 67, 68, 87, 151, 188
Singh, Sadhu Sundar 17
Smith, Milton 124
Soltau, George 8
Soukotta, Carol ....xviii, 8
Stanton, L .O. 9
Stenhouse, John 241
Stern, Fritz xviii
Strachan, Gordon 7
Sweet, Leonard 138
Synan, Vinson 303
Tamaki, Brian .... xvii, xviii, 196, 215, 217–21, 231–35, 238, 242, 265
Tamihana, Wiremu 232
Te Atairangikaahu, Queen 234, 235
Te Kooti Arikirangi Te Turuki 232
Te Whiti-o-Rongomai III, Erueti 232
Thompson, J. F. D. 49
Thompson, Muri 158
Thompson, Wallace 43, 44, 92, 117, 118
Thomson, Richard 1
Thrift, Allan 79, 94, 98
Thrift, Alva 98
Tiplady, John 178, 179
Toogood, Selwyn 87
Trebilco, Gill xix
Trebilco, Paul xix
Troeltsch, Ernst 2
Troughton, Geoff 96, 172, 193, 234
Turia, Tariana 231
Twain, Mark 141
Underwood, Phil 196
Uren, Bruce 93
Valdez, A. C. 26, 28–31, 34, 46, 55, 56, 97
van Rij, Bill 215
Veitch, Jim 140, 193
Vercoe, Whakahuihui 186, 209
Wales, H. R. H. Prince of 50, 51
See also Edward VIII, King
Walker, Harvey 8
Wallis, Arthur 124, 125
Walton, John 197, 220
Ward, Kevin 140, 142, 199, 200, 221, 249
Ward, Pete 138
Ward, Sir Joseph 42
Weber, Max 2, 29
Wesley, John 6
Weston, Edward R. 25, 27, 29, 30, 49, 53–55
Wheeler, Beryl 99
Wheeler, Rob .... xix, 74, 95, 97–101, 114, 116–18, 120–23, 125, 126, 143, 144, 156, 158, 177, 179, 197, 201, 220
White, Alice 44
White, Gilbert 44, 71, 93, 95
White, Gilbert, Jnr. 97, 115, 123, 125
White, Norman 97, 115, 116, 123, 125
Whiting, T. W. 98
Wigglesworth, Smith .... xvii, 5–12, 19–26, 29, 30, 34, 43, 46, 55, 56, 75, 97, 99, 170, 263
Wilkerson, David 125, 162
Williams, D. P. 52
Williams, Jim 180, 195, 198, 220
Williamson, Dale 127, 163
Wilson brothers 47, 51, 52
See also Wilson, Charles S.; Wilson, Frank; Wilson, Frederick A.; and Wilson, W.E.
Wilson, Bryan 139, 172
Wilson, Charles S. 51, 52
Wilson, Frank 51
Wilson, Frederick A. 45, 51, 72
Wilson, Margaret 218
Wilson, W. E. 51, 52
Wimber, John 199, 200
Wolfe, Tom 199
Wood, John 118
Wood, Larry xviii

Woodard, Christopher 100
Worley, A. S. 77, 115
Worsfold, Cecily 120
Worsfold, James ....xviii, 6–10, 20, 24, 25, 31–33, 53, 73, 78, 122, 171–73, 177, 195
Worsfold, Luke 48, 53, 78, 79, 94, 97, 173, 195, 196, 200, 217, 221, 238
Wright, Ken 125, 126
Wuthnow, Robert 155
Yaxley, Trevor 216
Yeats, W. B. 237
Yong, Amos 303

Place Index

Abyssinia 49
   See also Ethiopia
Aden 49
Afghanistan 229, 230
Alaska 45
America .... xvii, xviii, 1, 2, 7, 8, 17, 26, 27, 30, 34, 65–68, 72, 74–77, 79, 89, 91, 92, 97, 101, 110, 115, 123, 125, 126, 138, 141, 144, 155, 158, 159, 162, 199, 200, 202, 217, 221, 229, 239, 241
   See also United States
America, Latin 141
Ann Arbor, Michigan 162
Argentina 97, 174
Arrowtown 170
Ashburton 170
Asia 155, 211, 242, 303
Auckland ..... xix, 1, 10, 11, 18, 23, 25, 28, 31, 32, 42, 45–47, 49, 50, 54–56, 66, 70, 72, 73, 79, 90, 91, 93, 94, 96, 99, 116, 118, 127, 157, 158, 160, 162, 163, 169–71, 173, 176, 178, 179, 186–88, 191, 192, 195, 209, 210, 216, 217, 219, 222, 223, 232, 233, 235–37, 239, 241
Auckland, South 235
Australasia 9, 17, 20, 54, 78, 145, 175
Australia .... xvii, 3, 6, 8–10, 19, 20, 23, 26–28, 30, 33, 43, 47–49, 51–55, 65, 67, 71, 72, 74, 89, 93, 94, 98, 118–21, 126, 144, 145, 155, 175, 180, 181, 188, 194, 211, 219, 265, 303
Avondale, Auckland 47, 72
Bastion Point, Auckland 152, 186
Bay of Plenty 98, 239
Blenheim 23, 25, 26, 31, 32, 54–56, 79, 94, 170, 191, 214
Bosnia 212
Bradford, England 52, 71
Britain, Great 19, 47, 49, 52, 54, 57, 65–67, 69, 73, 94, 151, 158, 172, 199, 211, 230, 263–65
   See also United Kingdom
Buenos Aires, Argentina 97
Canada 45, 72, 77, 96, 211, 215
Canterbury 32, 249
Cape Reinga 214
Ceylon 8
   See also Sri Lanka
Chatham Islands 239
China 19, 20, 48, 68, 229
Chorleywood, England 199
Christchurch 11, 12, 21, 23, 26, 28, 31, 32, 43, 49–51, 69, 71, 79, 88, 90, 94, 95, 97, 99, 121, 123, 125, 127, 156, 158, 161, 162, 170, 171, 173, 179, 191, 215, 237–39, 249
Clyde 185
Corstorphine, Dunedin 90
Cumberland County, Kentucky 75
Denmark 19
Dunedin ...... xvii, 1, 8, 10–12, 22–

26, 32, 42, 43, 50, 66, 90, 99, 100, 116, 120, 159, 214, 239, 240, 242
Dunkirk 69
East Coast .... xvi, 98
East Timor 212, 230
Eden Park, Auckland 186
Ellerslie, Auckland 33, 96, 97, 114
Eltham 32
England 17, 19, 45, 46, 55, 71, 111, 152
English Channel 49
Ethiopia 49
  See also Abyssinia
Europe 1, 49, 65, 66, 151, 229
Foxton 116
Freeman's Bay, Auckland 11, 191
Geraldine 32
Germany 65, 211
Gibraltar 49
Gisborne .... xvi, 239
Gizeh, Egypt 47, 50
Gleneagles, Scotland 186
Gore 116
Hamilton 32, 33, 47, 186, 237, 239
Hastings 239
Hauraki xvi
Hawera 32
Hawkes Bay 32
Hicks Bay 98
Hollywood 17, 89
Hot Springs, Arkansas 30
Houston, Texas 76
Hutt Valley 51, 88
India 8, 11
Indonesia .... xix, 72, 73, 175, 303
Invercargill 50, 116
Iraq 229, 230
Israel 29, 47–50
Italy 48, 49
Japan 65, 67, 211
Java, Indonesia 303
Jeffersonville, Indiana 75

Jerusalem 303
Kaipara xvi
Kansas City 223
Kansu, China 48
Kawakawa 96
Kawarau Gorge 185
Kentucky 75
King Country xvi
Korea 68, 87, 88, 193, 242
Lake Taupo 218
Launceston, Tasmania 8
London 6
Los Angeles 23
Lower Hutt 44, 79, 94, 96, 124, 125, 127, 174
Lyttelton 42
Malacca, Straits of 49
Marchwiel, Timaru 90
Marlborough 32
Marsden Point, Whangarei 185
Masterton 32
Melbourne 20, 54, 121, 175
Middle East 48
Moscow 151
Motueka 170
Motunui 185
Motupiko 32
Mount Albert, Auckland 156, 179
Mount Maunganui 98
Mount Roskill, Auckland 45, 47, 51, 72, 93, 119
Mururoa Atoll 188
Napier 50, 239
Nelson 18, 31, 32, 52, 54, 55, 94, 117
New Plymouth 28, 31, 32, 54, 55, 70
New South Wales 120
New York 229
Newtown, Wellington 25
Ngaruawahia 6
North Battleford, Saskatchewan 72, 77, 79
North Island .... xvi, 79, 98, 116, 218

Place Index 297

North Shore, Auckland 191, 195
Northland 96, 239
Nuremburg 232
Oamaru 50
Onehunga, Auckland 31, 47, 54, 55, 57
Orakei, Auckland 187
Orkney Islands 54
Otago ...... xviii, xix, 3, 32, 66, 159, 303
Otara, Auckland 173
Pacific Islands 11, 119, 211
    See also Polynesia
Pacific Ocean 65, 67, 175, 188, 212
Palestine 48
Palmerston North 23, 25, 31–33, 43, 44, 49, 55, 161
Pearl Harbor, Hawaii 65
Pensacola, Florida 221
Penygroes, Wales 52
Perth, Australia 54
Picton 31, 32
Pleasant Point 32
Poland 65
Polynesia 212, 217
    See also Pacific Islands
Pounawea 6
Raglan 90
Rangitukia 99
Rātana Pa 18
Richmond, Nelson 94, 117
Rotorua 173, 196, 217
Russia 48
Seattle, Washington 73, 79
Seoul 242
Singapore 65, 66
Snell's Beach, Auckland 161, 176, 177, 181
South Africa 22, 50, 123, 124, 186, 221
South East Asia 175
South Island ..... xv, 18, 21, 23, 26, 79, 95, 116
South Yunnan, China 20
Southland 116
Springfield, Missouri ..... xvii, xviii

Sri Lanka 8
    See also Ceylon
Stewart Island 214
Suez 49
Sunderland, England 19
Surabaya, Indonesia 73
Sydenham, Christchurch 11, 21, 50, 71, 118, 121, 170, 173
Sydney 94, 195, 219, 242, 303
Taita, Wellington 90
Takapuna, Auckland 94, 191, 195
Tamaki, Auckland 96, 97
Taranaki 32
Tasman (Province) 239
Tasman Sea 20, 67, 90, 94
Tasmania 8
Taumarunui 43, 44
Tauranga 47, 79, 94, 98, 121, 126, 239
Tawangmangu, Indonesia 303
Te Araroa 98
Te Aro, Wellington 25
Te Awamutu 217
Te Hapua 186
Te Kuiti 54, 55
Te Teko 98
Temuka 32
Thames 47
Tikirau xvi
Timaru 33, 50, 79, 90, 95, 115, 116, 125, 170
Toronto 145, 200, 221–23
Tuatapere 116
Turkey 48
United Kingdom 1, 20, 54, 71
    See also Britain, Great
United States 1, 65, 67, 72, 74, 76, 77, 89, 98, 99, 111, 158, 174, 187, 188, 199, 211, 229, 230
    See also America
Van Nuys, California 176
Vancouver 45, 47
Victoria, Australia 8
Vietnam 110, 157
Waikato .... xvi, 186, 209, 237, 239
Waiomio 96, 97, 114

Waitangi 186, 209
Wales 50–52, 54
Wanganui/Whanganui 18, 32
Wellington ...... xix, 5, 7–9, 20–32,
　34, 42–44, 50, 51, 54–56, 68,
　70–73, 77, 90, 93, 94, 97, 100,
　158, 159, 172, 173, 192, 210,
　214, 237, 239, 241
Western Samoa 119
Whangaehu 18
Whangarei 11
Zion City, Illinois 235
Zurich 76

Select General Index

ACTs 259
  See also Apostolic Church
Anglican Church ..... xvi, 18, 25, 51, 69, 90, 100, 111–13, 123, 125, 127, 152, 156, 159, 163, 186, 191, 193, 194, 199, 212–14, 240, 241, 249
AOG 32, 96, 263–65
  See also Assemblies of God
APCNZ 177–80, 216, 265
  See also Associated Pentecostal Churches of New Zealand
Apostles/apostolic ministries 6, 53–57, 71, 77, 79, 115, 126, 145, 173, 194–97, 201, 212, 217, 221, 238
Apostolic Church 29, 33–35, 43–45, 49, 51–57, 70, 71, 77–79, 92–95, 97, 101, 115, 117, 119–23, 126, 145, 171–73, 177, 194–96, 212, 213, 216, 217, 219–21, 233, 234, 238, 251–53, 259, 264, 265
  See also ACTs
Apostolic Church, Australia 53, 54, 71
Apostolic Church, Britain 52–54
Apostolic Faith Church, Britain 52
Apostolic Faith Mission, Australia 11
Apostolic Faith Mission/ Movement, America 29
Assemblies of God 3, 6, 30–34, 43, 44, 51, 52, 54–57, 69–71, 77, 92, 93, 95–98, 101, 114, 115, 117–28, 144, 170–74, 176, 177, 179, 180, 191–95, 198, 212, 216, 217, 219, 220, 222, 223, 237–39, 241, 251–53, 259, 260, 263, 265
Assemblies of God, America 26, 30, 125, 126, 144, 145, 221
Assemblies of God, Australia ... 33, 118, 144, 219
Assemblies of God, Britain 92
Associated Churches of Christ 69, 213
Associated Fellowships 259
Associated Mission Churches of Australasia, Australia 175
Associated Pentecostal Churches of New Zealand 154, 161, 171, 177, 178, 181, 191, 194, 196, 237, 238, 259
  See also APCNZ
Baptism of the Spirit 6–11, 19–21, 23, 25, 29, 51, 56, 77, 79, 116, 120, 123, 124, 127, 161, 162, 169, 200
Baptist Church 18, 21, 25, 69, 75, 90, 112, 113, 120, 124, 163, 169, 172, 193, 212, 213, 222, 240
Bethel Temple 73, 74, 79, 94, 121
Bethel Temple, America 72–74, 79
Brethren assemblies 10, 51, 69,

124, 128, 144, 172, 236, 240
British Israel movement 44, 45, 47–52, 56, 57, 70–72, 93, 114, 251–53, 263, 264
Catholic Apostolic Church 6–8, 251–53, 263
Catholic Church 43, 69, 75, 126, 127, 152, 160–63, 189, 213, 236, 240
Celebration Centres 192, 260, 265
Charismatic Movement/ Renewal .... xvii, 72, 74, 76, 78–80, 92, 100, 101, 114, 117, 118, 120, 123–28, 141, 143–46, 152, 155, 158–64, 169–75, 180, 181, 190, 192–94, 196, 197, 199, 200, 212, 219, 236, 239, 240, 303
Charismatic spirituality/ethos 5–7, 25, 34, 55, 71, 77–79, 114, 115, 119, 124–26, 141, 143–46, 152, 160, 162, 163, 174, 175, 194, 195, 198–202, 216, 218, 221–23, 236
Christian Assemblies (Cooneyites) 69, 70
Christian City Churches 260, 265
Christian Covenant Churches 259
Christian Fellowships 251–53, 264
Christian Life Churches 219, 239, 260, 265
Christian Outreach Centres 192, 238, 251–53, 259, 265
Christian Revival Crusade 51, 52, 72, 93, 114, 177, 251–53, 259, 264
Church of Christ (New Zealand) 45, 47, 51, 52, 72, 93, 115, 251–53, 264
Church of God, America 145
City Impact Church 232, 242, 260, 265

Commonwealth Covenant Church 47, 51, 52, 114, 251–53, 264
Congregational Church 69, 90, 100
CRC New Zealand 51
   See also Christian Revival Crusade
Deinstitutionalization 139, 141, 143–46
Destiny Church ...... xvii, xviii, 172, 192, 215, 217, 221, 231–35, 237–39, 242, 259, 260, 265
Dutch Reformed Church 189, 215
Elim Church of New Zealand ... 92, 94, 97, 114, 121, 122, 170, 177, 191, 192, 213, 218, 239, 251–53, 259, 263, 264
Elim Foursquare Alliance of Great Britain 73, 94, 172
Exclusive Brethren 197
Foursquare Church, America ... 176
Full Gospel Churches 98, 251–53, 264
Hillsong Church, Australia 242
House Church movement, Britain 218, 221
Independent groups 25, 29, 52, 73, 77, 78, 94, 97, 98, 101, 114, 115, 117, 118, 122, 124, 125, 128, 143–45, 163, 174, 201, 237, 238, 242, 251–53, 264
Indigenous Churches 114, 115, 117, 119, 120, 122, 123, 128, 144, 158, 169, 170, 172, 175–77, 179, 190, 191, 194, 196, 197, 201, 249–53, 264
   See also New Life Churches
Institutions/institutionalization ... 2, 6, 7, 29, 89, 91, 92, 98, 100, 101, 110, 119, 123, 126, 128, 137–39, 141–46, 153, 155, 163, 190, 193, 197, 198, 202, 212, 219, 220, 231, 239, 240, 243, 263
Institutions, suspicion towards 29, 137, 139, 141,

Select General Index   301

142, 145, 146, 155, 202, 231
International Convention of
   Faith Ministries 259, 265
Jehovah's Witnesses 70
Latter Rain 47, 72, 75, 77–79,
   94, 97, 98, 101, 114, 115, 117,
   118, 121, 122, 124–26, 128,
   143–45, 175, 251–53, 264
Leadership modes,
   bureaucratic 2, 25, 29, 30
   34, 142–45, 190, 195–97, 202,
   217–23, 238, 242
Leadership modes,
   charismatic 2, 25, 29, 30,
   34, 119, 143–46, 172, 174, 181,
   190, 193, 195–98, 219–23, 232,
   234, 238, 242
Leadership modes, rational/
   legal 2, 29, 30
LinkNZ 260
Lutheran Church 213
Methodist Church 6, 9, 10, 18,
   43, 50, 69, 70, 90, 92, 111–13,
   120, 126, 152, 169, 194, 209,
   213, 240
Millennium Ministries 259
National Revival Crusade 51,
   72, 114, 122, 251–53, 264
Network of Christian
   Ministries 260, 265
New Covenant 72, 251–53, 264
New Frontiers 260, 265
New Life Churches 47, 89, 117,
   125, 157, 170, 171, 178, 179,
   191, 192, 197, 198, 213, 220,
   221, 236, 238, 250–53, 259, 260,
   264, 265
   See also Indigenous Churches
New Zealand Pentecostal
   Fellowship 73, 121–23, 176
PCNZ 32, 263, 264
   See also Pentecostal Church of
   New Zealand
Pentecostal Church of
   Australia 121
Pentecostal Church of New
   Zealand 10, 21, 23, 26–34,
   43, 44, 51, 52, 54–57, 70–73, 79,
   93, 94, 97, 121, 263
   See also PCNZ
Pentecostal groups, New Zealand
   See also Apostolic Church, Assemblies of God, Associated Fellowships, Associated Pentecostal Churches of New Zealand, Bethel Temple, Celebration Centres, Christian City Churches, Christian Covenant Churches, Christian Fellowships, Christian Life Churches, Christian Outreach Centres, Christian Revival Crusade, Church of Christ (New Zealand), City Impact Church, Commonwealth Covenant Church, Destiny Church, Elim Church of New Zealand, Full Gospel Churches, independent groups, Indigenous Churches, International Convention of Faith Ministries, Latter Rain, LinkNZ, Millennium Ministries, National Revival Crusade, Network of Christian Ministries, New Covenant, New Frontiers, New Life Churches, New Zealand Pentecostal Fellowship, Pentecostal Church of New Zealand, Revival Centres, Revival Fire Mission, Rhema Churches, Samoan Assemblies of God, South Pacific Churches, United Pentecostal Church and Vineyard Churches
Pentecostal Holiness Church,
   America 76
Presbyterian Church 6, 51, 69,
   89, 90, 100, 111–13, 125, 152,
   163, 169, 191, 194, 213, 215,
   240
Prophets/prophetic ministry 6,
   53–56, 71, 75, 77, 78, 118, 126,
   144, 145, 173, 194–96, 217, 218,
   223, 238, 242
Quasi-Pentecostal groups 250–
   53, 263

See also British Israel movement and Catholic Apostolic Church
Rātana Church 18, 214
Relocation of authority 101, 137, 141–43, 145, 146, 155
Revival Centres 251–53, 264
Revival Fire Mission 33, 45–47, 52, 70, 94, 263
Rhema Churches 260
Salvation Army 7, 69, 213, 236
Samoan Assemblies of God 119, 238, 239, 241, 259, 260, 265
Secularism/secularization 137, 139–42, 146, 153, 155, 156, 229, 241
Society of Friends (Quakers) 69, 213
South Pacific Churches 201, 220, 265
United Pentecostal Church 122, 251–53, 264
Vineyard Churches 251–53, 259, 264
Vineyard Churches, America 199, 200, 221

About the author

Brett Knowles has served the Pentecostal movement for more than fifty years as an elder, ordained pastor, missionary, Bible teacher and Bible School principal, speaker and National Ministry Training Coordinator. He holds three theological degrees—including a PhD in Church History—from the University of Otago, where he taught Church History in the Department of Theology and Religious Studies. He has also served on the staff of Sekolah Teologi Tinggi, Tawangmangu, Central Java, Indonesia and, latterly, as Director of Academic Resources and Senior Lecturer in Church History at Sydney College of Divinity in Australia, from post which he retired in 2008. He continues to contribute to teaching, the supervision and examination of postgraduate students and research.

Dr. Knowles' research interests include Pentecostal and Charismatic Movements, New Zealand Christianity and Culture, Cross-Cultural Aspects of Christianity in the Asian Region—especially prior to 1500 CE—and the Early Church. His primary area of expertise is New Zealand Pentecostalism. He has published *The History of a New Zealand Pentecostal Movement: The New Life Churches of New Zealand from 1946 to 1979* (Lewiston, NY: Edwin Mellen Press, 2000) and numerous articles in this field. He has also edited and coedited a number of academic publications for the University of Otago. He is currently involved in the E21 Global Scholars Consultation, a select group of international Pentecostal and Charismatic scholars—led by Chairman Dr. Vinson Synan and Co-Chairman Dr. Amos Yong—in preparation for the 2015 Empowered21Global Congress in Jerusalem.

Brett has been married to Adrienne for 39 years; they have two children and two grandchildren.

www.ingramcontent.com/pod-product-compliance
Lightning Source LLC
Chambersburg PA
CBHW022009300426
44117CB00005B/102